1969

W9-AED-686

THE STRATFORD-UPON-AVON LIBRARY

★

General Editors
JOHN RUSSELL BROWN
& BERNARD HARRIS

To
MY FATHER

THE STRATFORD-UPON-AVON LIBRARY 4

*

THOMAS DEKKER

The Wonderful Year
The Gull's Horn-Book
Penny-Wise, Pound-Foolish
English Villainies Discovered by Lantern and Candlelight

and

Selected Writings

edited by
E. D. PENDRY

HARVARD UNIVERSITY PRESS
Cambridge, Massachusetts
1968

First published 1968

First published in
the United States of America in 1968

First published in Great Britain by
Edward Arnold (Publishers) Ltd

Printed in Great Britain by
Butler & Tanner Ltd, Frome and London

General Preface

WE HOPE to form this Library for the student, teacher and general reader who is interested in Elizabethan and Jacobean life and literature. It will not provide further editions of Shakespeare's *Works*, or *The Faerie Queene*, or Jonson's *Works*, nor will it duplicate readily available editions of any poet or dramatist. We hope to reprint what is generally unavailable outside the great libraries and microfilm and photostat collections, or available only in expensive and rare complete editions; we want the *Stratford Library* to publish important parts of the staple literature of the period.

This present volume of Dekker's non-dramatic works is one of the first four to be published, the others being a selected Nashe (providing more than half his total writings and including four whole works), a collection of narrative poems, and *The Elizabethans' America* (reprinting letters, reports and pamphlets about the New World). In active preparation are volumes of Sir Thomas Wilson's *Art of Rhetoric* with generous selections from Fraunce's *Arcadian Rhetoric* and other works, a collection of Neo-Platonic writings, and another of pamphlets on Witchcraft and Demonology. We plan subsequent volumes of Sonnet Sequences, Lodge, Greene, Sermons, News Pamphlets, European Travel.

The texts are presented in modernized form. Editors have been asked to reparagraph, repunctuate, substitute italic type for roman, or *vice versa*, wherever they consider that such changes will avoid unnecessary confusions or obscurities. Modernization of spelling is sometimes difficult because of our slender knowledge of the spelling habits of authors and compositors, and our total ignorance of the many accidental decisions made during writing and printing: generally editors have retained archaic forms only where rhyme or metre requires, or where a modernized form does not give the required primary sense. Exceptions will sometimes be made where an author clearly distinguishes between two forms, for works surviving in autograph manuscript or for verse carefully printed from authorial manuscripts. Textual notes will define the editorial procedures for each volume. We believe that this presentation, in banishing the clumsiness of original editions and hyperconservative reprints, will often reveal liveliness and sometimes an added elegance.

Editors have provided brief annotations, a glossary or a glossarial index, whichever seems appropriate, and also textual notes, collating substantive changes to the copy-text and briefly discussing its textual authority. Each volume has an introduction dealing with any topics that will enhance the reading of the texts. We have not aimed at minute consistency between each volume, or even between each item in a single volume; editors have been encouraged to present these texts in the clearest practicable manner and with due consideration of the fact that many of the works reprinted have hitherto been 'known about' rather than known, more honoured or dishonoured in scholarly works than read and enjoyed as substantial achievements and records of Shakespeare's age.

JOHN RUSSELL BROWN
BERNARD HARRIS

Contents

List of Illustrations

Acknowledgments

THERE are many who have helped me with particular problems encountered in my work on this edition. I should like to thank by name Dr Giovanni Carsaniga, Professor P. G. Foote, Mr Derek Forbes, Mr J. P. Harthan, Mr F. M. Higman, the late Mr W. A. Jackson and his assistants, The Rev. R. Peter Johnston, Mr G. F. Jones, Miss E. D. Mercer, Dr Mary G. Morrison, Mr G. P. B. Naish, Mr R. A. Norman, The Rev. F. A. F. Poulden, Mr Robert Smallwood, Miss Susie Tucker, Miss Helen Wallis, and Dr and Mrs J. S. Wilders. Above all I am indebted to my wife for her assistance and encouragement.

I began the preparation of the texts while a Fellow at the Shakespeare Institute (University of Birmingham), and I am grateful to the Director, Professor T. J. B. Spencer, for allowing me to use its invaluable microfilms in the final as in the early stages of the work. Thanks are also due to the British Museum and the Bodleian Library for permission to reproduce the pictures specified in the List of Illustrations.

Introduction

THOUGH he always saw himself as a gentleman and a scholar, Thomas Dekker lived in the slums, scraped a livelihood by writing for the mass media of his day, fell into poverty and spent nearly seven abject years in gaol. The conviction that such a man emerged from such experiences with a soft heart and a smile of sweet certainty gratified the Victorians: it must irk us. 'He is so cheery and elastic,' wrote Grosart, 'so bright and pleasant in his style.' But this is the poet who could write in *Patient Grissil*, III. i. 157–9:

> Oh whats this world, but a confused throng
> Of fooles and mad men, crowding in a thrust
> To shoulder out the wise, trip downe the just.

or in *The Roaring Girl*, IV. ii. 206–7:

> What's this whole world but a gilt rotten pill?
> For at the heart lies the old chore still.

Any assessment of his work that makes too much of his piety, his gentleness, his cheeriness, his whimsy, seems to deny him those very qualities that might recommend him to the age we live in—his toughness and bitterness. He is a grown-up writer who feels pain, and can turn upon it with a snarl or a sneer; despair, bravado and indignation give an edge to much of his wit. There was for him no easy road to a faith in human goodness.

No one would claim for Dekker intellect or originality of the very first water. But he had such inborn talent that had luck done as well by him in the one case as in the other he would have left us as distinguished a tragedy as, in *The Shoemakers' Holiday*, he has left us a comedy; and moreover he had it in him to have become a major novelist. Luck seldom came his way. Yet much of what he achieved has great survival-value, and Dekker deserves to be re-appraised as a writer for today.

* * *

Dekker is a man we come to feel we know intimately; and yet the circumstances of his private life are obscure, and Dekker himself is almost completely silent about them. Even the dates of his birth and death are in doubt. In a late dedication to *Lantern and Candlelight* he gives his age as threescore. If that dedication was first published in 1632 (but see below, p. 326), then of course Dekker was born in or about 1572. This roughly corresponds with the chance remark of a

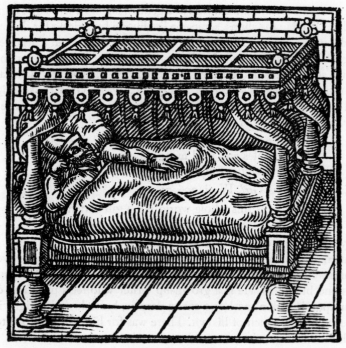

1. Thomas Dekker.

contemporary that he was not yet 40 in 1610.[1] He may well have been of Dutch extraction: there is the evidence of the name, his frequent allusions to Holland, and perhaps also an unusual familiarity with German literature, especially in his use of the Fortunatus legend for *Old Fortunatus*, of the Friar Rush legend for *If This Be Not a Good*

---

[1] S. R., *Martin Markall, Beadle of Bridewell* (London, 1610) in A. V. Judges, *The Elizabethan Underworld* (London, 1930), p. 406. A version of *Martin Markall* prior to *Lantern and Candlelight* in 1608 is possible; but the reference to Dekker's age occurs in a retort to *Lantern and Candlelight*.

Play, and of Friedrich Dedekind's *Grobianus* for *The Gull's Horn-Book*. But he does confirm that London was his mother and his nurse.[1]

External evidence is thin and uncertain. Thomas Dycker, Tom. Dykers and Th. Dickers are the names of the father or fathers of three girls, Dorcas, Elizabeth and Anne baptized at St Giles's, Cripplegate, on 27th October 1594, 29th November 1598 and 24th October 1602 respectively; and a Thomas Diccars was buried at St Botolph's, Bishopsgate, on 19th April 1598. J. P. Collier is the only known authority for his own assertion that Dekker's father died in Southwark in 1594, though a widow Dekker was certainly living in Maid Lane, Southwark, in 1596 and 1600. The relationships, if any, between these people and the poet remain conjectural.[2]

The mists clear when Dekker suddenly appears as an already fully established playwright. As a matter of fact we first find him in the early nineties associated with Shakespeare: the handwritings of both are believed to be amongst those of several playwrights to whom the manuscript play of *Sir Thomas More* was referred for revision: the censor had had qualms about the effect some passages might have on popular racial prejudice against immigrants. Then from January 1598 onwards Dekker's name figures prominently for several years in *Henslowe's Diary*—the memorandum and account books of Philip Henslowe, the speculator who set out to exploit London show business, and who himself put up the money for scripts that had been commissioned by the actors from a pool of regular writers. Mass-production was the rule. It may well be that the theatre-going public had an insatiable appetite for new plays: certainly pieces once completed were rapidly costumed and performed. But the writers' need for cash was probably the most pressing reason for the high speed at which plays were turned out, and for the common practice of setting up teams of as many as five collaborators to work on the same play at one time.

Dekker was in the main a team-writer. He is known to have written over sixty plays, and few of these were independent compositions. He had the experience of co-operating with most of the leading play-

---

[1] *A Rod for Runaways* in F. P. Wilson, *The Plague Pamphlets of Thomas Dekker* (Oxford, 1925), p. 146; *The Seven Deadly Sinnes of London*, ed. H. F. B. Brett-Smith (Oxford, 1922), p. 11.

[2] In *Un Peintre de la Vie Londonienne: Thomas Dekker*, 2 vols. (Paris, 1958), Professor M. T. Jones-Davies has done a service for Dekker comparable with that done for William Shakespeare by E. K. Chambers. All biographical references, if not separately cited, will readily be found in Jones-Davies, I, 27–72.

wrights of his time: Jonson, Webster, Middleton, Massinger, Hey-
wood, Ford—not to mention Shakespeare himself—are those most
famous today. But his favourites were Michael Drayton (with whom
he worked on 16 plays), Henry Chettle (15) and Robert Wilson (9).
It adds a poignancy to our reading of 'The Fields of Joy' to bear in
mind how much Dekker and Chettle must have been through together.
The recollection of his dead friend, at first so light-hearted, seems to
bring Dekker's fantasy to an abrupt end.

In 1598 and 1599, when the records are full, we see what it was to
write full-time for Henslowe. Dekker then worked on more than 25
plays, turning out the equivalent of a single-handed play in five or six
weeks. At some £6 or £7 each play, he is unlikely ever to have made
more than £40 a year (in an age when a cheap meal out cost 3d.).
Like Henslowe's other hacks he was paid advances on work in progress, so it may be assumed that his income was at once irregular,
insecure and inadequate. On 4th February 1598 Henslowe had to lend
him 40s. to discharge him from the Counter in the Poultry, one of the
Sheriffs' prisons to which presumably he had been committed on some
action of debt. A year later, on 30th January 1599, we find him under
arrest at the suit of the Chamberlain's Men, Shakespeare's company;
and since £3 10s. was needed to secure his release it is likely that
Dekker owed them money. Chettle was also in prison that month.[1]

Nevertheless Dekker was making a name for himself in the world of
the theatre. In September 1598, referring to plays none of which
survive, Francis Meres had described him as among the best in England
for tragedy. Two of his plays which do survive and which were in
fact his first to be printed, *Old Fortunatus* and *The Shoemakers' Holiday*,
had the distinction of being selected for performance at Court during
the Christmas season of 1599/1600. Then in 1601 it was he who was
asked by the Chamberlain's Men to write against the redoubtable Ben
Jonson in the so-called War of the Theatres. Strictly speaking it was
none of Dekker's business—although when Jonson heard of what was
afoot he quickly made Dekker one of his targets in *Poetaster*. What
the actors had in mind no doubt was to divert back to the arena of the
public theatre a controversy which drew large audiences but which
threatened to become exclusively the property of the children's companies in the private theatres. So far as is known Dekker's *Satiromastix*
was his first work for a company not backed by Henslowe; but in the

[1] *Henslowe's Diary*, ed. R. A. Foakes and R. T. Rickert (Cambridge, 1961),
pp. 86, 103, 104.

years to come he was to be much more of a free-lance. The play generously reveals his admiration for Jonson's genius, though not for his arrogance, and it seems surprising that Jonson should have felt himself worsted in the exchange.

The new reign seemed full of promise. Judging from lines reprinted in *The Wonderful Year*, Dekker must have been amongst those poets who pressed forward to offer verses to the new king, in hopes of winning his favour. And Dekker and Jonson uneasily shared the honours of preparing the pageantry for *The Magnificent Entertainment* to celebrate the Entry of King James into the City. But disaster overtook all hopes. A severe outbreak of plague in 1603 not only postponed the Entry but also led to the official closing of the theatres for so long that Dekker was obliged to look for a living in other work—in writing for publication. He probably stayed on in London. The satirical comments made by some actors[1] on his behaviour in the plague of 1625 may perhaps hold good for the earlier occasion also: Dekker, they said, would himself have fled from London like them if only he could have got hold of a horse; and if the theatres were opened he would give up his 'Trade of Pamphletts'.

It is by no means certain what Dekker may have been paid for a pamphlet—some £2 seems likely—but it is evident that work for the press was even less rewarding than work for the theatre. He can hardly have kept up a high rate of production, and indeed he tells us in *The Gull's Horn-Book* that it was no ambition of his to appear in print every Term. However, the reception given to what was probably his first pamphlet—*The Wonderful Year*—was no doubt encouraging, and recurrences of plague in the following years may have induced him to persevere in his 'Trade of Pamphletts', most of which lie within the comparatively narrow limits 1603–9.

In these years and those to follow he was again to come into conflict with the law. On two occasions he appeared before the magistrates. On 29th May 1608 he was himself in trouble for causing an unspecified breach of the peace against one Agnes Preston, described as a spinster of Whitechapel, the district in which he was then living. A year later, on 22nd June 1609, we find him standing as joint surety for the good behaviour of one married woman towards another. With these tantalizing glimpses of contentious East End neighbours we must at present be content.[2]

[1] B. V. *et al.*, *The Runaways' Answer* (London, 1625), sig. B1–B1ᵛ.
[2] Middlesex County Records, S.R. 462/14, 476/10; S. Reg. 1/188.

Worse was to come. In Michaelmas Term 1612 Dekker was arrested for debt and soon after committed to the King's Bench Prison, from which he was unable to extricate himself for nearly seven years. One of his creditors was his tailor, Thomas Cator, suing him for an unpaid bill. He complained to the Court of King's Bench that in Cheap Ward on 1st October 1612 Dekker had obtained a doublet and a pair of hose from him worth £4 6s., and had since repeatedly refused to settle up. Another case about this time was brought against him by John Crown and John Smithwick, who complained that as long ago as 3rd October 1611 he had entered into a bond for £10 which he had since failed to honour; Dekker and his attorney William Edwardes confessed a judgment and the Court proceeded to award the plaintiffs their £10 together with £1 damages.[1]

Dekker wrote little which we now know of while he was in prison. Perhaps he was writing for help, and painfully learning the lesson that 'Letters are a meat only to make hope fat and to starve a prisoner' (see below, p. 269). In November 1615 he was frankly confessing, in the dedication to *The Artillery Garden*, that after almost three years' imprisonment he personally had done all he could and that now his only chance of release lay in outside aid. Clearly he did not get it. Two of his letters, written to Edward Alleyn the famous actor, have survived: one of them, dated 12th September 1616, is a covering note for a poem (now lost) in praise of the building of Dulwich College, Alleyn's brain-child. In the second letter, which no doubt belongs with the first though it is undated, Dekker acknowledges with thanks that Alleyn had sent him some remembrance. But this fragmentary correspondence hardly makes it clear to what extent and in what way Dekker was beholden to Alleyn, who was now rich in his own right and was to inherit the estate of his father-in-law—none other than Philip Henslowe, who had died earlier that year. Another death in 1616, with (it may be) implications of a different sort, was that of Mary, wife of a Thomas Deckers; she was buried at St James's, Clerkenwell, on 24th July.[2]

The man who was Marshal of the King's Bench was Sir George Reynell. It may well be Reynell and his regime that Geffray Mynshul, who was a prisoner at the same time as Dekker, has in mind when he writes of those prison-keepers 'borne well, of gentle blood, and

---

[1] The pleas from which these facts are taken I hope to publish shortly, together with the Middlesex recognizances referred to above.

[2] Jones-Davies, I, 58–60.

extraordinary education'[1] but corrupted by their profession, and when he describes the filth, vice, extortion, cruelty and unrest in the King's Bench. In 1598, when Reynell (with the encouragement of the Bacons) was acting as Warden of the Fleet, the prisoners complained bitterly about his extortionate fees, and the case was heard in Star Chamber. He was cleared, but when he moved to the King's Bench similar complaints were to be made and in 1620, only a few months after Dekker's release, the prisoners rose in open mutiny and expelled their keepers. It was necessary for the High Sheriff of Surrey, acting on orders from the Privy Council, to raise a posse to quell them.

That Dekker's sufferings in prison were intense is revealed by the prison chapters which he added to *Lantern and Candlelight* in 1616. After enduring three more years 'amongst the Goths and Vandals' (a phrase he used to Alleyn and repeated in *Lantern and Candlelight*, p. 270) he wrote *Dekker His Dream*, which is a weird, faltering vision, mad with resentment and anguish, of a Hell which is and is not a prison:

> Why am I hell'd in Execution
> In this Damnd Jayle, ever to be Undone?
> If Hee layd downe his life to set me Cleere
> From all my Debts, why am I Dungeon'd Here?[2]

In November 1618 the king had at last revived the Elizabethan *Commissio pro Relevatione Debitorum*, the commission 'for compounding of debts between prisoners in the King's Bench and Fleet, and their creditors',[3] and it may be conjectured that it was through their agency that Dekker was reconciled with his creditor or creditors in 1619.

On his release from prison Dekker picked up the threads of his writing career once more, tackling both plays and pamphlets. Considering his past, he must have had some particularly bad moments in 1625, when he was summoned to Star Chamber on a charge of conspiracy and libel. The previous year he had joined with William Rowley, John Ford and John Webster in composing a highly topical play (now lost) called *Keep the Widow Waking*, which was based on

---

[1] *Essays and Characters of a Prison and Prisoners* (London, 1618), sig. E3ᵛ. This is the (revised) second edition of the year.

[2] A. B. Grosart, *The Non-Dramatic Works of Thomas Dekker*, The Huth Library (London, 1884–86), III, 55. Dekker twice refers to his past seven years asleep.

[3] Public Record Office, S.P. 14/141/234; Thomas Rymer, *Foedera* (London, 1704–35), XVII, 116–19.

two sordid cases then very much in the news. The plaintiff in one case, involving the forced marriage of his mother-in-law, an elderly widow, attempted to implicate the playwrights; he may have been actuated by a general grudge against the theatre community of the Red Bull, near which Dekker was now living, as well as by anger at the play itself. It came out that Dekker had no first-hand knowledge of the people and events in question.[1]

The year 1625 also saw the worst plague since 1603. Dekker scored something of a success with his *Rod for Runaways*, written on the lines of *The Wonderful Year* but castigating the refugees in stronger terms. A group of needy players thrown out of work by the plague took the opportunity to reply with *The Runaways' Answer*. They all needed the money: the theatrical profession was once again in chaos with the playhouses closed. It rather seems as if the discouragements proved too great for Dekker, and he gave up writing for the regular stage altogether. His work had been very much part of dramatic history for more than a quarter of a century, and in the give and take of changing fashions, registered so well in the tally of his surviving plays, it had not been his part only to take.

In the late twenties Dekker managed to establish himself in a line of semi-dramatic work in which he had long ago shown an interest, pageant writing for the City. With *The Magnificent Entertainment* in 1603 he had made a start, and he had been employed in 1612 on the Lord Mayor's Show just about the time of his arrest and imprisonment. Even while he was still in prison he was attempting to gain a foothold in a business that since the beginning of the reign had been the object of keen competition between two writers, Munday and Middleton. It was in fact the death of Middleton that gave Dekker his chance. We find him employed on the Shows in three successive years—1627, 1628 and 1629.

The degree of success which he thus seems to have attained in his last years was, as usual with him, offset by the fact that he was in trouble with the authorities for some reason, probably financial. Twice—on 1st December 1626 and 1st March 1628—Thomas Deckers of St James's, Clerkenwell, is reported to the magistrates for not going to church, a negligence on his part that may have been due to fear of arrest for debt. His last piece of writing was very probably the additions to *Lantern and Candlelight* that appeared in 1632. A Thomas Decker, householder, was buried on 25th August 1632 at St James's, Clerken-

[1] C. J. Sisson, *Lost Plays of Shakespeare's Age* (Cambridge, 1936), pp. 80–124.

well. On 4th September Elizabeth, described as the widow of Thomas Deckers of St James's, renounced the administration of his estate, an expedient sometimes taken to evade the inheritance of debts.[1]

What did the Elizabethans think of Dekker? One can answer immediately that he was the kind of writer whose lot it is to be honourably mentioned by his contemporaries in lists, and hardly ever on his own. He must have been an unobtrusive but not obscure figure on the literary scene. Jonson, it is true, has much more specific things to say about him in *Poetaster*: he sketches a seedy, incompetent hack, envious of Jonson's social and literary successes and prepared to libel anyone for money. But then Jonson was in the uncomfortable position of knowing that Dekker was at that moment engaged in writing against him.

* * *

What Dekker's personal feelings may have been about the difficulties of pleasing a theatre audience it is hard to say. The fact that, despite his long and varied experiences, he still keenly resented and feared criticism is evident enough; but if the Prologue and Epilogue to *If This Be Not a Good Play* are any guide, this uneasy mood must have given way to a very different one at times, when he looked back upon his labours with a settled, rueful resignation, and took pride in knowing that, whether he won applause or not, he had not prostituted his talent to the mob for money but had remained true to his vision. It was in just such complex and fluctuating moods that he ventured into writing directly for publication. He now had three sets of people to please—patrons, stationers and readers—and he was happy about his dealings with none of them.

It would be quite wrong to assume that Dekker normally writes the fulsome dedications that are common form in his day. On the contrary, he tends to be constrained, ill at ease: the apologetic, deprecatory tone, the insistent wish to do the correct thing, are deceptive. It clearly went against the grain with him to truckle to any reader, patron or not. And although he was in some ways, and the principal way economic, offended and disappointed at the decay of patronage in modern times (unhappily, there seems never to have been any incentive for him to use the same dedicatee twice) there is relish and relief in his disillusioned dedication of *The Gull's Horn-Book* to gulls, *The Raven's Almanac* to spendthrifts, and *News from Gravesend* (if this is his) to Nobody.

[1] Jones-Davies, I, 67–71.

And yet, had he found patronage, Dekker would have understood such a personal relationship much better than he did the newfangled publishing trade which depended on sales. He has a Jest which puts his problem in a pun:

> A Fellow that (to be a foole in print) had spent the stocke of his wits upon inke and paper, and made it into a booke, offred to sell at diverse Stationers stals, but none would buy it: At the length he came to one of the company, and swore to him he should not neede to feare to venture money upon it, for it would be to him an everlasting booke. Oh sayes the other, then I will not meddle with it: everlasting bookes are ill commodities in our trade: bring me a booke that will go away, and I am for you.[1]

He was well aware of the mass audience as a threat to his own 'everlasting' standards. And he was not even clear in his mind as to whether it was quite proper for a gentleman to publish frequently, or to write for gain at all. His frequent changes of publisher suggest, however, that he must himself have hawked his wares round from stationer to stationer in search of the best offer.

But what perhaps disturbed him most was revulsion—odd in a professional playwright—at having his work put on common display in Paul's Churchyard where any Tom, Dick or Harry could pass judgment on it. The general run of *lectores* were for him *lictores*.[2] The experience was best described as torture—to be torn on the rack or pressed to death:

> To come to the presse is more dangerous, then to bee prest to death, for the payne of those Tortures, last but a few minutes, but he that lyes upon the rack in print, hath his flesh torne off by the teeth of *Envy*, and *Calumny*, even when he meanes no body any hurt in his grave.[3]

More than once he refers to the existence of a particularly offensive group of would-be critics who are themselves writers. But whether it was a question of a coterie or the general public, it is quite certain that Dekker neither tolerated nor even understood criticism, and we cannot believe him when he declares that he does not let it worry him—that he is, in his telling word, 'snakeproof'. Snakeproof he never was.

[1] *Jests to Make You Merry* in Grosart, II, 274.
[2] *A Strange Horse-Race* in Grosart, III, 311.
[3] *News from Hell* in Grosart, II, 89. The two images occur below, pp. 28 (2), 95. For the sentiment, cf. p. 109, and Brett-Smith, p. 5.

Dekker tried to give value for money, but the extent to which he was a popular journalist has been exaggerated. In *A Strange Horse-Race* he admits, rather shamefacedly, to the need for titles that catch the eye even if they mislead,[1] and the eye-catching quality of his titles is undeniable. But titles are not contents, and it is hard to believe that buyers would be easily fooled by such advertising matter. Dekker seems to have scored few really resounding successes: rarely do any of his twenty or so pamphlets pass into a known second edition. It is fair to suppose that the name 'Dekker' counted for nothing in his own time: if it were otherwise, one would expect to find it on title-pages more frequently. The modern belief in his success as a popular journalist probably stems most unreasonably from the fact that he depicts the London of the common people.

* * *

Dekker is widely praised for his realism.

> in every street, carts and Coaches make such a thundring as if the world ranne upon wheeles: at everie corner, men, women, and children meete in such shoales, that postes are sette up of purpose to strengthen the houses, least with justling one another they should shoulder them downe. Besides, hammers are beating in one place, Tubs hooping in another, Pots clincking in a third, water-tankards running at tilt in a fourth: heere are Porters sweating under burdens, there Marchants-men bearing bags of money, Chapmen (as if they were at Leape-frog) skippe out of one shop into another: Tradesmen (as if they were daūcing Galliards) are lusty at legges and never stand still: all are as busie as countrie Atturneyes at an Assises: how then can *Idlenes* thinke to inhabit heere?[2]

Is this realistic? Of course not. It sounds realistic because it is written in something like the gimcrack style we all of us affect when we are overcome with enthusiasm for the richness of Elizabethan life. Dekker's style—which is not gimcrack—has gone to the making of our very mental picture of the period in which he lived, so that we are in danger of giving him (like Dickens) too little credit for literary creation, too much for realism. No, the passage quoted is not realistic. It is in fact a stylistic tour de force on the set subject of 'vigour', using a favourite device of Dekker's, the panoramic sentence, and it serves a precise rhetorical function in the definition of Sloth.

It is quite true that Dekker's works are full of London. Johnson's

[1] Grosart, III, 311–12. [2] Brett-Smith, pp. 37–8.

famous dictum that when a man is tired of London he is tired of life applies literally to Dekker, 'never going further out of town than a farthing candle will light'.[1] Even when he reaches out for a vision of the after-life it is as a busy city that he sees either Heaven or Hell. London sights and sounds, the eddying of crowds, the bustle of streets and shops, are constantly felt in the passing detail of his work, and they come as readily to his pen as rural imagery to other poets' pens; the precision of urban imagery—the names of streets, churches, taverns—is a technique he made his own. And yet, though it was probably an ever-present problem with him to know what to write about, the solution of writing description for its own sake seems never to have occurred to him. We must be on our guard against treating a work such as *The Gull's Horn-Book* as though it were a record of what was familiar and normal in the behaviour of men-about-town in Elizabethan London. Here and elsewhere Dekker was trying to do something which would seem to him both more difficult and more worthy than mere reportage—constructing his work on a moral plan.

In itself a moral vision is not dull, bleak and disdainful. Within its range lie invective, satire (often confused with realism) and the poetry of idealism, as well as the homily. Dekker's feeling for London is moral poetry—a deep sense of community. In the City that he knows, he glimpses a half-realized way of life in which people work hard side by side in harmony and happiness, proud of their skills, content with their stations, fond of one another. He is a socialist if by socialist we mean a man who sees society as offering not so much a challenge to individual initiative as an opportunity for service. He is a Tory in that he looks back to a perhaps fictitious time of greater social stability, and is a sentimental upholder of aristocracy and gentry. But he admires workpeople, and the prudent merchant classes most of all. All classes and vocations, in his view, have their dignity, their duties and their rights; they have their place in the scheme. 'Society,' he says in *Lantern and Candlelight*, 'is the string at which the life of man hangs' (p. 265). It is the traditional rôle of the rich to be charitable to the poor, including their own tenants; it is the traditional rôle of the soldier to defend the country, and of civilians to care for the disabled that return from the wars; it is the traditional rôle of the church to inculcate a contempt for the shortcomings of this world and to officiate with decorum at our departure from it. As a traditionalist Dekker is at

---

[1] *Martin Markall* in Judges, p. 392. Strictly speaking, this remark is made about the Bellman.

times surprisingly narrow-minded. He has a chronic distaste for ordinaries (restaurants) on the grounds that precedence is not observed there; nor does he care for the democracy of criticism—the freedom of speech—in a playhouse.

The plague is to him above all a calamity that strikes at the community. London is left 'forsaken like a lover, forlorn like a widow and disarmed of all comfort' (p. 48). Urban society crumbles; families are broken up, civic duties forgotten. Individuals, he reports admiringly, go to their deaths with acts of charity, but others simply look out for themselves. The citizen's place is in London, infection or no infection, to help as best he can, even if this is only to make sure that the dead receive a decent burial.

He was well aware that there might be occasions when the natural rights of an individual might be threatened by the abuse of a social authority legitimate in itself. Such problems had no simple answer; but they especially fascinated the dramatist, and produced some of his finest writing. Gwalter in *Patient Grissil*, Rufus in *Satiromastix*, the Duke of Milan in *1 Honest Whore*, Matheo in *2 Honest Whore*, the Earl in *Westward Ho*, perhaps Mother Sawyer in *The Witch of Edmonton* are not only themselves interesting characters because involved in external and internal conflict, they also figure in highly dramatic scenes written in correspondingly tense, at times obscure, verse. The element of protest and conflict is overlooked by critics who are intent on proving the existence of pathos in the plays. In *Patient Grissil* it is true that the heroine is a paragon of a long-suffering wife, but we must take into account the rebellious comments of her brother Laureo, not to mention the reversals of the underplot, before we declare Dekker's treatment of marital obedience a simple or stupid one. Similarly in the pamphlets: the poignancy of Dekker's prison chapters is due to complexity—the fact that, though he well knows the suffering inflicted, he is not prepared to deny the justice of the law.

For Dekker morality is largely a function of money. Virtue is the proper use, and vice the improper use, of money. Most of the hardships—and temptations—he takes note of may be attributed in one way or another to poverty. In an acquisitive society he remembers those who work hard for worthy causes and yet go without their due reward—such are the scholar and the soldier. Or he remembers those who from the nature of things cannot pull themselves up by their own boot-straps—such are the widows and the orphans, the destitute prisoners. For Dekker, as for so many of his contemporaries who were outside the business world, the usurer—we should say the financier or capitalist—was the arch-villain of the age. Dekker never understood the economic necessities of credit and investment, but he did understand the human consequences of bankruptcy. His detestation of usury colours his account of 1603. He shows how the threat of civil disorder and of sudden death destroys the value of money, undermines the economic foundations of society: the plague is a striking instance of Death the leveller, and Dekker feels a certain diabolic satisfaction in seeing the rich reduced to such shifts, and he thrills to the countryman's new-found impudence to his betters.

His pamphlet *Work for Armourers* is a curious half-prophetic allegory about the Two Nations (his own phrase) which well shows how deeply, with compassion rather than intellect, he saw into the malaise of his civilization. The Army of Poverty—in which he wryly regards himself as serving—assaults the Army of Money, which is entrenched in the City of London. But the class-war terminates not in victory for either side but in an uneasy truce, when it is agreed that in exchange for military service the poor can expect a paternalistic interest from the rich, and renewed efforts to bring financial rewards into line with merit. Dekker had no more visionary solution to offer. Have we?

There was of course another side to the coin. Poor as he was himself, he responded strongly to the imaginative appeal of riches, as in *Old Fortunatus*, I. i. 289–96:

> Gold is the strength, the sinnewes of the world,
> The Health, the soule, the beautie most divine,
> A maske of Gold hides all deformities;
> Gold is heavens phisicke, lifes restorative,
> Oh therefore make me rich: Not as the wretch,
> That onely serves leane banquets to his eye,
> Has Gold, yet starves: is famisht in his store:
> No, let me ever spend, be never poore.

One can understand his fascination with Fortunatus and his bottomless purse. Towards prodigality his tone tends to be much lighter than towards meanness. It is not just that prodigals are fools rather than rogues, or that they may be generous or charitable by accident: he enjoys lavishness of spirit in itself. He plainly admires the swashbuckling type of man—even if he be not a model of civic virtue, like Eyre who can feast his trade by the barrow-load, but a scapegrace like Matheo of *The Honest Whore*, intent (in his own amusing catchphrase) on 'flying high'. Admiration even qualifies his indictment of the criminal tricksters in *Lantern and Candlelight* whose daring and ingenuity are chiefly directed towards getting money. The fact that they are or appear to be gentlemen makes their conduct all the more piquant.

If Dekker has the makings of a rebel, it is because he finds so much injustice and suffering. But to the incurable ills of life endurance is his considered response. Candido has a famous speech on Patience in *1 Honest Whore*, V. ii. 497–505:

> It is the greatest enemy to law
> That can be, for it doth embrace all wrongs,
> And so chaines up, lawyers and womens tongues.
> Tis the perpetuall prisoners liberty:
> His walkes and Orchards: 'tis the bond-slaves freedome,
> And makes him seeme prowd of each yron chaine:
> As tho he wore it more for state then paine.
> It is the beggers Musick, and thus sings,
> Although their bodies beg, their soules are kings.

Patience is the abiding theme of his book of prayers, *Four Birds of Noah's Ark*, with its simple piety for high and low. And revealing in itself is the large number of allusions in his works to the Destinies or Fates who spin our lives and who decide quite arbitrarily the moment of our deaths. In his later pamphlets we find a more Puritanical and conscience-stricken Dekker, inclined to attribute suffering to sin— this at least made sense of it. Failing all else, there was the life to come; and towards the prospect of this he will sometimes turn weary eyes.

*   *   *

It was a godsend to English literature in the Elizabethan period that most of the great writers were attracted to the theatre, where they were initiated—how, is a mystery—in a tradition and discipline for the writing of the most complex literature of the time. Dekker's own intensive experience of composing plays was something that inevitably came to exert an influence upon him when he turned to the composing of pamphlets. There are reminiscences of the stage, both trivial and profound, throughout his non-dramatic work. The very devils of *Lantern and Candlelight* are in the old grotesque comedy convention associating the infernal and criminal underworlds, and when the post enters the hall it is to the cry 'Room!', as the Vice of the interludes had done generations before. The mythological and allegorical figures invoked in *The Gull's Horn-Book* are just the kind found in pageants, mummings and tournaments, while *The Seven Deadly Sins*, like the beginning of *The Wonderful Year*, is formally based on the staging of ceremonial entries into the City.

Penny-Wise and 'A Medicine' probably both derive from actual plays. *Penny-Wise*, the more elaborate piece, shows what can happen when a working dramatic method is applied successfully to prose fiction, in this case to the bare little didactic tale that serves as source. Most obviously, Dekker provides a new circumstantiality. Some modern readers might indeed value the story just for its quaintness— the background of the salt sea trade and piracy, of the grandly sinister city of Venice when it was still a commercial centre in which an English businessman could feel provincial, of the little tobacco-shop in Fleet St. But it is the select circumstantiality of drama, strictly subordinate to other concerns: without deviation Dekker takes us straight to each telling psychological moment, each essential climax of events; he keeps his eye on contrasts and parallels between times, places, events, people; he provides sinewy dialogue; he develops character.

In the source the main issue is the rather trite choice the unfaithful husband must make between his wife and his mistress, and what he buys (from an old man quite unknown to him) with his wife's penny is the stratagem by which he is enabled to find out their true worth: pretending to have suffered losses at sea and to be in urgent need of refuge, he is to appeal to them for assistance. The inevitable follows. And to crown it all, the valuable gifts which the merchant recovers from his mistress by another trick are represented as the financial return on the penny invested by his wife.

Dekker has obscured or sophisticated the simple outlines of the tale, while remaining true to the spirit of it to a degree inconceivable in the original. Out of a dramatic instinct, if not for an actual theatrical purpose, he reduces the wit bought for a penny to a mere moral warning, and saves up his account of the husband's stratagem until the occasion calls for it. He even quite frankly forgets for a time to tell us about the penny at all; and for our part we may well overlook the fact that the wife makes a handsome profit on her money. Dekker is not greatly interested in the folk wit so important to the structure of his source. The second part of his version, with the second voyage, the second courtesan, the second repentance, the second recovery, is not a mindless repetition of the original pattern: it makes of Ferdinand's weakness of character a kind of personal destiny from which he cannot extricate himself, and at the same time makes the counterclaim that, if there is something in him that will always make him fail, there is something in others that will always come to his aid when he does fail: there will be not only his wife but also the ubiquitous Theobald, a character whom Dekker has cleverly composed from the man-servant and the wise old man of the source and who is an important structural and thematic link between the two parts. It is a lesson in secular sin and secular grace, the grace being to some extent a force for good that Ferdinand himself has set in train and that he can avail himself of if he chooses.

The repetition of the pattern shifts the point of balance decisively away from the choice between women, one obviously good and to be espoused and the other obviously bad and to be eschewed, towards the much more moving relation between an incorrigibly feckless husband and his plucky wife who will in the event stick together regardless of moral blacks and whites. The pennyworth of wit is hers, the profit is for both of them.

The characterization is far from negligible. Annabell makes an attractive young woman, shrewd and forgiving, sweet of character and tart of tongue, soft of heart and—when need be—hard of hand. Ferdinand the ne'er-do-well hero, who for all his graceless escapades remains in Dekker's eyes forever a gentleman, is amusing for the thick-witted elegance with which he talks himself into wrongdoing. The inconsistent, unmotivated change of heart by the English courtesan, with her sentimental remembrance of 'the many jovial days and nights he and I have spent together', has the inexplicable effect of suddenly bringing her to full blowsy life. And the admirable British tar Theobald, oaken-hearted as a ship's figurehead, is a most heart-warming creation. The success of the tale depends very largely on its distinctive Dekkerian quality: the way in which sound prudential morals (generosity, hard work, thrift, marital loyalty do pay) are propounded with humour and kindness and are, furthermore, counter-balanced by a secret delight in 'flying high'.

There was no really settled form for the pamphlet, and Dekker was not farsighted enough to recognize that quasi-dramatic prose, which might have led him to the novel, was any more than one possibility amongst many. For models other than drama he could look at what had been achieved by his more eminent predecessors, Greene and Nashe. In the Bellman pamphlets, *The Bellman of London* and *Lantern and Candlelight*, he is the self-appointed heir of Greene, whose underworld exposures had been so successful more than fifteen years previously. With them Greene had developed what was in effect a new genre: he converted (one might say corrupted) into something much more literary and fictional the type of tract about criminals and their ways that had been based on first-hand knowledge and had served a useful social purpose. Like many another sensationalist, Greene (and Dekker after him) was only too glad to take over the moral sanctions for retailing spicy tales of trickery and debauchery, without greatly caring where the material was picked up. The authorities themselves nervously believed in the existence of confederacies or fraternities of rogues, but the imaginary world in which every confidence trick has its precise rules and rôles, designated by fanciful names, is in the main an invention of Greene's gladly adopted by Dekker.

Although in *News from Hell* Dekker wrote a sequel to Nashe's famous *Pierce Penniless*, it was in style rather than form that Nashe was to be his great master. His heady mixture of the impudent and the indignant, the colloquial and the learned, the solemn and the whimsical —all popular pamphleteers admired it and within their powers imitated it. As for form, Nashe had found a kind of form in invective. Dekker follows his example in, for instance, the opening of *The Gull's Horn-Book*; and the moral concern that animates much of his work is not unlike Nashe's. Perhaps the most modern characteristic of both writers is their sense of responsibility for culture and civilization in general. Distinct from academic scholars themselves, they are amongst our first 'intellectuals'.

The differences between Dekker and Nashe are differences of personality. Dekker is far less egotistic, far less arrogant: the very real gusto of which he is capable thus appears to lie in his subject instead of in himself, and it contributes to the illusion of realism. While Nashe craves personal recognition, Dekker would be satisfied with peace and quiet. While Nashe is angry and embittered, and would strike and strike hard if he could, Dekker is perplexed, dismayed, resentful. For Nashe the world is a cage; for Dekker it is a trap.

To some extent Dekker may be said to have responded to the great international movement in prose-style that in his day was beginning to reflect the process of re-thinking with which Bacon's name is so closely associated. The 'Anti-Ciceronian' style tends to be colloquial, disjointed, aphoristic and obscure, and often to consist of what might be called (in Lawrence Durrell's word) merely 'workpoints'. Dekker writes the new style, which was proper to essays and characters, with great success in the prison chapters of *Lantern and Candlelight*. But it was designed for original thinking at the expense (if necessary) of ornament and this ran counter to Dekker's more old-fashioned view of his art.

Dekker is not himself a prolific inventor. There are sources or at least starting-points for most of his best works and in, for instance, *The Bellman of London* and *The Double PP* imitation verges on what we would call plagiary. But Dekker would have regarded invention as primarily a stylistic process. As a dramatist nobody had expected him to be original: his skill lay, as Shakespeare's did, in 'digesting' scenes—in reducing story-material to a viable theatrical form. In *Poetaster*, III. iv. 322, Jonson punningly calls him 'a dresser of plaies'. He is also a decker of pamphlets.

We cannot wholly understand Dekker if we do not regard him as essentially a writer of artifice. He would have had difficulty in putting together some of his pieces at all if he had denied himself the use of variations in form and decorative formulae. In his pamphlets he often works from one set-piece to another (which in the margins of the original quartos will often be marked as such by some subtitle). We may find him, for instance, developing at length a paradox such as the praise of long, unkempt hair, or a fleeting allegory such as that of Confusion, or emblems such as those based on hunting images; while everywhere there is the sporadic rhetoric of apostrophes, soliloquies, comic hyperboles. What may seem to the modern to fall almost outside the range of artifice—the dramatic dialogue or the simple narrative, say—are properly to be considered further resources within it.

E. H. Miller has rightly pointed out that in rendering even his closest borrowing Dekker usually seems anxious to give something that is his own.[1] Hence, for example, the persona of the Bellman which Dekker invents as a vehicle of a good deal of second-hand material. And when in *Lantern and Candlelight* he copies out canting terms, Dekker goes to the trouble of at least putting them in alphabetical order and writing a piece on the Tower of Babel to introduce them. There may sometimes be some desperation in his attempts to freshen up his wares by whimsical or ingenious formal devices. Thus, the miscellaneous papers of *The Dead Term* are presented as a debate between London and Westminster personified. Most fantastic of all, *The Strange Horse-Race* describes all kinds of social phenomena as

[1] *The Professional Writer in Elizabethan England* (Cambridge, Mass., 1959), pp. 235–6.

allegorical races: a vicar versus benefices, a tailor versus pride, prodigality versus thrift, etc., whilst in 'The Catchpoles' Masque' and 'The Bankrupts' Banquet' we have sketches for devices that have scarcely got off the drawing-board.

Being a poet, he has his own favourite schemes and images, such as Hell and prison—the two being often equated. The imagery of war (a primary image for intellectual effort) comes readily to him. The actor-writers of *The Runaways' Answer* make fun of it: 'Hee would make us beleeve he has been a *Soldado* by his termes of Warre'; and concede dryly in the margin: 'He has seene Finsbury fields Mustering' (A4^v). The criticism hurt, and in *Wars, Wars, Wars* a year or two later Dekker feels obliged to admit twice that he was never a soldier, and anticipates ridicule for 'these my Martiall darings' (A4). There are many other images that recur in Dekker: conjuring in circles, angling with hooks and nets; fencing and the playing of the master's prize; voyaging (to savage lands); snakes, snails, birds and so on. One of his oddities is his fondness for the phrase 'up and down', which crops up no fewer than twenty-five times in *Lantern and Candlelight* alone. Runs of image are found in particular works. Thus when he tells comic tales of cobblers (as in *The Wonderful Year* and 'A Medicine') it is part of the fun that he should use metaphors derived from terms of the trade. But one might not consciously notice the frequent use of seafaring images in *Penny-Wise*—and of images inadvertently revealing the author's seasonable interest in a good fire. In 'An Excellent Stratagem' the sustained surgical and medical metaphor for the treatments administered to both the nuns and the friars conveys a sardonic irony which gives quite another dimension to the crudities of the story.

Dekker's pamphlets certainly tend to be bundles of sketches or stories or effects, but internal structure is by no means always or wholly lacking. He seems to have been attracted to the general pattern of the Fall, for instance. We have already seen one possible example of this in *Penny-Wise*; there is another in *The Gull's Horn-Book*. *The Bellman of London* is loosely organized on the proposition that, contrary to what one might expect, the low life of the countryside is no closer to the pastoral ideal than the low life of the city.[1] Paradise is a figment of the imagination. *Lantern and Candlelight* actually delineates a type of Fall in the story of Babel, a fall that in a narrow sense is a decay in the function of language from communication to mystification, but in a

[1] Did he get the idea from *The Return of the Knight of the Post From Hell* (London, 1606)?

larger sense helps to account doctrinally for the decadent human condition on which the rest of the book sheds light. Readers of Milton will not miss the curious resemblance of Chapter II, with its discussion of a destructive mission against the innocence of earth, to the Great Consult of *Paradise Lost*. A slender connecting thread between the tales that follow is the devastating joke of the emissary's discovery that Man, far from being innocent, has already fallen lower than the devils themselves.

The Wonderful Year begins with disillusionment like that of *The Bellman of London*: all is beautiful and peaceful and hopeful until disrupted by the savagery of real events. The imagery reveals a mind that has dwelt on the pageants of *The Magnificent Entertainment*, with its Vertumnus welcoming James to his Cheapside arbour, or the Dutch arch 'in which were to be seene, Sheepe browzing, Lambes nibbling, Byrds flying in the Ayre, with other arguments of a serene and untroubled season' (ll. 509–12). Dekker sees in the particular cancellation of his work a metaphor for the whole tragic fiasco of 1603. One can glimpse a half-realized myth of James as a sun-god bridegroom who is heralded as a regenerative force in the commonwealth but who proves to be an impotent king of cuckolds, ludicrously bringing death and disaster in his train.

Sheer variation of style and form within a work is not always one with desperate or dispirited muddle, but may be a kind of form in itself, a multiple form which, as much as any single literary form, is a valid strategy of attack upon experience. It allows a writer like Dekker —in a way extraordinary to the modern mind, which tends to be either too hidebound or too cavalier in its attitude to what is or is not decorous in literature—to respond sensitively and experimentally to a wide range of different aesthetic promptings that may indeed be irreconcilable one with another.

Given a solemn subject, he can test it to destruction. In *The Wonderful Year* Dekker describes the shock of bereavement felt by the nation when the Queen died, but then astonishingly goes on to fit together three silly little epigrams that dare to express the same emotion in the most precious of mannered poses. But the earlier treatment is not thereby nullified; this is not 'sick' humour. Similarly with his comic stories about plague-time. He knew the plague—it broke out in Whitechapel, where he may have been living at the time, and the death-roll was enormous. Around him stretched human devastation comparable to that from the fall-out of an atomic attack. But he could still reach for his pen and record not just horror and panic, but the foolish and ludicrous as well—all were 'wonderful' (he never entirely loses sight of his title). And so it was that he caught, as we have failed to do for ourselves, the very three-dimensional sense of what it was like to be alive and talking during the London blitz. He well understood what he was doing, as one can see from his expressly aiming at the same 'sad delight' as characterizes the very mixed tales soldiers tell after front-line action. Such multiconsciousness was rare enough even in his own day to meet with the disapproval of the earnest. When he comes to write *A Rod for Runaways* on similar lines to *The Wonderful Year* he feels obliged to excuse what may be thought 'idle or undecent merriment (for jests are no fruit for this season)'. And the author of *Lacrimae Londinenses* (London, 1626) writes disparagingly of 'Quacksalving Conceipts, to moove mirth, in time of a mightie Mortalitie', doubtless with Dekker partly in mind.[1]

But why seek further for form? One might well claim that throughout Dekker's work the constant figurativeness and allusiveness, the shifting conventions, devices and styles, the frequency of parentheses (giving an inner voice to so many sentences), and above all the puns and wordplay—in short, the ever-present tendency to explain or describe everything in terms of something else, makes up so rich and close-woven a linguistic fabric that it is all but self-sufficient and hardly needs any relation to real life or to any statement about real life to justify its existence.

[1] Wilson, pp. 153, 245–6n.

The Wonderful Year

1603.

THE VVON-
derfull yeare.

Wherein is shewed the picture of *London*, lying sicke of the Plague.

At the ende of all (like a mery Epilogue to a dull Play) cer-
taine Tales are cut out in sundry fashions, of purpose
to shorten the liues of long winters nights,
that lye watching in the darke for vs.

Et me rigidi legant Catones.

LONDON
Printed by Thomas Creede, and are to be solde
in Saint Donstones Church-yarde
in Fleet-streete.

To his Well Respected Good Friend,
Master Cuthbert Thuresby,
Water-Bailiff of London.

Books are but poor gifts, yet kings receive them; upon which I presume you will not turn this out of doors. You cannot for shame but bid it welcome, because it brings to you a great quantity of my love; which if it be worth little (and no marvel if love be sold underfoot when the god of love himself goes naked!) yet I hope you will not say you have a hard bargain, sithence you may take as much of it as you please for nothing. I have clapped the cognizance of your name on these scribbled papers; it is their livery. So that now they are yours, being free from any vile imputation save only that they thrust themselves into your acquaintance. But general errors have general pardons: for the title of other men's names is the common heraldry which all those lay claim to whose crest is a pen and inkhorn.

If you read, you may haply laugh. 'Tis my desire you should, because mirth is both physical and wholesome against the plague; with which sickness, to tell truth, this book is—though not sorely—yet somewhat infected. I pray, drive it not out of your company for all that. For, assure your soul, I am so jealous of your health that if you did but once imagine there were gall in mine ink, I would cast away the standish and forswear meddling with any more Muses.

To the Reader.

And why 'To the Reader'? O good sir, there's as sound law to make you give good words to the reader as to a constable when he carries his watch about him to tell how the night goes, though perhaps the one oftentimes may be served in for a goose and the other very fitly furnish the same mess. Yet to maintain the scurvy fashion and to keep custom in reparations he must be honeyed and come over with 'gentle reader', 'courteous reader' and 'learned reader' though he have no more gentility in him than Adam had, that was but a gardener, no more civility than a Tartar, and no more learning than the most arrant stinkard that except his own name could never find anything in the horn-book.

How notoriously therefore do good wits dishonour not only their calling but even their creation that worship glow-worms instead of the sun because of a little false glistering! In the name of Phœbus, what madness leads them unto it? For he that dares hazard a pressing to death—that's to say, to be a man in print—must make account that he shall stand like the old weathercock over Paul's steeple, to be beaten with all storms. Neither the stinking tobacco breath of a satin gull, the aconited sting of a narrow-eyed critic, the faces of a fantastic stage monkey, nor the 'Indeed-la!' of a puritanical citizen must once shake him; no, but desperately resolve like a French post to ride through thick and thin, endure to see his lines torn pitifully on the rack, suffer his Muse to take the *baston*—yea, the very stab—and himself like a new stake to be a mark for every haggler. And therefore, setting up all these rests, why should he regard what fool's bolt is shot at him? Besides, if that which he presents upon the stage of the world be good, why should he basely cry out, with that old poetical madcap in his *Amphitruo*, '*Iovis summi causa clare plaudite*'—beg a plaudit for God sake? If bad, who but an ass would entreat as players do in a cogging epilogue at the end of a filthy comedy that, be it never such wicked stuff, they would forbear to hiss or to damn it perpetually to lie on a stationer's stall? For he that can so cozen himself as to pocket up praise in that silly sort makes his brains fat with his own folly.

But *hinc pudor*—or rather *hinc dolor*: here's the Devil! It is not the rattling of all this former hail-shot that can terrify our band of Castalian penmen from entering into the field. No, no, the murdering artillery indeed lies in the roaring mouths of a company that look big as if they were the sole and singular commanders over the main army of poesy, yet if Hermes's muster-book were searched over they'll be found to be most pitiful pure freshwater soldiers! They give out that they are heirs apparent to Helicon but an easy herald may make them mere younger brothers or, to say truth, not so much. Bear witness all you whose wits make you able to be witnesses in this case that here I meddle not with your good poets: *nam tales nusquam sunt hic amplius*. If you should rake Hell or, as Aristophanes in his *Frog* says, in any cellar deeper than Hell, it is hard to find spirits of that fashion. But those goblins whom I now am conjuring up have bladder-cheeks puffed out like a Switzer's breeches—yet, being pricked, there comes out nothing but wind: thin-headed fellows that live upon the scraps of invention and 'travel' with such vagrant souls and so like ghosts in white sheets of paper that the Statute of Rogues may worthily be sued upon them because their wits have no abiding place and yet wander without a passport.

Alas poor wenches, the Nine Muses! How much are you wronged to have such a number of bastards lying upon your hands! But turn them out a-begging; or if you cannot be rid of their rhyming company, as I think it will be very hard, then lay your heavy and immortal curse upon them that whatsoever they weave in the motley loom of their rusty pates may like a beggar's cloak be full of stolen patches and yet never a patch like one another, that it may be such true lamentable stuff that any honest Christian may be sorry to see it. Banish these word-pirates, you sacred mistresses of learning, into the Gulf of Barbarism; doom them everlastingly to live among dunces; let them not once lick their lips at the Thespian bowl but only be glad—and thank Apollo for it, too—if hereafter, as hitherto they have always, they may quench their poetical thirst with small beer. Or if they will needs be stealing your Heliconian nectar, let them like the dogs of Nile only lap and away. For this goatish swarm are those that, where for these many thousand years you went for pure maids, have taken away your good names. These are they that deflower your beauties. These are those rank riders of art that have so spur-galled your lusty-winged Pegasus that now he begins to be out of flesh and, even only for provender sake, is glad to show tricks like Banks his curtal.

O you booksellers (that are factors to the liberal sciences) over whose stalls these drones do daily fly humming, let Homer, Hesiod, Euripides and some other mad-Greeks with a band of the Latins lie like musket shot in their way when these Goths and Getes set upon you in your paper fortifications. It is the only cannon upon whose mouth they dare not venture; none but the English will take their parts.

Therefore fear them not, for such a strong breath have these cheese-eaters that if they do but blow upon a book they imagine straight 'tis blasted: '*Quod supra nos, nihil ad nos,*' they say—'That which is above our capacity shall not pass under our commendation.' Yet would I have these Zoilists of all other to read me if ever I should write anything worthily, for the blame that known fools heap upon a deserving labour does not discredit the same but makes wise men more perfectly in love with it. Into such a one's hands therefore if I fortune to fall, I will not shrink an inch but, even when his teeth are sharpest and most ready to bite, I will stop his mouth only with this: *haec mala sunt, sed tu non meliora facis.*

Reader.

Whereas there stands in the rearward of this book a certain mingled troop of strange discourses fashioned into tales, know that the intelligence which first brought them to light was only flying report; whose tongue, as it often does, if in spreading them it have tripped in any material point and either slipped too far or fallen too short, bear with the error—and the rather because it is not wilfully committed. Neither let anyone whom those reports shall seem to touch cavil or complain of injury, sithence nothing is set down by a malicious hand. Farewell.

The Wonderful Year

Vertumnus, being attired in his accustomed habit of changeable silk, had newly passed through the first and principal court gate of heaven; to whom, for a farewell and to show how dutiful he was in his office, Janus that bears two faces under one hood made a very mannerly low leg and because he was the only porter at that gate presented unto this King of the Months all the New Year's gifts, which were more in number and more worth than those that are given to the Great Turk or the Emperor of Persia. On went Vertumnus in his lusty Progress—Priapus, Flora, the *dryades* and *hamadryades* with all the wooden rabble of those that dressed orchards and gardens perfuming all the ways that he went with the sweet odours that breathed from flowers, herbs and trees, which now began to peep out of prison. By virtue of which excellent airs the sky got a most clear complexion, looked smug and smooth, and had not so much as a wart sticking on her face. The sun likewise was freshly and very richly apparelled in cloth of gold like a bridegroom and instead of gilded rosemary the horns of the Ram, being the sign of that celestial bridehouse where he lay to be married to the Spring, were not like your common horns parcel-gilt but double-double-gilt with the liquid gold that melted from his beams.

For joy whereof the lark sung at his window every morning, the nightingale every night, the cuckoo—like a single-sole fiddler that reels from tavern to tavern—plied it all the day long, lambs frisked up and down in the valleys, kids and goats leaped to and fro on the mountains, shepherds sat piping, country wenches singing, lovers made sonnets for their lasses whilst they made garlands for their lovers. And as the country was frolic, so was the city merry. Olive-trees, which grow nowhere but in the garden of peace, stood as common as beech does at midsummer at every man's door, branches of palm were in every man's hand, streets were full of people, people full of joy, every house seemed to have a Lord of Misrule in it—in every house there was so much jollity; no screech-owl frighted the silly countryman at midnight nor any drum the citizen at noonday, but all was more calm than a still water, all hushed, as if the spheres

I   The Bower of Plenty in *The Magnificent Entertainment*

II   Fugitives from the Plague

had been playing in concert. In conclusion, heaven looked like a palace and the great hall of the earth like a paradise.

But oh! the short-lived felicity of man! O world, of what slight and thin stuff is thy happiness! Just in the midst of this jocund holiday a storm rises in the west. Westward from the top of a Rich-mount descended a hideous tempest that shook cedars, terrified the tallest pines and cleft in sunder even the hardest hearts of oak. And if such great trees were shaken, what think you became of the tender eglantine and humble hawthorn? They could not, doubtless, but droop; they could not choose but die with the terror. The element, taking the Destinies' part, who indeed set abroach this mischief, scowled on the earth and, filling her high forehead full of black wrinkles, tumbling long up and down like a great-bellied wife—her sighs being whirlwinds, and her groans thunder, at length she fell in labour and was delivered of a pale, meagre, weak child named Sickness, whom Death—with a pestilence!—would needs take upon him to nurse, and did so. This starveling being come to his full growth had an office given him for nothing (and that's a wonder in this age): Death made him his herald, attired him like a courtier and, in his name, charged him to go into the Privy Chamber of the English Queen to summon her to appear in the Star Chamber of Heaven.

The summons made her start but, having an invincible spirit, did not amaze her. Yet whom would not the certain news of parting from a kingdom amaze? But she knew where to find a richer, and therefore lightly regarded the loss of this, and thereupon made ready for that Heavenly coronation, being—which was most strange—most dutiful to obey, that had so many years so powerfully commanded. She obeyed Death's messenger and yielded her body to the hands of Death himself. She died, resigning her sceptre to posterity and her soul to immortality.

The report of her death, like a thunder-clap, was able to kill thousands. It took away hearts from millions. For having brought up even under her wing a nation that was almost begotten and born under her, that never shouted any other *ave* than for her name, never saw the face of any prince but herself, never understood what that strange outlandish word 'change' signified—how was it possible but that her sickness should throw abroad an universal fear, and her death an astonishment? She was the courtier's treasure: therefore he had cause to mourn. The lawyer's sword of justice: he might well faint. The merchant's patroness: he had reason to look pale. The citizen's mother: he might best lament. The shepherd's goddess: and should not he droop? Only the soldier, who had walked a long time upon wooden legs and was not able to give arms, though he were a gentleman, had bristled up the quills of his stiff porcupine mustachio and swore by no beggars that now was the hour come for him to bestir his stumps. Usurers and brokers, that are the Devil's ingles and dwell in the Long Lane of Hell, quaked like aspen leaves at his oaths; those that before were the only cut-throats in London now stood in fear of no other death. But my Signior Soldado was deceived. The tragedy went not forward.

Never did the English nation behold so much black worn as there was at her funeral. It was then but put on to try if it were fit, for the great day of mourning was set down in the book of Heaven to be held afterwards. That was but the dumb show: the tragical act hath been playing ever since. Her hearse, as it was borne, seemed to be an island swimming in water, for round about it there rained showers of tears: about her death-bed, none, for her departure was so sudden and so strange that men knew not how to weep because they had never been taught to shed tears of that making. They that durst not speak their sorrows whispered them; they that durst not whisper sent them forth in sighs. Oh, what an earthquake is the alteration of a state! Look from the Chamber of Presence to the farmer's cottage and you shall find nothing but distraction. The whole Kingdom seems a wilderness and the people in it are transformed to wild men. The map of a country so pitifully distracted by the horror of a change if you desire perfectly to behold, cast your eyes then on this that follows—which, being heretofore in private presented to the King, I think may very worthily show itself before you. And because you shall see them attired in the same fashion that they wore before His Majesty, let these few lines which stood then as Prologue to the rest enter first into your ears.

> Not for applauses, shallow fools adventure,
> I plunge my verse into a sea of censure,
> But with a liver dressed in gall to see
> So many rooks, catchpoles of poesy,
> That feed upon the fallings of high wit
> And put on cast inventions most unfit.
> For such, am I pressed forth in shops and stalls,
> Pasted in Paul's and on the lawyers' walls,
> For every basilisk-eyed critic's bait

To kill my verse or poison my conceit,
Or some smoked gallant who at wit repines
To dry tobacco with my wholesome lines
And in one paper sacrifice more brain
Than all his ignorant skull could e'er contain.
But merit dreads no martyrdom nor stroke:
My lines shall live when he shall be all smoke.

Thus far the Prologue who, leaving the stage clear, the fears that are bred in the womb of this altering Kingdom do next step up, acting thus:

The great impostume of the realm was drawn
Even to a head. The multitudinous spawn
Was the corruption which did make it swell
With hoped sedition, the burnt seed of Hell.
Who did expect but ruin, blood and death
To share our Kingdom and divide our breath?
Religions without religion
To let each other blood; Confusion
To be next Queen of England; and this year
The Civil Wars of France to be played here
By Englishmen—ruffians and pandering slaves
That fain would dig up gouty usurers' graves?
At such a time villains their hopes do honey
And rich men look as pale as their white money.
Now they remove and make their silver sweat,
Casting themselves into a covetous heat
And then, unseen, in the confederate dark
Bury their gold without or priest or clerk
And say no prayers over that dead pelf
(True, gold's no Christian but an Indian elf).
Did not the very Kingdom seem to shake
Her precious massy limbs? Did she not make
All English cities like her pulses beat
With people in their veins? The fear so great
That, had it not been physicked with rare peace,
Our populous bower had lessened her increase;
The spring-time, that was dry, had sprung in blood
A greater dearth of men than e'er of food:
In such a panting time and gasping year

Victuals are cheapest—only men are dear.
Now each wise-acred landlord did despair,
Fearing some villain should become his heir
Or that his son and heir before his time
Should now turn villain and with violence climb
Up to his life, saying 'Father, you have seen
King Henry, Edward, Mary and the Queen—
I wonder you'll live longer!' Then he tells him
He's loath to see him killed—therefore he kills him.
And each vast landlord dies like a poor slave:
Their thousand acres make them but a grave.
At such a time great men convey their treasure
Into the trusty City, wait the leisure
Of blood and insurrection which war clips
When every gate shuts up her iron lips.
Imagine now a mighty man of dust
Stands in a doubt what servant he may trust
With plate worth thousands, jewels worth far more.
If he prove false, then his rich lord proves poor.
He calls forth one by one to note their graces:
Whilst they make legs, he copies out their faces,
Examines their eyebrow, consters their beard,
Singles their nose out. Still he rests afeared.
The first that comes, by no means he'll allow—
Has spied three hairs starting between his brow:
Quite turns the word, names it celerity
For 'hares' do run away, and so may he.
A second shown, him he will scarce behold—
His beard's too red, the colour of his gold.
A third may please him, but 'tis hard to say
A rich man's pleased when his goods part away.
And now do chirrup by, fine golden nests
Of well-hatched bowls such as do breed in feasts;
For war and death cupboards of plate down pulls:
Then, Bacchus drinks not in gilt bowls but skulls.
Let me descend and stoop my verse a while
To make the comic cheek of poesy smile:
Rank penny-fathers scud, with their half hams
Shadowing their calves, to save their silver dams.
At every gun they start, tilt from the ground—

One drum can make a thousand usurers swound.
In unsought alleys and unwholesome places,
Back-ways and by-lanes where appear few faces,
In shamble-smelling rooms, loathsome prospects
And penny-lattice windows which rejects
All popularity—there the rich cubs lurk
When in great houses ruffians are at work,
Not dreaming that such glorious booties lie
Under those nasty roofs. Such they pass by
Without a search, crying 'There's nought for us!'
And wealthy men deceive poor villains thus.
Tongue-'travelling' lawyers faint at such a day,
Lie speechless for they have no words to say.
Physicians turn to patients, their arts dry
For then our fat men without physic die.
And to conclude, against all art and good
War taints the doctor, lets the surgeon blood.

Such was the fashion of this land when the great landlady thereof
left it. She came in with the fall of the leaf and went away in the
spring—her life, which was dedicated to virginity, both beginning
and closing up a miraculous maiden circle, for she was born upon a
Lady Eve and died upon a Lady Eve, her nativity and death being
memorable by this wonder, the first and last years of her reign by this:
that a Leigh was Lord Mayor when she came to the crown and a Lee
Lord Mayor when she departed from it. Three places are made famous
by her for three things: Greenwich for her birth, Richmond for her
death, Whitehall for her funeral. Upon her removing from whence (to
lend our tiring prose a breathing-time) stay and look upon these epigrams, being composed:

1. *Upon the Queen's Last Remove, being Dead.*

The Queen's removed in solemn sort,
Yet this was strange and seldom seen:
The Queen used to remove the Court
But now the Court removed the Queen.

2. *Upon her Bringing by Water to Whitehall.*

The Queen was brought by water to Whitehall;
At every stroke the oars tears let fall;
More clung about the barge; fish under water
Wept out their eyes of pearl and swam blind after.
I think the bargemen might with easier thighs
Have rowed her thither in her people's eyes—
For howsoe'er, thus much my thoughts have scanned:
She'd come by water had she come by land.

3. *Upon her Lying Dead at Whitehall.*

The Queen lies now at Whitehall dead
And now at Whitehall living.
To make this rough objection even:
Dead at Whitehall in Westminster
But living at white hall in Heaven.

Thus you see that both in her life and her death she was appointed to be the mirror of her time. And surely if, since the first stone that was laid for the foundation of this great house of the world, there was ever a year ordained to be wondered at, it is only this. The sibyls' *octogesimus octavus annus*, that same terrible '88 which came sailing hither in the Spanish Armada and made men's hearts colder than the Frozen Zone when they heard but an inkling of it; that '88 by whose horrible predictions almanac-makers stood in bodily fear their trade would be utterly overthrown, and poor Erra Pater was threatened—because he was a Jew—to be put to baser offices than the stopping of mustard pots; that same '88 which had more prophecies waiting at his heels than ever Merlin the magician had in his head was a year of Jubilee to this. Plato's *mirabilis annus* (whether it be past already or to come within these four years) may throw Plato's cap at *mirabilis* for that title of 'wonderful' is bestowed upon 1603. If that sacred aromatically-perfumed fire of wit out of whose flames Phoenix poesy doth arise were burning in any breast, I would feed it with no other stuff for a twelvemonth and a day than with kindling-papers full of lines that should tell only of the chances, changes and strange shapes that this Protean climacterical year hath metamorphosed himself into. It is able to find ten chroniclers a competent living and to set twenty printers at work.

You shall perceive I lie not if, with Peter Bales, you will take the pains to draw the whole volume of it into the compass of a penny. As first, to begin with the Queen's death; then the Kingdom's falling into an ague upon that. Next follows the curing of that fever by the wholesome receipt of a proclaimed king. That wonder begat more, for in an hour two mighty nations were made one, wild Ireland became tame on the sudden, and some English great ones that before seemed tame on the sudden turned wild—the same park which great Julius Caesar enclosed to hold in that deer whom they before hunted, being now circled by a second Caesar with stronger pales to keep them from leaping over. And last of all (if that wonder be the last and shut up the year) a most dreadful plague. This is the abstract and yet, like Stow's *Chronicle* in decimo-sexto to huge Holinshed, these small pricks in this sea-card of ours represent mighty countries. Whilst I have the quill in my hand, let me blow them bigger.

The Queen being honoured with a diadem of stars France, Spain and Belgia lift up their heads preparing to do as much for England by giving aim whilst she shot arrows at her own breast—as they imagined —as she had done many a year together for them. And her own nation betted on their sides, looking with distracted countenance for no better guests than Civil Sedition, Uproars, Rapes, Murders and Massacres. But the Wheel of Fate turned, a better lottery was drawn, *pro Troia stabat Apollo*—God stuck valiantly to us. For behold! up rises a comfortable sun out of the north whose glorious beams like a fan dispersed all thick and contagious clouds. The loss of a Queen was paid with the double interest of a King and Queen. The cedar of her government, which stood alone and bare no fruit, is changed now to an olive upon whose spreading branches grow both kings and queens. Oh, it were able to fill a hundred pair of writing-tables with notes but to see the parts played in the compass of one hour on the stage of this new-found world! Upon Thursday it was treason to cry 'God save King James, King of England!' and upon Friday high treason not to cry so. In the morning no voice heard but murmurs and lamentation; at noon nothing but shouts of gladness and triumph. St George and St Andrew, that many hundred years had defied one another, were now sworn brothers: England and Scotland, being parted only with a narrow river, and the people of both empires speaking a language less differing than English within itself, as though Providence had enacted that one

day those two nations should marry one another, are now made sure
together, and King James his Coronation is the solemn wedding-day.
Happiest of all thy ancestors, thou mirror of all princes that ever were
or are, that at seven of the clock wert a king but over a piece of a little
island and before eleven the greatest monarch in Christendom. Now

silver crowds
Of blissful angels and tried martyrs tread
On the star ceiling over England's head;
Now Heaven broke into a wonder and brought forth
Our *omne bonum* from the wholesome north—
Our fruitful sovereign James, at whose dread name
Rebellion swounded and e'er since became
Grovelling and nerveless, wanting blood to nourish,
For Ruin gnaws herself when kingdoms flourish.
Now are our hopes planted in regal springs
Never to wither, for our air breeds kings
And in all ages, from this sovereign time,
England shall still be called the royal clime.
Most blissful monarch of all earthen powers,
Served with a mess of kingdoms: four such bowers,
For prosperous hives and rare industrious swarms,
The world contains not in her solid arms.
O thou that art the meter of our days,
Poets' Apollo, deal thy Daphnean bays
To those whose wits are bay-trees evergreen
Upon whose high tops poesy chirps unseen;
Such are most fit t'apparel kings in rhymes
Whose silver numbers are the Muses' chimes,
Whose sprightly characters, being once wrought on,
Outlive the marble they're insculped upon.
Let such men chant thy virtues, then they fly
On learning's wings up to eternity.
As for the rest, that limp in cold desert,
Having small wit, less judgment and least art:
Their verse 'tis almost heresy to hear!
Banish their lines some furlong from thine ear
For 'tis held dang'rous (by Apollo's sign)
To be infected with a leprous line.
Oh, make some adamant Act, ne'er to be worn,

That none may write but those that are true-born;
So when the world's old cheeks shall rase and peel,
Thy Acts shall breathe in epitaphs of steel.

By these comments it appears that by this time King James is proclaimed. Now does fresh blood leap into the cheeks of the courtier; the soldier now hangs up his armour and is glad that he shall feed upon the blessed fruits of peace; the scholar sings hymns in honour of the Muses, assuring himself now that Helicon will be kept pure, because Apollo himself drinks of it. Now the thrifty citizen casts beyond the moon and, seeing the Golden Age returned into the world again, resolves to worship no saint but money. Trades that lay dead and rotten and were in all men's opinion utterly damned started out of their trance as though they had drunk of *aqua cælestis* or unicorn's horn and swore to fall to their old occupation. Tailors meant no more to be called 'merchant-tailors' but 'merchants', for their shops were all led forth in 'leases' to be turned into ships, and with their shears instead of a rudder would they have cut the seas like Levant taffeta and sailed to the West Indies for no worse stuff to make hose and doublets of than beaten gold. Or if the necessity of the time, which was likely to stand altogether upon bravery, should press them to serve with their iron and Spanish weapons upon their stalls, then was there a sharp law made amongst them that no workman should handle any needle but that which had a pearl in his eye, nor any copper thimble unless it were lined quite through or bombasted with silver. What mechanical hard-handed Vulcanist, seeing the dice of Fortune run so sweetly, and resolving to strike whilst the iron was hot, but persuaded himself to be Master or Head Warden of his Company ere half a year went about? The worst players' boy stood upon his good parts, swearing tragical and buskined oaths that, how villainously soever he ranted or what bad and unlawful action soever he entered into, he would in despite of his honest audience be half a sharer—at least—at home or else *stroll* (that's to say, 'travel') with some notorious wicked floundering company abroad.

And good reason had these time-catchers to be led into this fools' paradise. For they saw mirth in every man's face; the streets were plumed with gallants; tobacconists filled up whole taverns; vintners hung out spick and span new ivy-bushes (because they wanted good wine) and their old rain-beaten lattices marched under other colours, having lost both company and colours before. London was never in the highway to preferment till now. Now, she resolved to stand upon her pantofles. Now—and never till now—did she laugh to scorn that worm-eaten proverb of 'Lincoln was, London is, and York shall be' for she saw herself in better state than Jerusalem. She went more gallant than ever did Antwerp; was more courted by amorous and lusty suitors than Venice, the minion of Italy; more lofty towers stood like a coronet or a spangled head-tire about her temples than ever did about the beautiful forehead of Rome; Tyre and Sidon to her were like two thatched houses to Theobalds, the Grand Cairo but a hogsty.

Hinc illæ lacrimæ—she wept her bellyful for all this. Whilst Troy was swilling sack and sugar and mousing fat venison the mad-Greeks made bonfires of their houses. Old Priam was drinking a health to the wooden horse and, before it could be pledged, had his throat cut. Corn is no sooner ripe but, for all the pricking up of his ears, he is pared off by the shins and made to go upon stumps. Flowers no sooner budded but they are plucked and die. Night walks at the heels of the day, and sorrow enters like a tavern-bill at the tail of our pleasures. For in the Appenine height of this immoderate joy and security that like Paul's steeple overlooked the whole City—behold! that miracle-worker who in one minute turned our general mourning to a general mirth does now again in a moment alter that gladness to shrieks and lamentation.

Here would I fain make a full point because posterity should not be frighted with those miserable tragedies which now my Muse as Chorus stands ready to present. Time, would thou hadst never been made wretched by bringing them forth! Oblivion, would in all the graves and sepulchres whose rank jaws thou hast already closed up or shalt yet hereafter burst open, thou couldst likewise bury them forever!

A stiff and freezing horror sucks up the rivers of my blood. My hair stands on end with the panting of my brains. Mine eye-balls are ready to start out, being beaten with the billows of my tears. Out of my weeping pen does the ink mournfully and more bitterly than gall drop on the pale-faced paper even when I do but think how the bowels of my sick country have been torn. Apollo therefore, and you bewitching silver-tongued Muses, get you gone: I invoke none of your names. Sorrow and Truth, sit you on each side of me whilst I am delivered of this deadly burden: prompt me that I may utter ruthful and passion-ate condolement; arm my trembling hand that it may boldly rip up and anatomize the ulcerous body of this anthropophagized plague; lend me art, without any counterfeit shadowing to paint and delineate to the life the whole story of this mortal and pestiferous battle. And you the ghosts of those more by many than 40,000 that with the virulent poison of infection have been driven out of your earthly dwellings, you desolate hand-wringing widows that beat your bosoms over your departing husbands, you woefully distracted mothers that with dishevelled hair are fallen into swoons whilst you lie kissing the insensible cold lips of your breathless infants, you outcast and down-trodden orphans that shall many a year hence remember, more freshly to mourn, when your mourning garments shall look old and be forgotten, and you the Genii of all those emptied families whose habitations are now among the Antipodes: join all your hands together and with your bodies cast a ring about me; let me behold your ghastly visages, that my paper may receive their true pictures; echo forth your groans through the hollow trunk of my pen and rain down your gummy tears into mine ink, that even marble bosoms may be shaken with terror, and hearts of adamant melt into compassion.

What an unmatchable torment were it for a man to be barred up every night in a vast, silent charnel-house hung, to make it more hideous, with lamps dimly and slowly burning in hollow and glim-mering corners; where all the pavement should instead of green rushes be strewed with blasted rosemary, withered hyacinths, fatal cypress and yew, thickly mingled with heaps of dead men's bones—the bare ribs of a father that begat him lying there, here the chapless hollow skull of a mother that bore him; round about him a thousand corpses, some standing bolt upright in their knotted winding-sheets, others half mouldered in rotten coffins that should suddenly yawn wide open filling his nostrils with noisome stench and his eyes with the sight of nothing but crawling worms. And to keep such a poor wretch waking, he should hear no noise but of toads croaking, screech-owls howling, mandrakes shrieking. Were not this an infernal prison? Would not the strongest-hearted man beset with such a ghastly horror look wild? And run mad? And die?

And even such a formidable shape did the diseased City appear in. For he that durst in the dead hour of gloomy midnight have been so valiant as to have walked through the still and melancholy streets—what think you should have been his music? Surely the loud groans of raving sick men, the struggling pangs of souls departing; in every house grief striking up an alarum—servants crying out for masters, wives for husbands, parents for children, children for their mothers. Here, he should have met some franticly running to knock up sextons; there, others fearfully sweating with coffins to steal forth dead bodies lest the fatal handwriting of Death should seal up their doors. And to make this dismal concert more full, round about him bells heavily tolling in one place and ringing out in another. The dreadfulness of such an hour is inutterable. Let us go further.

If some poor man, suddenly starting out of a sweet and golden slumber, should behold his house flaming about his ears, all his family destroyed in their sleeps by the merciless fire, himself in the very midst of it woefully and like a madman calling for help—would not the misery of such a distressed soul appear the greater if the rich usurer dwelling next door to him should not stir, though he felt part of the danger, but suffer him to perish when the thrusting out of an arm might have saved him? Oh, how many thousands of wretched people have acted this poor man's part! How often hath the amazed husband, waking, found the comfort of his bed lying breathless by his side, his children at the same instant gasping for life, and his servants mortally wounded at the heart by sickness! The distracted creature beats at death's doors, exclaims at windows; his cries are sharp enough to pierce Heaven but on earth no ear is opened to receive them.

And in this manner do the tedious minutes of the night stretch out the sorrows of ten thousand. It is now day. Let us look forth and try what consolation rises with the sun. Not any, not any. For before the jewel of the morning be fully set in silver, a hundred hungry graves stand gaping and every one of them, as at a breakfast, hath swallowed down ten or eleven lifeless carcases. Before dinner in the same gulf are twice so many more devoured. And before the sun takes his rest those numbers are doubled. Threescore, that not many hours before had every one several lodgings very delicately furnished, are now thrust all together into one close room, a little, little, noisome room not fully ten foot square. Doth not this strike coldly to the heart of a worldly miser? To some the very sound of Death's name is instead of a passing-bell: what shall become of such a coward, being told that the selfsame body of his which now is so pampered with superfluous fare, so perfumed and bathed in odoriferous waters and so gaily apparelled in variety of fashions, must one day be thrown like stinking carrion into a rank and rotten grave where his goodly eyes, that did once shoot forth such amorous glances, must be eaten out of his head, his locks that hang wantonly dangling trodden in dirt underfoot? This, doubtless, like thunder must needs strike him into the earth! But, wretched man! when thou shalt see and be assured by tokens sent thee from Heaven that tomorrow thou must be fumbled into a muck-pit and suffer thy body to be bruised and pressed with threescore dead men lying slovenly upon thee, and thou to be undermost of all—yea, and perhaps half of that number were thine enemies, and see how they may be revenged, for the worms that breed out of their putrefying carcases shall crawl in huge swarms from them and quite devour thee— what agonies will this strange news drive thee into? If thou art in love with thyself this cannot choose but possess thee with frenzy.

But thou art gotten safe out of the civil City calamity to thy parks and palaces in the country, lading thy asses and thy mules with thy gold (thy god), thy plate and thy jewels; and, the fruits of thy womb thriftily growing up but in one only son, the young landlord of all thy careful labours, him also hast thou rescued from the arrows of infection. Now is thy soul jocund and thy senses merry. But open thine eyes, thou fool, and behold that darling of thine eye, thy son, turned suddenly into a lump of clay. The hand of pestilence hath smote him even under thy wing. Now dost thou rend thine hair, blaspheme thy Creator, cursest thy creation and basely descendest into brutish and unmanly passions, threatening in despite of Death and his plague to maintain the memory of thy child in the everlasting breast of marble. A tomb must now defend him from tempests. And for that purpose the sweaty hind that digs the rent he pays thee out of the entrails of the earth, he is sent for to convey forth that burden of thy sorrow. But note how thy pride is disdained. That weather-beaten sunburnt drudge that not a month since fawned upon thy worship like a spaniel, and like a bondslave would have stooped lower than thy feet, does now stop his nose at thy presence and is ready to set his mastiff as high as thy throat to drive thee from his door. All thy gold and silver cannot hire one of those whom before thou didst scorn, to carry the dead body to his last home.

The country round about thee shun thee as a basilisk; and therefore to London, from whose arms thou cowardly fledst away, post upon post must be galloping to fetch from thence those that may perform that funeral office. But there are they so full of grave matters of their own that they have no leisure to attend thine. Doth not this cut thy very heart-strings in sunder? If that do not, the shutting up of this tragical act I am sure will. For thou must be enforced with thine own hands to wind up that blasted flower of youth in the last linen that ever he shall wear. Upon thine own shoulders must thou bear part of him, thy amazed servant the other. With thine own hands must thou dig his grave, not in the church or common place of burial—thou hast not favour, for all thy riches, to be so happy; but in thine orchard or in the proud walks of thy garden, wringing thy palsy-shaken hands instead of bells, most miserable father, must thou search him out a sepulchre.

My spirit grows faint with rowing in this Stygian ferry. It can no longer endure the transportation of souls in this doleful manner. Let us therefore shift a point of our compass and, since there is no remedy but that we must still be tossed up and down in this *Mare Mortuum*, hoist up all our sails and on the merry wings of a lustier wind seek to arrive on some prosperous shore.

Imagine then that all this while Death, like a Spanish leaguer—or rather, like stalking Tamburlaine—hath pitched his tents, being nothing but a heap of winding-sheets tacked together, in the sinfully polluted suburbs. The plague is muster-master and marshal of the field; burning fevers, boils, blains and carbuncles the leaders, lieutenants, sergeants and corporals; the main army consisting like Dunkirk of a mingle-mangle, viz. dumpish mourners, merry sextons, hungry coffin-sellers, scrubbing bearers and nasty grave-makers (but indeed they are the pioneers of the camp, that are employed only like moles in casting up of earth and digging of trenches); fear and trembling, the two catchpoles of Death, arrest everyone.

No parley will be granted, no composition stood upon. But the alarum is struck up, the tocsin rings out for life, and no voice heard but '*Tue! Tue!*'—'Kill! Kill!' The little bells only, like small shot, do yet go off and make no great work for worms—a hundred or two lost in every skirmish or so. But alas, that's nothing. Yet by these desperate sallies, what by open setting upon them by day and secret ambuscadoes by night, the skirts of London were pitifully pared off by little and little. Which they within the gates perceiving, it was no boot to bid them take their heels, for away they trudge thick and threefold—some riding, some on foot, some without boots, some in their slippers, by water, by land. In shoals swam they westward. Marry, to Gravesend none went unless they were driven, for whosoever landed there never came back again. Hackneys, watermen and wagons were not so terribly employed many a year, so that within a short time there was not a good horse in Smithfield nor a coach to be set eye on: for after the world had once run upon the wheels of the pest-cart neither coach nor caroach durst appear in his likeness.

Let us pursue these runaways no longer but leave them in the unmerciful hands of the country hard-hearted Hobbinolls who are ordained to be their tormentors, and return back to the siege of the

City, for the enemy, taking advantage by their flight, planted his ordnance against the walls. Here the cannons, like their great bells, roared. The Plague took sore pains for a breach; he laid about him cruelly ere he could get it, but at length he and his tyrannous band entered. His purple colours were presently—with the sound of Bow-bell instead of a trumpet—advanced and joined to the Standard of the City. He marched even through Cheapside and the capital streets of Troynovant. The only blot of dishonour that stuck upon this invader being this, that he played the tyrant not the conqueror, making havoc of all when he had all lying at the foot of his mercy. Men, women and children dropped down before him. Houses were rifled, streets ransacked, beautiful maidens thrown on their beds and ravished by sickness, rich men's coffers broken open and shared amongst prodigal heirs and unthrifty servants, poor men used poorly but not pitifully. He did very much hurt, yet some say he did very much good. Howsoever he behaved himself, this intelligence runs current, that every house looked like St Bartholomew's Hospital and every street like Bucklersbury, for poor Mithridatum and Dragon-Water, being both of them in all the world scarce worth threepence, were boxed in every corner and yet were both drunk every hour at other men's cost. Lazarus lay groaning at every man's door—marry, no Dives was within to send him a crumb, for all your goldfinches were fled to the woods, nor a dog left to lick up his sores for they, like curs, were knocked down like oxen and fell thicker than acorns.

I am amazed to remember what dead marches were made of three thousand trooping together: husbands, wives and children being led as ordinarily to one grave as if they had gone to one bed. And those that could shift for a time and shrink their heads out of the collar, as many did, yet went they most bitterly miching and muffled up and down with rue and wormwood stuffed into their ears and nostrils, looking like so many boars' heads stuck with branches of rosemary to be served in for brawn at Christmas.

This was a rare world for the Church, who had wont to complain for want of living and now had more living thrust upon her than she knew how to bestow. To have been clerk now to a Parish Clerk was better than to serve some foolish Justice of Peace or than, the year before, to have had a benefice. Sextons gave out if they might, as they hoped, continue these doings but a twelvemonth longer they and their posterity would all ride upon foot-cloths to the end of the world. Amongst which worm-eaten generation the three bald sextons of

limping St Giles', St Sepulchre's and St Olave's ruled the roast more
hotly than ever did the *triumviri* of Rome. Johanan, Simon and
Eleazar never kept such a plaguy coil in Jerusalem among the hunger-
starved Jews as these three sharkers did in their parishes among naked
Christians. Cursed they were, I am sure, by some to the pit of Hell for
tearing money out of their throats that had not a cross in their purses.
But, alas, they must have it—it is their fee—and therefore give the
Devil his due. Only herb-wives and gardeners, that never prayed
before unless it were for rain or fair weather, were now day and night
upon their marrowbones that God would bless the labours of these
molecatchers, because they suck sweetness by this: for the price of
flowers, herbs and garlands rose wonderfully, insomuch that rosemary,
which had wont to be sold for twelvepence an armful, went now for
six shillings a handful.

A fourth sharer likewise of these winding-sheet weavers deserves
to have my pen give his lips a Jew's letter. But because he worships
the bakers' good lord and master, charitable St Clement, whereas
none of the other three ever had to do with any saint, he shall scape
the better. Only let him take heed that, having all this year buried his
prayers in the bellies of fat ones and plump capon-eaters, for no worse
meat would down this sly fox's stomach—let him, I say, take heed lest,
his flesh now falling away, his carcase be not plagued with lean ones—
of whom, whilst the bill of 'Lord have mercy upon us' was to be denied
in no place, it was death for him to hear.

In this pitiful or rather pitiless perplexity stood London, forsaken
like a lover, forlorn like a widow and disarmed of all comfort: 'disarmed' I may well say, for five rapiers were not stirring all this time,
and those that were worn had never been seen if any money could
have been lent upon them—so hungry is this ostrich disease that it
will devour even iron.

Let us therefore with bag and baggage march away from this
dangerous sore city and visit those that are fled into the country. But
alas! *decidis in Scyllam*—you are peppered if you visit them, for they
are visited already. The broad arrow of Death flies there up and down
as swiftly as it doth here. They that rode on the lustiest geldings
could not outgallop the plague. It overtook them and overturned
them too, horse and foot. You whom the arrows of pestilence have
reached at eighteen and twentyscore, though you stood far enough,
as you thought, from the mark; you that, sickening in the highway,
would have been glad of a bed in an hospital and, dying in the open

fields, have been buried like dogs: how much better had it been for you to have lain fuller of boils and plague-sores than ever did Job, so you might in that extremity have received both bodily and spiritual comfort which, there, was denied you? For those misbelieving pagans, the plough drivers, those worse than infidels that, like their swine, never look up so high as Heaven: when citizens boarded them they wrung their hands and wished rather they had fallen into the hands of Spaniards. For the sight of a flat cap was more dreadful to a lob than the discharging of a caliver; a treble ruff, being but once named 'the merchant's set', had power to cast a whole household into a cold sweat. If one new suit of sackcloth had been but known to have come out of Birchin Lane (being the common wardrobe for all their clown-ships) it had been enough to make a market town give up the ghost. A crow that had been seen in a sunshine day standing on the top of Paul's would have been better than a beacon on fire to have raised all the towns within ten miles of London for the keeping her out.

Never let any man ask me what became of our physicians in this massacre. They hid their synodical heads as well as the proudest. And I cannot blame them. For their phlebotomies, lozenges and electuaries, with their diacatholicons, diacodions, amulets and antidotes had not so much strength to hold life and soul together as a pot of Pinder's ale and a nutmeg. Their drugs turned to dirt; their simples were simple things. Galen could do no more good than Sir Giles Goosecap. Hippocrates, Avicenna, Paracelsus, Rhazes, Fernelius, with all their succeeding rabble of doctors and water-casters, were at their wits' end —or I think rather at the world's end, for not one of them durst peep abroad or, if any one did take upon him to play the venturous knight, the plague put him to his *nonplus*. In such strange and such changeable shapes did this chameleon-like sickness appear that they could not, with all the cunning in their budgets, make purse-nets to take him napping.

Only a band of desperviews, some few empirical madcaps (for they could never be worth velvet caps) turned themselves into bees—or, more properly, into drones—and went humming up and down with honey-brags in their mouths sucking the sweetness of silver and now and then of *aurum potabile* out of the poison of blains and carbuncles. And these jolly mountebanks clapped up their bills upon every post like a fencer's challenge, threatening to canvas the plague and to fight with him at all his own several weapons. I know not how they sped but some they sped, I am sure, for I have heard them banned for the

Heavens because they sent those thither that were wished to tarry longer upon earth.

I could in this place make your cheeks look pale and your hearts shake with telling how some have had eighteen sores at one time running upon them, others ten and twelve, many four and five, and how those that have been four times wounded by this year's infection have died of the last wound, whilst others that were hurt as often go up and down now with sounder limbs than many that come out of France and the Netherlands. And, descending from these, I could draw forth a catalogue of many poor wretches that in fields, in ditches, in common cages and under stalls, being either thrust by cruel masters out of doors, or wanting all worldly succour but the common benefit of earth and air, have most miserably perished. But to chronicle these would weary a second Fabyan.

We will therefore play the soldiers who, at the end of any notable battle, with a kind of sad delight rehearse the memorable acts of their friends that lie mangled before them: some showing how bravely they gave the onset, some how politicly they retired, others how manfully they gave and received wounds; a fourth steps up and glories how valiantly he lost an arm: all of them making by this means the remembrance even of tragical and mischievous events very delectable. Let us strive to do so, discoursing as it were at the end of this mortal siege of the plague, of the several most worthy accidents and strange births which this pestiferous year hath brought forth: some of them yielding comical and ridiculous stuff, others lamentable, a third kind upholding rather admiration than laughter or pity.

As first, to relish the palate of lickerish expectation and withal to give an item how sudden a stabber this ruffianly swaggerer Death is, you must believe that, amongst all the weary number of those that on their bare feet have 'travelled' in this long and heavy vacation to the Holy Land, one (whose name I could for need bestow upon you but that I know you have no need of it—though many want a good name), lying in that common inn of sick men, his bed, and seeing the black and blue stripes of the plague sticking on his flesh, which he received as tokens from Heaven that he was presently to go dwell in the upper world, most earnestly requested and in a manner conjured his friend, who came to interchange a last farewell, that he would see him go handsomely attired into the wild Irish country of worms, and for that purpose to bestow a coffin upon him. His friend loving him, not because he was poor—yet he was poor—but because he was a scholar (alack that the West Indies stand so far from universities! and that a mind richly apparelled should have a threadbare body!) made faithful promise to him that he should be nailed up—he would board him; and for that purpose went instantly to one of the new-found trade of coffin-cutters, bespake one and, like the surveyor of Death's buildings, gave direction how this little tenement should be framed, paying all the rent for it beforehand. But note upon what slippery ground life goes! Little did he think to dwell in that room himself which he had taken for his friend. Yet it seemed the common law of mortality had so decreed, for he was called into the cold company of his grave neighbours an hour before his infected friend and had a long lease, even till Doomsday, in the same lodging which in the strength of health he went to prepare for the other.

What credit therefore is to be given to breath which like a harlot will run away with every minute? How nimble is sickness, and what skill hath he in all the weapons he plays withal! The greatest cutter that takes up the Mediterranean Aisle in Paul's for his gallery to walk in cannot ward off his blows. He's the best fencer in the world—Vincentio Saviolo is nobody to him. He has his *mandrittos*, *imbroccatas*, *stramaῳῳones* and *stoccatas* at's fingers' ends. He'll make you give him ground though you were never worth foot of land, and beat you out of breath though Æolus himself played upon your windpipe.

To witness which, I will call forth a Dutchman (yet now he's past calling for—he's lost his hearing, for his ears by this time are eaten off with worms) who though he dwelt in Bedlam was not mad, yet the very looks of the plague, which indeed are terrible, put him almost out of his wits. For when the snares of this cunning hunter, the pestilence, were but newly laid—and yet laid, as my Dutchman smelt it out, well enough to entrap poor men's lives that meant him no hurt—away sneaks my clipper of the King's English; and, because musket shot should not reach him, to the Low Countries (that are built upon butter-firkins and Holland cheese) sails this plaguy fugitive. But Death, who hath more authority there than all the Seven Electors, and to show him that there were other Low Countries besides his own, takes a little frokin, one of my Dutch runaway's children, and sends her packing: into those Netherlands she departed. Oh, how pitifully looked my burgomaster when he understood that the sickness could swim! It was an easy matter to scape the Dunkirks, but Death's galleys made out after him swifter than the Great Turk's. Which he, perceiving, made no more ado but drunk to the States five or six healths (because he would be sure to live well) and back again comes he to try the strength of English beer. His old rendezvous of madmen was the place of meeting; where he was no sooner arrived but the plague had him by the back and arrested him upon a *ne exeat regnum* for running to the enemy. So that, for the mad tricks he played to cozen our English worms of his Dutch carcase which had been fatted here, sickness and death clapped him up in Bedlam the second time, and there he lies. And there he shall lie till he rot before I'll meddle any more with him.

But being gotten out of Bedlam, let us make a journey to Bristol, taking an honest known citizen along with us; who, with other company travelling thither only for fear the air of London should conspire to poison him, and setting up his rest not to hear the sound of Bow-bell till next Christmas, was notwithstanding in the highway singled out from his company and set upon by the plague, who bid him stand and deliver his life. The rest at that word shifted for themselves and went on; he, amazed to see his friends fly, and being not able to defend himself (for who can defend himself meeting such an enemy?), yielded and, being but about forty miles from London, used all the sleights he could to get loose out of the hands of Death and so to hide himself in his own house.

Whereupon he called for help at the same inn where not long before he and his fellow pilgrims obtained for their money—marry, yet with more prayers than a beggar makes in three Terms—to stand and drink some thirty foot from the door. To this house of tippling iniquity he repairs again, conjuring the *lares* or walking sprites in it, if they were Christians (that 'if' was well put in) and in the name of God, to succour and rescue him, to their power, out of the hands of infection which now assaulted his body. The Devil would have been afraid of this conjuration but they were not. Yet afraid they were, it seemed: for presently the doors had their wooden ribs crushed in pieces by being beaten together, the casements were shut more close than an usurer's greasy velvet pouch, the drawing windows were hanged, drawn and quartered; not a crevice but was stopped, not a mouse-hole left open, for all the holes in the house were most wickedly dammed up. Mine host and hostess ran over one another into the backside, the maids into the orchard, quivering and quaking and ready to hang themselves on the innocent plum-trees, for hanging to them would not be so sore a death as the plague (and to die maids, too! Oh, horrible!). As for the tapster, he fled into the cellar, rapping out five or six plain country

oaths that he would drown himself in a most villainous stand of ale if
the sick Londoner stood at the door any longer. But stand there he
must, for to go away well he cannot, but continues knocking and
calling in a faint voice which in their ears sounded as if some staring
ghost in a tragedy had exclaimed upon Rhadamanth. He might knock
till his hands ached and call till his heart ached, for they were in a
worse pickle within than he was without: he being in a good way to
go to Heaven, they being so frighted that they scarce knew whereabout
Heaven stood. Only they all cried out 'Lord have mercy upon us!',
yet 'Lord have mercy upon us' was the only thing they feared. The
doleful catastrophe of all is: a bed could not be had for all Babylon,
not a cup of drink—no, nor cold water—be gotten though it had been
for Alexander the Great; if a draught of *aqua-vitæ* might have saved
his soul, the town denied to do God that good service.

What misery continues ever? The poor man standing thus at death's
door and looking every minute when he should be let in—behold,
another Londoner that had likewise been in the *frigida zona* of the
country and was returning, like Æneas out of Hell, to the Heaven of
his own home makes a stand at this sight to play the physician and,
seeing by the complexion of his patient that he was sick at heart,
applies to his soul the best medicines that his comforting speech could
make, for there dwelt no pothecary near enough to help his body.
Being therefore driven out of all other shifts, he leads him into a field,
a bundle of straw which with much ado he bought for money serving
instead of a pillow. But the Destinies, hearing the diseased party complain and take on because he lay upon a field-bed when before he would
have been glad of a mattress, for very spite cut the thread of his life;
the cruelty of which deed made the other, that played Charity's part,
at his wit's end because he knew not where to purchase ten foot of
ground for his grave. The church nor churchyard would let none of
their lands. Master Vicar was struck dumb and could not give the dead
a good word, neither clerk nor sexton could be hired to execute their
office—no, they themselves would first be executed. So that he that
never handled shovel before got his implements about him, ripped up
the belly of the earth and made it like a grave, stripped the cold carcase,
bound his shirt about his feet, pulled a linen night-cap over his eyes
and so laid him in the rotten bed of the earth, covering him with
clothes cut out of the same piece. And, learning by his last words his
name and habitation, this sad traveller arrives at London, delivering
to the amazed widow and children instead of a father and a husband

only the outside of him, his apparel. But by the way note one thing: the bringer of these heavy tidings (as if he had lived long enough when so excellent a work of piety and pity was by him finished) the very next day after his coming home departed out of this world to receive his reward in the Spiritual Court of Heaven.

It is plain therefore, by the evidence of these two witnesses, that Death like a thief sets upon men in the highway, dogs them into their own houses, breaks into their bedchambers by night, assaults them by day, and yet no law can take hold of him. He devours man and wife, offers violence to their fair daughters, kills their youthful sons and deceives them of their servants. Yea, so full of treachery is he grown since this plague took his part that no lovers dare trust him nor by their good wills would come near him, for he works their downfall even when their delights are at the highest.

Too ripe a proof have we of this in a pair of lovers. The maid was in the pride of fresh blood and beauty. She was that which to be now is a wonder—young and yet chaste. The gifts of her mind were great, yet those which Fortune bestowed upon her, as being well descended, were not much inferior. On this lovely creature did a young man so steadfastly fix his eye that her looks kindled in his bosom a desire whose flames burnt the more brightly because they were fed with sweet and modest thoughts. Hymen was the god to whom he prayed day and night that he might marry her. His prayers were received and at length, after many tempests of her denial and the frowns of kinsfolk, the element grew clear and he saw the happy landing-place where he had long sought to arrive: the prize of her youth was made his own, and the solemn day appointed when it should be delivered to him. Glad of which blessedness, for to a lover it is a blessedness, he wrought by all the possible art he could use to shorten the expected hour and bring it nearer. For, whether he feared the interception of parents, or that his own soul with excess of joy was drowned in strange passions, he would often with sighs mingled with kisses, and kisses half sinking in tears, prophetically tell her that sure he should never live to enjoy her.

To discredit which opinion of his, behold! the sun has made haste and wakened the bridal morning. Now does he call his heart traitor that did so falsely conspire against him; lively blood leaps into his cheeks; he's got up and gaily attired to play the bridegroom. She likewise does as cunningly turn herself into a bride. Kindred and friends are met together. Sops and muscadine run sweating up and down till they drop again to comfort their hearts. And, because so many coffins pestered London churches that there was no room left for weddings, coaches are provided and away rides all the train into the country. On a Monday morning are these lusty lovers on their journey, and before noon are they alighted, entering instead of an inn, for more state, into a church; where they no sooner appeared but the priest fell to his business, the holy knot was a-tying. But he that should fasten it, coming to this—'in sickness and in health'—there he stopped, for suddenly the bride took hold of 'in sickness', for 'in health' all that stood by were in fear she should never be kept. The maiden blush into which her cheeks were lately dyed now began to lose colour. Her voice like a coward would have shrunk away but that her lover, reaching her a hand, which he brought thither to give her (for he was not yet made a full husband), did with that touch somewhat revive her. On went they again so far till they met with 'for better, for worse'. There was she worse than before, and had not the holy officer made haste the ground on which she stood to be married might easily have been broken up for her burial. All ceremonies being finished, she was led between two not like a bride but like a corpse to her bed: that must now be the table on which the wedding-dinner is to be served up, being at this time nothing but tears and sighs and lamentation; and Death is chief waiter.

Yet at length her weak heart, wrestling with the pangs, gave them a fall, so that up she stood again and in the fatal funeral coach that carried her forth was she brought back as upon a bier to the City. But see the malice of her enemy that had her in chase: upon the Wedsday following being overtaken, was her life overcome. Death rudely lay with her and spoiled her of a maidenhead in spite of her husband. Oh, the sorrow that did round beset him! Now was his divination true: she was a wife, yet continued a maid; he was a husband and a widower, yet never knew his wife; she was his own, yet he had her not; she had him, yet never enjoyed him. Here is a strange alteration, for the rosemary that was washed in sweet water to set out the bridal is now wet in tears to furnish her burial. The music that was heard to sound forth dances cannot now be heard for the ringing of bells. All the comfort that happened to either side being this: that he lost her before she had time to be an ill wife, and she left him ere he was able to be a bad husband.

Better fortune had this bride to fall into the hands of the plague than one other of that frail female sex, whose picture is next to be

c

drawn, had to scape out of them. An honest cobbler (if, at least, cobblers can be honest, that live altogether amongst wicked soles) had a wife who, in the time of health treading her shoe often awry, determined in the agony of a sickness, which this year had a saying to her, to fall to mending as well as her husband did. The bed that she lay upon being as she thought—or rather feared—the last bed that ever should bear her (for many other beds had borne her, you must remember) and the worm of sin tickling her conscience, up she calls her very innocent and simple husband out of his virtuous shop where like Justice he sat distributing among the poor—to some, halfpenny pieces, penny pieces to some, and twopenny pieces to others so long as they would last, his provident care being always that every man and woman should go upright. To the bed's side of his plaguy wife approaches Monsieur Cobbler to understand what deadly news she had to tell him and the rest of his kind neighbours that there were assembled, such thick tears standing in both the gutters of his eyes to see his beloved lie in such a pickle that in their salt water all his utterance was drowned. Which she perceiving wept as fast as he. But by the warm council which sat about the bed the shower ceased, she wiping her cheeks with the corner of one of the sheets and he his sullied face with his leathern apron.

At last two or three sighs like a Chorus to the tragedy ensuing stepping out first, wringing her hands (which gave the better action), she told the pitiful Actæon her husband that she had often done him wrong. He only shook his head at this and cried 'Humph!'; which 'Humph!' she taking as the watchword of his true patience unravelled the bottom of her frailty at length, and concluded that with such a man (and named him, but I hope you would not have me follow her steps and name him, too) she practised the universal and common art of grafting and that upon her good man's head they two had planted a monstrous pair of invisible horns. At the sound of the horns my cobbler started up like a March hare and began to look wild. His awl never ran through the sides of a boot as that word did through his heart. But being a politic cobbler and remembering what piece of work he was to underlay, stroking his beard like some grave headborough of the parish and giving a nod as who should say 'Go on!', bade her go on indeed, clapping to her sore soul this general salve that 'All are sinners, and we must forgive, etc.'. For he hoped by such wholesome physic, as shoemaker's wax being laid to a boil, to draw out all the corruption of her secret villainies.

She, good heart, being tickled under the gills with the finger of these kind speeches, turns up the white of her eye and fetches out another. Another, O thou that art trained up in nothing but to handle pieces! another hath discharged his artillery against thy castle of fortification! Here was passion predominant. Vulcan struck the cobbler's ghost (for he was now no cobbler) so hard upon his breast that he cried 'Oh!'. His neighbours, taking pity to see what terrible stitches pulled him, rubbed his swelling temples with the juice of patience which, by virtue of the blackish sweat that stood reeking on his brows and had made them supple, entered very easily into his now parlous-understanding skull, so that he left wincing and sat quiet as a lamb, falling to his old vomit of counsel which he had cast up before and swearing, because he was in strong hope this shoe should wring him no more, to seal her a general acquittance.

Pricked forward with this gentle spur, her tongue mends his pace so that in her confession she overtook others whose boots had been set all night on the cobbler's last, bestowing upon him the posy of their names, the time and place, to the intent it might be put into his next wife's wedding ring. And although she had made all these blots in his tables, yet the bearing of one man false, whom she had not yet discovered, stuck more in her stomach than all the rest.

'O valiant cobbler!' cries out one of the auditors, 'How art thou set upon! How art thou tempted! Happy art thou that thou art not in thy shop, for instead of cutting out pieces of leather thou wouldst doubtless now pare away thy heart. For *I* see—and so do all thy neighbours here, thy wife's ghostly fathers, see—that a small matter would now make thee turn Turk and to meddle with no more patches. But to live within the compass of thy wit, lift not up thy choler, be not horn-mad, thank Heaven that the murder is revealed, study thou Balthazar's part in *Hieronimo*, for thou hast more cause though less reason than he to be glad and sad. Well, I see thou art worthy to have Patient Griselda to thy wife, for thou bearest more than she. Thou showst thyself to be a right cobbler, and no souter, that canst thus cleanly clout up the broken and seam-rent sides of thy affection.'

With this learned oration the cobbler was tutored, laid his finger on his mouth and cried '*Pocas palabras!*': he had sealed her pardon and therefore bid her not fear.

Hereupon she named the malefactor (I could name him, too, but that he shall live to give more cobblers' heads the *bastinado*) and told that on such a night when he supped there (for a lord may sup with a cobbler that hath a pretty wench to his wife), when the cloth (O treacherous linen!) was taken up and Menelaus had for a parting blow given the other his fist, down she lights this half-sharer, opening the wicket but not shutting him out of the wicket; but conveys him into a by-room, being the wardrobe of old shoes and leather. From whence (the unicorn cobbler, that dreamed of no such spirits, being over head and ears in sleep, his snorting giving the sign that he was cock-sure) softly out steals Sir Paris and to Helena's teeth proved himself a true Trojan.

This was the cream of her confession; which being skimmed off from the stomach of her conscience, she looked every minute to go thither where she should be far enough out of the cobbler's reach. But the Fates, laying their heads together, sent a reprieve. The plague, that before meant to pepper her, by little and little left her company. Which news being blown abroad—oh, lamentable! never did the old buskined tragedy begin till now! For the wives of those husbands with whom she had played at fast and loose came with nails sharpened for the nonce like cats, and tongues forkedly cut like the stings of adders, first to scratch out false Cressida's eyes and then, which was worse, to worry her to death with scolding. But the matter was took up in a tavern: the case was altered and brought to a new reckoning— marry, the blood of the Bordeaux grape was first shed about it, but in the end all anger on every side was poured into a pottle-pot and there burned to death. Now whether this recantation was true or whether the steam of infection fuming up like wine into her brains made her talk thus idly, I leave it to the jury.

And whilst they are canvassing her case, let us see what doings the sexton of Stepney hath; whose warehouses being all full of dead commodities saving one, that one he left open a whole night, yet was it half-full, too, knowing that thieves this year were too honest to break into such cellars. Besides, those that were left there had such plaguy pates that none durst meddle with them, for their lives. About twelve of the clock at midnight, when spirits walk and not a mouse dare stir because cats go a-caterwauling, Sin—that all day durst not show his head—came reeling out of an alehouse in the shape of a drunkard, who no sooner smelt the wind but he thought the ground under him danced the canaries: houses seemed to turn on the toe, and all things went round, insomuch that his legs drew a pair of indentures between his body and the earth, the principal covenant being that he for his part would stand to nothing whatever he saw; every tree that came in his way did he jostle and yet challenge it the next day to fight with him. If he had clipped but a quarter so much of the King's silver as he did of the King's English his carcase had long ere this been carrion for crows. But he lived by gaming and had excellent casting, yet seldom won, for he drew reasonable good hands but had very bad feet that were not able to carry it away. This setter up of maltmen, being troubled with the staggers, fell into the selfsame grave which stood gaping wide open for a breakfast next morning; and imagining, when he was in, that he had stumbled into his own house and that all his bedfellows as they were indeed were in their dead sleep he, never complaining of cold nor calling for more sheet, soundly takes a nap till he snorts again.

In the morning the sexton comes plodding along and casting upon his fingers' ends what he hopes the dead pay of that day will come to, by that which he received the day before (for sextons now had better doings than either taverns or bawdy-houses). In that silver contemplation, shrugging his shoulders together, he steps ere he be aware on the brims of that pit into which this worshipper of Bacchus was fallen; where finding some dead men's bones and a skull or two that lay scattered here and there, before he looked into this coffer of worms those he takes up and flings them in. One of the skulls battered the sconce of the sleeper whilst the bones played with his nose. Whose blows waking his musty worship, the first word that he cast up was an oath and, thinking the cans had flown about, cried 'Zounds! What, do you mean to crack my mazer?' The sexton smelling a voice (fear being stronger than his heart) believed verily some of the corpses spake to him; upon which, feeling himself in a cold sweat, took his heels whilst the goblin scrambled up and ran after him. But it appears the sexton had the lighter foot, for he ran so fast that he ran out of his wits—which being left behind him, he had like to have died presently after.

A merrier bargain than the poor sexton's did a tinker meet withal in a country town; through which a citizen of London being driven, to keep himself under the lee shore in this tempestuous contagion, and casting up his eye for some harbour spied a bush at the end of a pole, the ancient badge of a country alehouse; into which (as good luck was, without any resistance of the barbarians that all this year used to keep such landing-places) vailing his bonnet, he struck in. The host had been a mad-Greek (marry, he could now speak nothing but English). A goodly fat burgher he was, with a belly arching out like a beer barrel; which made his legs, that were thick and short like two piles driven under London Bridge, to straddle half as wide as the top of Paul's, which upon my knowledge hath been burned twice or thrice. A leathern pouch hung at his side that opened and shut with a snaphance, and was indeed a flask for gunpowder when King Henry went to Boulogne. An antiquary might have picked rare matter out of his nose but that it was worm-eaten—yet that proved it to be an ancient nose. In some corners of it there were bluish holes that shone like shells of mother-of-pearl and, to do his nose right, pearls had been gathered out of them. Other were richly garnished with rubies, chrysolites and carbuncles, which glistered so oriently that the Hamburgers offered I know not how many dollars for his company in an East Indian voyage to have stood a-nights in the poop of their admiral, only to save the charges of candles. In conclusion, he was an host to be led before an emperor, and though he were one of the greatest men in all the shire, his bigness made him not proud, but he humbled himself to speak the base language of a tapster and upon the Londoner's first arrival cried 'Welcome! A cloth for this gentleman!' The linen was spread and furnished presently with a new cake and a can, the room voided and the guest left like a French lord, attended by nobody; who drinking half a can in conceit to the health of his best friend the City, which lay extreme sick and had never more need of health, I know not what qualms came over his stomach but immediately he fell down without uttering any more words and never rose again.

Anon, as it was his fashion, enters my puffing host to relieve with a fresh supply out of his cellar the shrinking can if he perceived it stood in danger to be overthrown. But seeing the chief leader dropped at his feet, and imagining at first he was but wounded a little in the head, held up his gouty golls and blessed himself that a Londoner, who had wont to be the most valiant rob-pots, should now be struck down only with two hoops; and thereupon jogged him, fumbling out these comfortable words of a soldier, 'If thou art a man stand o' thy legs!' He stirred not for all this, whereupon the maids, being raised as it had been with a hue and cry, came hobbling into the room like a flock of geese and, having upon search of the body given up this verdict, that the man was dead and murdered by the plague—oh, daggers to all their hearts that heard it! Away trudge the wenches and one of them, having had a freckled face all her lifetime, was persuaded presently that now they were the tokens and had like to have turned up her heels upon it. My gorbelly host, that in many a year could not without grunting crawl over a threshold but two foot broad, leaped half a yard from the corpse (it was measured by a carpenter's rule) as nimbly as if his guts had been taken out by the hangman. Out of the house he wallowed presently, being followed with two or three dozen of napkins to dry up the lard that ran so fast down his heels that all the way he went was more greasy than a kitchen-stuff wife's basket. You would have sworn it had been a barrel of pitch on fire if you had looked upon him, for such a smoky cloud, by reason of his own fatty hot steam, compassed him round that but for his voice he had quite been lost in that stinking mist. Hanged himself he had without all question in this pitiful taking but that he feared the weight of his intolerable paunch would have burst the rope and so he should be put to a double death.

At length the town was raised, the country came down upon him— and yet not upon him neither, for after they understood the tragedy every man gave ground, knowing my pursy aleconner could not follow them. What is to be done in this strange alarum? The whole village is in danger to lie at the mercy of God and shall be bound to curse none but him for it; they should do well therefore to set fire on his house before the plague scape out of it, lest it forage higher into the country and knock them down man, woman and child like oxen: whose blood, they all swear, shall be required at his hands.

At these speeches my tender-hearted host fell down on his marrow-bones, meaning indeed to entreat his audience to be good to him. But they, fearing he had been peppered, too, as well as the Londoner, tumbled one over another and were ready to break their necks for haste to be gone. Yet some of them, being more valiant than the rest because they heard him roar out for some help, very desperately stepped back and with rakes and pitchforks lifted the gulch from the ground; concluding, after they had laid their hogsheads together to draw out some wholesome counsel, that whosoever would venture upon the dead man and bury him should have forty shillings out of the common town purse, though it would be a great cut to it, with the love of the churchwardens and sidemen during the term of life. This was proclaimed, but none durst appear to undertake the dreadful execution. They loved money well—marry, the plague hanging over any man's head that should meddle with it in that sort, they all vowed to die beggars before it should be chronicled they killed themselves for forty shillings. And in that brave resolution everyone with bag and baggage marched home, barricadoing their doors and windows with fir bushes, fern and bundles of straw to keep out the pestilence at the stave's end.

At last a tinker came sounding through the town, mine host's house being the ancient watering-place where he did use to cast anchor. You must understand he was none of those base rascally tinkers that, with a bandog and a drab at their tails and a pikestaff on their necks, will take a purse sooner than stop a kettle: no, this was a devout tinker—he did honour God Pan; a musical tinker that upon his kettledrum could play any country-dance you called for, and upon holidays had earned money by it when no fiddler could be heard of. He was only feared when he stalked through some towns where bees were, for he struck so sweetly on the bottom of his copper instrument that he would empty whole hives and lead the swarms after him only by the sound.

This excellent egregious tinker calls for his draught, being a double jug. It was filled for him but, before it came to his nose, the lamentable tale of the Londoner was told, the chamber-door where he lay being thrust open with a long pole because none durst touch it with their hands, and the tinker bidden if he had the heart to go in and see if he knew him. The tinker, being not to learn what virtue the medicine had which he held at his lips, poured it down his throat merrily and crying 'Trillil!' he feared no plagues. In he stepped, tossing the dead body to and fro, and was sorry—he knew him not.

Mine host, that with grief began to fall away villainously, looking very ruefully on the tinker and thinking him a fit instrument to be played upon, offered a crown out of his own purse if he would bury the party. A crown was a shrewd temptation to a tinker: many a hole might he stop before he could pick a crown off it. Yet being a subtle tinker (and to make all sextons pray for him, because he would raise their fees) an angel he wanted to be his guide: and under ten shillings, by his ten bones, he would not put his finger in the fire. The whole parish had warning of this presently. Thirty shillings was saved by the bargain, and the town likely to be saved, too: therefore ten shillings was levied out of hand, put into a rag which was tied to the end of a long pole and delivered in sight of all the parish, who stood aloof stopping their noses, by the headborough's own self in proper person to the tinker, who with one hand received the money and with the other struck the board, crying 'Hey! a fresh double pot!' Which armour of proof being fitted to his body, up he hoists the Londoner on his back like a schoolboy, a shovel and pickaxe standing ready for him.

And thus furnished, into a field some good distance from the town he bears his deadly load and there throws it down, falling roundly to his tools—upon which the strong beer having set an edge, they quickly cut out a lodging in the earth for the citizen. But the tinker, knowing that worms needed no apparel saving only sheets, stripped him stark naked; but first dived nimbly into his pockets to see what linings they had, assuring himself that a Londoner would not wander so far without silver. His hopes were of the right stamp, for from one of his pockets he drew a leathern bag with £7 in it. This music made the tinker's heart dance. He quickly tumbled his man into the grave, hid him over head and ears in dust, bound up his clothes in a bundle and, carrying that at the end of his staff on his shoulder, with the purse of £7 in his hand, back again comes he through the town, crying aloud 'Have ye any more Londoners to bury? Hey down a down derry! Have ye any more Londoners to bury?'—the Hobbinolls running away from him as if he had been the dead citizen's ghost, and he marching away from them in all the haste he could with that song still in his mouth.

You see therefore how dreadful a fellow Death is, making fools even of wise men, and cowards of the most valiant—yea, in such a base slavery hath it bound men's senses that they have no power to look higher than their own roofs, but seem by their Turkish and barbarous actions to believe that there is no felicity after this life and that like beasts their souls shall perish with their bodies. How many, upon sight only of a letter sent from London, have started back and durst have laid their salvation upon it that the plague might be folded in that empty paper, believing verily that the arm of Omnipotence could never reach them unless it were with some weapon drawn out of the infected City? Insomuch that even the western pugs receiving money here have tied it in a bag at the end of their barge and so trailed it through the Thames lest, plague-sores sticking upon shillings, they should be nailed up for counterfeits when they were brought home.

More venturous than these blockheads was a certain Justice of Peace to whose gate, being shut (for you must know that now there is no open house kept), a company of wild fellows being led for robbing an orchard, the stout-hearted Constable rapped most courageously and would have about with none but the Justice himself, who at last appeared in his likeness above at a window, enquiring why they summoned a parley. It was delivered why: the case was opened to his examining wisdom and that the evil-doers were only Londoners. At the name of 'Londoners' the Justice, clapping his hand on his breast as who should say 'Lord have mercy upon us!', started back and, being wise enough to save one, held his nose hard between his fore-finger and his thumb and, speaking in that wise (like the fellow that described the villainous motion of Julius Caesar and the Duke of Guise who, as he gave it out, fought a combat together), pulling the casement close to him, cried out in that quail-pipe voice that if they were Londoners 'Away with them to limbo! Take only their names!' They were sore fellows and he would deal with them when time should serve—meaning when the plague and they should not be so great together. And so they departed, the very name of 'Londoners' being worse than ten whetstones to sharpen the sword of justice against them.

I could fill a large volume and call it the Second Part of *The Hundred Merry Tales* only with such ridiculous stuff as this of the Justice. But *di meliora*, I have better matters to set my wits about. Neither shall you wring out of my pen, though you lay it on the rack, the villainies of that damned keeper who killed all she kept. It had been good to have made her keeper of the common gaol and the holes of both Counters, for a number lie there that wish to be rid out of this motley world. She would have tickled them and turned them over the thumbs. I will likewise let the churchwarden in Thames St sleep (for he's now past waking) who, being requested by one of his neighbours to suffer his wife or child that was then dead to lie in the churchyard, answered in a mocking sort, he kept that lodging for himself and his household; and within three days after was driven to hide his head in a hole himself. Neither will I speak a word of a poor boy, servant to a chandler dwelling thereabouts, who being struck to the heart by sickness was first carried away by water to be left anywhere but, landing being denied by an army of brown bill men that kept the shore, back again was he brought and left in an out-cellar where, lying grovelling and groaning on his face amongst faggots (but not one of them set on fire to comfort him), there continued all night and died miserably for want of succour. Nor of another poor wretch in the Parish of St Mary Overy's who, being in the morning thrown, as the fashion is, into a grave upon a heap of carcases that stayed for their complement, was found in the afternoon gasping and gaping for life. But by these tricks imagining that many a thousand have been turned wrongfully off the ladder of life, and praying that Derrick or his executors may live to do those a good turn that have done so to others, *hic finis Priami*, here's an end of an old song; *et iam tempus equum fumantia solvere colla*.

FINIS

The Gull's Horn-Book:

Or,
Fashions to Please
All Sorts of Gulls.

THE GVLS

Horne·booke:

Stultorum plena junt omnia.

Al Sauio meza parola,
Basta.

By T. Deckar.

6
Imprinted at London for R. S. 1609.

To All Gulls in General:
Wealth and Liberty!

Whom can I choose, my most worthy Mæcen*asses*, to be patrons to this labour of mine fitter than yourselves? Your hands are ever open, your purses never shut: so that you stand not in the common rank of dry-fisted patrons who give nothing, for you give all. Scholars therefore are as much beholden to you as vintners, players and punks are. Those three trades gain by you more than usurers do by thirty in the hundred: you spend the wines of the one, you make suppers for the other, and change your gold into white money with the third. Who is more liberal than you? Who but only citizens are more free? Blame me not therefore if I pick you out from the bunch of book-takers to consecrate these fruits of my brain, which shall never die, only to you. I know that most of you, O admirable gulls, can neither write nor read. A horn-book have I invented because I would have you well schooled. Paul's is your Walk, but this your guide. If it lead you right, thank me; if astray, men will bear with your errors because you are gulls. Farewell.

T.D.

To the Reader.

Gentle reader, I could willingly be content that thou shouldest neither be at cost to buy this book nor at the labour to read it. It is not my ambition to be a man in print thus every Term. *Ad prælum tanquam ad prælium*—we should come to the press as we come to the field, seldom. This tree of gulls was planted long since but, not taking root, could never bear till now. It hath a relish of Grobianism and tastes very strongly of it in the beginning. The reason thereof is that, having translated many books of that into English verse and not greatly liking the subject, I altered the shape and of a Dutchman fashioned a mere Englishman. It is a table wherein are drawn sundry pictures. The colours are fresh: if they be well laid on, I think my workmanship well bestowed; if ill, so much the better, because I draw the pictures only of gulls.

T.D.

The Chapters Contained
in this Book.

The Gull's Horn-Book

I sing, like the cuckoo in June, to be laughed at. If therefore I make a scurvy noise and that my tunes sound unmusically, the ditty being altogether lame in respect of the bad feet, and unhandsome in regard of the worm-eaten fashion, you that have authority under the broad seal of mouldy custom to be called 'the gentle audience' set your goodly great hands to my pardon! Or else, because I scorn to be upbraided that I profess to instruct others in an art whereof I myself am ignorant, do your worst! Choose whether you will let my notes have you by the ears or no; hiss or give plaudits, I care not a nutshell which of either. You can neither shake our comic theatre with your stinking breath of hisses nor raise it with the thunder-claps of your hands. Up it goes *in dispetto del fato*. The motley is bought, and a coat with four elbows for anyone that will wear it is put to making in defiance of the Seven Wise Masters. For I have smelled out of the musty sheets of an old almanac that, at one time or other, even he that jets upon the neatest and sprucest leather, even he that talks all Adage and Apophthegm, even he that will not have a wrinkle in his new satin suit though his mind be uglier than his face, and his face so ill-favouredly made that he looks at all times as if a tooth-drawer were fumbling about his gums, with a thousand lame heteroclites more that cozen the world with a gilt spur and a ruffled boot, will be all glad to fit themselves in Will Summers his wardrobe and be driven like a Flemish hoy in foul weather to slip into our school and take out a lesson. Tush, *cælum petimus stultitia*—all that are chosen constables for their wit go not to Heaven.

A fig, therefore, for the new-found College of Critics! You courtiers that do nothing but sing the *gamut A re* of complimental courtesy and, at the rustical behaviour of our country Muse, will screw forth worse faces than those which God and the painter has bestowed upon you: I defy your perfumed scorn and vow to poison your musk-cats if their civet excrement do but once play with my nose. You ordinary gulls that, through a poor and silly ambition to be thought you inherit the revenues of extraordinary wit, will spend your shallow censure upon the most elaborate poem so lavishly that all the painted tablemen about you take you to be heirs apparent to rich Mid*ass*, that had more skill in alchemy than Kelley with the philosopher's stone, for all that he could lay his fingers on turned into beaten gold: dry tobacco with my leaves, you good dry-brained polypragmonists, till your pipe-offices smoke with your pitifully stinking girds shot out against me. I conjure you, as you come of the right Goosecaps, stain not your house: but when at a new play you take up the twelvepenny room next the stage (because the lords and you may seem to be hail-fellow-well-met) there draw forth this book, read aloud, laugh aloud and play the antics that all the garlic-mouthed stinkards may cry out 'Away with the fool!' As for thee, Zoilus, go hang thyself! And for thee, Momus, chew nothing but hemlock and spit nothing but the syrup of aloes upon my papers till thy very rotten lungs come forth for anger. I am snakeproof. And though with Hannibal you bring whole hogsheads of vinegar railings, it is impossible for you to quench or come over my Alpine resolution. I will sail boldly and desperately alongst the shore of the Isle of Gulls and in defiance of those terrible blockhouses, their logger-heads, make a true discovery of their wild yet habitable country.

Sound an alarum therefore, O thou my courageous Muse, and like a Dutch crier make proclamation with thy drum, the effect of thine 'Oyez' being:

'That if any man, woman or child, be he lord, be he loon, be he courtier, be he carter, of the Inns o' Court or inns of City, that, hating from the bottom of his heart all good manners and generous education, is really in love or rather dotes on that excellent country lady, Innocent Simplicity, being the first, fairest and chiefest chambermaid that our great-grandam Eve entertained into service; Or if any person afore-said, longing to make a voyage in the Ship of Fools, would venture all the wit that his mother left him to live in the country of gulls, cockneys and coxcombs to the intent that, haunting theatres, he may sit there like a popinjay only to learn play speeches which afterward may furnish the necessity of his bare knowledge to maintain table-talk, or else, haunting taverns, desires to take the Bacchanalian degrees and to write himself *in arte bibendi magister*; that at ordinaries would sit like Bi*ass* and in the streets walk like a braggart; that on foot longs to go like a French lackey and on horseback rides like an English tailor; Or that from seven years and upward till his dying day has a month's mind to have *The Gull's Horn-Book* by heart, by which in time he may be promoted to serve any lord in Europe as his crafty fool or his bawdy jester—yea, and to be so dear to his lordship as for the excellency of his fooling to be admitted both to ride in coach with him and to lie at his very feet on a truckle-bed: **Let** all such (and I hope the world has not left her old fashions but there are ten thousand such) repair hither.'

Never knock, you that strive to be ninny-hammers, but with your feet spurn open the door and enter into our school. You shall not need to buy books—no, scorn to distinguish a B from a battledore. Only look that your ears be long enough to reach our rudiments and you are made for ever. It is by heart that I would have you to con my lessons, and therefore be sure to have most devouring stomachs. Nor be you terrified with an opinion that our rules be hard and indigestible, or that you shall never be good graduates in these rare sciences of Barbarism and Idiotism. Oh, fie upon any man that carries that ungodly mind! Tush, tush! Tarlton, Kempe nor Singer, nor all the litter of fools that now come drawling behind them never played the clowns more naturally than the arrantest sot of you all shall, if he will but boil my instructions in his brainpan.

And lest I myself, like some pedantical vicar stammering out a most false and cracked Latin oration to Master Mayor of the Town and his Brethren, should cough and hem in my deliveries, by which means you my auditors should be in danger to depart more like woodcocks than when you came to me: O thou venerable father of ancient and therefore hoary customs, Silvanus, I invoke thy assistance! thou that first taughtest carters to wear hobnails and lobs to play Christmas gambols and to show the most beastly horse-tricks, oh, do thou or, if thou art not at leisure, let thy mountebank goat-footed *fauni* inspire me with the knowledge of all those silly and ridiculous fashions which the old dunstical world wore even out at elbows, draw for me the pictures of the most simple fellows then living, that by their patterns I may paint the like.

Awake, thou noblest drunkard Bacchus! Thou must likewise stand to me—if at least thou canst, for reeling. Teach me, you sovereign skinker, how to take the Germany's *upsy Friese*, the Danish *ruse*, the Switzer's stoup of Rhenish, the Italian's *Parmesan*, the Englishman's healths, his hoops, cans, half-cans, gloves, frolics and flap-dragons, together with the most notorious qualities of the truest tosspots: as, when to cast, when to quarrel, when to fight and where to sleep. Hide not a drop of thy moist mystery from me, thou plumpest swill-bowl, but like an honest red-nosed wine-bibber lay open all thy secrets and the mystical hieroglyphic of rashers o' th' coals, modicums and shoeing-horns and why they were invented, for what occupations and when to be used.

Thirdly (because I will have more than two strings to my bow) Comus, thou clerk of Gluttony's kitchen, do thou also bid me 'Proface!' and let me not rise from table till I am perfect in all the general rules of epicures and cormorants. Fatten thou my brains that I may feed others and teach them both how to squat down to their meat and how to munch so like loobies that the wisest Solon in the world shall not be able to take them for any other.

If there be any strength in thee, thou beggarly monarch of Indians and setter up of rotten-lunged chimney-sweepers, Tobacco, I beg it at thy smoky hands! Make me thine adopted heir that, inheriting the virtues of thy whiffs, I may distribute them amongst all nations and make the fantastic Englishmen above the rest more cunning in the distinction of thy roll Trinidado, leaf and pudding than the whitest-toothed blackamoor in all Asia. After thy pipe shall ten thousands be taught to dance if thou wilt but discover to me the sweetness of thy snuffs, with the manner of spawling, slavering, spitting and drivelling in all places and before all persons. Oh, what songs will I 'charm' out in praise of those valiantly strong stinking breaths which are easily purchased at thy hands if I can but get thee to travel through my nose! All the 'fohs!' in the fairest lady's mouth that ever kissed lord shall not fright me from thy brown presence. For thou art humble, and from the courts of princes hast vouchsafed to be acquainted with penny galleries and like a good fellow to be drunk for company with watermen, carmen and colliers whereas before, and so still, knights and wise gentlemen were and are thy companions.

Last of all, thou lady of clowns and carters, schoolmistress of fools and wiseacres, thou homely but harmless Rusticity, oh, breathe thy dull and dunstical spirit into our gander's quill! Crown me thy poet not with a garland of bays—oh no! the number of those that steal laurel is too monstrous already—but swaddle thou my brows with those unhandsome boughs which like Autumn's rotten hair hang dangling over thy dusty eyelids. Help me, thou midwife of unmannerliness, to be delivered of this embryon that lies tumbling in my brain. Direct me in this hard and dangerous voyage that, being safely arrived on the desired shore, I may build up altars to thy unmatchable rudeness, the excellency whereof I know will be so great that groutnolls and momes will in swarms fly buzzing about thee.

So Herculean a labour is this that I undertake that I am enforced to bawl out for all your succours, to the intent I may aptly furnish this Feast of Fools—unto which I solemnly invite all the world, for at it shall sit not only those whom Fortune favours but even those whose wits are naturally their own; yet because your artificial fools bear away the bell, all our best workmanship at this time shall be spent to fashion such a creature.

The old world and the new weighed together: the tailors of those times and these compared; the apparel and diet of our first fathers.

Good clothes are the embroidered trappings of Pride, and good cheer the very eryngo root of Gluttony: so that fine backs and fat bellies are coach-horses to two of the Seven Deadly Sins, in the boots of which coach Lechery and Sloth sit like the waiting-maid. In a most desperate state therefore do tailors and cooks stand by means of their offices, for both those trades are apple-squires to that couple of Sins: the one invents more fantastic fashions than France hath worn since her first stone was laid; the other, more lickerish epicurean dishes than were ever served up to Gallonius's table.

Did man, think you, come wrangling into the world about no better matters than all his lifetime to make privy searches in Birchin Lane for whalebone doublets, or for pies of nightingale tongues in Elagabalus his kitchen? No, no! the first suit of apparel that ever mortal man put on came neither from the mercer's shop nor the merchant's warehouse. Adam's bill would have been taken then sooner than a knight's bond now; yet was he great in nobody's books for satin and velvets. The silkworms had something else to do in those days than to set up looms and be free of the Weavers. His breeches were not so much worth as King Stephen's, that cost but a poor noble. For Adam's holiday hose and doublet were of no better stuff than plain fig-leaves, and Eve's best gown of the same piece; there went but a pair of shears between them. An antiquary in this town has yet some of the powder of those leaves, dried, to show. Tailors then were none of the Twelve Companies. Their Hall, that now is larger than some dorps among the Netherlands, was then no bigger than a Dutch butcher's shop. They durst not strike down their customers with large bills. Adam cared not an apple-paring for all their lousy hems. There was then neither the Spanish slop nor the skipper's galligaskin, the Switzer's blistered cod-piece nor the Danish sleeve sagging down like a Welsh wallet, the Italian's close strosser nor the French standing collar; your treble-quadruple Dædalian sffur nor your stiff-necked rebatoes, that have more arches for Pride to row under than can stand under five London Bridges, durst not then set themselves out in print, for the patent for starch could by no means be signed. 'Fashions' then was counted a disease, and horses died of it. But now, thanks to folly, it is held the only rare physic and the purest Golden Asses live upon it.

As for the diet of that Saturnian Age, it was like their attire— homely. A salad and a mess of leek porridge was a dinner for a far greater man than ever the Turk was. Potato-pies and custards stood like the sinful suburbs of cookery and had not a wall so much as a handful high built round about them. There were no daggers then, nor no chairs. Crookes his ordinary in those parsimonious days had not a capon's leg to throw at a dog. Oh, golden world! the suspicious Venetian carved not his meat with a silver pitchfork, neither did the sweet-toothed Englishman shift a dozen of trenchers at one meal. Piers Plowman laid the cloth, and Simplicity brought in the voider. How wonderfully is the world altered! And no marvel, for it has lain sick almost five thousand years, so that it is no more like the old *théâtre du monde* than old Paris Garden is like the King's Garden at Paris.

What an excellent workman, therefore, were he that could cast the globe of it into a new mould! And not to make it look like Molyneux his globe, with a round face sleeked and washed over with whites of eggs, but to have it *in plano* as it was at first, with all the ancient circles, lines, parallels and figures, representing indeed all the wrinkles, cracks, crevices and flaws that, like the mole on Helen's cheek, being *cos amoris*, stuck upon it at the first creation and made it look most lovely. But now those furrows are filled up with ceruse and vermilion; yet all will not do—it appears more ugly. Come, come, it would be but a bald world but that it wears a periwig. The body of it is foul like a birding-piece by being too much heated. The breath of it stinks like the mouths of chambermaids by feeding on so many sweetmeats. And though to purge it will be a sorer labour than the cleansing of Augeas's stable or the scouring of Moorditch, yet *ille ego, qui quondam*—I am the Pasquil's Madcap that will do't.

Draw near therefore, all you that love to walk upon single and simple souls and that wish to keep company with none but innocents and the sons of civil citizens! Out with your tables, and nail your ears, as it were to the pillory, to the music of our instructions. Nor let the title 'gullery' fright you from school. For mark what an excellent ladder you are to climb by: how many worthy, and men of famous memory for their learning, of all offices from the scavenger and so upward, have flourished in London of the ancient family of the Wise-acres, being now no better esteemed than fools and younger brothers? This gear must be looked into lest in time (oh, lamentable time when that hour-glass is turned up!) a rich man's son shall no sooner peep out of the shell of his minority but he shall straightways be begged for a concealment or set upon as it were by freebooters, and ta'en in his own purse-nets by fencers and coney-catchers; to drive which pestilent infection from the heart, here's a medicine more potent and more precious than was ever that mingle-mangle of drugs which Mithridates boiled together. Fear not to taste it; a caudle will not go down half so smoothly as this will. You need not call the honest name of it in question, for Antiquity puts off his cap and makes a bare oration in praise of the virtues of it. The receipt hath been subscribed unto by all those that have had to do with simples, with this moth-eaten motto, *probatum est*. Your *diacatholicon aureum*, that with gunpowder threatens to blow up all diseases that come in his way, smells worse than *ass*afœtida in respect of this. You therefore, whose bodies either overflowing with the corrupt humours of this age's fantasticness or else, being burnt up with the inflammation of upstart fashions, would fain be purged, and to show that you truly loathe this polluted and mangy-fisted world, turn Timonists, not caring either for men or their manners: do you pledge me! Spare not to take a deep draught of our homely counsel. The cup is full, and so large that I boldly drink a health unto all comers.

CHAPTER II

How a young gallant shall not only keep his clothes (which many of them can hardly do, for brokers) but also save the charges of taking physic; with other rules for the morning. The praise of sleep and of going naked.

You have heard all this while nothing but the Prologue and seen no more but a dumb show. Our *vetus comœdia* steps out now. The fittest stage upon which you that study to be an actor there are first to present yourself is in my approved judgment the softest and largest down-bed; from whence, if you will but take sound counsel of your pillow, you shall never rise till you hear it ring noon at least. Sleep, in the name of Morpheus, your bellyful—or, rather, sleep till you hear your belly grumbles and waxeth empty. Care not for those coarse painted-cloth rhymes made by the University of Salerno that come over you with

> *Sit brevis, aut nullus, tibi somnus meridianus—*
> Short let thy sleep at noon be
> Or, rather, let it none be.

Sweet candied counsel! But there's ratsbane under it. Trust never a Bachelor of Art of them all, for he speaks your health fair but to steal away the maidenhead of it. Salerno stands in the luxurious country of Naples—and who knows not that the Neapolitan will, like Derrick the hangman, embrace you with one arm and rip your guts with the other? There's not a hair in his mustachio but if he kiss you will stab you through the cheeks like a poniard. The slave, to be avenged on his enemy, will drink off a pint of poison himself, so that he may be sure to have the other pledge him but half so much. And it may be that upon some secret grudge to work the general destruction of all mankind those verses were composed.

Physicians, I know, and none else took up the bucklers in their defence, railing bitterly upon that venerable and princely custom of Long Lying Abed. Yet now I remember me, I cannot blame them: for they which want sleep, which is man's natural rest, become either mere naturals or else fall into the doctor's hands, and so consequently into the Lord's. Whereas he that snorts profoundly scorns to let Hippocrates himself stand tooting on his urinal, and thereby saves that charges of a groatsworth of physic. And happy is that man that saves it, for physic is *non minus venefica quam benefica*—it hath an ounce of gall in it for every dram of honey. Ten Tyburns cannot turn men over the perch so fast as one of these brewers of purgations, the very nerves of their practice being nothing but *ars homicidiorum*, an art to make poor souls kick up their heels, insomuch that even their sick grunting patients stand in more danger of Master Doctor and his drugs than of all the cannon-shots which the desperate disease itself can discharge against them. Send them packing therefore, to walk like Italian mountebanks. Beat not your brains to understand their parcel-Greek, parcel-Latin gibberish. Let not all their sophistical buzzing into your ears, nor their satirical canvassing of feather-beds and tossing men out of their warm blankets, awake you till the hour that here is prescribed.

For do but consider what an excellent thing sleep is. It is so inestimable a jewel that, if a tyrant would give his crown for an hour's slumber, it cannot be bought; of so beautiful a shape is it that, though a man lie with an empress, his heart cannot be at quiet till he leaves her embracements to be at rest with the other; yea, so greatly indebted are we to this kinsman of Death that we owe the better tributary half of our life to him. And there's good cause why we should do so, for sleep is that golden chain that ties health and our bodies together. Who complains of want, of wounds, of cares, of great men's oppressions, of captivity, whilst he sleepeth? Beggars in their beds take as much pleasure as kings. Can we therefore surfeit on this delicate ambrosia? Can we drink too much of that, whereof to taste too little tumbles us into a churchyard, and to use it but indifferently throws us into Bedlam? No, no! Look upon Endymion, the moon's minion, who slept threescore and fifteen years and was not a hair the worse for it. Can lying abed till noon, then, being not the threescore and fifteenth thousand part of his nap, be hurtful?

Besides, by the opinion of all philosophers and physicians it is not good to trust the air with our bodies till the sun with his flame-coloured wings hath fanned away the misty smoke of the morning, and refined that thick tobacco-breath which the rheumatic night throws abroad of purpose to put out the eye of the element; which work questionless cannot be perfectly finished till the sun's car-horses stand prancing on the very top of highest noon. So that then, and not till then, is the most healthful hour to be stirring. Do you require examples to persuade you? At what time do lords and ladies use to rise but then? Your simpering merchants' wives are the fairest liers in the world, and is not eleven o'clock their common hour? They find no doubt unspeakable sweetness in such lying, else they would not day by day put it so in practice. In a word, midday slumbers are golden: they make the body fat, the skin fair, the flesh plump, delicate and tender; they set a russet colour on the cheeks of young women, and make lusty courage to rise up in men; they make us thrifty both in sparing victuals, for breakfasts thereby are saved from the Hell-mouth of the belly, and in preserving apparel, for whilst we warm us in our beds our clothes are not worn.

The casements of thine eyes being then at this commendable time of the day newly set open, choose rather to have thy windpipe cut in pieces than to salute any man. Bid not 'Good morrow' so much as to thy father, though he be an emperor. An idle ceremony it is, and can do him little good. To thyself it may bring much harm, for if he be a wise man that knows how to hold his peace, of necessity must he be counted a fool that cannot keep his tongue! Amongst all the wild men that run up and down in this wide forest of fools, the world, none are more superstitious than those notable Hebricians, the Jews. Yet a Jew never wears his cap threadbare with putting it off, never bends i' th' hams with casting away a leg, never cries 'God save you!' though he sees the Devil at your elbow. Play the Jews therefore in this and save thy lips that labour.

Only remember that so soon as thy eyelids be unglued thy first exercise must be, either sitting upright on thy pillow or rarely lolling at thy body's whole length, to yawn, to stretch and to gape wider than any oyster-wife. For thereby thou dost not only send out the lively spirits like vaunt-couriers to fortify and make good the uttermost borders of the body, but also as a cunning painter thy goodly lineaments are drawn out in their fairest proportion.

This lesson being played, turn over a new leaf and, unless that Friesland cur, cold winter, offer to bite thee, walk a while up and down thy chamber either in thy thin shirt only or else, which at a bare word is both more decent and more delectable, strip thyself stark naked. Are we not born so? And shall a foolish custom make us to break the laws of our creation? Our first parents so long as they went naked were suffered to dwell in Paradise, but after they got coats to their backs they were turned out o' doors. Put on therefore either no apparel at all or put it on carelessly. For look, how much more delicate liberty is than bondage, so much is the looseness in wearing of our attire above the imprisonment of being neatly and tailor-like dressed up in it. To be ready in our clothes is to be ready for nothing else. A man looks as if he hung in chains or like a scarecrow. And as those excellent birds (whom Pliny could never have the wit to catch in all his springes) commonly called woodcocks, whereof there is great store in England, having all their feathers plucked from their backs and being turned out as naked as Plato's cock was before all Diogenes his scholars, or as the cuckoo in Christmas, are more fit to come to any knight's board and are indeed more serviceable than when they are lapped in their warm liveries: even so stands the case with man. Truth (because the bald-pate her father Time has no hair to cover his head) goes, when she goes best, stark naked. But Falsehood has ever a cloak for the rain. You see likewise that the lion being the King of Beasts, the horse being the lustiest creature, the unicorn whose horn is worth half a city—all these go with no more clothes on their backs than what nature hath bestowed upon them. But yon baboons and yon jackanapes, being the scum and rascality of all the hedge-creepers, they go in jerkins and mandilions—marry, how? They are put into these rags only in mockery.

Oh, beware therefore both what you wear and how you wear it. And let this heavenly reason move you never to be handsome: for, when the sun is arising out of his bed does not the element seem more glorious then, being only in grey, than at noon when he's in all his bravery? It were madness to deny it. What man would not gladly see a beautiful woman naked or at least with nothing but a lawn or some loose thing over her, and even highly lift her up for being so? Shall we then abhor that in ourselves which we admire and hold to be so excellent in others? *Absit.*

CHAPTER III

How a young gallant should warm himself by the fire; how attire himself. The description of a man's head; the praise of long hair.

But if, as it often happens unless the year catch the sweating-sickness, the morning like charity waxing cold thrust his frosty fingers into thy bosom, pinching thee black and blue with her nails made of ice, like an invisible goblin, so that thy teeth as if thou wert singing prick-song stand coldly quavering in thy head and leap up and down like the nimble jacks of a pair of virginals: be then as swift as a whirlwind, and as boisterous, in tossing all thy clothes in a rude heap together. With which bundle filling thine arms, step bravely forth crying, 'Room! What a coil keep you about the fire!' The more are set round about it, the more is thy commendation if thou either bluntly ridest over their shoulders or tumblest aside their stools to creep into the chimney-corner. There toast thy body till thy scorched skin be speckled all over, being stained with more motley colours than are to be seen on the right side of the rainbow. Neither shall it be fit for the state of thy health to put on thy apparel till by sitting in that hot-house of the chimney thou feelest the fat dew of thy body like basting run trickling down thy sides. For by that means thou mayst lawfully boast that thou livest by the sweat of thy brows.

As for thy stockings and shoes, so wear them that all men may point at thee and make thee famous by that glorious name of a 'malcontent'. Or if thy quick silver can run so far on thy errand as to fetch thee boots out of St Martin's, let it be thy prudence to have the tops of them wide as the mouth of a wallet, and those with fringed boot-hose over them to hang down to thy ankles. Doves are accounted innocent and loving creatures; thou in observing this fashion shalt seem to be a rough-footed dove and be held as innocent. Besides, the strolling which of necessity so much leather between thy legs must put thee into will be thought not to grow from thy disease but from that gentlemanlike habit.

Having thus apparelled thee from top to toe according to that simple fashion which the best goosecaps in Europe strive to imitate, it is now high time for me to have a blow at thy head, which I will not cut off with sharp documents but rather set it on faster, bestowing upon it such excellent carving that, if all the wise men of Gotham should lay their heads together, their jobbernowls should not be able to compare with thine.

To maintain, therefore, that sconce of thine strongly guarded and in good reparation never suffer comb to fasten his teeth there. Let thy hair grow thick and bushy like a forest or some wilderness, lest those six-footed creatures that breed in it and are tenants to that Crown Land of thine be hunted to death by every base barbarous barber and so that delicate and tickling pleasure of scratching be utterly taken from thee. For the head is a house built for Reason to dwell in, and thus is the tenement framed: the two eyes are the glass windows at which light disperses itself into every room, having goodly penthouses of hair to overshadow them; as for the nose, though some most injuriously and improperly make it serve for an Indian chimney, yet surely it is rightly a bridge with two arches under which are neat passages, to convey as well perfumes to air and sweeten every chamber, as to carry away all noisome filth that is swept out of unclean corners; the cherry lips open, like the new-painted gates of a Lord Mayor's house, to take in provision; the tongue is a bell hanging just under the middle of the roof and, lest it should be rung out too deep, as sometimes it is when women have a peal, whereas it was cast by the First Founder but only to toll softly, there are two even rows of ivory pegs like pales set to keep it in; the ears are two music rooms into which as well good sounds as bad descend down two narrow pair of stairs that for all the world have crooked windings like those that lead to the top of Paul's steeple and, because when the tunes are once gotten in they should not too quickly slip out, all the walls of both places are plastered with yellow wax round about them.

Now as the fairest lodging, though it be furnished with walls, chimneys, chambers and all other parts of architecture, yet if the ceiling be wanting it stands subject to rain and so consequently to ruin, so would this goodly palace which we have modelled out unto you be but a cold and bald habitation were not the top of it rarely covered. Nature therefore has played the tiler and given it a most curious covering—or, to speak more properly, she has thatched it all over, and that thatching is hair. If then thou desirest to reserve that fee-simple of wit, thy head, for thee and the lawful heirs of thy body, play neither the scurvy part of the Frenchman that plucks up all by the roots nor that of the spending Englishman who, to maintain a paltry warren of unprofitable coneys, disimparks the stately swift-footed wild deer; but let thine receive his full growth that thou mayest safely and wisely brag 'tis thine own 'bush natural'.

And withal consider that as those trees of cobweb lawn, woven by spinners the fresh May mornings, do dress the curled heads of the mountains and adorn the swelling bosoms of the valleys, or as those snowy fleeces which the naked brier steals from the innocent nibbling sheep to make himself a warm winter livery are to either of them both an excellent ornament, so make thou account that to have feathers sticking here and there on thy head will embellish and set thy crown out rarely. None dare upbraid thee that like a beggar thou has lain on straw or like a travelling pedlar upon musty flocks, for those feathers will rise up as witnesses to choke him that says so, and to prove that thy bed was of the softest down. When your noblest gallants consecrate their hours to their mistresses and to revelling, they wear feathers then chiefly in their hats, being one of the fairest ensigns of their bravery. Be thou a reveller and a mistress-server all the year by wearing feathers in thy hair; whose length before the rigorous edge of any puritanical pair of scissors should shorten the breadth of a finger, let the three housewifely spinsters of Destiny rather curtail the thread of thy life.

Oh no, long hair is the only net that women spread abroad to entrap men in. And why should not men be as far above women in that commodity as they go beyond men in others? The merry Greeks were called καρηκομόωντες 'long-haired'. Lose not thou, being an honest Trojan, that honour, sithence it will more fairly become thee. Grass is the hair of the earth which, so long as it is suffered to grow, it becomes the wearer and carries a most pleasing colour but when the sunburnt clown makes his mows at it and like a barber shaves it off to the stumps, then it withers and is good for nothing but to be trussed up and thrown amongst jades.

How ugly is a bald pate! It looks like a face wanting a nose or like ground eaten bare with the arrows of archers, whereas a head all hid in hair gives even to a most wicked face a sweet proportion and looks like a meadow newly married to the spring. Which beauty in men the Turks envying, they no sooner lay hold on a Christian but the first mark they set upon him to make him know he's a slave is to shave off all his hair close to the skull. A Mahommedan cruelty therefore is it to stuff breeches and tennis balls with that which when 'tis once lost all the hare-hunters in the world may sweat their hearts out and yet hardly catch it again.

You, then, to whom chastity has given an hair apparent, take order that it may be apparent, and to that purpose let it play openly with the lascivious wind even on the top of your shoulders. Experience cries out in every city that those selfsame critical Saturnists whose hair is shorter than their eyebrows take a pride to have their hoary beards hang slavering like a dozen of foxtails down so low as their middle. But, alas! Why should the chins and lips of old men lick up that excrement which they violently clip away from the heads of young men? Is it because those long besoms, their beards, with sweeping the soft bosoms of their beautiful young wives may tickle their tender breasts and make some amends for their masters' unrecoverable dullness? No, no! There hangs more at the ends of those long grey hairs than all the world can come to the knowledge of.

Certain I am that when none but the Golden Age went current upon earth it was higher treason to clip hair than to clip money. The comb and scissors were condemned to the currying of hackneys. He was disfranchised for ever that did but put on a barber's apron. Man, woman and child wore their hair longer than a lawsuit. Every head, when it stood bare or uncovered, looked like a butter-box's noll having his thrummed cap on. It was free for all nations to have shaggy pates as it is now only for the Irishman. But since this polling and shaving world crept up, locks were locked up and hair fell to decay. Revive thou, therefore, the old buried fashion and in scorn of periwigs and sheep-shearing keep thou that quilted head-piece on continually. Long hair will make thee look dreadfully to thine enemies and manly to thy friends. It is in peace an ornament; in war, a strong helmet— it blunts the edge of a sword and deads the leaden thump of a bullet. In winter it is a warm night-cap; in summer, a cooling fan of feathers.

D

CHAPTER IV

How a gallant should behave himself in Paul's Walks.

Being weary with sailing up and down alongst these shores of
Barbaria, here let us cast our anchor and nimbly leap to land in our
coasts, whose fresh air shall be so much the more pleasing to us if the
ninny-hammer whose perfection we labour to set forth have so much
foolish wit left him as to choose the place where to suck in. For that
true humorous gallant that desires to pour himself into all fashions, if
his ambition be such to excel even compliment itself must as well
practise to diminish his walks as to be various in his salads, curious in
his tobacco, or ingenious in the trussing up of a new Scotch hose. All
which virtues are excellent and able to maintain him, especially if the
old worm-eaten farmer his father be dead and left him five hundred a
year only to keep an Irish hobby, an Irish horse-boy, and himself like
a gentleman. He therefore that would strive to fashion his legs to his
silk stockings and his proud gait to his broad garters, let him whiff
down these observations. For if he once get but to walk by the book
(and I see no reason but he may, as well as fight by the book) Paul's
may be proud of him, Will Clarke shall ring forth encomiums in his
honour, John in Paul's Churchyard shall fit his head for an excellent
block, whilst all the Inns of Court rejoice to behold his most handsome
calf.

Your Mediterranean Aisle is then the only gallery wherein the
pictures of all your true fashionate and complimental gulls are and
ought to be hung up. Into that gallery carry your neat body. But take
heed you pick out such an hour when the main shoal of Aislanders
are swimming up and down. And first observe your doors of entrance
and your exit not much unlike the players at the theatres, keeping your
decorums even in fantasticality: as for example, if you prove to be a
northern gentleman I would wish you to pass through the North
Door more often especially than any of the other; and so, according
to your countries, take note of your entrances.

Now for your venturing into the Walk, be circumspect and wary
what pillar you come in at and take heed in any case, as you love the

88

III   A Tobacco Shop

IV   Paul's Walk

reputation of your honour, that you avoid the Servingman's Log and approach not within five fathom of that pillar but bend your course directly in the middle line, that the whole body of the church may appear to be yours. Where in view of all you may publish your suit in what manner you affect most, either with the slide of your cloak from the one shoulder (and then you must, as 'twere in anger, suddenly snatch at the middle of the inside if it be taffeta at the least, and so by that means your costly lining is betrayed) or else by the pretty advantage of compliment. But one note by the way do I especially woo you to, the neglect of which makes many of our gallants cheap and ordinary: that by no means you be seen above four turns, but in the fifth make yourself away either in some of the sempsters' shops, the new tobacco office or amongst the booksellers where, if you cannot read, exercise your smoke and enquire who has writ against 'this divine weed', etc. For this withdrawing yourself a little will much benefit your suit, which else by too long walking would be stale to the whole spectators.

But howsoever, if Paul's jacks be once up with their elbows and quarrelling to strike eleven, as soon as ever the clock has parted them and ended the fray with his hammer, let not the Duke's Gallery contain you any longer, but pass away apace in open view. In which departure if by chance you either encounter or aloof off throw your inquisitive eye upon any knight or squire being your familiar, salute him not by his name of 'Sir Such-a-one' or so but call him 'Ned' or 'Jack', etc.: this will set off your estimation with great men. And if (though there be a dozen companies between you, 'tis the better) he call aloud to you (for that's most genteel) to know where he shall find you at two o'clock, tell him at such an ordinary or such (and be sure to name those that are dearest and whither none but your gallants resort). After dinner you may appear again, having translated yourself out of your English cloth cloak into a light Turkey grogram (if you have that happiness of shifting) and then be seen for a turn or two to correct your teeth with some quill or silver instrument and to cleanse your gums with a wrought handkerchief. It skills not whether you dined or no (that's best known to your stomach) or in what place you dined, though it were with cheese of your own mother's making in your chamber or study.

Now if you chance to be a gallant not much crossed amongst citizens—that is, a gallant in the mercers' books exalted for satins and velvets: if you be not so much blessed to be crossed (as I hold it the greatest blessing in the world to be great in no man's books), your Paul's Walk is your only refuge. The Duke's Tomb is a sanctuary and will keep you alive from worms and land-rats that long to be feeding on your carcase. There you may spend your legs in winter a whole afternoon: converse, plot, laugh and talk anything, jest at your creditor even to his face, and in the evening, even by lamplight, steal out and so cozen a whole covey of abominable catchpoles.

Never be seen to mount the steps into the Choir but upon a high festival day, to prefer the fashion of your doublet, and especially if the singing boys seem to take note of you, for they are able to buzz your praises above their anthems if their voices have not lost their maidenheads. But be sure your silver spurs dog your heels, and then the boys will swarm about you like so many white butterflies when you in the open Choir shall draw forth a perfumed embroidered purse —the glorious sight of which will entice many countrymen from their devotion, to wondering; and quoit silver into the boys' hands that it may be heard above the first lesson, although it be read in a voice as big as one of the great organs. This noble and notable act being performed, you are to vanish presently out of the Choir and to appear again in the Walk. But in any wise be not observed to tread there long alone, for fear you be suspected to be a gallant cashiered from the society of captains and fighters.

Suck this humour up especially: put off to none unless his hatband be of a newer fashion than yours and three degrees quainter. But for him that wears a trebled cypress about his hat, though he were an alderman's son, never move to him, for he's suspected to be worse than a gull and not worth the putting off to, that cannot observe the time of his hatband nor know what fashioned block is most kin to his head. For in my opinion that brain that cannot choose his felt well, being the head ornament, must needs pour folly into all the rest of the members and be an absolute confirmed fool *in summa totali*.

All the diseased horses in a tedious siege cannot show so many 'fashions' as are to be seen for nothing every day in Duke Humphrey's Walk. If therefore you determine to enter into a new suit, warn your tailor to attend you in Paul's; who with his hat in his hand shall like a spy discover the stuff, colour and fashion of any doublet or hose that dare be seen there and, stepping behind a pillar to fill his tablebooks with those notes, will presently send you into the world an accomplished man: by which means you shall wear your clothes in print with the first edition.

But if fortune favour you so much as to make you no more than a mere country gentleman or but some three degrees removed from him (for which I should be very sorry, because your London experience will cost you dear before you shall have the wit to know what you are) then take this lesson along with you: the first time that you venture into Paul's, pass through the body of the church like a porter, yet presume not to fetch so much as one whole turn in the Middle Aisle— no, nor to cast an eye to Si-quis Door, pasted and plastered up with servingmen's supplications—before you have paid tribute to the top of Paul's steeple with a single penny. And when you are mounted there, take heed how you look down into the yard, for the rails are as rotten as your great-grandfather. And thereupon it will not be amiss if you enquire how Kit Woodroffe durst vault over, and what reason he had for't to put his neck in hazard of reparations. From hence you may descend to talk about the horse that went up, and strive if you can to know his keeper; take the day of the month and the number of the steps, and suffer yourself to believe verily that it was not a horse but something else in the likeness of one. Which wonders you may publish when you return into the country, to the great amazement of all farmers' daughters, that will almost swoon at the report and never recover till their banns be asked twice in the church.

But I have not left you yet. Before you come down again, I would desire you to draw your knife and grave your name—or, for want of a name, the mark which you clap on your sheep—in great characters upon the leads by a number of your brethren, both citizens and country gentlemen: and so you shall be sure to have your name lie in a coffin of lead when yourself shall be wrapped in a winding-sheet. And indeed the top of Paul's contains more names than Stow's *Chronicle*.

These lofty tricks being played and you, thanks to your feet, being safely arrived at the stairs' foot again, your next worthy work is to repair to my Lord Chancellor's Tomb. And if you can but reasonably spell, bestow some time upon the reading of Sir Philip Sidney's brief epitaph—in the compass of an hour you may make shift to stumble it out. The great dial is your last monument. There bestow some half of the threescore minutes to observe the sauciness of the jacks that are above the man in the moon there. The strangeness of the motion will quit your labour. Besides, you may here have fit occasion to discover your watch by taking it forth and setting the wheels to the time of Paul's, which I assure you goes truer by five notes than St Sepulchre's chimes. The benefit that will arise from hence is this, that you publish your charge in maintaining a gilded clock, and withal the world shall know that you are a timepleaser.

By this I imagine you have walked your bellyful and, thereupon being weary or (which rather I believe) being most gentlemanlike hungry, it is fit that, as I brought you into the Duke: so, because he follows the fashion of great men in keeping no house and that therefore you must go seek your dinner, suffer me to take you by the hand and lead you into an ordinary.

CHAPTER V

How a young gallant should behave himself in an ordinary.

First having diligently enquired out an ordinary of the largest reckoning whither most of your courtly gallants do resort, let it be your use to repair thither some half-hour after eleven, for then you shall find most of your fashion-mongers planted in the room waiting for meat. Ride thither upon your Galloway nag or your Spanish jennet a swift ambling pace in your hose and doublet, gilt rapier and poniard bestowed in their places and your French lackey carrying your cloak and running before you; or rather in a coach, for that will both hide you from the basilisk eyes of your creditors and outrun a whole kennel of bitter-mouthed sergeants.

Being arrived in the room, salute not any but those of your acquaintance. Walk up and down by the rest as scornfully and as carelessly as a gentleman-usher. Select some friend, having first thrown off your cloak, to walk up and down the room with you. Let him be suited if you can worse by far than yourself: he will be a foil to you, and this will be a means to publish your clothes better than Paul's, a tennis-court or a playhouse.

Discourse as loud as you can, no matter to what purpose; if you but make a noise and laugh in fashion, and have a good sour face to promise quarrelling, you shall be much observed. If you be a soldier, talk how often you have been in action—as, the Portugal Voyage, Cadiz Voyage, the Island Voyage, besides some eight or nine employments in Ireland and the Low Countries. Then you may discourse how honourably your Graf used you (observe that you call your Graf Maurice *your Graf*), how often you have drunk with Count Such-a-one and such a count on your knees to your Graf's health— and let it be your virtue to give place neither to St Cynog nor to any Dutchman whatsoever in the Seventeen Provinces for that soldier's compliment of drinking. And if you perceive that the untravelled company about you take this down well, ply them with more such stuff—as, how you have interpreted between the French King and a great lord of Barbary when they have been drinking healths together.

And that will be an excellent occasion to publish your languages if you have them. If not, get some fragments of French or small parcels of Italian to fling about the table. But beware how you speak any Latin there; your ordinary most commonly hath no more to do with Latin than a desperate town of garrison hath.

If you be a courtier, discourse of the obtaining of suits, of your mistress's favours, etc.; make enquiry if any gentleman at board have any suit, to get which he would use the good means of a great man's interest with the King; and withal (if you have not so much grace left in you as to blush) that you are, thanks to your stars, in mighty credit (though in your own conscience you know and are guilty to yourself that you dare not, but only upon the privileges of handsome clothes, presume to peep into the Presence). Demand if there be any gentleman whom any there is acquainted with that is troubled with two offices, or any vicar with two church livings: which will politicly insinuate that your enquiry after them is because you have good means to obtain them. Yea, and rather than your tongue should not be heard in the room but that you should sit like an ass with your finger in your mouth and speak nothing, discourse how often this lady hath sent her coach for you and how often you have sweat in the tennis-court with that great lord—for indeed the sweating together in France (I mean the society of tennis!) is a great argument of most dear affection even between noblemen and peasants.

If you be a poet and come into the ordinary (though it can be no great glory to be an ordinary poet) order yourself thus: observe no man, doff not cap to that gentleman today at dinner to whom not two nights since you were beholden for a supper. But after a turn or two in the room take occasion, pulling out your gloves, to have some epigram or satire or sonnet fastened in one of them that may, as it were unwittingly to you, offer itself to the gentlemen. They will presently desire it, but without much conjuration from them and a pretty kind of counterfeit loathness in yourself do not read it. And though it be none of your own, swear you made it. Marry, if you chance to get into your hands any witty thing of another man's that is somewhat better, I would counsel you then, if demand be made who composed it, you may say, 'Faith, a learned gentleman, a very worthy friend', and this seeming to lay it on another man will be counted either modesty in you or a sign that you are not ambitious of praise, or else that you dare not take it upon you for fear of the sharpness it carries with it.

Besides, it will add much to your fame to let your tongue walk faster than your teeth though you be never so hungry and, rather than you should sit like a dumb coxcomb, to repeat by heart either some verses of your own or of any other man's, stretching even very good lines upon the rack of censure; though it be against all law, honesty or conscience, it may chance save you the price of your ordinary and beget you other supplements. Marry, I would further entreat our poet to be in league with the mistress of the ordinary because from her, upon condition that he will but rhyme knights and young gentlemen to her house and maintain the table in good fooling, he may easily make up his mouth at her cost *gratis*.

Thus much for particular men. But in general let all, that are in ordinary pay, march after the sound of these directions: before the meat come smoking to the board our gallant must draw out his tobacco-box, the ladle for the cold snuff into the nostril, the tongs and prining-iron—all which artillery may be of gold or silver if he can reach to the price of it (it will be a reasonable useful pawn at all times when the current of his money falls out to run low). And here you must observe to know in what state tobacco is in town better than the merchants, and to discourse of the pothecaries where it is to be sold and to be able to speak of their leaves as readily as the pothecary himself reading the barbarous hand of a doctor. Then let him show his several tricks in taking it—as, the whiff, the ring, etc. For these are compliments that gain gentlemen no mean respect and for which indeed they are more worthily noted, I ensure you, than for any skill that they have in learning.

When you are set down to dinner you must eat as impudently as can be, for that's most gentlemanlike. When your knight is upon his stewed mutton, be you presently (though you be but a captain) in the bosom of your goose. And when your Justice of Peace is knuckle-deep in goose, you may without disparagement to your blood (though you have a lady to your mother) fall very manfully to your woodcocks.

You may rise in dinner-time to ask for a close-stool, protesting to all the gentlemen that it costs you a hundred pound a year in physic besides the annual pension which your wife allows her doctor. And if you please you may, as your great French lord doth, invite some special friend of yours from the table to hold discourse with you as you sit in that withdrawing-chamber; from whence being returned again to the board, you shall sharpen the wits of all the eating gallants about you, and do them great pleasure, to ask what pamphlets or poems a man might think fittest to wipe his tail with (marry, this talk will be somewhat foul if you carry not a strong perfume about you) and in propounding this question you may abuse the works of any man, deprave his writings that you cannot equal, and purchase to yourself in time the terrible name of a severe critic—nay, and be one of the College if you'll be liberal enough, and when your turn comes pay for their suppers.

After dinner every man as his business leads him—some to dice, some to drabs, some to plays, some to take up friends in the Court, some to take up money in the City, some to lend testers in Paul's, others to borrow crowns upon the Exchange. And thus, as the people is said to be a beast of many heads, yet all those heads like Hydra's ever growing as various in their horns as wondrous in their budding and branching, so in an ordinary you shall find the variety of a whole kingdom in a few apes of the kingdom.

You must not swear in your dicing, for that argues a violent impatience to depart from your money and in time will betray a man's need. Take heed of it! No, whether you be at primero or hazard you shall sit as patiently, though you lose a whole half-year's exhibition, as a disarmed gentleman does when he's in the unmerciful fingers of sergeants. Marry, I will allow you to sweat privately, and tear six or sevenscore pair of cards, be the damnation of some dozen or twenty bale of dice, and forswear play a thousand times in an hour; but not swear. Dice yourself into your shirt and, if you have a beard that your friend will lend but an angel upon, shave it off and pawn that rather than to go home blind to your lodging. Further it is to be remembered, he that is a great gamester may be trusted for a quarter's board at all times, and apparel provided if need be.

At your twelvepenny ordinary you may give any Justice of Peace or young knight, if he sit but one degree towards the equinoctial of the salt-cellar, leave to pay for the wine; and he shall not refuse it though it be a week before the receiving of his quarter's rent—which is a time, albeit of good hope, yet of present necessity.

There is another ordinary, to which your London usurer, your stale bachelor and your thrifty attorney do resort—the price threepence, the rooms as full of company as a gaol and indeed divided into several wards like the beds of an hospital. The compliment between these is not much, their words few, for the belly hath no ears. Every man's eye here is upon the other man's trencher to note whether his fellow lurch him or no. If they chance to discourse it is of nothing but of statutes, bonds, recognizances, fines, recoveries, audits, rents, subsidies, sureties, enclosures, liveries, indictments, outlawries, feoffments, judgments, commissions, bankrupts, amercements, and of such horrible matter that when a lieutenant dines with his punk in the next room he thinks verily the men are conjuring. I can find nothing at this ordinary worthy the sitting down for, therefore the cloth shall be taken away. And those that are thought good enough to be guests here shall be too base to be waiters at your grand ordinary, at which your gallant tastes these commodities: he shall fare well, enjoy good company, receive all the news ere the post can deliver his packet, be perfect where the best bawdy-houses stand, proclaim his good clothes, know this man to drink well, that to feed grossly, the other to swagger roughly; he shall, if he be minded to travel, put out money upon his return and have hands enough to receive it upon any terms of repayment; and, no question, if he be poor he shall now and then light upon some gull or other whom he may skelder, after the genteel fashion, of money.

By this time the parings of fruit and cheese are in the voider, cards and dice lie stinking in the fire, the guests are all up, the gilt rapiers ready to be hanged, the French lackey and Irish footboy shrugging at the doors with their masters' hobby-horses to ride to the new play—that's the rendezvous, thither they are galloped in post. Let us take a pair of oars and now lustily after them.

CHAPTER VI

How a gallant should behave himself in a playhouse.

The theatre is your poets' Royal Exchange upon which their Muses—that are now turned to merchants—meeting, barter away that light commodity of words for a lighter ware than words—plaudits and the breath of the great beast which, like the threatenings of two cowards, vanish all into air. Players are their factors who put away the stuff and make the best of it they possibly can, as indeed 'tis their parts so to do. Your gallant, your courtier and your captain had wont to be the soundest paymasters and I think are still the surest chapmen. And these by means that their heads are well stocked deal upon this comical freight by the gross when your groundling and gallery commoner buys his sport by the penny and like a haggler is glad to utter it again by retailing.

Sithence then the place is so free in entertainment, allowing a stool as well to the farmer's son as to your Templar, that your stinkard has the selfsame liberty to be there in his tobacco fumes which your sweet courtier hath, and that your carman and tinker claim as strong a voice in their suffrage, and sit to give judgment on the play's life and death as well as the proudest Momus among the Tribe of Critic, it is fit that he whom the most tailors' bills do make room for when he comes should not be basely, like a viol, cased up in a corner.

Whether, therefore, the gatherers of the public or private playhouse stand to receive the afternoon's rent, let our gallant, having paid it, presently advance himself up to the throne of the stage. I mean not into the Lords' Room, which is now but the stage's suburbs (no—those boxes, by the iniquity of custom, conspiracy of waiting-women and gentlemen-ushers that there sweat together, and the covetousness of sharers, are contemptibly thrust into the rear and much new Satin is there damned by being smothered to death in darkness), but on the very rushes where the comedy is to dance—yea, and under the state of Cambyses himself—must our feathered ostrich, like a piece of ordnance, be planted valiantly because impudently, beating down the mews and hisses of the opposed rascality.

For do but cast up a reckoning what large comings-in are pursed up by sitting on the stage. First, a conspicuous eminence is gotten by which means the best and most essential parts of a gallant—good clothes, a proportionable leg, white hand, the Persian lock, and a tolerable beard—are perfectly revealed.

By sitting on the stage you have a signed patent to engross the whole commodity of censure; may lawfully presume to be a girder; and stand at the helm to steer the passage of scenes. Yet no man shall once offer to hinder you from obtaining the title of an insolent overweening coxcomb.

By sitting on the stage you may, without travelling for it, at the very next door ask whose play it is and, by that quest of enquiry, the law warrants you to avoid much mistaking. If you know not the author, you may rail against him and peradventure so behave yourself that you may enforce the author to know you.

By sitting on the stage, if you be a knight, you may haply get you a mistress; if a mere Fleet St gentleman, a wife; but assure yourself by continual residence you are the first and principal man in election to begin the number of 'We Three'.

By spreading your body on the stage and by being a Justice in examining of plays you shall put yourself into such true scenical authority that some poet shall not dare to present his Muse rudely upon your eyes without having first unmasked her, rifled her and discovered all her bare and most mystical parts before you at a tavern, when you most knightly shall for his pains pay for both their suppers.

By sitting on the stage you may with small cost purchase the dear acquaintance of the boys; have a good stool for sixpence; at any time know what particular part any of the infants present; get your match lighted; examine the play-suits' lace, and perhaps win wagers upon laying 'tis copper, etc..

And to conclude, whether you be a fool or a Justice of Peace, a cuckold or a captain, a Lord Mayor's son or a dawcock, a knave or an under-sheriff: of what stamp soever you be, current or counterfeit, the stage (like Time) will bring you to most perfect light and lay you open. Neither are you to be hunted from thence though the scarecrows in the yard hoot at you, hiss at you, spit at you—yea, throw dirt even in your teeth. 'Tis most gentlemanlike patience to endure all this and to laugh at the silly animals. But if the rabble with a full throat cry 'Away with the fool!' you were worse than a madman to tarry by it, for the gentleman and the fool should never sit on the stage together.

Marry, let this observation go hand in hand with the rest—or rather, like a country servingman, some five yards before them: present not yourself on the stage, especially at a new play, until the quaking Prologue hath by rubbing got colour into his cheeks and is ready to give the trumpets their cue that he's upon point to enter. For then it is time, as though you were one of the properties or that you dropped out of the hangings, to creep from behind the arras with your *tripos* or 'three-footed stool' in one hand and a teston mounted between a forefinger and a thumb in the other. For if you should bestow your person upon the vulgar when the belly of the house is but half full, your apparel is quite eaten up, the fashion lost, and the proportion of your body in more danger to be devoured than if it were served up in the Counter amongst the Poultry. Avoid that as you would the *baston*.

It shall crown you with rich commendation to laugh aloud in the middest of the most serious and saddest scene of the terriblest tragedy and to let that clapper, your tongue, be tossed so high that all the house may ring of it. Your lords use it, your knights are apes to the lords and do so too, your Inn o' Court man is zany to the knights and—marry, very scurvily—comes likewise limping after it; be thou a beagle to them all and never lin snuffing till you have scented them, for by talking and laughing like a ploughman in a morris you heap Pelion upon Ossa, glory upon glory. As, first, all the eyes in the galleries will leave walking after the players and only follow you; the simplest dolt in the house snatches up your name and, when he meets you in the streets or that you fall into his hands in the middle of a watch, his word shall be taken for you. He'll cry 'He's such a gallant!', and you pass. Secondly, you publish your temperance to the world, in that you seem not to resort thither to taste vain pleasures with a hungry appetite but only as a gentleman to spend a foolish hour or two because you can do nothing else. Thirdly, you mightily disrelish the audience and disgrace the author. Marry, you take up (though it be at the worst hand) a strong opinion of your own judgment, and enforce the poet to take pity of your weakness and by some dedicated sonnet to bring you into a better paradise, only to stop your mouth.

If you can, either for love or money provide yourself a lodging by the waterside for, above the conveniency it brings to shun shoulder-clapping and to ship away your cockatrice betimes in the morning, it adds a kind of state unto you to be carried from thence to the stairs of your playhouse. Hate a sculler (remember that) worse than to be acquainted with one o' th' Scullery. No, your oars are your only sea-

crabs. Board them and take heed you never go twice together with one
pair: often shifting is a great credit to gentlemen, and that dividing of
your fare will make the poor watersnakes be ready to pull you in
pieces to enjoy your custom. No matter whether upon landing you
have money or no: you may swim in twenty of their boats over the
River upon ticket. Marry, when silver comes in, remember to pay
treble their fare, and it will make your flounder-catchers to send more
thanks after you when you do not draw than when you do, for they
know it will be their own another day.

Before the play begins, fall to cards. You may win or lose as fencers
do in a prize, and beat one another by confederacy, yet share the money
when you meet at supper. Notwithstanding, to gull the ragamuffins
that stand aloof gaping at you, throw the cards, having first torn four
or five of them, round about the stage just upon the third sound, as
though you had lost. It skills not if the four knaves lie on their backs
and outface the audience: there's none such fools as dare take exceptions at them because, ere the play go off, better knaves than they will
fall into the company.

Now, sir, if the writer be a fellow that hath either epigrammed you
or hath had a flirt at your mistress, or hath brought either your feather
or your red beard or your little legs, etc., on the stage you shall
disgrace him worse than by tossing him in a blanket or giving him the
bastinado in a tavern if in the middle of his play, be it pastoral or
comedy, moral or tragedy, you rise with a screwed and discontented
face from your stool to be gone. No matter whether the scenes be good
or no: the better they are, the worse do you distaste them. And, being
on your feet, sneak not away like a coward but salute all your gentle
acquaintance that are spread either on the rushes or on stools about
you, and draw what troop you can from the stage after you. The
mimics are beholden to you for allowing them elbow-room. Their
poet cries perhaps 'A pox go with you!' but care not you for that—
there's no music without frets.

Marry, if either the company or indisposition of the weather bind
you to sit it out, my counsel is then that you turn plain ape, take up a
rush and tickle the earnest ears of your fellow gallants to make other
fools fall a-laughing; mew at passionate speeches, blare at merry, find
fault with the music, whew at the children's action, whistle at the songs
and above all curse the sharers that, whereas the same day you had
bestowed forty shillings on an embroidered felt and feather, Scotch
fashion, for your mistress in the Court or your punk in the City,

within two hours after, you encounter with the very same block on the stage, when the haberdasher swore to you the impression was extant but that morning.

To conclude, hoard up the finest play-scraps you can get, upon which your lean wit may most savourly feed for want of other stuff when the Arcadian and Euphuized gentlewomen have their tongues sharpened to set upon you. That quality, next to your shuttlecock, is the only furniture to a courtier that's but a new-beginner and is but in his ABC of Compliment. The next places that are filled after the playhouses be emptied are, or ought to be, taverns. Into a tavern then let us next march, where the brains of one hogshead must be beaten out to make up another.

CHAPTER VII

How a gallant should behave himself in a tavern.

Whosoever desires to be a man of good reckoning in the City and
like your French lord to have as many tables furnished as lackeys
(who, when they keep least, keep none): whether he be a young quat
of the first year's revenue; or some austere and sullen-faced steward
who, in despite of a great beard, a satin suit and a chain of gold wrapped
in cypress, proclaims himself to any but to those to whom his lord
owes money for a rank coxcomb; or whether he be a country gentleman that brings his wife up to learn the fashion, see the tombs at
Westminster, the lions in the Tower, or to take physic; or else is some
young farmer who many times makes his wife in the country believe
he hath suits in law, because he will come up to his lechery: be he of
what stamp he will that hath money in his purse and a good conscience
to spend it, my counsel is that he take his continual diet at a tavern,
which out of question is the only rendezvous of boon company, and
the drawers the most nimble, the most bold and most sudden pro-
claimers of your largest bounty.

Having therefore thrust yourself into a case most in fashion (how
coarse soever the stuff be, 'tis no matter so it hold fashion) your office
is, if you mean to do your judgment right, to enquire out those taverns
which are best customed, whose masters are oftenest drunk (for that
confirms their taste and that they choose wholesome wines) and such
as stand furthest from the Counters. Where landing yourself and your
followers, your first compliment shall be to grow most inwardly
acquainted with the drawers: to learn their names—as 'Jack' and 'Will'
and 'Tom'; to dive into their inclinations—as whether this fellow
useth to the fencing school, this to the dancing school, whether that
young conjuror in hogsheads at midnight keeps a gelding now and
then to visit his cockatrice, or whether he love dogs, or be addicted
to any other eminent and citizen-like quality; and protest yourself to
be extremely in love and that you spend much money in a year upon
any one of those exercises which you perceive is followed by them.

The use which you shall make of this familiarity is this: if you want money five or six days together you may still pay the reckoning with this most gentlemanlike language—'Boy, fetch me money from the bar!'—and keep yourself most providently from a hungry melancholy in your chamber. Besides you shall be sure, if there be but one faucet that can betray neat wine to the bar, to have that arraigned before you sooner than a better and worthier person.

The first question you are to make, after the discharging of your pocket of tobacco and pipes and the household-stuff thereto belonging, shall be for an inventory of the kitchen. For it were more than most tailor-like, and to be suspected you were in league with some kitchen wench, to descend yourself, to offend your stomach with the sight of the larder and haply to grease your accoutrements. Having therefore received this bill you shall, like a captain putting up dear pays, have many salads stand on your table, as it were for blanks to the other more serviceable dishes. And according to the time of the year vary your fare—as, capon is a stirring meat some time, oysters are a swelling meat sometimes, trout a tickling meat sometimes, green goose and woodcock a delicate meat sometimes, especially in a tavern, where you shall sit in as great state as a churchwarden amongst his poor parishioners at Pentecost or Christmas.

For your drink, let not your physician confine you to any one particular liquor. For, as it is requisite that a gentleman should not always be plodding in one art but rather be a general scholar—that is, to have a lick at all sorts of learning, and away—so 'tis not fitting a man should trouble his head with sucking at one grape, but that he may be able, now there is a general peace, to drink any stranger drunk in his own element of drink or, more properly, in his own mist language.

Your discourse at the table must be such as that which you utter at your ordinary; your behaviour the same, but somewhat more careless. For where your expense is great let your modesty be less and, though you should be mad in a tavern, the largeness of the items will bear with your incivility. You may without prick to your conscience set the want of your wit against the superfluity and sauciness of their reckonings.

If you desire not to be haunted with fiddlers (who by the Statute have as much liberty as rogues to travel into any place, having the passport of the house about them) bring then no women along with you. But if you love the company of all the drawers, never sup without your cockatrice for, having her there, you shall be sure of most officious attendance.

2. Fiddlers at a Tavern.

Enquire what gallants sup in the next room and, if they be any of your acquaintance, do not you after the City fashion send them in a pottle of wine and your name sweetened in two pitiful papers of sugar, with some filthy apology crammed into the mouth of a drawer. But rather keep a boy in fee who underhand shall proclaim you in every room what a gallant fellow you are, how much you spend yearly in taverns, what a great gamester, what custom you bring to the house, in what witty discourse you maintain a table, what gentlewomen or citizens' wives you can with a wet finger have at any time to sup with you, and suchlike. By which encomiastics of his they that know you not shall admire you and think themselves to be brought into a paradise but to be meanly in your acquaintance. And if any of your endeared friends be in the house and beat the same ivy-bush that yourself does, you may join companies and be drunk together most publicly.

But in such a deluge of drink take heed that no man counterfeit himself drunk to free his purse from the danger of the shot: 'tis an usual thing now amongst gentlemen—it had wont be the quality of cockneys. I would advise you to leave so much brains in your head as to prevent this. When the terrible reckoning, like an indictment, bids you hold up your hand, and that you must answer it at the bar, you must not abate one penny in any particular—no, though they reckon cheese to you when you have neither eaten any nor could ever abide it, raw or toasted. But cast your eye only upon the *totalis* and no further: for to traverse the bill would betray you to be acquainted with the rates of the market—nay, more, it would make the vintners believe you were *paterfamilias* and kept a house (which I assure you is not now in fashion).

If you fall to dice after supper let the drawers be as familiar with you as your barber, and venture their silver amongst you—no matter where they had it: you are to cherish the unthriftiness of such young tame pigeons if you be a right gentleman. For when two are yoked together by the purse-strings and draw the chariot of Madam Prodigality, when one faints in the way and slips his horns, let the other rejoice and laugh at him.

At your departure forth the house, to kiss mine hostess over the bar or to accept of the courtesy of the cellar when 'tis offered you by the drawers (and, you must know, that kindness never creeps upon them but when they see you almost cleft to the shoulders) or to bid any of the vintners goodnight, is as commendable as for a barber after trimming to lave your face with sweet water.

To conclude, count it an honour either to invite or to be invited to any rifling for, commonly though you find much satin there, yet you shall likewise find many citizens' sons and heirs and younger brothers there, who smell out such feasts more greedily than tailors hunt upon Sundays after weddings. And let any hook draw you either to a fencer's supper or to a player's that acts such a part for a wager. For by this means you shall get experience by being guilty to their abominable shaving.

CHAPTER VIII

*How a gallant is to behave himself passing through the City at all
hours of the night, and how to pass by any watch.*

After the sound of pottle-pots is out of your ears and that the spirit
of wine and tobacco walks in your brain, the tavern-door being shut
upon your back, cast about to pass through the widest and goodliest
streets in the City. And if your means cannot reach to the keeping of
a boy, hire one of the drawers to be as a lantern unto your feet and to
light you home. And still as you approach near any night-walker that
is up as late as yourself curse and swear, like one that speaks High
Dutch, in a lofty voice, because your men have used you so like a
rascal in not waiting upon you, and vow the next morning to pull
their blue cases over their ears—though if your chamber were well
searched, you give only sixpence a week to some old woman to make
your bed, and that she is all the serving creatures you give wages to.

If you smell a watch (and that you may easily do, for commonly
they eat onions to keep them in sleeping, which they account a
medicine against cold): but if you come within danger of their brown
bills, let him that is your candlestick and holds up your torch from
dropping (for to march after a link is shoemaker-like), let *Ignis Fatuus*,
I say, being within the reach of the Constable's staff, ask aloud, 'Sir
Giles' or 'Sir Abr'am, will you turn this way' or 'down that street?' It
skills not though there be none dubbed in your bunch, the watch will
wink at you only for the love they bear to arms and knighthood.
Marry, if the sentinel and his court of guard stand strictly upon his
martial law and cry 'Stand!', commanding you to give the word and
to show reason why your ghost walks so late, do it in some jest, for
that will show you have a desperate wit and perhaps make him and his
halberdiers afraid to lay foul hands upon you; or if you read a *mittimus*
in the Constable's look, counterfeit to be a Frenchman, a Dutchman
or any other nation whose country is in peace with your own, and
you may pass the pikes; for being not able to understand you, they
cannot by the customs of the City take your examination and so by
consequence they have nothing to say to you.

If the night be old and that your lodging be in some place into which no artillery of words can make a breach, retire and rather assault the doors of your punk—or, not to speak broken English, your 'sweet mistress'—upon whose white bosom you may languishingly consume the rest of darkness that is left in ravishing, though not restorative, pleasures without expenses, only by virtue of four or five oaths, when the siege breaks up and at your marching away with bag and baggage, that the last night you were at dice and lost so much in gold, so much in silver, and seem to vex most that two such Elizabeth twenty-shilling pieces or four such spur-royals (sent you with a cheese and a baked meat from your mother) rid away amongst the rest. By which tragical yet politic speech you may not only have your night-work done *gratis* but also you may take diet there the next day and depart with credit only upon the bare word of a gentleman to make her restitution.

All the way as you pass, especially being approached near some of the gates, talk of none but lords, and such ladies with whom you have played at primero or danced in the Presence the very same day. It is a chance to lock up the lips of an inquisitive bellman. And being arrived at your lodging door, which I would counsel you to choose in some rich citizen's house, salute at parting no man but by the name of 'Sir', as though you had supped with knights, albeit you had none in your company but your *perinado* or your 'ingle'.

Haply it will be blown abroad that you and your shoal of gallants swam through such an ocean of wine, that you danced so much money out at heels, and that in wild fowl there flew away thus much; and, I assure you, to have the bill of your reckoning lost of purpose, so that it may be published, will make you to be held in dear estimation. Only the danger is if you owe money, and that your revealing gets your creditors by the ears. For then look to have a peal of ordnance thundering at your chamber door the next morning. But if either your tailor, mercer, haberdasher, silkman, cutter, linen-draper or sempster stand like a guard of Switzers about your lodging watching your uprising or, if they miss of that, your down-lying in one of the Counters, you have no means to avoid the galling of their small shot than by sending out a light horseman to call your pothecary to your aid; who, encountering this desperate band of your creditors only with two or three glasses in his hand, as though that day you purged, is able to drive them all to their holes like so many foxes. For the name of taking physic is a sufficient *quietus est* to any endangered gentleman and gives an acquittance for the time to them all, though the Twelve Companies stand with their hoods to attend your coming forth, and their officers with them.

I could now fetch you about noon, the hour which I prescribed you before to rise at, out of your chamber and carry you with me into Paul's Churchyard: where planting yourself in a stationer's shop, many instructions are to be given you what books to call for, how to censure of new books, how to mew at the old, how to look in your tables and enquire for such and such Greek, French, Italian or Spanish authors whose names you have there but whom your mother for pity would not give you so much wit as to understand. From thence you should blow yourself into the tobacco ordinary, where you are likewise to spend your judgment like a quacksalver upon that mystical wonder to be able to discourse whether your cane or your pudding be sweetest, and which pipe has the best bore and which burns black, which breaks in the burning, etc. Or if you itch, to step into the barber's: a whole dictionary cannot afford more words to set down notes what Dialogues you are to maintain whilst you are Doctor of the Chair there. After your shaving, I could breathe you in a fence school and out of that cudgel you into a dancing school, in both which I could weary you by showing you more tricks than are in five galleries or fifteen prizes. And, to close up the stomach of this feast, I could make cockneys whose fathers have left them well acknowledge themselves infinitely beholden to me for teaching them by familiar demonstration how to spend their patrimony and to get themselves names when their fathers are dead and rotten. But lest too many dishes should cast you into a surfeit I will now take away; yet so that if I perceive you relish this well, the rest shall be in time prepared for you. Farewell.

FINIS

Penny-Wise, Pound-Foolish:

Or,
A Bristol Diamond Set in Two Rings,
and Both Cracked.

PENNY-VVISE
POVND FOOLISH.

Or, a Bristovv Diamond, set in two
Rings, and both Crack'd.

Profitable for Married men, pleasant for young men, and a
rare example for all good Women.

VENICE.

LONDON.

BRISTOW

At London Printed by *A. M.* for *Edward Blackmore*, and are to be
sould in *Pauls* Church-yard, at the signe of the Angell. 1631.

To the Reader.

The title of this book is printed in many a man's face. Some walk early into the fields to glean ears of corn who, before the harvest of their wit was in, scattered abroad whole sheaves. Wealth is not regarded till we come to beggary; beauty, an enticing bavin fire to warm fools, and not set by when 'tis out; nay, life itself knows not her own precious value till sickness lays it in the balance.

How many courtiers may here see their pictures! How many brave soldiers! How many citizens! How many countrymen! All which were drunk with pleasures when they swum in the full sea of them but, now at a low ebb, count a glass of cold water more wholesome than healths in canary before. The lavish and slavish spending of pounds begets but sorrow; the true saving of a penny buys wisdom.

In these few papers is the map of the whole world. London, Bristol and Venice are here the figures of all other cities: in all other cities are courtesans; and all courtesans have idolatrous fools to adore them. The discourse is hid, like our ladies' heads in taffeta purse-nets, under the masks of Ferdinand and Annabell. Their lives and their loves are enclosed in this nutshell; which if you crack without hurting your teeth, the kernel is sweet in the chewing. The apples plucked from this little tree may serve to turn in the fire in your Christmas nights, and not much amiss all the winter after. So fall to; and fare well.

The Excellent Worth of a Penny.

A penny is a small piece of silver and therefore soonest spent. A penny is a very faithful messenger, and the best errand it goes upon is when a rich man sends his commendations by it to a beggar. The rich man gives and the poor man takes—no, the poor man gives and the rich man takes, for the prayers of the poor increase the blessings of the rich. Poor penny! how much good therefore art thou able to do—nay, how much good dost thou, daily and hourly—when those that are thy betters and a thousand times beyond thee in substance and estate will not part from a farthing. A penny is the dole for which a wretched creature cries, 'Good master, bestow a penny upon me!' He does not beg twopence but a penny, a single penny. A penny will content a carrier when a pound will not satisfy a curmudgeon.

Land in old times no doubt was sold good cheap, for men used to say they bought it 'with their penny', but in these days 'the case is altered,' quoth Plowden: law hath taught land buyers to speak another language. A penny had wont to pay for a pot of nappy ale, but now a pot of ale defies the company of a penny. And yet, for all this, a penny will be a brave companion still. Old men love it, and are therefore called 'penny-fathers'; tradesmen love it, for they cry 'Take it for a penny more!'; watermen love it, for they ask but a penny to cross the water; and when a man hath not a penny in his purse, then he swears he hath not one 'cross' about him—so that, as a penny is the least cross that a man can carry, there can be no greater cross than for a man to go without a penny. A black wench, if she be penny-white, passes for current money where a fair wench that hath no pence shall be nailed up for a counterfeit.

A penny, then, being in such extraordinary request for the general good it does to so many, how much more ought we to make of it when for a penny a man may buy wit! That market does now begin, and how much wit a merchant had for so small a piece of silver, lend your attention, and the history of that penny bargain shall be worth at least twopence to any man that hears it.

Penny-Wise, Pound-Foolish

In the City of Bristol, not much above two twelve-months past, did live a merchant in the bravery of his youth, in the height of full fortunes and in the excellency of all perfection both for a comely proportion of body and unmatchable ornaments of mind. He had all those things which in this world make a man to be counted happy, and wanted none of those the lack of which teach men to believe they are miserable. One only blessing was absent whose possession would have set a crown upon all the other: and that was the marriage of some delicate fair young woman to so wealthy and handsome a young man. (This gentleman's name will we call 'Ferdinand'; his true both Christian name and surname for divers reasons shall be concealed.) And albeit he might have had in Bristol the choice of many maidens both answerable to himself in state and beauty, that city being as richly stored with fair and sweet-proportioned women as any be in the world, yet Master Ferdinand, using often by way of traffic in merchandise to repair to London, happened to cast his eye on the most beautiful face of a very worthy and very wealthy citizen's daughter of London, her name being 'Annabell' (but how she was called otherwise, her succeeding fortunes forbid me to discover).

The parents and friends of this beauteous damsel, who was called the star of this city as well for her delicacy of body as for modesty, giving way to a match so suitable to their own desires and their daughter's liking, little wooing needed, so that the marriage was not so joyfully on all sides appointed as it was with pompous ceremony of friends invited, feastings, masques, dancing and revelling solemnized. No couple through the whole City of London were held so happy as these beauteous pair. Ferdinand and Annabell drew all eyes after them wheresoever they went.

But it was not enough for Ferdinand to be thus followed with praises in London, nor to have his delicate young wife gazed at and envied by the curious dames of this city. No, there was a fire of vain-glory in him to have all the eyes of Bristol behold what gallant prize he had taken at London. Nor was the beauty of his fair bedfellow behindhand with him in the same pride and ambition: her longings that way were as great as his. Their desires thus spreading the same wing, the parents and friends loath to lose two such jewels, yet necessity snatching them from them, away do they hasten to Bristol. Wonder there looks upon them; joy and ten thousand welcomes embrace them. It was hard to tell whether the merchants of that town did think him more happy in being master of such a treasure as so delicate a wife, or whether the brave dames of that city did hold her more fortunate in being lodged every night within the arms of so handsome a husband.

But admiration being never long-lived, let us after a quarter or half a year's entertainment of Mistress Annabell amongst her husband's friends in Bristol leave her there, attended upon with all those commendable glories which set forth excellent women, whilst we follow him back again from Bristol to London; whither being come and welcomed by his wife's father and kindred, joys were redoubled to hear of her health and to see his welfare. In a short time had he despatched the business for which he came, touching his merchandise, to finish which he made the more haste as thinking every day spent here a thousand years lost at home until again he might rest in the bosom of his beloved.

But though the sails of his desire and affection were spread fair, yet the winds grew churlish: they blustered, and conspired to part our two new-married lovers asunder. For, the bravery of this Bristol merchant's mind being observed by our gallants here in the City, his comeliness of person, affability in language and royalty in expenses kindled a fire of good liking in many to be partners in his society. And he took as great a glory to enjoy their appointments and meetings as they did his. Youth led him on to these engagements of pleasure. New acquaintance, which still grew faster and faster upon him, begat new invitations; those invitations brought forth new delights; and those delights served as pulleys to draw on fresher and larger expenses; all these serving together as so many hooks—nay, as so many cast anchors—to fasten him from setting forward in his intended voyage homeward.

In this multiplicity of acquaintance, jollities and jovial meetings Ferdinand did often happen into the familiarity of divers merchants' wives of London whose beauties, though they were excellent, and behaviours able to tempt any man to admire and dote upon them, yet to him they were but as colours to a blind man, the music of their enchanting tongues but songs to the deaf. He had, as he thought, a brighter star of his own to sail by. These painted fires gave to him no heat. The sunbeams that lent warmth to him were those which were shot from the sparkling eyes of his most dearly-beloved Annabell. The Fates had spun good and even threads for him had they still continued winding upon this white bottom; but then altered the distaff and so drew out his misery and his wife's misfortune. This constancy of his was but a watery sunshine. It seemed built upon a rock, but the foundation was not sound. This oak that stood up so high and strong, in resolution never to be shaken with any allurements, is now in danger to be riven in sunder and cleft even to the root by the lightning flying from the eyes of a strange woman.

For one day, chancing in a company of young gallants like himself to fall into private discourse with a delicate creature rich in attire, costly in jewels, rare in the proportion both of face and body, sweet in voice and of a winning, bewitching behaviour, Ferdinand was on a sudden taken prisoner by her beauty. Her charms were strong, and he lay fast bound in them. He upon this first coming into the field made suit to be her servant; and she, after a few slight skirmishing words, yielded herself to be his mistress. The next day he wooed his young mistress that her servant might be so happy as to be suffered to visit her at her own lodging; and she, feeling what fish nibbled at her bait, gave him line and leave enough to play, and told him she was not so unworthy as not to bid so new and so noble a servant welcome. The day wearing away, and the assembly in which Ferdinand and his new-found lady had been merry together being weary of their pleasures— as feasting, dancing, drinking healths, courting and suchlike—the spell brake and dissolved those chains which had almost a whole day bound them within this circle. Night approached and all parted.

Ferdinand being come home and locking himself into his private chamber, he begins thus to contemplate upon the beauties, graces and perfections of his rare and most admired mistress: 'If ever man met an angel upon earth in the shape of a woman, this is she!' If ever woman was too worthy to be touched by any man, this was she! Had she been born when idolatry was first committed, to her only had the heathen given adoration. In fashioning her Idea or the figure of her body in his fantasy, her eyes through the windows of his soul presented themselves to him like a pair of stars; her face he called the masterpiece of all art, sweetness and proportion, to equal which—nay, to come but near it in picture—it was not possible for any painter in the world

E

to do it with his pencil; her hand he called his book of palmistry, her foot the first step to the stateliest measure that ever was prosecuted by motion. In brief her whole body, to the eye of his imagination, appeared a mine stored with treasures beyond all valuation. No arithmetic could sum up her excellencies, no figures set down the hopes of that happiness which he conceived in his unmatchable mistress.

But after his cogitations had thus ran division on her praises, his understanding began to fall into another tune and his memory to be set to this note, to call to mind his dear and disconsolated Annabell in Bristol. Presenting her therefore to his remembrance, and the full volume of all her virtues being printed in his soul, he thus brake forth into a passionate reprehension of his new-conceived folly:

'And shall thy youth, thy beauty, thy integrity, modesty and innocence, O my dearest sweetheart, be by me forgotten? Can I prove a traitor to thy pillow who, I dare swear it, art most true to mine? Must all my vows made to thee when I wooed thee, all those matrimonial obligations which I sealed to thee before angels in the holy temple, and all those protestations I left in kisses upon thy lips when I late and last parted from thee—must all this be forgotten, all written in sand, and left floating on the water? O villain that I am, to fix mine eye on a bead of worthless crystal and prefer it before the rarest diamond in the world! This woman, sure, who hath made choice of me to be her servant is some mermaid enticing me to run upon the rocks of destruction. Stop, then, thine ears and avoid the danger by not listening to her enchantments. A goddess is ready to receive thee into her arms at home, and a painted witch opens hers to kill thee in her false embraces abroad. I will not be caught by this sorcerous woman. I must not. I dare not.'

At this he fetched a deep sigh. And then, his soul and her entering into conference together: 'Why,' quoth he, 'though I have all the delicatest meats standing on mine own table, may not I sit down at another man's board? What wife is true to her husband? Why then should any husband be true to his wife? We are all born free—why should marriage make us bondslaves? Shall the ceremony only of a golden ring be a charm to bind me from enjoying my pleasures? I am satisfied with a wife, cloyed with her enjoyments. My appetite is young and must taste varieties. The fishes in the sea are not married; birds in the air choose their valentines, and that's their wedding; all the beasts upon earth have a liberty in desires to range how they will, and to take whom they will. Why then should man be made a captive to any woman? O my sweetest, dearest, most delicious mistress, I die if I live not to do thee service. I cannot be beaten from thee with frowns, with swords, with death—yes, death only can force our separation, nothing else shall.'

Having thus spent the night in these passionate perturbations, the morning summoned him to appear before the saint he so honoured. Up in all haste he rises and hastens to the lodging of his mistress who, not willing to lose such a golden fly as she made account this her new burring servant would prove, was weaving her curious loom-works with the best and surest art she could. For she left her bed betimes to make her face, by painting, show more excellent, which of itself was absolute before. He came and saluted and kissed her, and in that kiss felt all his blood put into a terrible burning. He saw her in bravery, rich as a queen, bright in jewels as the morning sun, breathing from her apparel perfumes more precious than those which the spring gives to the earth. He saw her and stood astonished to behold her. He saw her and forgat that ever he saw a wife to whom his eyes did owe that duty and tribute which he paid to a courtesan. But she, to put him out of this trance, took her lute, which she touched sweetly and sung to it more sweetly, and by this striving to awaken him she cast him into a deeper sleep, out of which again she startled him by the magic of her enticing lips, on which, dwelling with a languishing delightful pleasure, he tasted—nay, was so filled with sweets that he thought one apple in this garden worth a whole orchard of his wife's at home. Dalliance thus charming them into a liking one of another, Ferdinand vows ever to be hers and none but hers, she swears ever to be his and none but his.

Days, weeks and months were consumed between these two unchaste lovers in all kinds of varied pleasures that riot could invent. There was no new fashions in apparel but she had them; no jewel how costly soever but she was mistress of it. A caroach and coach-horses he bought for her in which he and she together were sometimes hurried to playhouses, sometimes to Brentford to lie there, then to Barnet to lie there, then to Bow to be merry there, then to Blackwall to see the ships there, and then to Bloomsbury to solace themselves there—and so to all bawdy B's lying near and about London.

His wife, seeing her beloved stay beyond the time limited by himself for his return, at first began to wonder, then to mistrust, then to lament for his absence. But ill news, being swifter of wing than any other bird, came flying into Bristol and, alighting in Annabell's ear, that was open day and night listening for some good tidings of her lost husband, did there sing to her a sad note of the lewd and lascivious courses of Ferdinand with a courtesan. Hereupon she tore her hair, beat her white breasts, cursed her hard fortunes and wished that either she had been born deformed, that none might ever have loved her, or that her face had been made as enticing as that strumpet's on whom her husband dotes, for then she had kept him to herself, where now in this wandering she is in danger to lose him forever.

To post after him to London would but proclaim his faults, which she was willing to hide from the world. To come and tear out those bewitching eyes of his harlot, she had not a heart to hurt that which her husband had chosen to love so dearly. Wavering thus betwixt many doubts and fears, fed with hopes that yet he would come home, and frighted with despair that she should never more see him, for sin is a luscious meat and the more we taste it the more we desire it; it is a sea and, being once got into it without a good pilot, 'tis not so easy to return again to shore; upon these considerations she writ many loving letters to call and recall her dear husband home. But he, as the papers came, still showing them to his mistress, the passions of a wife were comical plays to a strumpet; the tears which the one sent, dropping on the letters as she writ them, were pledged in kisses by the other on her husband's cheeks, and in claret wine and sugar. The young woman's father and friends, likewise hearing of these dissolute courses taken by Ferdinand, found him out and both by soft persuasions and harsh threatenings did their best to win him to his wife. But he laughed to scorn their counsel.

At last the bonfires of his prodigality being almost burnt out, his purse shrinking, his money melting, his credit decaying, and his debts increasing to such a mountain it was not possible for him to climb well over them without tumbling into one of the Counters, he privately, with many ostentations and oaths to his mistress to return from Bristol so soon as he could furnish himself there with moneys, took his leave of her, she distilling from her eyes some few drops of hot waters which her feigned sorrow drank off to him to comfort his heart at the farewell. But she having other sickles to cut down her corn than his, the shower of tears which she rained upon her whorish cheeks being soon dried up, the storm was quickly blown over and she was to provide for another golden harvest.

But leave we her, plucking pleasure and diseases out of one and the same well, and let us follow him to Bristol. Whither being secretly come and with all expressions of a noble, loving and forgiving wife welcomed by the virtuous Annabell, she wept for joy and, as she wept, mildly chid him and, as she chid him, gave him a thousand kisses. He, ashamed to abuse such an excellent goodness, shut up his wrongs to her in as sweet language as he could handsomely meet with, and told her there was no staying for him in safety either in Bristol or London. His estate, he said, was weak, yet not so weak but that he had a staff to hold it up from falling—and that was certain bags of money left in a trusty friend's hands when he departed for London. Which money he would closely and instantly disburse in merchandise and in some good ship, of which he himself would be captain and with a ging of good fellows try his fortune at sea. She, unwillingly willing, yields to this. So into the Straits he ventures.

At Iskenderun he goes on shore and vents such commodities as he had by caravans, up at Aleppo amongst the Turks and such Christian merchants as there were in traffic, insomuch that by his industry and knowledge in commerce he might have made a reasonable good voyage if, upon the sale of his wares brought thither, and lading his ship with commodities from thence, he had returned home without encountering any second fortune.

But Heaven, smiling upon him, appointed a Turkish pirate, richly furnished, to set upon our captain of Bristol and his mad merry company, who were all Englishmen—courageous, skilful, resolute and tall seamen, every one of them swearing to live and die with their noble captain. The Turk set upon them; they bravely returned an English defiance. The Turks called upon Mohammed, the Christians cried 'St George!' but called upon Him whom they knew could help them. The fight was short but cruel, the victory doubtful but speedy: for the Turkish pirate being boarded and as fast thrown overboard as the English could enter, a noble and rich spoil was made: the true man robbed the thief. Captain Ferdinand's ship was doubly laden with treasure, and with acclamations of joy the Turks went sneaking to their holes, and the English put in at a hither part of Christendom to refresh their wounded men and to give them good victuals.

I must here put you in mind of one thing which before, when Ferdinand was to come from Bristol, I should have remembered, and that was this: at the time when he was ready to prepare for his sea-voyage, he told his wife all that he could get together was little enough to furnish him forth for so weighty a business, yet he would leave sufficient to maintain her in his absence; and then, merrily asking her what she would venture with him, she answered she would adventure all that she had—and that was her body and her poor life.

'No,' says her husband, 'you shall not. I will not hazard all our substance in one bottom.'

'Why then,' quoth she, 'though my body must stay at home, my heart shall go with you, and upon what shore soever you land, my good wishes for your prosperity and prayers for your health shall ever wait upon you as your servants. And yet, because it shall not be said but that both by sea and land my fortunes shall still set their foot by yours, I will put in my share in your adventure.'

'What, my good sweetheart?' said her husband.

'Sir,' replied his wife, 'you have often laid out much money which never brought home any profit. I dare therefore not trust you with much. All that I put into your hands is only one single penny.' He, smiling upon her, asked what he should do with that penny. 'Marry,' quoth she, 'only buy and bring home for that money a pennyworth of wit.' He, glad to see her so pleasantly conceited, protested he would lay out her money to the best advantage he could. And so took his leave of her.

You heard before that, after the fight was ended between Ferdinand and the Turkish pirates, our Bristol captain went on shore to refresh his men. During his absence in a port-town of Spain called Sanlúcar de Barrameda in Andalucia (for there his ship put in), one of the mariners who stayed aboard, being a merry conceited fellow, and one that knew all the passages of Ferdinand's life, all his wild humours and mad fits played between him, his wife and his courtesan; intending to pin some merriment upon his captain's shoulder, disguised his face like to a tanned gypsy and put himself into nothing but rags like a beggar, and in this manner stood waiting on the shore till his captain was to come back to take shipping.

Ferdinand being then passing by him, this supposed rogue, setting out a wide throat, cried out in a big voice, 'Noble captain! brave honest captain! bestow one single penny upon a poor man, upon an Englishman, upon your countryman, that shall pray you may have a *bon voyage*. Good worthy captain, one penny, one poor single penny!' Ferdinand, hearing the name of Englishman and that word 'single penny', cast his eye back upon my counterfeit beggar, and the sound of 'single penny' put him in mind of his wife and her venture of a penny, and what he was to buy with it.

So turning to the fellow, 'Troth, honest countryman,' said he, 'for so I perceive thou art by thy tongue, what thou begg'st for I have about me,' and so drew forth his wife's penny. 'Look thou, here's a new single penny. But I have other employment for it than to bestow it on a beggar, for it is an adventure put into my hands by my wife, and I am to buy with it for her a pennyworth of wit.'

'O master,' cries the beggar, 'you were better give me the penny than travail so long till you buy so rich a commodity as wit for so poor a sum of money. Many come into this country, and others on this side the seas, and spend they care not what, only to get wit and knowledge and experience, but in the end return home as arrant coxcombs as I did when I came from travel. Many a thousand pound have I laid out to purchase wit, but I could never reach to so much as a farthing's worth.'

'Thou? Many a hundred pounds?' said Ferdinand.

'Yes, captain,' answered the beggar. 'No dispraise to your person, I once held myself as brave a gallant as yourself. My silks and satins on my back, men at my heels, roaring boys at my beck, my comrades at a call.'

'And how,' quoth the captain, 'comest thou to be so poor?'

'I will tell you how,' said t'other. 'One part of my money ran away with "Come on, six!" and "Come on, seven!". I could play at novum, passage, in-and-in, mumchance; at tables—Irish, tick-tack . . . anything! at cards—maw, cent, primero, prima vista, gleek, post and pair, whist . . . all games! noddy, and any game where a knave was to be turned up. All the money I either won or lost this way went sure to the Devil, for I had it with damnable swearing and parted from it with abominable tearing of God, blasphemy and cursing. Another part of my money melted away in sack and claret, but I licked my lips prettily well at this feast, for I met for my money wine, good cheer, good fires, good wenches, good music—and good knocking reckonings. A third part of my money I spent—nay, cast away—upon a whore, a dainty one, a young one, a proud one. So long as my silver lasted her brazen face was always at my nose kissing me. But when my cheeks grew lean and my pockets empty, away flies my wagtail. Now, my noble captain, if (as I know most of our English gallants do) you have a lickerish tooth in your head and keep a punk: hang her, damn her, trust her not—she'll graze upon thy meadow so long as there's a blade of grass; that gone, she leaps over hedge and ditch into any butcher's pasture. But if, my brave captain and countryman, thou hast a wife: kiss her, coll her, trust her, try her—for she will run for *aqua-vitae* to recover thy fortunes, when thy cockatrice shall cast them into a swoon. Should thy ship lie here upon a sand and could not stir for want of water to fetch thee off, thy strumpet would not throw out the basin in which she washes her hands unless for her own benefit, where thy wife (if thou hast a good one) would draw a sea out of her eyes to save thee from sinking.'

The captain, hearing the beggarman talk thus, with a smiling countenance gave him his wife's single penny and told him he did not think but that the money was laid out as she desired, for that penny should peradventure send him and his ship home with a richer lading than five hundred pound could furnish him with. And so, thanking the poor fellow for his discourse, he gave him besides at parting four pieces of eight for a farewell to drink his health; which the beggar swore he would do. Ferdinand presently gets aboard to make for England, and the mad mariner as nimbly tears off his rags unknown to any man and leaps into the ship almost as soon as the captain.

In this interim of Ferdinand's being at sea his fair mistress, wondering at his long absence, considering his vehement oaths with all speed possible to return, and being loath to lose such a goldfinch that sung so sweetly in her ear, she (partly for a kind of love she bare him, he being a very proper man, but chiefly for his estate, which she knew was great and to catch which she did angle) came in her thundering caroach like some great lady to Bristol with this resolution: if Ferdinand were there, then to enjoy him as before; if not there, yet she would repair her losses and charge of the journey upon any other whom she next lighted on fit to be made a property, as no doubt but Bristol had store of such tame fowl as well as any other city. Her wishes and intentions hit the marks she shot at, for tercel-gentle in abundance came to the fist of our she-falconer.

By this time, wind and weather favouring him, Ferdinand is as secretly arrived at Bristol as he departed closely from thence and, stepping privately to a dear friend, enquires what news in the town, how all the mad girls did and what new wenches were come to Bristol, so that in the end by way of merry discourse and descanting upon other women, he perceived, but concealed it, that his mistress had followed him thither; and his heart, leaning to his old bias, began almost to leap for joy to think that he found his noble sweetheart so kind.

But then remembering his wife's single penny and the beggar's counsel, he meant to make trial what his wife's venture would come to: and so, putting himself into rags like a beggar, with a short cudgel in his hand, he found out her lodging and knocked to speak with her. One of her servants, seeing such a tatterdemalion rascal, enquired scurvily what he would have.

T'other replied as scurvily, 'I must speak with your lady or mistress.'

'Away, you lousy slave!' cried the pander. 'My mistress a companion for such a nitty-breech as thou art to talk to her?' But my counterfeit Bristol *maunderer* in a very pitiful voice told him that he had letters from one Ferdinand, a merchant, and somewhat else by word of mouth to deliver to her.

Upon this he was called up into her chamber and then, requesting to deliver his message in private, all were commanded out of the room but himself and her. And then asking if she knew him not by his voice (for by his tattered attire and face she could not), he told her he was that Ferdinand whom once she loved so dearly, and she that mistress of his that commanded both his life and fortunes; all the happiness he had on earth was to enjoy her presence; tells her how he was taken prisoner by the Turk, made a galley-slave, tugged at the oar, had an hundred blows on the naked back with a bull's pizzle, fed on coarse brown bread and water, and hardly got away but most miraculously with life; entreats her—what needs entreaties? he presumes she is so noble that she will lodge him in her bosom as she had wont; prays her to send into the town for clothes to make him brave, for good cheer to fill his belly, for some clean linen (for he was lousy) and that he might have a good fire to shift himself by.

But she, casting an eye of scorn at his baseness, reviled him, kicked at him, bid him 'Avaunt!', called for her servants to thrust him out of doors.

But he, falling on his knees, begged as she was a woman to let him lie in some hayloft, in some stable, upon a heap of horse-dung, for since his coming to shore he had killed a man that misused him, and if she turned him out of doors it was his assured death and confusion.

'Nay, you base scum!' cried she and so, tumbling him into the street, shut the doors upon him.

He then, all ragged as he was, went in private home to his wife. She, for all the misery round about him, knew his face, hung about his neck, wept for joy, and enquired what mischance sent him to her in this pitiful estate.

He told her his ship was burnt by pirates, his goods taken from him, his men slain, and himself only scaped with life.

'And that's all,' quoth his wife, 'which I desire! Let ship, goods and all be lost, so I find thee. My rings, jewels, plate—nay, my own apparel—I'll presently pawn or sell outright to furnish my dear husband fitting to his worth.'

But he, overjoyed at this her admirable love and unfeigned expressions of a noble wife, plucked off his rags and under them discovered a fair habit. But entreating her to pardon his absence for an hour or two for the despatch of a most especial business, he leaves her full of joy both at his unexpected arrival and at his prosperous voyage, of which in some few words he gave her a firm assurance.

Ferdinand then richly attiring himself and taking four or five of his mariners, neatly apparelled, passed by the courtesan's door once or twice. She, spying him, sent after him, the servant saying his mistress entreated him by any means to come back and speak with her. He did so, when she at his entrance into her chamber ran and fell upon his cheeks, printing on them and his lips an hundred kisses, and telling him that a base rascal in shape of a beggar came to her and took his name upon him.

'That very beggar, sweetest mistress,' quoth Ferdinand, 'was I myself, and came to you in that poverty to try if you would relieve me. But it was an easy matter for you to scorn me, as not knowing me in that loathsome appearance. I therefore pardon it. And to show how deeply even in absence you were printed in my memory, and that you are to me the same beloved mistress that heretofore you have been, behold! as a part of my good voyage, I present to your white hands this rich cabinet full of the most precious jewels that are to be found in this part of the world.' She was reaching out her hands to lay hold upon them—'But!' quoth he, 'my most endeared mistress, I remember I have given you many rings, bracelets of diamonds, chains of pearls and gold, and many costly jewels. I doubt in my absence you have bestowed these upon some other sweethearts. Show me these, therefore, and I shall be in the better hope that for my sake you will preserve these likewise.'

Hereupon she fetches all the braveries and costly gifts that he ever presented to her. Which seen, he seized upon them, told her he found her to be a Bristol diamond—she was a cunning, a cheating and hardhearted courtesan. And so, giving her sufficient means and money, for his own reputation sake, to rid her from Bristol and ship her for London, on his wife he bestowed all those jewels and told her that the wit which he bought with the single penny she ventured in his ship was worth all the merchandise he brought home besides.

The bed where a husband and wife lies is that music room where the souls of them both play in the most excellent consort. All discords before are here put into tune, all jars so winded up with the strings of concord that no harmony can be sweeter. Such a bed is an altar where a pair of loving hearts are offered, and no gall mingled with the sacrifice. Such a bed is a cradle where pleasure, content and all earthly happiness rock man and wife asleep, kisses perfuming the pillows as if they were banks of roses, and warm tears of joy, there to be reconciled one to another, being the soft showers that make those rosy kisses grow fairer and in more abundance.

Ferdinand, our young and now rich merchant of Bristol, enjoying his beauteous Annabell a whole night together, the pleasure of their embraces were increased by his relation of his wild courses, dalliances and delights which he took at London in that bewitching mistress of his, the courtesan, but ten times more doubled in her free and noble forgiveness of whatsoever had passed between them. He thereupon promised to be to his wife a new man, a new-moulded husband; and she vowed to him to be an ever-loyal and ever-loving wife.

Whilst thus they lay talking the sun, casting his eye upon them in at the window, told them it was time to rise and that the mariners who ventured their lives and fortunes with him in his voyage were all attending for him. Upon this summons of the sun they both forsook their beds, made them ready and came down, Ferdinand delivering to every one of them whatsoever in right they could claim for wages or anything else, and withal, because they should not report they met with an unworthy or ingrateful person, he bestowed upon them as his bounteous gift twenty pounds amongst them all over and above their due, to drink his wife's health and his at a dinner or supper; which they with merry countenances swore to perform. And then Ferdinand, his wife the fair Annabell being by, relating how happily he met with a poor beggar at his return to his ship when they went ashore in Spain and that, bestowing his wife's single penny upon that poor man, he found since that the pennyworth of wit which the beggar gave him there—and served him well, too, for so little money—had done him a great deal of good since his arrival, and that to the last day of his life he would be a fair gainer by the beggar's bargain.

Annabell, smiling, told him he was as much or more beholding to her as to that poor man, for that her venture of a single penny was the first and principal occasion of meeting so excellent and unvaluable a commodity as wit. He confessed it, and told his wife before all those witnesses that he was deep in her debt.

But then the mariner who counterfeited the beggar, not being able to glue up his lips any longer, told them all that he was that ragamuffin who begged an alms on the shore, only to put his captain in mind of his wife and her penny, because he knew how the single penny was delivered; and therefore in his beggarly oration to him he touched him to the quick, as knowing into how many wild and crooked currents the stream of his captain's life had run. Yet if this bold attempt of his had succeeded well, he hoped his offence was the more easily pardoned.

'Pardoned!' quoth Annabell. 'Yes, and rewarded, too!'And thereupon remembering and putting her husband in mind of his own words in bed to her—which were that, but for the advice the supposed beggar gave him for his penny, he had never put that trial upon his courtesan but doubtless, coming home so rich, had both poured and rained down golden showers into her lap, and his soul—as before—into her bosom; she therefore hung about her husband's neck and, for the content she herself encountered with by this mariner (whose name was Theobald) as also for the blessing Heaven crowned his own life with by the hands of that good seaman, she entreated—nay, importunately begged—nay, by all the bonds of affection between them conjured him to make up that single penny he gave him a full one hundred pounds, and so set him afloat in the world.

Ferdinand being willing to win his Annabell to him by any means, sithence he had given her just cause forever to lose her, and considering the request easy in regard it was but a drop to the full sea his riches swum in, and just in respect of the golden harvest his wife's penny and the mariner's counsel brought him, he not only very nobly, freely, and cheerfully delivered an hundred pounds as his wife's gift but, to show how much he desired to make her joys full in all things, he lent one hundred pound more to Theobald without script or scroll, to be paid him when it should please the Heavens to command the winds and the waves to send him home a merry, a prosperous and a wealthy voyager.

Theobald, with infinite thanks for these undeserved courtesies on her part, and unexpected on his, acknowledges his life ever to be their debtor. And so in a very short time, having so many golden stars to sail by, away puts he to sea; where we will leave him, carefully, industriously and like a toiling ant providing sufficient in the summer of his youth how to maintain him in the winter of his age.

And now let us cast our eyes once more upon Ferdinand and Annabell, who grew up in Bristol like two fair trees, looked at by all, admired by all and loved by all. That reputation of his, which ran aground at London, is in Bristol fetched off safely from all shelves and sands. A harlot undid his fortunes there, a wife restores them here. His former riots are now turned to good husbandry, his feasting in taverns to a civil entertainment in his own house, his roaring boys' companies to a brave society of merchants, and his roguing beggarly noises of scraping fiddlers to the most excellent music of sweet and harmless stories told between him and his wife, or else to the cunning touch of her hand upon the strings of her lute, guided by the echoes of a ravishing voice, in both of which she exceeded even skilful musicians. What wounds he got in his estate by borrowing he now cured by paying every penny, so that upon his word he might either in Bristol or London have taken up more money than many that carried their heads higher in the air, and more proudly jet on the stage of opinion, could procure upon their bonds.

Abundance filled his bags, rich merchandise his cellars and warehouses, cupboards of plate waited on his table, and both men-servants and maid-servants on him and his wife. Superfluity of all worldly blessings thus casting his youthful mind into a surfeit, he began not only to be weary of Bristol but of his own natural country, burning with an immoderate and unquenchable desire to travel beyond the seas, to come acquainted with the manners, fashions and conditions of foreign nations. The bellows that kindled these flames within him were the praises, given to him by young merchants and gallants that had travelled, of the delicate faces of other women abroad, of their quaint dressings, curious attires and most bewitching compliments— our English ladies and merchants' wives of London being but coarse creatures, dowdies and doddypolls, either to the German *Frau*, the French pretty parleying *mademoiselle* or the cherry-lipped, wanton-eyed, plump Italian *buonaroba*. And besides these spurs of longings clapped to his heels to set him going, his wife (albeit a delicate creature) began, after this frenzy of dreaming after other women, though he never saw them, not to seem so handsome in his eye as she was wont— or, if she did, let our own pasture be never so fat, never so full, never such wholesome feeding, we think our neighbour's better, though far worse. As in taverns when fault is found in the wine though there be none in it, if the drawer goes but to change it and brings the same again—'Oh!' cries all the company. 'Now, drawer, thou hast gone right indeed!' So that the sick part about us is our opinion: 'tis our judgment is poisoned.

Ferdinand therefore, being thus, as it were, with child to see fashions abroad, could find no ease in mind or body until he fell into 'travel', and for that purpose he freighted a ship with rich and vendible commodities to be sent to Venice, and himself to go as chief in her. His wife was much against his going—she feared her bird whom she had kept so long, getting now out of the cage, would fly she knew not whither and grow wild. But he showing many reasons for his venturing in person, as that it was hard trusting factors—his gains might be trebled by his being there—the eye of the master fats the horse—it would, besides the double profit, return to his mind an infinite pleasure to behold other cities, other people, and converse with other merchants—his knowledge would hereby grow perfect, his experience be confirmed, and that little knowledge he hath in the Italian tongue be much bettered—his ambition having ever been to be cunning in that language; these reasons and others, being put into the balance, weighed down her fears and so she yielded at length to let him go.

Ferdinand, having wind and water as swift as his own wishes, in a short time arrived at Venice, one of the wonders, for a city, in the world, as having the foundation laid in, and the whole frame of the building raised out of, the Mediterranean Sea. His commodities, being excellent good and exceeding rich, dwelt not long in the ship but on silver pulleys were drawn into Venetian merchants' houses, who paid him down for them presently. So that his purse was soon full, but his eyes and longings empty of enjoying the rarities of that renowned city. Some few days made him master of them all. The Rialto was as familiar to him as the Exchange in Cornhill is to merchants, or the New Bourse in the Strand is to courtiers and lawyers. St Mark's Church he knew as well as Paul's steeple. And the Murano, where all the Venice glasses are made, he visited more often than vintners do the glasshouse in Broad St to furnish themselves there with these brittle carousing bowls. The Arsenal, which is a storehouse to arm both men and galleys with all warlike provision, by money and friendship he went into with desire, and came forth with admiration. The many thousands of bridges which cross every street through the whole city put him into as much wonder as London Bridge did a northern man who, at first gaping at it, swore he thought in his conscience 'it cost above vorty shillings'.

His eyes could never have been bloodshotten had they only fed

AVGVSTI APVD VENETOS TEMPLI D. MARCI ACCVRATISSIMA
EFFIGVRATIO   *Depinxit Georgius Houfnaglius*

Oriens

V   St Mark's, Venice

Il Signior Tomaso Odcombiano   Margarita Emiliana bella
Cortesana di Venetia

Gu: Hole sculp

VI   The Englishman and the Venetian Courtesan

upon these objects, as it was no hurt for him to look upon wood and stone and workmen, nor to have been carried in one of their Venetian gondolas, rowing up and down the river that embraces the city called the Grand Canal. None of these enticing flowers carried poison in their scent. No, as before in London he was ensnared by one English whore, so here found he ten thousand Venetian courtesans, the worst of them all having sorcery enough in her eyes and behaviour to enchant him. With the butterfly, he flew from herb to herb and from weed to weed, but in the end alighted upon one which he liked above all the rest. Here he stayed, here he set up his rest. It was a creature sufficiently fair had she been indifferently good, and reasonably good she might have been but that the custom of the country which authoriseth brothelry makes her believe it is not sin in her so to sell and prostitute her body and, in her body, her soul. You talk of the poor catamountains in Turnbull who venture upon the pikes of damnation for single money, and you wonder at the feathered ostriches in Westminster, Strand, Bloomsbury, etc., how they can live! Where these Venetian madonnas carry the ports of ladies, live in houses fair enough to entertain lords. Into such a lodging was 'Ferdinando' received; upon such a courtesan did he fasten his lustful affection.

No gold was spared to warm her white hands with the fires of such sparkling sunbeams, no music kept dumb by her whose voice, she knew, would entice him to hear it. This strumpet's name was Livia Ferramonti—well-descended and therefore taught by her education how to win and how to hold fast when once she had a man in her nets. Her behaviour was pleasing, her compliments courtly, her appearance stately. Yet, how strongly guarded soever this castle of beauty seemed by her eyes, in show disdainful, and a tongue proud in parleys, yet Ferdinand mounting his silver ordnance charged with golden bullets, the fort of womanish frailty quickly yielded, but upon this composition: that he should suffer no other Italian dame but herself share in her embraces.

'Jealousy is a book that all our Italian dames and signiors read. And if,' quoth she, 'you ever give me cause to open that book strung with yellow ribbon, I shall give you cause to curse my acquaintance, and you will teach me hereafter to hate forever an Englishman.' He told her—nay, most vehemently protested by the faith of a gentleman and by all those fires burning in the breast of a lover—that she should have no cause to speak to him that language.

And so she, being a merchantess for the flesh, and to sell her ware as dear as she could hold it up, agreed with Ferdinand that for five hundred crowns a month he should enjoy her body, her bed, her house and all that belonged to her command. The greatest *magnifico* in Venice, she told him, would be glad to be sharer with two more and so enjoy her by turns, yet each of them to allow her so poor a sum— nay, the bravest *clarissimo*, to enjoy her as now she comes to him, alone—would into her apron every month cast a thousand crowns. But he being an Englishman and gracious in her eye, she would exact but that slender hire (it being the custom of Venice that whatsoever a courtesan and a whoremaster bargains for, be it for a day, a night, a week, a month or a year, she has law on her side to recover it and make him pay it; and she is his, for that time, as absolutely as a beast bought in Smithfield or a rotten joint of mutton sold at Pie Corner, her *inamorato* being likewise, during the continuance of this agreement, more sure of his Italian hackney than many Englishmen are of their wives though a household full of eyes be fixed upon them, for if she flies out from him to any other, an action at the case here is nothing to that case which the *buonaroba* shall be in there if once she be found faulty).

Months and months were consumed in libidinous and adulterous embraces by these two, Ferdinand ever and anon sending into England some slight Italian toys to his wife with letters, expressing his great care to increase his estate kept him so long from her, and that the delight he took in seeing those cities, and noble entertainment he found amongst those merchants, had carried him up higher into the country but that he would shorten his journey and cut off much of his employment out of a desire to be again in the arms of his Annabell. She, good soul, believed all this upon receipt of her husband's letters. But he intended no such matter. He was too fast entangled in the allurements of a wanton and too far engaged in purse and reputation to get off without exceeding loss, if not danger of life. For when an Italian strumpet feels her lover flying from her and in disdain leaving her, a poisoned banquet or a stab from a panderly bravo soon ends her discontentment.

But our Bristol merchant was too far plunged in affection to fall off or grow cool in desires to her upon whose beauties he did more than dote. And therefore, to show that he was a right Englishman, who will venture life and living and all that he hath in the world before he will lose his wench, he not only (more than his bargain tied him of five hundred crowns a month) had, in banquets, costly dinners and suppers, and rich new gowns and tires for her, spent a world of money upon her, but also—the faster, as he thought, to tie her to him (though he could not easily shake her off)—he bestowed a company of admirable fair jewels upon his dearest Livia.

Fair were those jewels in outward show, as the wearer of them was. But many—or, rather, most—of the stones were counterfeit. For Ferdinand, by means of keeping company with many brave Italian merchants, came acquainted with a Venetian Jew whose name was Caleb Mosolomon. This Jew was wondrous wealthy and wondrous wary, and as wicked in his ways to get money, especially from Christians, as any of his Hebrew tribes could be. Ferdinand came oft to his house and was as often welcomed, but this feast of Jewish welcomes should be paid for at last in the tail of the reckoning. Mosolomon had abundance of as costly, true and precious jewels of all fashions as could be made or bought for gold and silver in the world, for it was his trade to deal with most princes in Christendom by his factors for such commodities; but, as amongst men and women, some are good, some bad. So Caleb, our subtle Jew, perceiving Ferdinand to be an unthrift, that his ship's rich lading was swallowed up in a Venetian Gulf—a Venetian whore—and that to fill such a barn a fool cared not what cornfield he reaped nor from whose sheaves he stole, were it but a handful, he saw he would sink and therefore, to rid him out of his pain, he would tie some of his plummets to his heels.

Hereupon, showing one day to our Bristol lapidary, that dealt in none but false stones, a goodly heap of counterfeit jewels as fair to the eye as any that were worn in Italy (and the falsehood not easy to be found out but by a very cunning workman), he liked them so well that, being wondrous importunate to buy them, albeit the Jew held them at an unreasonable rate, yet he had them for time, a bond being drawn to pay to Mosolomon double the value if he had not his money just upon the day. The match pleased them both: the Jew laughed in his sleeve to see how he had over-reached a lecherous Christian; and the other, as proudly, hastened to his Italian hen-sparrow to show what costly and glorious feathers he had bought to stick her with. The jewels were with thousands of thanks received, and as many kisses paid back to him on his lips; which he accepted as a sufficient satisfaction.

The day of payment for these jewels being come, the Jew—as busy as a kite over his prey—soars over Ferdinand's lodging, still looking when the money would be tendered. But a day or two being past over, and no cash appearing, Caleb leaps for joy that now he shall have the double. The forfeiture to him would be as a feast. A Christian to lie in prison at his suit was a braver triumph than when Turkish galleys board English pirates. He swears by his Hebrew tribe from whence he is descended he will flay him alive with miseries if he hath not his moneys; not a Christian farthing of copper or brass— no, not an old leaden chandler's token—should be abated.

An officer—nay, a whole kennel of hounds—are let loose to seize upon him and to drag him to prison. But Ferdinand, being an Englishman and understanding by his experience of London and Bristol what it was to fall into catchpoles' hands, and how such beagles where they fastened did not only bite but draw blood, kept himself out of the way, so that Ben Mosolomon was ready to run mad with anger. That jew's-trump in his mouth—his tongue—played nothing but curses; his great nose swelled twice so much as it was before by his thumping and plucking it almost off from his face in rage, to think he should be so cozened by a wenching rascal, a Christian whoremaster; and yet he said to himself, it was no wonder for him to be so gulled, sithence 'twas too well known that Englishmen are as cunning as any cheaters in the world.

In this interim of Ferdinand his wasting of his youth, his estate and his honour, and the hazarding both of life and soul upon an enticing strumpet, did one Signior Giovanni Guidanes return to Venice from travel. He had, before he went, made choice amongst all the faces in that city of this Livia Ferramonti to be his mistress. She, perceiving by the Jew and others of whom Ferdinand had taken up round sums of money, how the winds blew and that the breath of his fortunes grew colder and colder, and being glad to hear that Giovanni was come home, writ a few wanton but witty verses (for the Italian women are excellent in those qualities) to welcome him from travel and to invite him to her lodging unknown to her English sweetheart, who now hung the wing as being full of sick feathers.

A stately banquet one appointed evening was prepared at the courtesan's house to which Signior Giovanni, attended upon with one man only, came with resolution to renew his love to his sweetest mistress, and that night to pay such tribute to her embraces as was due to her by his so long absence. Ferdinand, not daring in the day to walk the streets, came muffled in his cloak in the dark with a rapier by his side to visit his lady and, spying every room so full of lights as if all the stars had forsook the moon to come and shine in her lodging, and withal hearing admirable voices and instruments within (for she had provided all content to please Giovanni), Ferdinand boldly knocked at door, presuming he had paid dear enough for the opening of her wicket.

A bravo or ruffianly he-bawd comes and tells him there was no cushion for him to sit upon tonight; another was made Doctor of his Italian Chair; the ringtail which he loved to cut up was to be served up and be laid on a Venetian gentleman's trencher, one Signior Giovanni Guidanes, son to rich Antonio Guidanes, one of the chiefest *clarissimoes*; and so bidding him to be packing—or, if he were so hot for a whore, there were enough i' th' city; and if he could not fall upon them, stand there still and cool his heels—and with that shut the doors upon him.

Jealousy and Revenge, the Furies that haunt every Italian, laid hold, upon this base affront of the pander, on Ferdinand: the custom of the people and the inconstancy of the women teaching even strangers, if they dwell but a while amongst them, to snatch the firebrands out of those two Furies' hands, and to be as mad as the Venetians themselves. Taking therefore this abuse, offered to him by the bravo, for an act of the mistress, as knowing he durst not have done so without her consent, he vows to kill this Giovanni, whatsoever he should be, leaving his body at her very doors as the monument of a strumpet's falsehood and an Englishman's noble revenge upon a corrival; and, this done, by the aid of darkness to escape, get a gondola and so, shifting from Venice, to fly first into France over the Alps and after that into England. For this purpose the spleenful Ferdinand walks up and down watching when this gallant should come forth. But he was too fast locked in his mistress's arms to take any danger from a naked rapier. Yet, going to bed with his beloved madonna, he commanded his man to get him to his lodging and attend for him next morning.

The fellow being lighted out of doors and Ferdinand, who stood watching, not knowing the master from the man, took this to be the gentleman that wronged him; and so, running at him, the glimpse of the candle made him spy the weapon; which nimbly though he put by, yet was he wounded in two or three places. 'Murder!' then being cried, and more candles being held out at several windows, the servant that was hurt was carried off and Ferdinand haled to prison.

The next morning, criminal judges having the examination of this business, the bravo giving in evidence that he came to his mistress's house to quarrel and do some mischief, and Ferdinand being half mad that his revenge fell so unluckily on a poor unworthy fellow, his aim being (as he confessed freely) to have sped that Giovanni who lodged there that night in the arms of a strumpet whose flesh he had bought and paid dearly for: the matter then grew more foul in that, besides the drawing blood from one, his intent was to murder another —yea, and to murder such a gentleman so nobly descended as Guidanes was. For the love which all Venice bare both to father and son, the whole Senate set a heavy fine on Ferdinand's head for his intent of murder and, albeit the fellow's wounds were not mortal, yet was he, besides a doom of imprisonment, adjudged to pay for the cure and to satisfy the servant for his hurts.

The Jew, hearing of this imprisonment, laughed and leaped for joy that the great fish was taken which brake through his net; but sithence he was in, he would wear out his fingers' ends with tying knots but he should be fast enough: and so laid an action upon him of 14,000 crowns.

He then hoping, for all this, to find some comfort at his mistress's hands, writ in Italian to her, but she understood not his language. To him she could not send without losing an Italian friend worth twenty English, and come to him she would not.

Upon this, casting his eyes back at his forepast fortunes and his now present miseries, he began to think that Heaven had justly laid this shame and these crosses upon him for not still making use of that counsel which the mariner in shape of a beggar gave to him for his wife's single penny. Had he followed it coming to this courtesan in Venice as he did when he tried that other in England, he had never met such occasion to curse his folly in making himself a mockery to all his countrymen, especially to merchants, but most especially to the merchants in Bristol. To call to mind the wrongs done to his wife was to him more than a death. To think what sums of money his lust and riot had in Venice consumed, every piece of silver fetched drops of blood from his heart. He that flung away pounds would now be glad of a penny. He wished himself in his own country sitting in some highway begging one single farthing, with no worse a conscience than those poor wretches his countrymen do that so live upon good men's charity. Would he, he cries out, had lived so ever! He should not then answer for the lavish wasting of that which was sufficient to maintain thousands, where now the remembrance of those fond expenses as much torment his soul as the want of the money afflicts his body.

'Happy,' he protests, 'are those that, begging a farthing token and making up four of them, peradventure sit now in England by a good fire with a cup of strong drink in their hand, where I in this noisome and stinking dungeon would be glad of clean water to quench my thirst and of a coal of fire to blow my nails over.'

Being driven almost to the very doors of despair by these miseries, the last refuge he had was to send for his wife from Bristol and to persuade her with all possible speed to turn all the estate he left with her, all his plate, all her chains, rings and jewels—yea, even to sell all his household-stuff; to turn it into money and, if ever she loved him, now to show it by redeeming him from a miserable captivity. That word *if ever she did love him* was a charm strong enough to make her fly over worlds of waters and wildernesses of land to find him out and, found, to set him at liberty and, being free from Jews, harlots, hard-hearted Christians, to lay him in her warm bosom, to forgive what's past, to upbraid him with nothing, and in his wants to love him as dearly as ever she did in his greatest abundance. And all this did the virtuous woman his wife.

Suppose then you see them both come from beyond seas not so beaten with winds and waves as bitten by hunger, his dissolute courses causing all his own friends to scorn to cast an eye of pity on him, and the constant love she carried to her distressed husband taking from her friends all desire to help or comfort her, lest he should be a sharer in those benefits. So that not a sunbeam of compassion shining from any friends, kindred or acquaintance upon either of them, in the end they both, by the intercession and tears and modest countenance of the woman, got to be trusted with a few pipes, a little tobacco and a small narrow shop which was both their hall, bed-chamber, kitchen and cellar.

This was but a poor living for him that had wont to freight ships with rich commodities, now to sit filling a pipe of tobacco—and for a penny: that single penny comes oft into his mind and upbraids him with his ill husbandry. The world is changed with him. It runs not now upon wheels as once it did. He that was wont to make taverns roar with the noise of gallon pots, and drawers to run upstairs and downstairs crying 'Anon! Anon!' only at his call is now glad without any roaring or noise-making to be any man's drawer for a penny-pot of ale. His brave fires in a tavern chimney are turned to a little pan of small coals over which he sits blowing to light his customers' pipes. His riotous dinners and suppers are forgotten and instead of them a poor dinner of sprats now and then for fish-days and a sheep's gather or a sheep's head on flesh-days—and very good cheer, too. In former times neither he or his wife could tell what a fasting day meant, but now they could hardly meet with any other. And albeit a man that has ever gone with full pockets, continually fed at full tables and never felt what want was, could not without much repining, cursing and disdain undergo so low and wretched a course of life, yet with such a noble patience did his virtuous wife both bear her own sorrows and counselled him not to sink under his that he by her example was as jovial in this his poverty as ever before he was in plenty and, how great soever their wants were known to themselves, yet would she set a good face upon't and not once show a sad or heavy countenance for fear to displease or discomfort her husband.

It was a wonder to see and hear how people would descant upon these two for their making shift to live in this order. Some laughed him to scorn and said pride had now caught a fall, the peacock's feathers were plucked, and suchlike; others were glad to see him take any honest course to live, considering in what high bravery he spread his sails before; but all persons both men and women did mightily commend the wife, who in all these misfortunes was never seen to knit a brow or heard to upbraid her husband with any of his dissolute former courses by which they were both brought to this beggary.

It being then bruited up and down the City that Ferdinand, the brave young merchant that came from Bristol, was fallen to decay and lived in that mean manner as you have heard before, a gentleman who knew him when he was in his jollity and had taken notice of the state he was in now, came to the courtesan upon whom he spent so much in London when he called her 'mistress', and as a most strange news told her that her servant Ferdinand, whom she followed to Bristol, was in London, but exceeding poor.

'A pox on him!' quoth she. 'So when I was in Bristol, he put a trick upon me and came like a rogue to me in his Plymouth cloak and cheated me of all the rings, jewels, bracelets and anything of any worth that ever he gave me, sending me home like a sheep new-shorn with scarce any wool on my back.'

'Why, then,' said the gentleman, 'he's paid in the same cracked money which he delivered to you. He that shaved is now shaven, and so close cut that—what wool you carried on your back, I know not— but I fear he has scarce wool or skin on his back, for he is so poor that his wife and he are glad to keep a tobacco-shop.'

'A tobacco-shop?' cried his quondam mistress, 'O strange! It shall never be said that I loved a man in his bravery, and would not look upon him in his necessity. The injury he did me at Bristol—I deserved it, and pardon it. His wrongs I forget, but not him: the many jovial days and nights he and I have spent together are so freshly and deeply printed in my memory that if I should not with gladness call them to mind I would count myself ingrateful. It shall never be reported that a man—a gentleman, a noble-minded young fellow—spent his money upon me when he was full of golden pieces and let them fly, but now he wants those pieces and is become poor, I will spend part of what I have upon him. This is not the common humour of mad wenches such as I am about the City, that get their living by the labour of their thighs, and care not so they suck men's estates, like their bodies, to the bare bones. I am altered from the creature I was at Bristol.'

And so, entreating the gentleman to direct her to the shop which Ferdinand kept, she, making herself very gallant, went thither; whom he, beholding, blushed as red as fire for shame she came upon him so unwares into so homely a room, his wife and he being so meanly habited. But this mistress of his, being a wench of a lusty spirit, stepped to his wife and, kissing her, told her she was come to beg pardon for a robbery she had committed—in stealing away her husband some days from her board and some nights from her pillow; but protests he shall never play the truant more with her; is sorry for what was past; and wishes he had laid out his riots at no worse a market in Venice than he met with in London, and that his Italian banquet had been no dearer than that which she invited him to in England.

Annabell in a mild voice tells her partner that she has crossed the book of all former reckonings; the debt of her anger, both at her and her husband, is all paid; she forgives them both so they run no more upon a new score with her. Which both of them vow never to do. And then the courtesan, swearing likewise never again to break into her orchard to steal away those apples which are for her own eating nor, if she can help it, never hereafter to come into the company of her husband, in some part of satisfaction towards all expenses between them she delivers to his wife as a free gift twenty pieces, and so takes her leave in this unexpected kindness, conquering all ill opinion conceived against her, and that small sum of money of twenty pieces redeeming all the lavish spendings upon his mistress and making more amends to Ferdinand's wife than all his riotous layings out did do her hurt before.

Misfortunes seldom walk alone; and so when blessings do knock at a man's door, they lightly are not without followers and fellows. For just upon this golden visitation—not usually put in practice by creatures of her quality—came home Theobald the mariner from sea upon whom our Bristol merchant at his wife's request bestowed one hundred pound for the good he received by the single penny, and trusted him with another hundred pound to be repaid if ever Heavens should send him a *bon voyage*, that he might be able to spare it. With those two hundred pounds this mariner, playing the good husband beyond the seas in Barbary and other places with the Straits, had so increased his stock that he was esteemed a rich man, and his credit very good upon the Exchange.

He, coming to this tobacco-shop, his face much sunburnt with travel and his cheeks grown over with hair, called for a pipe of smoke, and was not known. Ferdinand, perceiving by his tanned complexion and habit that he was a seaman, asked in what part of the world he had lately been, and the other replying, 'Both in Barbary and some other places within the Straits', Ferdinand prays him to tell him if he knows not one Theobald and whether he saw him not in Barbary.

'Yes,' quoth Theobald, 'I both knew him and saw him. But now he's past either my knowledge or sight in this world, for these very hands helped to bury him in the bottom of the sea where he died.'

Ferdinand started at this and, looking pale, with a deep sigh from his heart expressed a great deal of sorrow for the loss of so faithful and honest a friend. And his wife hearing the sad story, clapping her hand on her knee as she sat, 'O sweetheart!' said she, 'if Theobald be gone, the best of our hopes lie a-dying, for it was likely if ever Heaven had prospered him he would not have shown himself unthankful to you or to me for the courtesies you and I did him.'

'No remedy,' quoth her husband. 'We must all die one day, and since one of our best cards is out of the bunch, let us shuffle and cut in the world as well as we can. One good, true friend as he was—reckoning the treachery amongst men in these days—is worth a rock of diamonds, and though we are cheated of him by death, yet let us two be true to one another, for the love of man and wife is the noblest friendship.'

By this time our mariner—or, rather, now our merchant—had whiffed off three pipes of tobacco for which he was to pay threepence and, drawing out a whole handful of gold, told them he had no white money. And they could not change any one piece. Yet looking in another pocket, he asked if they would take tokens.

'Yes,' said Ferdinand, 'they are as welcome to me now as angels and double sovereigns have been *in diebus illis*, in my mad days—for I have spent some.'

The other then told him he could make but eight tokens, and that was but twopence, a penny less than his due.

'No matter, sir,' answered our new tobacco-man. 'For his sake whom you say you knew and saw him buried at sea, let it alone; you shall pay nothing and, if you please, drink as much more.'

'Nay!' cried t'other, 'shall I go o' th' score or drink *in forma pauperis*, my pockets having such gay linings in them? See, see, I now can make up your money, for there's eight tokens and a single penny in silver, look you, tied with a string through the hole in it for fear of running away. And I can tell you, I part very unwillingly with that penny.'

Ferdinand and his wife seeing the silk string and noting the penny, 'Oh!' cried she. 'Husband, this is the single penny you had of me when you went to sea and which afterwards you tied about his arm that is dead!'

'I did indeed!' said he. 'And he swore it should never from his arm so long as there was any breath in his body.'

'He was as good as his word, then,' replied Theobald, 'for when he yielded up the ghost I—as before he bid me—took it from his arm. And because you shall know I am no counterfeit messenger, look upon me well. Hath my kissing the sun so altered my face? I am that Theobald, this is the same penny for which you gave me an hundred pound in gold for the good it did you. That penny hath done me good, too. I am a made man by it, and shall not only myself ever love a penny, but counsel every man else to make much of a penny when he hath it. It is a beggar's stock and a rich man's stewardship. You, my noble captain and worthy master, made one lucky voyage with it and brought home wit for it—though since, I hear, by your travelling without it you came home a loser. I have made another voyage with the same penny and, praise be given to Heaven, I have brought home wealth by it. Much am I in your debt, but am come honestly to pay you all. You bestowed this single penny upon me when you took me for a beggar. I return your own penny back again upon you, whom I now take not to be very rich. The one hundred pound my good mistress wooed you to give me—behold! I lay for them an hundred golden pictures in her lap, with the other hundred pound you trusted me with to be paid when, the seas and I playing together, I should get a lucky hand. That hour's come: I now have it. And all that I am owner of coming to me by your means, not only every penny that is mine shall be yours but every pound be sent of an errand to fetch in profit.'

He was as good as his word, for he lent them so much money as put him again into his trade of merchandise. And at this hour is he a very worthy merchant in London.

FINIS

Tales

THE
RAVEVENS
Almanacke

Foretelling of a {Plague,
{Famine. and
{Ciuill Warre.

That shall happen this present yeare
1609. not only within this Kingdome of great
Brittaine, but also in *France, Germany, Spayne*, &
other parts of Christendome.

With certaine remedies, rules, and receipts,
how to preuent or at least to abate the edge of these
vniuersall Calamities.

Printed by *E. A.* for *Thomas Archer*, and are to sold at
his shop in the *Popes-head-Pallace*, neere the Royall
Exchange. 1609.

A Medicine to Cure the Plague of a Woman's Tongue, Experimented on a Cobbler's Wife.

from *The Raven's Almanac.*

A merry cobbler there was dwelling at Ware who for joy that he mended men's broken and corrupted soles did continually sing, so that his shop seemed a very bird-cage and he sitting there in his foul linen and greasy apron showed like a blackbird. It was this poor souter's destiny, not to be hanged but—worse than that—to be married. And to what creature, think you? To a fair, to a young, to a neat, delicate country lass that for her good parts was able to put down all Ware.

But with this honey that flowed in her did there drop such abundance of gall and poison from her scorpion-like tongue that Monsieur Shoe-Mender wished his wife were set upon the shortest last; and a thousand times a day was ready to die Cæsar's death, O valiant cordwainer, and to stab himself not with a bodkin but with his furious awl—because he knew that would go through stitch. He never took up the ends of his thread but he wished those to be the ends of his thread of life. He never pared his patches but he wished his knife to be the shears of the Fatal Sisters Three. He never handled his balls of wax but he compared them to his wife and sighed to think that he that touches pitch must be defiled. Now did his songs as heavily come from him as music does from a fiddler when in a tavern he plays for nothing. Now did Signior Cobbler stand no more on his pantofles, but at his shutting in of shop could have been content to have had all his neighbours have thrown his old shoes after him when he went home, in sign of good luck.

But alas, he durst not do that neither, for she that played the devil in woman's apparel (his wife I mean) made her Cavaliero Cobbler to give her account every night of every patch that went through his fingers. In this purgatory did our graduate in the gentle craft live a long time. But at length he was thrust into 'hell': for his wife, not following the steps of her husband—who was ever on the mending hand—but growing from bad into worse, cast aside her wedding stockings and drew on a pair of yellow hose. Then was my miserable cobbler more narrowly watched than a mouse by a cat or a debtor by a catchpole. He durst not unlock his lips after a wench but his teeth were ready to fly out of his head with her beating, nor have touched any petticoat but his wife was more dangerous than for a cat to eat fire. If any maid brought but her shoes to mending, his wife swore presently that he had the length of her foot and that he sewed love-stitches into every piece, though it were no bigger than a chandler's token.

Wearied therefore with this, worse than a bear-baiting, and being almost worn to the bare bones, his heart fretting out even to the elbows by rubbing up and down in this misery, at the length my brave boot-haler sifted his wits to the very bran for some hook to fasten into his wife's nostrils.

And the pill which he found either to choke her or purge her was this. A doctor, of whom all Ware was afraid because the vicar of the town sucked more sweetness out of his patients whom he sent to him (by reason all that came under his hands went the way of all flesh) than out of all his tithe-pigs, happened to dwell close by this distressed cobbler. To him, having saved his water overnight, repairs my reformer of decayed shoe leather betimes in the morning. The *bonjour* being given and returned, the cobbler's water was looked into. Much tossing and tumbling of it there was for a pretty while and at last it was demanded whose the urine should be.

'Mine,' quoth the cobbler.

'So it may be,' replied our Galenist, 'for I spy neither any disease swimming about thy body in this water, and thy very looks show that thou art sound.'

'Sound!' cries out the infected cobbler. 'Alas, sir, I see now that some diseases have power to make dunces of doctors themselves. "Sound," quoth a! Why, sir, I am sick at heart. I am struck with the plague; I have such a plague-sore upon me your doctor's cap is not able to cover it, 'tis so broad; it eats and spreads more and more into my flesh and, if you apply not some present remedy, Ware must and shall trudge to some other when their old shoes want mending—for the cobbler's but a dead man.'

At this the doctor stood amazed and wondered that his skill should shoot so wide as not to find out a grief so common, so dangerous and so palpable. Whereupon, he bidding the cobbler to open his breast and not to fear to show him that plague-sore whereof he so complained, the cobbler presently told him he would but step forth of doors and at his return he should see it.

At length the cobbler comes back again with his wife borne on his back like a sow new-scalded on the back of a butcher. And for all her kicking, railing, cursing and swearing, yet to the doctor he came with her, crying: 'Look you here, Master Doctor! This is my plague-sore that so torments me! In the night it keeps me from sleep, in the day it makes me mad; in my bed this serpent stings me, at my board she stabs me. And all with one weapon—her villainous tongue, her damnable tongue! If I reply, she fights; if I say nothing, she raves. If you call not this a plague, Master Doctor, then such a plague light on you, Master Doctor! Teach me therefore how to cure it, or else if you give me over I shall grow desperate and cut mine own throat.'

The doctor at this laughed; the cobbler's wife railed. The cobbler himself bid her lie still and held her so long till a number of his neighbours came about him to behold this scene of mirth—all of them, knowing how dangerously the cobbler was infected with this marriage plague, desiring the doctor to play the right physician and to cure their neighbour.

The doctor hereupon swore he would do it and, stepping into his study, he returned immediately with a paper in one hand and a fair cudgel in the other, delivering both to the cobbler, protesting that neither Galen, Averroës nor Hippocrates can prescribe any other remedy than this; and that if this medicine cure not the woman's evil, nothing can.

The cobbler, having neither the writing nor reading tongue, requested the doctor to read the receipt—as for the cudgel, he understood that well enough. The paper therefore, after a solemn 'Oyez!', by all the standers-by was read, and contained thus much:

> Take this salve, cobbler, for thy plague-sore!
> A crabbed cudgel fits a froward whore.
> Beat her well and thriftily
> Whilst she cries out lustily.
> Never let thy hand give o'er
> Till she swears to scold no more.

At the end of this the audience gave a plaudit in token they liked well of the doctor's physic. The cobbler thanked him and thus, instead of an Epilogue, spake to his neighbours: 'Neighbours,' quod he, 'you know and I know—nay, the Devil himself knows—that my wife

F

hath stuck upon me like a plague thus many years. To apply either the syrup of a salt eel or the oil of holly to her shoulders I hitherto was afraid, because I had no warrant that a man might lawfully beat his wife. But now sithence Master Doctor, who wears not a velvet night-cap for nothing, having turned over his books, finds that no herb, mineral, salve nor plaster, no purging nor any other blood-letting will cure or take out that worm under a woman's tongue which makes her mad, but only a sound beating: I will, God willing, give her the diet he sets down and, if ever I complain hereafter to any physician for the grief of this plague, let all Ware laugh at me for an ass and swear that my wife wears the breeches.'

Upon this resolution bravely does the cobbler march home, his wife like a Fury following, railing, reviling and casting dirt and stones as well at him as at the youths of the parish that went shouting after her heels. But being within doors and the locks made fast by my valiant cobbler, her tongue served as a drum or trumpet to sound an alarum whilst my brave desperview prepared for the onset with a good *bastinado*. The assault was not so furious but the cobbler's wife was as ready to receive it. To the skirmish fall they pell-mell, the cobbler's cockscomb being first broken; but he, being no Welshman to faint at sight of his own blood, so plied his business and so thrashed out all the chaff in his wife—who was nothing but rye—that in the end she fell on her knees, cried for the crumbs of the cobbler's mercy and fed upon them hungerly; he living ever after more quietly for her scolding than if he had dwelt in a steeple full of bells that had lost their claps.

*the Time of Famine to be Well
Provided of Flesh, How to Preserve
it a Long Time from Corruption
and How, when Hunger is most Sharp-
Set, a Man shall have no Lust to
Fall to but may Grow Abstinent.*

from *The Raven's Almanac.*

In the city of Cadiz, being an island bordering and belonging to the Kingdom of Spain, there was built a College of Friars amongst whom there was one lusty churchman above the rest who was better limbed than learned and could better skill in composing an amorous sonnet than in saying solemn dirges. This friar notwithstanding bare such a holy show, was so demure in his manners and so covertly cloaked his holiness that he was supposed the holiest friar of all the fraternity and therefore was appointed a confessor to a nunnery that was famous in this island for women of most severe form of life and godly conversation.

Under the jurisdiction of the Abbess there were some twenty nuns, all young, lusty and full of favour—very devout, and yet no such recluses but they had eyes as other, secular women had to judge of beauty, and hearts to wish wanton thoughts; which after grew to light, as Time is the discoverer of most hidden secrets.

For it so fell out amongst these holy she-saints that one was either more wise or more wanton than the rest, called Madonna Barbadora, issued of good parentage, and only daughter though not only child to Senor Ideaques Bartolos, a man of great reputation in the city of Cadiz. This Barbadora coming oftentimes to be confessed of this friar, whose name was Father Pedro Ragazoni, noted that he was a man of comely personage and so began somewhat favourably to conceit of him. Till at length Friar Pedro, marking her glances, perceived them to be amorous and, with that, hearing her sigh sundry times ere he had confessed her, did straight imagine that either she was a great sinner and deeply repentant or else sore overladen with the maiden's plague (which is over-large chastity) and therefore so full of outward sorrow and contrition.

The friar, taking her one day by the hand as she was alone with him in a pew, wished her to uncover her face. Barbadora obeying her ghostly father's command threw off her veil and blushed.

Which Friar Pedro espying, kissing her cheek, began to salute her in this manner: 'Fair nun and fair maid, as I am your confessor and have power to absolve, so if you conceal any sin from me it will crave the greater punishment. Therefore briefly and faithfully answer me to my question. There be many sins that trouble maids which may be eased if they be prevented by some friend or faithful counsellor—as, unchaste wishes, wanton glances, amorous thoughts and such venial scapes, which are engrafted by nature and therefore crave pardon by course, and yet all deserving penance; but seeing they are but sins of the mind, they are but motions. What say you, Barbadora? Are you troubled with any of these trifling follies?'

The nun, holding down her head, only answered she was a woman and her mother's daughter.

Friar Pedro, smelling a pad in the straw, prosecuted thus pleasantly: 'And is it, sweet maiden,' quod he, 'for those sins you sigh?'

'Oh no, holy father!' quoth she, 'for they be deeper passions that make me so sorrowful.'

'Why,' says the friar, 'is it pride, covetousness, gluttony, envy, wrath, sloth or any such Deadly Sins that drive you into those dumps?'

'I would,' said Barbadora, 'I were as free from all other as from these.'

'Then,' said the friar, 'my life for yours, it is some woman's plague you are troubled withal! And if it be so, take heed—it is dangerous: the sin is more easy than the sickness.'

'I pray you, sir,' saith she, 'what term you that plague?'

'Marry,' answers the friar, 'that plague is when a maiden is fair, young, of ripe years and hath never a faithful friend to her love but must in so great distress die a virgin.'

'That! That, my reverend confessor,' quoth the nun, 'is my grief. You have censured right of my sorrow. I am troubled with that burning plague and, if your counsel comfort me not, I am like to fall into greater inconvenience. Seeing therefore you are privy to my disease as you are a ghostly father and have care of my soul to absolve my sins; for I hold you as a surgeon, therefore yours be the charge to provide for the health of my body.'

The friar, hearing the nun in so good a mind, whispered in her ear (but what, I cannot tell—but I am sure he applied such plasters to help her that she complained no more of the 'plague' a long time after).

Barbadora, being thus set free from her often sighs, could not keep her own counsel, but she revealed it unto her bedfellow (for the closet of a woman's thoughts hangs at her tongue's end); in such sort discoursed the conceit of her cure unto her that Juliana longed for the confessing day (for so was the nun's bedfellow called).

Which being once come and she in secret with Friar Pedro, after he had questioned her of many sins and given much devout and holy counsel, at last she burst forth into plain terms and told him she was troubled with the same sickness her bedfellow Barbadora was, and therefore craved the like assistance at his hands.

The friar, smiling at this, was content to play the surgeon to cure this 'plague', still under the colour of auricular confession shadowing his villainy, till of twenty nuns fifteen were with child.

At last time began to babble and the nuns' bellies to grow big, so that before three months were past they began to feel that for the amending of their plague they had a spice of tympany. Not long after, the world was quick that the nuns grew big. And, to be brief, they feared their fellows should perceive their fault and so bewray it to the Abbess. Whereupon with a general consent they all agreed, at their next confession to bewray it to the friar; which was not long before it happened.

So Barbadora, cunningly dissembling the matter, being foremost of the rest because she was eldest and of greatest account with the Abbess, came to confession and—when Friar Pedro began with many a smiling look and holy kiss to greet her and question her about her sins— fetching a great sigh, made him this answer: 'Devout father, to make a rehearsal of my sins is folly, to tell what particular offences have scaped from me is needless: because in one brief word, as he that sins in one of the Ten Commandments breaks all, so she that by a friar is gotten with child hath blemished all her other virtues. And, sir, therefore I confess here that my belly is big and your sweet surgery hath wrought it. So either you must bestir your wits to help now at a pinch or else your discredit will be as great as my dishonour.'

The friar, although this motion had greatly amazed him, yet he would not show it in countenance lest he might discourage his fair leman, but bade her be of good cheer and not to fear, for he would be chary of her honour and credit, and salve what was amiss, to both their contents.

'Aye, sir,' quod she, 'were myself only in this perplexity I would not doubt of your present device. But there is fourteen more besides myself all troubled with the like swelling.'

'What, sister!' quod the friar, and with that he fetched a great sigh and said, 'I have made the old saying true—who sows shall reap.'

'Aye,' quoth Barbadora, 'if it be but a whip and a white sheet! And therefore, good friar, take heed that your penance be not worse than our punishment, for your ghostly surgery hath brought us to this devilish sickness.'

'Fear nothing, darling,' quoth he, and smiled. 'Friars have wit, as women have wills. And therefore doubt not of any conceit, but tell me what is your greatest care?'

'Marry,' quoth she, 'that the five that are free perceive us not and so discover our faults to the Abbess.'

'Leave that to me,' quoth he. 'I will take order for that, to your high content.' And so with great comfort to his holy sister he sent her away with a kind confession and took himself to the rest, who all sung the same song that Barbadora did; which put the poor friar to his shifts.

But when he had confessed them all, subtly he went to the Abbess and saluted her; and she, returning him as kindly greetings, questioned how her twenty nuns profited in virtue.

'Truly, madam,' said Pedro, 'well. But amongst Twelve Disciples there was one Judas. And when Adam had but two sons one proved a murderer. In Noah's Ark there was one Ham. And where God hath a church, the Devil hath a chapel.'

The Abbess, hearing the holy father beginning such an enigmatical exordium, began to suspect that there was some mischance amongst her nuns, and therefore called him into the dortour and desired him to bewray unto her what was amongst the sisters.

The fox, that had fed upon so much mutton, cunningly began to insinuate himself under the shape of Habakkuk thus: 'Madam, you know that it behoves a confessor to be as secret as severe, and to conceal offences as well as he appoints correction for sins. Therefore I may not nor dare not for mine oath reveal what either I know or they have confessed. But this in private I give you as a caveat: if they stay long in your cloister, they will discredit your house and bring it in great opprobratious question.' With that he named the five honest nuns and with a solemn protestation admonished the Abbess as speedily as might be to convey them out of the nunnery with credit.

She, thanking the holy father for his care he had of her honour, gave him gold for his pains and bade him farewell, still imagining what this matter might be. And examine them she durst not lest they should suspect their confessor had discovered their confession and so upon their complaint bring the friar to further trouble. Yet willing to have them removed so to save her house from blemish, she sent for their friends and dealt so covertly and cunningly with them that they were taken home for a time till further trial of their fortunes might be had. Their friends and parents, sorrowful and grieving that they above the rest should miscarry, yet concealed all and shadowed their home-coming by sundry excuses. And yet not so cunningly but the common people began to imagine diversely of their departure. But none durst censure openly, though they muttered in secret, so that after many days all was whisht.

And the other nuns were glad, for all were feathered of one wing, and did so closely comfort themselves that the Abbess suspected nothing and Friar Pedro had more free access to clergify his holy virgins and confessants; and made an agreement that which of them was brought to bed first should give him their child and he would convey it away, to their content and his own credit.

Living thus as pleasantly as a cock amongst so many hens, it fell so out at the last that Barbadora's good hour was come, and that at such an unhappy time that neither the device of the friar nor the secrecy of the nuns nor her own policy could save her honesty. For, rising as their custom is at twelve o'clock at night to sing certain hymns, Barbadora in the midst of the choir fell in travail and, though she fought by all means to conceal and to bide many sore pangs, yet at last she was fain with a loud alarum to cry higher than they sung.

Which the Abbess, hearing, stayed their matins and went to Barbadora, asking her what she ailed and what extreme disease pained her so, that she made such heavy shrieking.

The great-bellied nun, half-dead with pain, would give the Abbess no answer but 'Oh, my belly, my belly! Friar Pedro, Pedro! Oh, my belly!'

The old matron perhaps in her youth had been cured of the maid's plague; perceived straight where her shoe wrung her, and therefore charged the nuns to hold her back. And she played so cunningly the midwife's part that Barbadora was delivered of a pretty boy. Which the

Abbess seeing, after she knew that all danger was past, she raged and
railed against the poor nun, laying open not only the grievousness of
the sin but also her own discredit, and chiefly that blemish that should
redound to her, to the house and all her fellow nuns through her only
lightness of her life. After she had almost chased herself out of breath
she questioned who was the father, and Barbadora in great contrition
of mind told her how her holy father Friar Pedro did it.

The Abbess swearing a mortal revenge against the friar for the love
she bare to Barbadora's father Senor Ideaques Bartolos and for the
care she had lest, if this fact were known, her nunnery should grow in
open contempt, she began to salve the matter amongst the nuns: 'I
cannot deny, sisters,' quoth she, 'but as your vow is holy, so the breach
of virginity in this case deserves no less than Hell-fire, and without
repentance can have no absolute pardon. For the scape of a nun is
more than of another ordinary woman; and for that course, only upon
suspicion, I removed five of your fellows which I thought faulty. Yet
flesh is frail, and women are weak vessels, especially tempted by such a
subtle serpent as Friar Pedro is. And therefore the fault is the less, and
the more willingly to be shadowed. So that I charge you here to conceal the matter both for your own and mine honour. And if any of you
all have been by him persuaded to the like folly, tell it to me now in
secret, and I will be as silent as yourselves to salve and save your
honesties.'

The nuns hearing this, all fourteen fell down on their knees before
the Abbess and cried out upon Friar Pedro, lecherous Friar Pedro,
and cursed him.

The Abbess, suspecting nothing of the whole fourteen, bade them
beware not only of him—for he should no more come within their
dortour—but of all others that hereafter should be their confessors.

'Alas, madam!' quod Juliana, 'it is too late, for we all fourteen are
with child by him.'

'Marry, God forbid!' quod the Abbess, and blessed her. 'What?'
quod she, 'fifteen at a clap with child, and only by one friar? Then I
see well the Devil is grown devout, when friars deal their alms so
frankly. But by sweet St Anne,' said she, 'I will be revenged on the
friar, and all the convent shall pay sweetly for engrossing the market
and buying so much flesh for his own diet.' So she fell to more strict
examination of them, whether any more friars came with him or no.
And they confessed that he had procured every one of them a lover,
and delivered their names.

Which she taking note of deferred not revenge very long lest suspicion might be had, but thus cunningly sought to acquit the wrongs proffered both to her and her house. She sent her steward abroad to buy great provision of victuals, and then her own self went to the Abbot and desired that her confessor and fourteen of his friends might take part of a feast which she had provided. The Abbot granted, and the friars gave her great thanks and promised to come, all laughing in their sleeves that she should give the fair nuns and them leave to have one merry supper together, seeing in secret they had so many nights' lodging with them.

The Abbess went home smiling and provided certain tall sturdy knaves for that purpose that were tenants and belonging to the lands of the nunnery, and conveyed them all near unto the back-place of the chapel and had given them her mind out plainly to deal with the friars as she had decreed; and thereupon placed in that back-room fifteen great blocks all standing one by another as orderly as might be.

Having thus fitted all things to the purpose, she put up the nuns every one into their cells lest they should give any inkling unto the friars of her determination. At the hour appointed these frolic friars came clad in their cowls with smooth faces and dissembling hearts, having great show of prayers in their eyes and hope of lechery in their thoughts. But howsoever, the old Abbess gave them a most courteous and friendly welcome, telling them that the nuns were all this day busy cooks about the feast; only herself was left to give entertainment.

They gratulated her courtesies and she led them all into a great parlour where she caused the steward to bring them in wine. Then, the place being strong, she went forth and called the confessor to her. And then leading him into the back-room appointed for the purpose, the tall knaves laid hold on him and there stripping him into his shirt they took a great three-forked nail and fastened the friar's doucets of dimissaries fast to the block, to the great pain and amazing of the friar.

Well, howsoever he complained, he could not get any answer of the Abbess but that she laughed heartily. And thus by one and one she drew out the friars and nailed them fast in their shirts to the blocks. Then laying down by every one of them a sharp knife, she began to make her oration thus: 'Gentle Father Pedro and you the rest of the holy friars, you know the smallest sin craves some penance in the lay people; then what do great offences in friars? He which knows his master's will and doth it not must be beaten with many stripes; so you that know Lechery was a Deadly Sin and had all by solemn oaths vowed chastity have gotten all the nuns of my house with child. Therefore I in charity have for your souls' health appointed you this penance.' At that word all the country fellows set fire in the thatch and the house began to burn. 'You see,' quoth she, 'either burn to death or else, here lie knives to free yourselves. Now it is at your own choice whether you will burn or geld yourselves. And hereafter endeavour to keep chastity.'

The friars hearing this hard resolution began with humble looks to entreat her, but in vain. She made them all a low curtsy and went her ways.

The friars in great perplexity seeing the house all on fire and that they began to fry in their shirts and the house ready to fall about their ears, Friar Pedro learning first to play the man took the knife and whipped off his genitories, and away he runs towards the Abbey. And every friar, fearing the fire, played the like part, and away they run bleeding, as fast as their legs would carry them.

The fire grew great and it was perceived afar off, so that Senor Ideaques Bartolos, Barbadora's father, espied it; fearing his daughter's mishap, ran thither himself. The Abbot being told the nunnery was on fire made no little haste for fear of his friars, and an infinite of other people being devoutly minded to the nunnery ran thither. And as they went Senor Bartolos and the Abbot met the friars running away in their shirts.

Which amazing them, the Abbot said, 'What news, Friar Pedro? What, the nunnery afire and you run away in your shirts? What meaneth this?'

'I know not, I know not, sir,' said he. 'We were there late enough. The Devil burn house, Abbess, nuns and all!' And away trudged the convent, every man to his lodging and sending speedily for a skilful surgeon.

The Abbot with the rest of the townsmen and Senor Bartolos came thither. And by that time the roof was pulled down and all quenched, and they found the Abbess ready to entertain them friendly. They, wondering at this, demanded how the fire came and what the reason was the friars ran away in their shirts.

The Abbess recounted unto them from point to point what had happened and how fifteen of the nuns were with child under the shadow of confession by those fifteen friars, and therefore she had sought revenge to clear herself of that crime: 'And because your eyes shall witness what bitter punishment I have appointed them for penance, come all with me.' And so she led them into the back-room, where she showed them the knives and what the friars for fear had left behind them.

At this they all fell into a great laughter—except Bartolos, who grieved for his daughter Barbadora. Yet he highly commended the Abbess for her revenge. And she was honoured through the city, the nuns banished their religious house, the friars put out of their dortours, and the five poor nuns that were thrust out without cause entertained again. And ever after the nunnery was in great fame and credit.

A
KNIGHTS
Coniuring.

Done in earneſt:

Diſcouered in Ieſt.

By *Thomas Dekker*.

LONDON,

Printed by *T. C.* for *William Barley*, and
are to be ſolde at his Shop in
Gratious ſtreete,
1607.

*'The Fields of Joy' Described. None
there must Dwell
But Purgéd Souls and Such as have
Done Well:
Some Soldiers there, and Some that
Died in Love;
Poets Sit Singing in 'The Bay-Tree
Grove' . . . .*

from *A Knight's Conjuring.*

Let me carry you into those *Insulae Fortunatae* ordained to be the abidings for none but blessed souls. The walls that encompass these goodly habitations are white as the forehead of Heaven. They glister like polished ivory, but the stuff is finer. High they are like the pillars that uphold the court of Jove, and strong they are as towers built by enchantment. There is but one gate to it all, and that's of refined silver; so narrow it is that but one at once can enter. Round about wears it a girdle of waters that are sweet, redolent and crystalline—the tears of the vine are not so precious, the nectar of the gods nothing so delicious.

Walk into the groves: you shall hear all sorts of birds melodiously singing; you shall see swains deftly piping and virgins chastely dancing. Shepherds, there, live as merrily as kings, and kings are glad to be companions with shepherds. The widow, there, complains of no wrong; the orphan sheds no tears, for Covetousness cannot carry it away with his gold, nor Cruelty with the sway of greatness; the poor client needs fee no lawyer to plead for him, for there's no jury to condemn him nor judges to astonish him. There, is all mirth without immodesty, all health without base abusing of it, all sorts of wines without intemperance, all riches without sensuality, all beauty without painting, all love without dissimulation. Winter there plays not the tyrant, neither is the summer's breath pestilent, for spring is all the year long tricking up the boughs, so that the trees are ever flourishing, the fruits ever growing, the flowers ever budding. Yea, such cost and such art is bestowed upon the arbours that the very benches whereon these blessed inhabitants sit are sweet beds of violets, the beds whereon they lie banks of musk-roses, their pillows' hearts are heart's-ease, their sheets the silken leaves of willow.

Neither is this a common inn to all travellers, but the very palace where Happiness herself maintains her court; and none are allowed to follow her but such as are of merit. Of all men in the world landlords dare not quarter themselves here, because they are rackers of rents. A pettifogger that has taken bribes will be damned ere he come near the gates. A fencer is not allowed to stand within twelvescore of the place. No more is a vintner nor a farmer nor a tailor—unless he creep through the eye of his needle; no, and but few gentlemen-ushers. Women, for all their subtlety, scarce one amongst five hundred has her pew there—especially old midwives, chambermaids and waiting wenches: their doings are too well known to be let into these lodgings. No, no! none can be free of these liberties but such as have consciences without cracks, hands not spotted with uncleanness, feet not worn out with walking to mischief, and hearts that never were hollow. Listen therefore and I will tell you what passengers have licence to land upon these shores.

Young infants that die at the breast and have not sucked of their parents' sins are most welcome thither for their innocency. Holy singers whose divine anthems have bound souls by their charms, and whose lives are tapers of virgin wax set in silver candlesticks to guide men out of error's darkness: they know their places there, and have them for their integrity.

Some scholars are admitted into this society. But the number of them all is not half so many as are in one of the colleges of an university; and the reason is they either kindle firebrands in the sanctified places by their contention or kill the hearts of others by their coldness.

One field there is amongst all the rest set round about with willows. It is called The Field of Mourning; and in this, upon banks of flowers that wither away even with the scorching sighs of those that sit upon them, are a band of malcontents. They look for all the world like the mad folks in Bedlam and desire, like them, to be alone. And these are forlorn lovers such as pined away to nothing for nothing: such as for the love of a wanton wench have gone crying to their graves whilst she in the meantime went, laughing to see such a kind coxcomb, into another's bed. All the joy that these poor fools feed upon is to sit singing lamentable ballads to some doleful tunes. For, though they have changed their old lives, they cannot forget their young loves. They spend their time in making of myrtle garlands and shed so much water out of their eyes that it hath made a pretty little river which lies so soaking continually at the roots of the willow trees that half the leaves of them are almost washed into a whiteness.

There is another piece of ground where are encamped none but soldiers; and of those, not all sorts of soldiers neither, but only such as have died nobly in the wars; and yet of those but a certain number, too: that is to say such that in execution were never bloody, in their country's revenge severe but not cruel; such as held death in one hand and mercy in the other; such as never ravished maidens, never did abuse no widows, never gloried in the massacre of babes, were never drunk of purpose before the battle began because they would spare none, nor after the battle did never quarrel about pledging the health of his whore. Of this garrison there are but a few in pay, and therefore they live without mutiny.

Beyond all these places is there a grove which stands by itself like an island, for a stream that makes music in the running clasps it round about like a hoop-girdle of crystal. Laurels grew so thick on all the banks of it that lightning itself if it came thither hath no power to pierce through them. It seems, without, a desolate and unfrequented wood, for those within are retired into themselves; but from them came forth such harmonious sounds that birds build nests only in the trees there to teach tunes to their young ones prettily.

This is called The Grove of Bay-Trees, and to this concert-room resort none but the children of Phœbus, poets and musicians: the one creates the ditty and gives it the life or number, the other lends it voice and makes it speak music. When these happy spirits sit asunder their bodies are like so many stars, and when they join together in several troops they show like so many heavenly constellations.

Full of pleasant bowers and quaint arbours is all this walk. In one of which old Chaucer, reverend for priority, blithe in cheer, buxom in his speeches and benign in his haviour, is circled around with all the makers or poets of his time, their hands leaning on one another's shoulders and their eyes fixed seriously upon his whilst their ears are all tied to his tongue by the golden chains of his numbers. For here like Evander's mother they spake all in verse. No Attic eloquence is so sweet. Their language is so pleasing to the gods that they utter their oracles in none other.

Grave Spenser was no sooner entered into this chapel of Apollo but these elder fathers of the divine fury gave him a laurel and sung his welcome. Chaucer called him his son and placed him at his right hand; all of them, at a sign given by the whole choir of the Muses that brought him thither, closing up their lips in silence and tuning all their ears for attention to hear him sing out the rest of his *Faerie Queene's* praises.

In another company sat learned Watson, industrious Kyd, ingenious Acheley and (though he had been a player, moulded out of their pens, yet because he had been their lover and a register to the Muses) inimitable Bentley. These were likewise carousing to one another at the holy well, some of them singing pæons to Apollo, some of them hymns to the rest of the gods; whilst Marlowe, Greene and Peele had got under the shades of a large vine, laughing to see Nashe (that was but newly come to their college) still haunted with the sharp and satirical spirit that followed him here upon earth.

For Nashe inveighed bitterly, as he had wont to do, against dry-fisted patrons, accusing them of his untimely death: because if they had given his Muse that cherishment which she most worthily deserved he had fed to his dying day on fat capons, burnt sack and sugar and not so desperately have ventured his life and shortened his days by keeping company with pickle herrings.

The rest asked him 'What news in the world?' He told them that barbarism was now grown to be an epidemial disease and more common than the toothache.

Being demanded how poets and players agreed now, 'Troth,' says he, 'as physicians and patients agree: for the patient loves his doctor no longer than till he get his health, and the player loves a poet so long as the sickness lies in the twopenny gallery when none will come into it. Nay,' says he, 'into so low a misery, if not contempt, is the sacred art of poesy fallen that though a writer who is worthy to sit at the table of the Sun waste his brains to earn applause from the more worthy spirits, yet when he has done his best he works but like Ocnus, that makes ropes in Hell: for as he twists, an ass stands by and bites them in sunder—and that ass is no other than the audience with hard hands.'

He had no sooner spoken this but in comes Chettle sweating and blowing by reason of his fatness. To welcome whom, because he was of old acquaintance, all rose up and fell presently on their knees to drink a health to all the lovers of Helicon; in doing which they made such a mad noise that, all this *Conjuring* which is past being but a dream, I suddenly started up and am now awake.

FINIS

English Villainies
Discovered by
Lantern and Candlelight

LANTHORNE

and Candle-light.

Or

The Bell-mans second Nights walke.

In which

Hee brings to light, a Broode of more ſtrange Villanies,
then euer were till this yeare diſcouered.

--Decet nouiſſe malum; feciſſe, neſandum.

LONDON
Printed for *Iohn Busbie*, and are to be ſold at his ſhop in
Fleet-ſtreet, in Saint Dunſtans Church-yard.
1608.

The Bellman's Cry.

Men and children, maids and wives,
'Tis not late to mend your lives!
Lock your doors, lie warm in bed—
Much loss is in a maidenhead;
Midnight feastings are great wasters,
Servants' riots undo masters.
When you hear this ringing bell,
Think it is your latest knell.
When I cry 'Maid in your smock',
Do not take it for a mock;
Well I mean, if well 'tis taken:
I would have you still awaken.
Four o'clock! the cock is crowing;
I must to my home be going.
When all other men do rise
Then must I shut up mine eyes.

A Table of All the Matters that are Contained in this Discourse.

To the Very Worthy Gentleman,
Master Francis Muschamp of
Peckham.

Sir,

It may haply seem strange unto you that such an army of idle words should march into the open field of the world under the ensign of your name, you being not therewith made acquainted till now. You may judge it in me an error. I myself confess it a boldness. But such an ancient and strong charter hath custom confirmed to this printing age of ours, by giving men authority to make choice of what patrons they like, that some writers do almost nothing contrary to that custom and some by virtue of that privilege dare do anything. I am neither of that first order nor of this last. The one is too fondly ceremonious, the other too impudently audacious. I walk in the midst so well as I can between both. With some fruits that have grown out of my brain have I been so far from being in love that I thought them not worthy to be tasted by any particular friend, and therefore have they been exposed only to those that would entertain them. Neither did I think the fairest that ever was mine so worthy that it was to be looked upon with the eye of universal censure.

Two sorts of madmen trouble the stationers' shops in Paul's Churchyard: they that out of a mere and idle vainglory will ever be pamphleting, though their books, being printed, are scarce worth so much brown paper—and this is a very poor and foolish ambition; of the other sort are they that being free of wit's merchant-venturers do every new moon for gain only make five or six voyages to the press, and every Term-time upon booksellers' stalls lay whole litters of blind invention—fellows that if they do but walk in the Middle Aisle spit nothing but ink and speak nothing but poem. I would keep company with neither of these two madmen if I could avoid them. Yet I take the last to be the wisest and less dangerous, for sithence all the arrows that men shoot in the world fly to two marks only, either pleasure or profit, he is not much to be condemned that, having no more acres to live upon than those that lie in his head, is every hour hammering out one piece or other out of this rusty Iron Age, sithence the golden

176

and silver globes of the world are so locked up that a scholar can hardly be suffered to behold them.

Some perhaps will say that this lancing of the pestilent sores of a kingdom so openly may infect those in it that are sound, and that in this our school, where close abuses and gross villainies are but discovered and not punished, others that never before knew such evils will be now instructed by the book to practise them. If so, then let not a traitor or a murderer be publicly arraigned, lest the one laying open to the world how his plots were woven to contrive a treason, or the other what policies he was armed with for the shedding of blood, the standers-by that are honest be drawn by their rules to run headlong into the same mischiefs. No, our strong physic works otherwise. What more makes a man to loathe that mongrel madness, that half-English, half-Dutch sin, drunkenness, than to see a common drunkard acting his beastly scenes in the open street? Is any gamester so foolish to play with false dice when he's assured that all who are about him know him to be a sworn cheater? The letting therefore of vice's blood in these several veins which the Bellman hath opened cannot by any judicial rules of physic endanger the body of the commonwealth or make it feeble, but rather restore those parts to perfect strength which by disorder have been diseased.

Give me leave to lead you by the hand into a wilderness where are none but monsters—whose cruelty you need not fear, because I teach the way to tame them. Ugly they are in shape and devilish in conditions. Yet to behold them afar off may delight you, and to know their qualities if ever you should come near them may save you from much danger. Our country breeds no wolves nor serpents, yet these engender here and are either serpents or wolves, or worse than both. Whatsoever they are, I send unto you not the herd of the one or the bed of the other, but only a picture of either. View them, I pray, and where the colours are not well laid on, shadow them with your finger. If you spy any disproportion, thus excuse it: such painting is fit for monsters. How rudely soever the piece is drawn, call it a picture. And when one more worthy your view lies under the workman's pencil, this bad one shall bring you home a better. In the meantime I cease, and begin to be, if you please,

All yours,

THOMAS DEKKER

To the Glory of Middlesex, the Honourable
and Worthily Deserving Gentlemen,
His Majesty's Justices for
the Peace in that
Populous County.

To whom but to you, noble gentlemen and worthy patriots of your county, should I dedicate these my labours? The sick man sends to his doctor, the wounded man to his surgeon: you are both, and the commonwealth cries out to you for remedy. Petty enormities are the diseases, and grand impieties are the stabs, that go deep into her body. I but open the sores and show how foul they are; the balm is yours, and yours the skill to drop it in. It is better to empty gaols than to fill hospitals—to hang a thief, save the true man; but corruption fed fattens mischief.

Few saints walk up and down the City, fewer in the suburbs—they are the limbs infected: there, many a leg is fit to be cut off. If therefore there were not sessions-houses we should scarce have houses to dwell in. Should not such as you sit there it were no walking anywhere, for so our forefathers did complain, so we do complain, and so posterity shall complain, that fresh villainies and abuses are begotten, born and grow up in all parts of this kingdom. And for that cause Justice had need to have many hands to strike and many swords to strike home. Were she born blind as the painters say she is, the wickedness of this age is able to lift her eyelids open. But she sits by you clear-sighted, and Mercy by her with a hand as soft as ever signed pardon to a condemned prisoner. Yet to such a monstrous and ugly body is iniquity grown that if the voice of Justice should every hour in the day and every day in the week sentence offenders to their deservings the whip and the halter would never lie quiet; a beadle would not be able to lift his arms to his head, nor the hangman to walk on foot to Tyburn.

You have strong hands over the people and are feared where you dwell. Get as strong hearts and care not how the many-headed beast roars, so the republic loves you. He is a true Justice that can search the disease to the bottom and has medicines to cure it; and such are you.

Are there any of that character not such? *Di meliora!* But as in an army all are not soldiers that fight and bear arms, no more is everyone a Justice that bears the name but he that is so both *nomine et re*, such a one as is furnished with learning, law, equity, judgment, integrity, discretion. If you are all such, as it is not for me to doubt, you are a brave company. I often see, for petty crimes, people hurried along the streets. What a noise keeps them company! How those bells in women's mouths jangle! How they cry out to go, not before such a one, but before such a one! Why should the face of one Justice be more terrible than another? Why his name? Why his warrant? It is as when crazy bodies are driven to apothecaries: juleps go down smoothly, bitter pills choke. They love to see Naomi in your parlours, not Mara.

I preach without a pulpit. This is no sermon but an Epistle Dedicatory which dedicates these discoveries and my threescore years devotedly.

Yours in my best service,
THOS. DEKKER

To my own Nation.

Readers, after it was proclaimed abroad that under the conduct of the Bellman of London new forces were once more to be levied against certain wild and barbarous rebels that were up in open arms against the tranquillity of the weal public, it cannot be told what numbers of voluntaries offered themselves daily to fight against so common, so bold, so strange and so dangerous an enemy. Light horsemen came in hourly with discovery where these mutineers lay entrenched, delivering in brief notes of intelligence who were their leaders, how they went armed, and that they served both on horse and foot. Only their strengths could not be descried, because their numbers were held infinite. Yet instructions were written and sent every minute by those that were favourers of goodness showing what military discipline the foe used in his battles and what forts if he were put at any time to flight he would retire to, what stratagems he would practise, and where he did determine to lie in ambuscado. They that could not serve in person in this noble quarrel sent their auxiliary forces well armed with counsel. So that the Bellman, contrary to his own hopes, seeing himself so strongly and strangely seconded by friends doth [in a fourth set battle once again] bravely advance forward in main battalion. The day of encounter is appointed to be in this Easter Term and Trinity Term; the place, Paul's Churchyard, Fleet St and other parts of the City. [To furnish this army the better with soldiers have I opened a prison, out of which what troops issue and how practised in discipline, let but a drum beat to call up the rear and thou shalt easily in one light skirmish know of what mettle they are.]

But before they join let me give you note of one thing, and that is this. There is an usurper that of late hath taken upon him the name of the Bellman but, being not able to maintain that title, he doth now call himself the Bellman's brother. His ambition is, rather out of vainglory than the true courage of an experienced soldier, to have the leading of the van. But it shall be honour good enough for him, if not too good, to come up with the rear. You shall know him by his habiliments, for by the furniture he wears he will be taken for a Beadle of Bridewell. It is thought he is rather a neuter than a friend to the cause, and therefore the Bellman doth here openly protest that he comes into the field as no fellow in arms with him.

Howsoever it be struck, or whosoever gives the first blow, the victory depends upon the valour of you that are the wings to the Bellman's army; for which conquest he is in hope you will valiantly fight, sithence the quarrel is against the head of monstrous abuses and the blows which you must give are in defence of law, justice, order, ceremony, religion, peace and that honourable title of goodness.

St George! I see the two armies move forward, and behold! the Bellman himself first chargeth upon the face of the enemy thus.

To the Reader.

It is now about eighteen years past since a bed of strange snakes were found. They were then but in the shell, yet when they were fully hatched and began to crawl out their poison spread itself into all the parts and veins of the kingdom; but the stench of the venom brake out most in and about London. Candlelight was then the first that discovered that cursed nursery of vipers. What was the brood, think you? All sorts of witty cheaters, tame coney-catchers and subtle crossbiters, etc. But this were, as the Spaniard says, *peccadilla*—petty sins, pygmy villainies to these giants which after roared about the world. And the honest intelligencer that first opened the den of these monsters was the Bellman of London. Here he shows you their pictures and not the pictures only, but the mis-shapen persons themselves. In drawing of whose filthy proportions, albeit the poor Bellman took infinite pains, yet when it was once famed what an excellent work he was in hand with, a curious number of noble gentlemen joined their counsels to the Bellman's undertakings. Some sent him delicate pencils, some notes how and where to lay on such and such colours; others taught him how to shadow some of these villainies by setting off the abuses wet but not hanging forth the party for a sign. So that where at the beginning the Bellman feared he should have wanted work, in the end he had more than he could turn his hands to.

Heartened with these auxiliary forces he came bravely into the field, not caring what cannons of mischief this army of Furies, here mustered together, could or durst discharge against him. But now whole acres of new and as yet unknown weeds are crept up which the Bellman with his finger points to, and shows them to the eye of Justice that she, being the best and ablest gardener to weed the republic and, having cleansed it, to dress it up neatly and in order, may so pluck them up by the root they may no more be seen to deface so goodly a commonwealth.

All that before was written or is now newly added is to yield thee profit and pleasure. Neither wonder how the Bellman should lay open such a number of villainies unless he himself should in his own person cry 'Guilty!' to all. No, an apothecary may know all poisons, yet practise them upon none. He never poisons, himself. Yet after the strongest and most killing ones are corrected he gives them physically for his patients' preservation. So they are prescribed to thee here, to the end that by knowing the secret mischiefs, abuses, villainies and treacheries of the world, thou mayest arm thyself against them or guard thy friend by advice from them. He says as the wanton poet does of himself: *lasciva est nobis pagina, vita proba est.*

Read and laugh; read and learn; read and loathe. Laugh at the knavery; learn out the mystery; loathe the base villainy. Farewell.

To the Author.

Howe'er thou may'st by blazing all abuse
Incur suspect thou speak'st what thou hast proved—
Though then to keep it close it thee behooved,
So Reason makes for thee a just excuse;
Yet of thy pains the best may make good use.
Then of the best thy pains should be approved
And, for the same, of them should'st be beloved,
Sith thou of falsehoods' flood dost ope the sluice
That they at waste continually may run
By showing men the reaches that they have,
That honest men may so o'er-reach a knave
Or sound their swallowing deeps, the same to shun.
But if from hence a knave more cunning grows,
That spider sucks but poison from thy rose.

Thy friend if thine own,

JO. DA.

To his Friend.

Of vice, whose countermine a state confounds
Worse than sedition; of those mortal wounds
Which, throughly searched, do kingdoms' hearts endanger;
Of plagues that o'er-run cities; of those stranger
Big-swoll'n impostumes poisoning the strong health
Of the most sound, best-dieted commonwealth—
Thou tell'st the causes and dost teach the cure
By med'cine well-compounded, cheap and sure,
And, as one read in deep chirurgery,
Draw'st of these evils the true anatomy.
Then on thy plainness let none lay reproof:
Thou tak'st sin's height as men do stars, aloof.

M. R.

To my Industrious Friend.

In an ill time thou writ'st, when tongues had rather
Spit venom on thy lines than from thy labours,
As druggists do from poison, medicines gather.
This is no age to crown desert with favours.
But be thou constant to thyself and care not
What arrows malice shoots. The wise will never
Blame thy loud singing, and the foolish dare not;
None else but wolves will bark at thine endeavour.
When thou in thy dead sleep liest in thy grave,
These charms to after-ages up shall raise thee.
What here thou leav'st, alive thy name shall save
And what thou now dispraisest shall then praise thee.
Though not to know ill be wise ignorance
Yet thou, by reading evil, dost goodness teach
And of abuse the colours dost advance
Only upon abuse to force a breach.
The honour that thy pen shall earn thereby
Is this: that though knaves live, their sleights here die.

E. G.

Lantern and Candlelight:

Or,

The Bellman's Second
Night's Walk.

CHAPTER I

Of canting: how long it hath been a language; how it comes to be a language; how it is derived; and by whom it is spoken.

When all the world was but one kingdom all the people in that kingdom spake but one language. A man could travel in those days neither by sea nor land but he met his countrymen and none others. Two could not then stand gabbling with strange tongues and conspire together, to his own face, how to cut a third man's throat but he might understand them. There was no Spaniard in that age to brave his enemy in the rich and lofty Castilian; no Roman orator to plead in the rhetorical and fluent Latin; no Italian to court his mistress in the sweet and amorous Tuscan; no Frenchman to parle in the full and stately phrase of Orleans; no German to thunder out the high and rattling Dutch; the unfruitful crabbed Irish and the voluble significant Welsh were not then so much as spoken of; the quick Scottish dialect, sister to the English, had not then a tongue.

Neither were the strings of the English speech in those times untied. When she first learned to speak it was but a broken language. The singlest and the simplest words flowed from her utterance, for she dealt in nothing but in monosyllables, as if to have spoken words of greater length would have cracked her voice; by which means her eloquence was poorest, yet hardest to learn and so, but for necessity, not regarded amongst strangers. Yet afterwards those noblest languages lent her words and phrases and, turning those borrowings into good husbandry, she is now as rich in elocution and as abundant as her proudest and best-stored neighbours.

Whilst thus, as I said before, there was but one alphabet of letters for all the world to read by, all the people that then lived might have

187

wrought upon one piece of work in countries far distant asunder without mistaking one another, and not needing an interpreter to run between them. Which thing Nimrod the first idolater perceiving, and not knowing better how to employ so many thousand millions of subjects as bowed before him, a fire of ambition burned within him to climb up so high that he might see what was done in Heaven. And for that purpose workmen were summoned from all the corners of the earth who presently were set to build the Tower of Babel.

But the Master Workman of this great universe, to check the insolence of such a saucy builder that durst raise up pinnacles equal to His own above, commanded the selfsame spirit that was both bred in the Chaos and had maintained it in disorder to be both surveyor of those works and controller of the labourers. This messenger was called Confusion. It was a spirit swift of flight and faithful of service, her looks wild, terrible and inconstant, her attire carelessly loose and of a thousand several colours. In one hand she griped a heap of storms with which at her pleasure she could trouble the waters; in the other she held a whip to make three spirits that drew her to gallop faster before her. The spirits' names were Treason, Sedition and War, who at every time when they went abroad were ready to set kingdoms in an uproar. She rode upon a chariot of clouds which was always furnished with thunder, lightning, winds, rain, hailstones, snow and all the other artillery belonging to the service of divine vengeance, and when she spake her voice sounded like the roaring of many torrents boisterously struggling together, for between her jaws did she carry a hundred thousand tongues.

This strange linguist, stepping to every artificer that was there at work, whispered in his ear; whose looks were thereupon presently filled with a strange distraction. And on a sudden, whilst every man was speaking to his fellow, his language altered and no man could understand what his fellow spake. They all stared one upon another, yet none of them all could tell wherefore so they stared. Their tongues went and their hands gave action to their tongues, yet neither words nor action were understood. It was a noise of a thousand sounds, and yet the sound of the noise was nothing. He that spake knew he spake well, and he that heard was mad that the other could speak no better. In the end they grew angry one with another, as thinking they had mocked one another of purpose, so that the mason was ready to strike the bricklayer, the bricklayer to beat out the brains of his labourer, the carpenter took up his axe to throw at the carver, whilst the carver was stabbing at the smith because he brought him a hammer when he should have made him a chisel; he that called for timber had stones laid before him and when one was sent for nails he fetched a tray of mortar.

Thus Babel should have been raised, and by this means Babel fell. The frame could not go forward, the stuff was thrown by, the workmen made holiday. Everyone packed up his tools to be gone, yet not to go the same way that he came. But glad was he that could meet another whose speech he understood, for to what place soever he went, others that ran madding up and down, hearing a man speak like themselves, followed only him, so that they who when the work began were all countrymen, before a quarter of it was finished fled from one another as from enemies and strangers. And in this manner did men at the first make up nations. Thus were words coined into languages, and out of those languages have others been moulded since only by the mixture of nations after kingdoms have been subdued.

But I am now to speak of a people and of a language of both which, many thousands of years since that wonder wrought at Babel, the world till now never made mention. Yet Confusion never dwelt more amongst any creatures. The Bellman in his first voyage which he made for discoveries found them to be savages, yet living in an island very temperate, fruitful, full of a noble nation and rarely governed. The laws, manners and habits of these wild men are plainly set down as it were in a former painted table. Yet lest haply a stranger may look upon this second picture of them who never beheld the first, it shall not be amiss in this place to repeat over again the names of all the tribes into which they divide themselves both when they serve abroad in the open fields and when they lie in garrison within towns and walled cities. And these are their ranks as they stand in order, viz.

rufflers	prigs
upright men	swadders
hookers, *alias* anglers	curtails
rogues	Irish toyles
wild rogues	swigmen
priggers of prancers	jarkmen
palliards	patricoes
fraters	kinchin coes
Abraham men, *alias* mad	glimmerers
Tom of Bedlam	bawdy-baskets
whipjacks	autem morts

counterfeit cranks	doxies
dommerars	dells
	kinchin morts

Into thus many regiments are they now divided. But in former times, above four hundred years now past, they did consist of five squadrons only, viz.

(i) cursitors, *alias* vagabonds
(ii) faitors
(iii) Robert's men
(iv) draw-latches
(v) sturdy beggars

And as these people are strange both in names and in their conditions, so do they speak a language proper only to themselves called *canting*, which is more strange. By none but the soldiers of these tattered bands is it familiarly or usually spoken, yet within less than fourscore years now past not a word of this language was known. The first inventor of it was hanged, yet left he apt scholars behind him who have reduced that into method which he on his death-bed (which was a pair of gallows) could not so absolutely perfect as he desired.

It was necessary that a people so fast increasing and so daily practising new and strange villainies should borrow to themselves a speech which, so near as they could, none but themselves should understand, and for that cause was this language which some call 'pedlars' French' invented, to th' intent that, albeit any spies should secretly steal into their companies to discover them, they might freely utter their minds one to another, yet avoid that danger. The language therefore of *canting* they study even from their infancy, that is to say from the very first hour that they take upon them the names of *kinchin coes* till they are grown *rufflers* or *upright men*, which are the highest in degree amongst them.

This word *canting* seems to be derived from the Latin verb *canto*, which signifies in English 'to sing' or 'to make a sound with words', that's to say 'to speak'. And very aptly may *canting* take his derivation *a cantando* 'from singing' because amongst these beggarly consorts, that can play upon no better instruments, the language of *canting* is a kind of music and he that in such assemblies can *cant* best is counted the best musician.

Now as touching the dialect or phrase itself, I see not that it is grounded upon any certain rules. And no marvel if it have none, for sithence both the father of this new kind of learning and the children that study to speak it after him have been from the beginning and still are the breeders and nourishers of all base disorder in their living and in their manners, how is it possible they should observe any method in their speech and especially in such a language as serves but only to utter discourses of villainies?

And yet even out of all that irregularity, unhandsomeness and fountain of barbarism do they draw a kind of form and in some words, as well simple as compounds, retain a certain salt tasting of some wit and some learning. As for example, they call a 'cloak' in the canting tongue a *togeman*, and in Latin *toga* signifies a 'gown' or an 'upper garment'. *Pannam* is 'bread', and *panis* in Latin is likewise 'bread'. *Cassan* is 'cheese', and is a word barbarously coined out of the substantive *caseus*, which also signifies 'cheese'. And so of others.

Then by joining of two simples do they make almost all their compounds. As for example, *nab* in the canting tongue is a 'head', and *nab cheat* is a 'hat' or a 'cap'. Which word *cheat*, being coupled to other words, stands in very good stead and does excellent service, for a *smelling cheat* signifies a 'nose', a *prattling cheat* is a 'tongue', *crashing cheats* are 'teeth', *hearing cheats* are 'ears'; *fambles* are 'hands', and thereupon a 'ring' is called *fambling cheat*; a *muffling cheat* signifies a 'napkin', a *belly cheat* an 'apron', a *grunting cheat* a 'pig', a *cackling cheat* a 'cock' or a 'capon', a *quacking cheat* a 'duck', a *lowing cheat* a 'cow', a *bleating cheat* a 'calf' or a 'sheep', and so may that word be married to many others besides.

The word *cove* or *cofe* or *cuffin* signifies a 'man', a 'fellow', etc., but differs something in his property according as it meets with other words, for a 'gentleman' is called a *gentry cove* or *cofe*, a 'good fellow' is a *bene cofe*, a 'churl' is called a *queer cuffin* (*queer* signifies 'naught' and *cuffin*, as I said before, a 'man') and in canting they term a 'Justice of Peace' (because he punisheth them, belike) by no other name than by *queer cuffin*, that's to say a 'churl' or a 'naughty man'; and so, *ken* signifying a 'house', they call a 'prison' a *queer ken*, that's to say an 'ill house'. Many pieces of this strange coin could I show you, but by these small stamps you may judge of the greater.

Now because a language is nothing else than heaps of words orderly woven and composed together, and that within so narrow a circle as I have drawn to myself it is impossible to imprint a dictionary of all the canting phrases, I will at this time not make you surfeit on too much but, as if you were walking in a garden, you shall only pluck here a flower and there another; which, as I take it, will be more delightful than if you gathered them by handfuls.

But before I lead you into that walk, stay and hear a canter in his own language making rhythms—albeit I think those charms of poesy which at the first made the barbarous tame and brought them to civility can upon these savage monsters work no such wonder. Yet thus he sings, upon demand whether any of his own crew did come that way, to which he answers 'Yes,' quoth he,

Canting Rhythms.

'Enough! With boozy cove maund nase,
Tower the patring cove in the darkman case,
Docked the dell for a copper make,
His watch shall feng a prounce's nab cheat,
Cyarum, by Salmon, and thou shalt peck my jeer
In thy gan, for my watch it is nase gear,
For the bene booze my watch hath a win, etc.'.

This short lesson I leave to be construed by him that is desirous to try his skill in the language, which he may do by help of the following dictionary; into which way that he may more readily come I will translate into English this broken French that follows in prose. Two canters having wrangled a while about some idle quarrel, at length growing friends, thus one of them speaks to the other, viz.

A Canter in Prose.

Stow you, bene cofe, and cut benar whids, and bing we to Romeville to nip a bung. So shall we have lower for the boozing ken, and when we bing back to the Deuce-a-ville we will filch some duds off the ruffmans or mill the ken for a lag of duds.

Thus in English.

Stow you, bene cofe,   hold your peace, good fellow
and cut benar whids,   and speak better words
and bing we to Romeville,   and go we to London
to nip a bung,   to cut a purse

So shall we have lower, so shall we have money
for the boozing ken, for the alehouse
and when we bing back, and when we come back
to the Deuce-a-ville, into the country
we will filch some duds, we will filch some clothes
off the ruffmans, from the hedges
or mill the ken, or rob the house
for a lag of duds, for a buck of clothes

Now turn to your dictionary; and because you shall not have one dish twice set before you, none of those canting words that are Englished before shall here be found, for our intent is to feast you with variety.

The Canter's Dictionary.

autem, a church
autem mort, a married woman
bung, a purse
bord, a shilling
half a bord, sixpence
booze, drink
boozing ken, an alehouse
bene, good
beneship, very good
bufe, a dog
bing awast, get you hence
caster, a cloak
a commission, a shirt
chates, the gallows
to cly the jerk, to be whipped
to cut, to speak
to cut bene, to speak gently
to cut bene whids, to speak good words
to cut queer whids, to give evil language
to cant, to speak
to couch a hogshead, to lie down asleep
drawers, hosen
duds, clothes
darkmans, the night

Deuce-a-ville,   the country
dup the jigger,   open the door
fambles,   hands
fambling cheat,   a ring
flag,   a groat
glaziers,   eyes
gan,   a mouth
gage,   a quart pot
grannam,   corn
gybe,   a writing
glimmer,   fire
jigger,   a door
gentry mort,   a gentlewoman
gentry cofe's ken,   a nobleman's house
harman beck,   a constable
harmans,   the stocks
heave a bough,   rob a booth
iark,   a seal
ken,   a house
lag of duds,   a buck of clothes
libbege,   a bed
lower,   money
lap,   butter, milk or whey
libken,   a house to lie in
lag,   water
lightmans,   the day
mint,   gold
a make,   a halfpenny
Margery prater,   a hen
maunding,   asking
to mill,   to steal
mill a ken,   rob a house
nosegent,   a nun
niggling,   companying with a woman
prat,   a buttock
peck,   meat
poplars,   pottage
prancer,   a horse
prigging,   riding
patrico,   a priest

pad, a way
quaroms, a body
ruff peck, bacon
Roger or *Tib of the buttery,* a goose
Romeville, London
Rome booze, wine
Rome mort, a queen
ruffmans, the woods or bushes
Ruffian, the Devil
stamps, legs
stampers, shoes
slate, a sheet
skew, a cup
Solomon, the Mass
stuling ken, a house to receive stolen goods
skipper, a barn
strommel, straw
smelling cheat, an orchard or garden
to scour the cramp-ring, to wear bolts
stalling, making or ordaining
trining, hanging
to tower, to see
win, a penny
yarum, milk

And thus have I builded up a little mint where you may coin words for your pleasure. The payment of this was a debt, for the Bellman at his farewell in his first round which he walked promised so much. If he keep not touch by tendering the due sum, he desires forbearance and if any that is more rich in this canting commodity will lend him any more or any better he will pay his love double. In the meantime receive this and, to give it a little more weight, you shall have a canting song wherein you may learn how this cursed generation pray or, to speak truth, curse such officers as punish them.

A Canting Song.

The Ruffian cly the nab of the harman beck!
If we maund pannam, lap or ruff peck
Or poplars of yarum, he cuts 'Bing to the ruffmans!'

Or else he swears by the lightmans
To put our stamps in the harmans.
The Ruffian cly the ghost of the harman beck!
If we heave a booth we cly the jerk.

If we niggle or mill a boozing ken
Or nip a bung that has but a win
Or dup the jigger of a gentry cofe's ken,
To the queer cuffin we bing
And then to the queer ken to scour the cramp-ring,
And then to be trined on the chates in the lightmans.
The bube and Ruffian cly the harman beck and harmans!

Thus Englished.

The Devil take the Constable's head!
If we beg bacon, buttermilk or bread
Or pottage, 'To the hedge!' he bids us hie
Or swears 'by this light!' i' th' stocks we shall lie.
The Devil haunt the Constable's ghost!
If we rob but a booth we are whipped at a post.

If an alehouse we rob or be ta'en with a whore
Or cut a purse that has just a penny and no more
Or come but stealing in at a gentleman's door,
To the Justice straight we go
And then to the gaol to be shackled, and so
To be hanged on the gallows i' th' day-time. The pox
And the Devil take the Constable and his stocks!

We have canted, I fear, too much. Let us now give ear to the Bell-man and hear what he speaks in English.

The Bellman's Second Night's Walk

CHAPTER II

It was Term-time in Hell (for you must understand a lawyer lives there as well as here) by which means Don Lucifer, being the Justice for that County where the brimstone mines are, had better doings and more rapping at his gates than all the doctors and empirical quack-salvers of ten cities have at theirs in a great plague-time. The Hall where these Termers were to try their causes was very large and strongly built but it had one fault: it was so hot that people could not endure to walk there. Yet to walk there they were compelled by reason they were drawn thither upon occasions, and such jostling there was of one another that it would have grieved any man to be in the throngs amongst 'em. Nothing could be heard but noise and nothing of that noise be understood but that it was a sound as of men in a kingdom when on a sudden it is in an uproar. Everyone brabbled with him that he walked with, or if he did but tell his tale to his council he was so eager in the very delivery of that tale that you would have sworn he did brabble. And such gnashing of teeth there was when adversaries met together that the filing of ten thousand saws cannot yield a sound more horrible.

The Judge of the Court had a devilish countenance, and as cruel he was in punishing those that were condemned by law as he was crabbed in his looks whilst he sat to hear their trials. But albeit there was no pity to be expected at his hands, yet was he so upright in justice that none could ever fasten bribe upon him, for he was ready and willing to hear the cries of all comers. Neither durst any pleader at the infernal bar or any officer of the Court exact any fee of plaintiffs and such as complained of wrongs and were oppressed, but only they paid that were the wrong-doers—those would they see damned ere they should get out of their fingers. Such fellows they were, appointed to vex at the very soul.

The matters that here were put in suit were more than could be bred in twenty vacations. Yet should a man be despatched out of hand.

In one Term he had his judgment, for here they never stand upon returns but presently come to trial. The causes decided here are many, the clients that complain many, the counsellors that plead till they be hoarse many, the attorneys that run up and down infinite, the Clerks of the Court not to be numbered. All these have their hands full. Day and night are they so plagued with the bawling of clients that they never can rest.

The ink wherewith they write is the blood of conjurors. They have no paper, but all things are engrossed in parchment, and that parchment is made of scriveners' skins flayed off after they have been punished for forgery. Their standishes are the skulls of usurers; their pens the bones of unconscionable brokers and hard-hearted creditors that have made dice of other men's bones, or else of perjured executors and blind overseers that have eaten up widows and orphans to the bare bones, and those pens are made of purpose without nibs because they may cast ink but slowly, in mockery of those who in their lifetime were slow in yielding drops of pity.

Would you know what actions are tried here? I will but turn over the records and read them unto you as they hang upon the file. The courtier is sued here and condemned for riots. The soldier is sued here and condemned for murders. The scholar is sued here and condemned for heresies. The citizen is sued here and condemned for the City-sins, [their wives for pride and servants for stealth]. The farmer is sued here upon penal statutes and condemned for spoiling the markets. Actions of battery are brought against swaggerers, and here they are bound to the peace. Actions of waste are brought against drunkards and epicures, and here they are condemned to beg at the grate for one drop of cold water to cool their tongues or one crumb of bread to stay their hunger; yet are they denied it. Harlots have process sued upon them here and are condemned to howling, to rottenness and to stench.

No 'Acts of Parliament' that have passed the 'Upper House' can be broken but here the breach is punished, and that severely and that suddenly. For here they stand upon no demurs; no *audita querela* can here be gotten; no writs of error to reverse judgment; here is no flying to a Court of Chancery for relief; yet everyone that comes hither is served with a *subpoena*. No, they deal altogether in this Court upon the *habeas corpus*, upon the *capias*, upon the *ne exeat regnum*, upon writs of rebellion, upon heavy fines (but no recoveries), upon writs of outlawry to attach the body forever, and last of all upon executions after judgment which, being served upon a man, is his everlasting undoing.

Such are the customs and courses of proceedings in the offices belonging to the Prince of Darkness. These hot doings hath he in his Termtimes.

But upon a day when a great matter was to be tried between an Englishman and a Dutchman, which of the two were the foulest drinkers, and the case being a long time in arguing by reason that strong evidence came in reeling on both sides (yet it was thought that the Englishman would carry it away and cast the Dutchman) on a sudden all was stayed by the sound of a horn that was heard at the lower end of the Hall. And everyone looking back, as wondering at the strangeness—'Room! room!' was cried and made through the thickest of the crowd for a certain spirit in the likeness of a post who made way on a little lean nag up to the Bench where Judge Rhadamanth with his two grim brothers Minos and Aeacus sat. This spirit was an intelligencer sent by Beelzebub of Barathrum into some countries of Christendom to lie there as a spy, and had brought with him a packet of letters from several liegers that lay in those countries for the service of the Tartarean their lord and master. Which packet being opened, all the letters, because they concerned the general good and state of those Low Countries in Hell, were publicly read. The contents of that letter which stung most and put them all out of their law cases were to this purpose:

'That whereas the Lord of the Fiery Lakes had his ministers in all kingdoms above the earth whose offices were not only to win subjects of other princes to his obedience but also to give notice when any of his own sworn household or any other that held league with him should revolt or fly from their duty and allegiance, as also discover from time to time all plots, conspiracies, machinations or underminings that should be laid, albeit they that durst lay them should dig deep enough, to blow up his great infernal city, so that if his horned regiment were not suddenly mustered together and did not lustily bestir their cloven stumps his territories would be shaken, his dominions left in time unpeopled, his forces looked into, and his authority which he held in the world contemned and laughed to scorn: the reason was that a certain fellow, the child of darkness, a common night-walker, a man that had no man to wait upon him but only a dog, one that was a disordered person and at midnight would beat at men's doors bidding them in mere mockery to look to their candles when they themselves were in their dead sleeps and, albeit he was an officer, yet he was but of light carriage, being known by the name of the Bellman of London, had of late not only drawn a number of the Devil's own kindred into question for their lives but had also, only by the help of the lantern and candle, looked into the secrets of the best trades that are taught in Hell, laying them open to the broad eye of the world, making them infamous, odious and ridiculous—yea, and not satisfied with doing this wrong to his Devilship, very spitefully hath he set them out in print, drawing their pictures so to the life that now a horse-stealer shall not show his head but a halter with the hangman's noose is ready to be fastened about it, a *foist* nor a *nip* shall not walk into a fair or a playhouse but every crack will cry "Look to your purses!", nor a poor common rogue come to a man's door but he shall be examined if he can cant. If this bawling fellow therefore have not his mouth stopped, the light angels that are coined below will never be able to pass as they have done but be nailed up for counterfeits, Hell will have no doings and the Devil be nobody.'

This was the lining of the letter, and this letter drave them all to a *nonplus* because they knew not how to answer it. But at last advice was taken, the Court brake up, the Term was adjourned by reason that the hell-hounds were thus plagued, and a Common Council in Hell was presently called how to redress these abuses.

The satanical synagogue being set, up starts the Father of Hell and Damnation and, looking very terribly with a pair of eyes that stared as wide as *The Mouth* gapes at Bishopsgate, fetching four or five deep sighs which were nothing else but the smoke of fire and brimstone boiling in his stomach and showed as if he were taking tobacco, which he oftentimes does, told his children and servants and the rest of the citizens that dwelt within the freedom of Hell and sat there before him upon narrow low forms that they never had more cause to lay their heads together and to grow politicians. He and they all knew that from all the corners of the earth some did every hour in a day creep forth to come and serve him—yea, that many thousands were so bewitched with his favours and his rare parts that they would come running quick to him. His dominions, he said, were great and full of people; emperors and kings in infinite numbers were his slaves; his Court was full of princes. If the world were divided, as some report, but into three parts two of those three were his; or if, as others affirm, into four parts in almost three of that four had he firm footing.

But if such a fellow as a treble-voiced Bellman should be suffered [with his night rimes] to pry into the infernal mysteries and into those black acts which command the spirits of the deep and, having sucked what knowledge he can from them, to turn it all into poison and to spit it in the very faces of the professors with a malicious intent to make them appear ugly and so to grow hateful and out of favour with the world: if such a conjuror at midnight should dance in their circles and not be driven out of them, Hell in a few years would not be worth the dwelling in. The great Lord of Limbo did therefore command all his black guard that stood about him to bestir them in their places and to defend the Court wherein they lived, threatening besides that his curse and all the plagues of stinking Hell should fall upon his officers, servants and subjects unless they either advised him how or took some speedy order themselves to punish that saucy intelligencer, the Bellman of London. Thus he spake and then sat.

At last a foolish devil rose up and shot the bolt of his advice, which flew thus far: that the Black Dog of Newgate should again be let loose and afar off follow the bawling Bellman to watch into what places he went and what deeds of darkness every night he did. *Hinc risus!* The whole synodical assembly fell a-laughing at this wiseacre, so that neither he nor his Black Dog durst bark any more.

Another, thinking to cleave the very pin with his arrow, drew it home to the head of wisdom, as he imagined, and yet that lighted wide, too. But thus shot his counsel: that the ghosts of all those thieves, cheaters and others of the damned crew who by the Bellman's discovery had been betrayed, were taken and sent westward should be fetched from those fields of horror where every night they walk disputing with Doctor Story, who keeps them company there in his corner-cap, and that those wry-necked spirits should have charge given them to haunt the Bellman in his walks and so fright him out of his wits. This devil for all his roaring went away neither with a plaudit nor with a hiss. Others stepped up, some pronouncing one verdict, some another. But at the last, it being put into their devilish heads that they had no power over him farther than what should be given unto them, it was thus concluded and set down as a rule in Court that some one strange spirit who could transform himself into all shapes should be sent up to London and, scorning to take revenge upon so mean a person as a bell-ringer, should thrust himself into such companies as in a warrant, to be signed for that purpose, should be nominated and, being once grown familiar with them, he was to work and win them by all possible means to fight under the dismal and black colours of the Grand Sophy, his lord and master. The fruit that was to grow upon this Tree of Evil would be great, for it should be fit to be served up to Don

Lucifer's table as a new banqueting dish, sithence all his other meats, though they fatted him well, were grown stale.

Hereupon Pamersiel the messenger was called, a passport was drawn, signed and delivered to him with certain instructions how to carry himself in this travel. And thus much was openly spoken to him by word of mouth:

'Fly, Pamersiel, with speed to the great and populous city in the west; wind thyself into all shapes: be a dog to fawn, a dragon to confound, be a dove—seem innocent, be a devil as thou art, and show that thou art a journeyman to Hell. Build rather thy nest amongst willows that bend every way than on tops of oaks whose hearts are hard to be broken. Fly with the swallow close to the earth when storms are at hand, but keep company with birds of greater talents when the weather is clear, and never leave them till they look like ravens. Creep into bosoms that are buttoned up in satin and there spread the wings of thine infection. Make every head thy pillow to lean upon, or use it like a mill only to grind mischief. If thou meetst a Dutchman, drink with him; if a Frenchman, stab; if a Spaniard, betray; if an Italian, poison; [if an Irishman, flatter;] if an Englishman, do all this.

'Haunt taverns; there shalt thou find prodigals. Pay thy twopence to a player; in his gallery may'st thou sit by a harlot. At ordinaries may'st thou dine with silken fools. When the day steals out of the world thou shalt meet rich drunkards. Under welted gowns search for threescore in the hundred; hug those golden villains—they shine bright and will make a good show in Hell. Shriek with a cricket in the brew-house and watch how they conjure there. Ride up and down Smithfield and play the jade there. Visit prisons and teach gaolers how to make nets of iron there. Bind thyself prentice to the best trades. But if thou canst grow extreme rich in a very short time honestly, I banish thee my kingdom—come no more into Hell! I have read thee a lecture; follow it. Farewell.'

No sooner was 'Farewell' spoken but the spirit to whom all these matters were given in charge vanished, the cloven-footed orator arose and the whole assembly went about their damnable business.

CHAPTER III

Gull Groping: how gentlemen are cheated at ordinaries.

The Devil's footman was very nimble of his heels, for no wild Irishman could outrun him; and therefore in a few hours was he come up to London, the miles between Hell and any place upon earth being shorter than those between London and St Albans to any man that travels from hence thither or to any lackey that comes from thence hither on the Devil's errands, but to any other poor soul that dwells in those Low Countries they are never at an end and by him are not possible to be measured.

No sooner was he entered into the City but he met with one of his master's daughters called Pride dressed like a merchant's wife who, taking acquaintance of him and understanding for what he came, told him that the first thing he was to do he must put himself in good clothes such as were suitable to the fashion of the time, for that here men were looked upon only for their outsides; he that had not ten pounds' worth of wares in his shop would carry twenty marks on his back; that there were a number of sumpter-horses in the City who cared not how coarsely they fed so they might wear gay trappings— yea, that some pied fools, to put on satin and velvet but four days in the year, did oftentimes undo themselves, wives and children ever after.

The spirit of the Devil's buttery, hearing this, made a leg to Pride for her counsel and, knowing by his own experience that every tailor hath his 'hell' to himself under his shop-board where he damns new Satin, amongst them he thought to find best welcome and therefore into Birchin Lane he stalks very mannerly, Pride going along with him and taking the upper hand. No sooner was he entered into the ranks of the linen armourers whose weapons are Spanish needles but he was most terribly and sharply set upon: every prentice boy had a pull at him. He feared they had been all sergeants, because they all had him by the back. Never was poor devil so tormented in Hell as he was amongst them. He thought it had been St Thomas his Day and that he had been called upon to be Constable, there was such bawling in his ears. And no strength could shake them off but that they must show him some suits of apparel, because they saw what gentlewoman was in his company, whom they all knew. Seeing no remedy, into a shop he goes, was fitted bravely and, beating the price, found the lowest to be unreasonable, yet paid it and departed—none of them, by reason of their crowding about him before, perceiving what customer they had met with. But now the tailor, spying the devil, suffered him to go, never praying that he would know the shop another time. But looking round about his warehouse if nothing were missing, at length he found that he had lost his conscience. Yet remembering himself that they who deal with the Devil can hardly keep it, he stood upon it the less.

The Fashions of an Ordinary.

The Stygian traveller being thus translated into an accomplished gallant with all accoutrements belonging—as, a feather for his head, gilt rapier for his sides and new boots to hide his polt-foot (for in Bedlam he met with a shoemaker, a mad slave that knew the length of his last)—it rested only that now he was to enter upon company suitable to his clothes. And knowing that your most selected gallants are the only tablemen that are played withal at ordinaries, into an ordinary did he most gentlemanlike convey himself in state.

It seemed that all who came thither had clocks in their bellies, for they all struck into the dining-room much about the very minute of feeding. Our new cavalier had all the eyes that came in thrown upon him as being a stranger, for no ambassador from the Devil ever dined amongst them before. And he as much took especial notes of them: in observing of whom and of the place, he found that an ordinary was the only rendezvous for the most ingenious, most terse, most travelled and most fantastic gallant, the very Exchange for news out of all countries, the only bookseller's shop for conference of the best editions; that if a woman to be a lady would cast away herself upon a knight, there a man should hear a catalogue of most of the richest London widows; and, last, that it was a school where they were all fellows of one form and that a country gentleman was of as great reckoning as the proudest Justice that sat there on the Bench above him, for he that had the grain of the table with his trencher paid no more than he that placed himself beneath the salt. [Here he heard fools prate, perceived knaves solicit and beheld wise men dumb.]

The Devil's intelligencer could not be contented to fill his eye only with these objects, and to feed his belly with delicate cheer, but he drew a larger picture of all that were there and in these colours. The voider having cleared the table, cards and dice (for the last mess) are served up to the board. They that are full of coin draw; they that have little stand by and give aim. They shuffle and cut on one side; the bones rattle on the other. Long have they not played but oaths fly up and down the room like hail-shot. If the poor dumb dice be but a little out of square, 'the pox!' and 'a thousand plagues!' break their necks out at window. Presently after, the four knaves are sent packing the same way, or else like heretics are condemned to be burnt.

In this battle of cards and dice are several regiments and several officers:

They that sit down to play are at first called 'Leaders'.

They that lose are the 'Forlorn Hope'.

He that wins all is the 'Eagle'.

He that stands by and ventures is the 'Woodpecker'.

The fresh gallant that is fetched in is the 'Gull'.

He that stands by and lends is the 'Gull Groper' [or 'Impost-Taker'.]

The Gull Groper.

This Gull Groper is commonly an old moneymonger who, having travelled through all the follies of the world in his youth, knows them well and shuns them in his age, his whole felicity being to fill his bags with gold and silver. He comes to an ordinary to save charges of housekeeping and will eat for his two shillings more meat than will serve three of the Guard at a dinner, yet swears he comes thither only for the company and to converse with travellers. It's a goldfinch that seldom flies to these ordinary nests without a hundred or two hundred pound in twenty-shilling pieces about him.

After the tearing of some seven pair of cards or the damning of some ten bale of dice, steps he upon the stage. And this part he plays: if any of the Forlorn Hope be a gentleman of means either *in esse* or *in posse* (and that the old fox will be sure to know, to half an acre) whose money runs at a low ebb, as may appear by his scratching of the head and walking up and down the room as if he wanted an ostler, the Gull Groper takes him to a side-window and tells him he's sorry to see his hard luck, but the dice are made of women's bones and will cozen any man; yet for his father's sake—whom he hath known so long—if it please him he shall not leave off play for a hundred pound or two. If my young ostrich gape to swallow down this metal (and for the most part they are very greedy, having such provender set before them) then is the gold poured on the board, a bond is made for repayment at the next quarter-day, when exhibition is sent in; and because it is all gold and cost so much the changing, the scrivener (who is a whelp of the old mastiff's own breeding) knows what words will bite, which thus he fastens upon him.

And in this net the Gull is sure to be taken howsoever. For if he fall to play again and lose, the hoary goat-bearded satyr that stands at his elbow laughs in his sleeve. If his bags be so recovered of their falling sickness that they be able presently to repay the borrowed gold, then Monsieur Gull Groper steals away of purpose to avoid the receipt of it. He hath fatter chickens in hatching; 'tis a fairer mark he shoots at. For the day being come when the bond grows due, the within-named Signior Avaro will not be within or, if he be at home, he hath wedges enough in his pate to cause the bond to be broken. Or else, a little before the day, he feeds my young master with such sweet words that, surfeiting upon his protestations, he neglects his payment, as presuming he may do more. But the law, having a hand in the forfeiture of the bond, lays presently hold of our young gallant with the help of a couple of sergeants, and just at such a time when old Erra Pater the Jew that lent him the money knows by his own Prognostication that the moon with the silver face is with him in the wane. Nothing then can free him out of the fangs of those bloodhounds but he must presently confess a judgment for so much money or for such a manor or lordship three times worth the bond forfeited, to be paid or to be entered upon by him by such a day or within so many months after he comes to his land. And thus are young heirs cozened of their acres before they well know where they lie.

The Woodpecker.

The Woodpecker is a bird that sits by upon a perch, too, but is nothing so dangerous as this vulture spoken of before. He deals altogether upon returns, as men do that take three for one at their coming back from Jerusalem, etc. For, having a jewel, a clock, a ring with a diamond, or any suchlike commodity, he notes him well that commonly is best acquainted with the dice and hath ever good luck. To him he offers his prize, rating it at ten or fifteen pound when haply 'tis not worth above six, and for it he bargains to receive five shillings or ten shillings, according as it is in value, at every hand, second, third or fourth hand he draws; by which means he perhaps in a short time makes that yield him forty or fifty pound which cost not half twenty. Many of these merchant-venturers sail from ordinary to ordinary, being sure always to make saving voyages when they that put in ten times more than they, are for the most part losers.

The Gull.

Now if either the Leaders or the Forlorn Hope or any of the rest chance to hear of a young freshwater soldier that never before followed these strange wars and yet hath a charge, newly given him by the old fellow Soldado Vecchio his father when Death had shot him into the grave, of some ten or twelve thousand in ready money, besides so many hundreds a year, first are scouts sent out to discover his lodging. That known, some lie in ambush to note what apothecary's shop he resorts to every morning, or in what tobacco-shop in Fleet St he takes a pipe of smoke in the afternoon. That fort which the puny holds is sure to be beleaguered by the whole troop of the old weather-beaten gallants, amongst whom some one whose wit is thought to be of a better block for his head than the rest is appointed to single out our novice. And, after some four or five days spent in compliment, our heir to seven hundred a year is drawn to an ordinary, into which he no sooner enters but all the old ones in that nest flutter about him, embrace, protest, kiss the hand, congé to the very garter, and in the end (to show that he is no small fool but that he knows his father left him not so much money for nothing) the young cub suffers himself to be drawn to the stake.

To flesh him, Fortune and the dice, or rather the false dice that cozen Fortune and make a fool of him too, shall so favour him that he marches away from a battle or two the only winner. But afterwards, let him play how warily soever he can, the damned dice shall cross him, and his silver crosses shall bless those that play against him. For even they that seem dearest to his bosom shall first be ready and be the foremost to enter with the other Leaders into conspiracy how to make spoil of his golden bags. By such ransacking of citizens' sons' wealth the Leaders maintain themselves brave. The Forlorn Hope that drooped before do now gallantly come on. The Eagle feathers his nest, the Woodpecker picks up his crumbs, the Gull Groper grows fat with good feeding, and the Gull himself, at whom everyone has a pull, hath in the end scarce feathers enough to keep his own back warm.

[To these there is another to be added no less pernicious than any, and indeed somewhat more in the Devil's favour by as much as the deceit is commonly covered with the greatest persons: and this is the 'Impostor' or 'Impost-Taker'. This fellow is ever of the greatest eminence and as an Atlas supports the ordinary on his shoulders. He looks for no favour from Heaven, for he will use no courtesy on earth; civil speech he accounts the fool's language, and rudeness he loves more than meat, drink or humanity. He cares not on whom he spits, whose cloak he tears with his spurs, nor whose name he dirties with foul reproaches. This Signior Glorius, being as it were the *corregidor* of the ordinary, as soon as the young Gull is fallen amongst these ravens, after he hath abused him some five or six times and made other fools bold to do him the like injury, seeing he hath possessed him with a fear of his humours and admiration of his valour, presently he falls into an insinuation with the young Gull and from a tyrant becomes a flatterer. No man then shall dare to do the Gull disgrace but he is his champion. He defends his carriage, makes his folly wisdom, his cowardice discretion, his impudence audacity, his unmannerliness courtly education, and all his simplicity a most imitable form of outlandish behaviour, so that the poor Gull, proud of his intimacy, hides himself under this Eagle's wing and thinks there is no Heaven but that to which his friendship bears him.

As soon as the Impostor perceives this, presently he animates the Gull to all courses of unthriftiness, especially to game—as to primero, gleek or the like, in which he dignifies his cunning so much that the Gull thinks himself a graduate ere he know ABC in the Devil's hornbook. Then to make him more valiant in his own undoing this Impostor, who is the loadstone that directs the Gull's compass, will be his half in game and, sitting close by his elbow so as he may look into his cards, having formerly made his match with a third person who is the opposite gamester and the Impostor's friend and half also, no game of likelihood comes into the Gull's hand but the Impostor by several signs tells it to the adverse party—as, such a motion with his glove for five and fifty, such a curling of his hair for prime, such a rubbing of his nose for nine and thirty, such a finger for such a number, and such a finger for such, so that the poor Gull shall not have a game that he will not discover.

When thus they have cheated him of all his substance, then the

Impostor lends him more money till the Gull's credit be on the uttermost tenter. Then he makes him take money for jewels, cloaks, garments or anything upon impost, which is to pay so much upon every stake till such a sum be raised or, if it be at dice, so much upon every main till such a sum be repaid. And having sucked whilst one drop of blood will come, the Impostor begins to quarrel in the Gull's behalf, and in that tumult game is broke off, all are dispersed and the Impostor and his companion share the Gull's goods between them.

There is also another which is called a 'Deluder'. This fellow for the most part is a man of substance. He commonly wears on the little finger of his left hand a fair table diamond or a square topaz which, turning inwards as he draws the cards, will discover every card he pulleth; and then, stopping those which are for his purpose, he maketh his game as sure as if he had leave to choose what cards him pleaseth. If this Deluder be not able to compass such a ring, then he will have a most excellent hatched silver rapier so purely polished and trimmed that no looking-glass can show any figure fairer. This rapier he lays cross his waist just under his left hand and, in it seeing what cards he draweth, makes the same use was spoke of the diamond. And thus Simplicity being made a lean fool and his Plain Dealing a beggar, knaves grow rich as the Devil and feed with the curses of undone people.]

The postmaster of Hell, seeing such villainies to go up and down in cloaks lined clean through with velvet, was glad he had such news to send over and therefore, sealing up a letter full of it, delivered the same to filthy-bearded Charon, their own waterman, to be conveyed first to the Porter of Hell and then by him to the Master Keeper of the Devils.

CHAPTER IV

Of Ferreting, or the manner of undoing gentlemen by taking up of commodities.

Hunting is a noble, a manly and a healthful exercise. It is a very true picture of war—nay, it is a war in itself, for engines are brought into the field, stratagems are contrived, ambushes are laid, onsets are given, alarums struck up, brave encounters are made, fierce assailings are resisted by strength, by courage or by policy. The enemy is pursued and the pursuers never give over till they have him in execution. Then is a retreat sounded; then are spoils divided; then come they home wearied but yet crowned with honour and victory.

And as in battles there be several manners of fight, so in the pastime of hunting there are several degrees of game. Some hunt the lion: and that shows as when subjects rise in arms against their king. Some hunt the unicorn for the treasure on his head: and they are like covetous men that care not whom they kill for riches. Some hunt the spotted panther and the freckled leopard: they are such as to enjoy their pleasures regard not how black an infamy sticks upon them. All these are barbarous and unnatural huntsmen, for they range up and down the deserts, the wilderness and inhabitable mountains. Others pursue the long-lived hart, the courageous stag or the nimble-footed deer; these are the noblest hunters and they exercise the noblest game; these by following the chase get strength of body, a free and undisquieted mind, magnanimity of spirit, alacrity of heart and an unwearisomeness to break through the hardest labours. Their pleasures are not insatiable but are contented to be kept within limits, for these hunt within parks enclosed or within bounded forests. The hunting of the hare teaches Fear to be bold and puts Simplicity so to her shifts that she grows cunning and provident. The turnings and cross-windings that she makes are emblems of this life's uncertainty: when she thinks she is furthest from danger it is at her heels, and when it is nearest to her the hand of Safety defends her. When she is wearied and has run her race, she takes her death patiently, only to teach man that he should make himself ready when the grave gapes for him.

All these kinds of hunting are abroad in the open field, but there is a close City hunting, only within the walls, that pulls down parks, lays open forests, destroys chases, wounds the deer of the land and makes such havoc of the goodliest herds that, by their wills who are the rangers, none should be left alive but the rascals. This kind of hunting is base and ignoble. It is the meanest, yet the most mischievous, and it is called 'Ferreting'. To behold a course or two at this did the light horseman of Hell one day leap into the saddle.

City Hunting.

This Ferret Hunting hath his seasons as other games have, and is only followed at this time of year: when the gentry of our kingdom, by riots having chased themselves out of the fair revenues and large possessions left to them by their ancestors, are forced to hide their heads like coneys in little caves and in unfrequented places or else, being almost windless by running after sensual pleasures too fiercely, they are glad, for keeping themselves in breath so long as they can, to fall to Ferret Hunting—that is to say, to take up commodities.

No warrant can be granted for a buck in this forest but it must pass under these five hands:

   (i) He that hunts up and down to find game is called the 'Tumbler'.
  (ii) The commodities that are taken up are called 'Purse-Nets'.
 (iii) The citizen that sells them is the 'Ferret'.
  (iv) They that take up are the 'Rabbit-Suckers'.
   (v) He upon whose credit these Rabbit-Suckers run is called the 'Warren'.

How the Warren is Made.

After a rain coneys use to come out of their holes and to sit nibbling on weeds or anything in the cool of the evening. And after a revelling when younger brothers have spent all or in gaming have lost all, they sit plotting in their chambers with necessity, how to be furnished presently with a new supply of money. They would take up any commodity whatsoever, but their names stand in too many texted letters already in mercers' and scriveners' books. Upon a hundred pounds' worth of roasted beef they could find in their hearts to venture, for that would away in turning of a hand; but where shall they find a butcher or a cook that will let any man run so much upon the score for flesh only?

Suppose, therefore, that four of such loose-fortuned gallants were tied in one knot and knew not how to fasten themselves upon some wealthy citizen. At the length it runs into their heads that such a young novice who daily serves to fill up their company was never entangled in any City lime-bush. They knew his present means to be good and those to come to be great. Him therefore they lay upon the anvil of their wits till they have wrought him like wax—or indeed till they have won him to do anything in wax for himself as well as for them. To slide upon this ice, because he knows not the danger, is he easily drawn, for he considers within himself that they are all gentlemen well descended, they have rich fathers, they wear good clothes, have been gallant spenders, and do now and then still let it fly freely; he is to venture upon no more rocks than all they—what then should he fear? He therefore resolves to do it, and the rather because his own exhibition runs low and that there lack a great many weeks to the quarter-day at which time he shall be refurnished from his father. The match being thus agreed upon, one of them that has been an old Ferret-monger and knows all the tricks of such Hunting seeks out a 'Tumbler', that is to say a fellow who beats the bush for them till they catch the birds—he himself being contented, as he protests and swears, only with a few feathers.

The Tumbler's Hunting Dry-Foot.

This Tumbler being let loose runs snuffing up and down close to the ground in the shops either of mercers, goldsmiths, drapers, haberdashers, or of any other trade where he thinks he may meet with a Ferret. And though upon his very first course he can find his game, yet to make his gallants more hungry and to think he wearies himself in hunting the more, he comes to them sweating and swearing that the City Ferrets are so coped—that's to say, how their lips are stitched up so close—that he can hardly get them open to so great a sum as five hundred pounds, which they desire. This herb, being chewed down by the Rabbit-Suckers, almost kills their hearts and is worse to them than dabbing on the necks to coneys. They bid him, if he cannot fasten his teeth upon plate or cloth or silks, to lay hold on brown paper or tobacco, Bartholomew-babies, lute-strings or hobnails or two hundred pounds in St Thomas onions, and the rest in money. The onions they could get wenches enough to cry and sell them by the rope, and what remains should serve them with mutton. Upon this, their Tumbler trots up and down again. And at last, lighting on a citizen that will deal, the names are received and delivered to a scrivener who, enquiring whether they be good men and true that are to pass upon the life and death of five hundred pounds, finds that four of the five are wind-shaken and ready to fall into the Lord's hands; marry, the fifth man is an oak and there's hope that he cannot be hewed down in haste. Upon him, therefore, the citizen builds so much as comes to five hundred pounds, yet takes in the other four for to make them serve as scaffold-ing till the frame be furnished; and if then it hold, he cares not greatly who takes them down. In all haste are the bonds sealed and the com-modities delivered. And then does the Tumbler fetch his second career, and that's this.

The Tumbler's Hunting Counter.

The wares which they fished for, being in the hands of the five shavers, do now more trouble their wits how to turn these wares into ready money than before they were troubled to turn their credits into wares. The tree being once more to be shaken, they know it must lose fruit, and therefore their factor must barter away their merchandise though it be with loss. Abroad into the City he sails for that purpose and deals with him that sold, to buy his own commodities again for ready money. He will not do it under £30 loss in the hundred. Other archer's bows are tried at the same mark, but all keep much about one scantling. Back therefore comes their carrier with this news that no man will disburse so much present money upon any wares whatsoever. Only he met by good fortune with one friend (and that friend is him-self) who for £10 will procure them a chapman—marry, that chapman will not buy unless he may have them at £30 loss in the hundred.

'Foh!' cry all the sharers. 'A pox on these fox-furred curmudgeons! Give that fellow, your friend, £10 for his pains and fetch the rest of the money.' Within an hour after, it is brought and poured down in one heap upon a tavern table, where making a goodly show as if it could never be spent, all of them consult what fee the Tumbler is to have for hunting so well and conclude that less than £10 they cannot give him; which £10 is the first money told out.

Now let us cast up this account. In every £100 is lost £30— which being five times £30 makes £150. That sum the Ferret puts up

clear besides his overpricing the wares. Unto which £150 lost add
£10 more which the Tumbler gulls them of and another £10 which he
hath for his voyage—all which makes £170; which deducted from
£500, there remaineth only £330 to be divided amongst five. So that
every one of the partners shall have but £66. Yet this they all put up
merrily, washing down their losses with sack and sugar, whereof they
drink that night profoundly.

[Nay, it hath been verily reported that one gentleman of great hopes
took up £100 in brown paper and sold it for £40, another £100 in
hobby-horses and sold them for £30, and £16 in joints of mutton and
quarters of lamb ready roasted and sold them for £3. *Hinc lacrimae!*
This was strange but not wonderful.]

How the Warren is Spoiled.

Whilst this fair weather lasteth and that there is any grass to nibble
upon, these Rabbit-Suckers keep to the Warren wherein they fattened.
But the cold day of repayment approaching, they retire deep into their
caves so that, when the Ferret makes account to have five before him
in chase, four of the five lie hidden and are stolen into other grounds.
No marvel, then, if the Ferret grow fierce and tear open his own jaws
to suck blood from him that is left; no marvel if he scratch what wool
he can from his back. The Purse-Nets that were set are all taken up and
carried away. The Warren therefore must be searched; that must pay
for all; over that does he range like a little lord. Sergeants, Marshal's
men and bailiffs are sent forth who lie scouting at every corner and
with terrible paws haunt every walk. In conclusion, the bird that these
hawks fly after is seized upon; then are his feathers plucked—his
estate looked into; then are his wings broken—his lands made over to
a stranger; then must our young son and heir pay £500 for which he
never had but £66, or else lie in prison; to keep himself from which he
seals to any bond, enters into any statute, morgageth any lordship,
does anything, says anything, yields to pay anything. And these City
storms, which will wet a man till he have never a dry thread about
him though he be kept never so warm, fall not upon him once or twice
but, being a little way in, he cares not how deep he wades. The greater
his possessions are, the apter he is to take up and to be trusted; the
more he is trusted, the more he comes in debt; the farther in debt, the
nearer to danger. Thus gentlemen are wrought upon; thus are they
cheated; thus are they Ferreted; thus are they undone.

CHAPTER V

*Falconers: of a new kind of hawking, teaching how to catch birds by
books.*

Hunting and hawking are of kin and therefore it is fit they should
keep company together. Both of them are noble games and recreations,
honest and healthful, yet they may so be abused that nothing can be
more hurtful. In hunting, the game is commonly still before you or
i' th' hearing and within a little compass. In hawking, the game
flies far off and oftentimes out of sight. A couple of rooks therefore,
that were birds of the last feather, conspired together to leave their nest
in the City and to flutter abroad into the country. Upon two lean
hackneys were these Doctor Doddypolls horsed, civilly suited that
they might carry about them some badge of a scholar.

The Devil's rank rider that came from the last City hunting, understanding that two such light horsemen were gone a-hawking, posts
after and overtakes them. After some ordinary highway talk he begins
to question of what profession they were. One of them, smiling scornfully in his face as thinking him to be some gull (and indeed such
fellows take all men for gulls who they think to be beneath them in
quality) told him they were 'falconers'. But the fox that followed them,
seeing no properties belonging to a falconer about them, smelt knavery,
took them for a pair of mad rascals and therefore resolved to see at
what these 'falconers' would let fly.

How to Cast up the Lure.

At last on a sudden says one of them to him, 'Sir, we have sprung
a partridge, and so fare you well!'—which words came stammering
out with the haste that they made, for presently the two foragers of
the country were upon the spur. Pluto's post, seeing this, stood still
to watch them and at length saw them in main gallop make toward a
goodly fair place where either some knight or some great gentleman
kept. And this goodly house belike was the 'partridge' which those
falconers had sprung. He, being loath to lose his share in this hawking,

and having power to transform himself as he listed, came thither as soon as they, but beheld all which they did invisibly.

They both like two knights errant alighted at the gate, knocked and were let in. The one walks the hackneys in an outward court as if he had been but squire to Sir Dagonet. The other, as boldly as St George when he dared the dragon at his very den, marcheth undauntedly up into the hall where, looking over these poor creatures of the house that wear but the bare blue coats (for *aquila non capit muscas*—what, should a falconer meddle with flies?), he only salutes him that in his eye seems to be a gentlemanlike fellow. Of him he asks for this good knight or so; and so it was that he is a gentleman come from London on a business which he must deliver to his own worshipful ear. Up the stairs does brave Mount Dragon ascend, the knight and he encounter, and with this staff does he valiantly charge upon him.

How the Bird is Caught.

'Sir, I am a poor scholar, and the report of your virtues hath drawn me hither, venturously bold to fix your worthy name as a patronage to a poor short discourse which here I dedicate, out of my love, to your noble and eternal memory.' This speech he utters barely.

The hawking pamphleteer is then bid to put on whilst his miscellanean Maecenas opens a book fairly apparelled in vellum with gilt fillets, and four-penny silk ribbon—at least—like little streamers on the top of a marzipan castle hanging dangling by at the four corners. The title being superficially surveyed, in the next leaf he sees that the author he hath made him one of his gossips, for the book carries his worship's name and under it stands an Epistle just of the length of a henchman's grace before dinner (which is long enough for any book, in conscience, unless the writer be unreasonable).

The knight, being told beforehand that this little sunbeam of Phoebus shining thus briskly in print hath his mite or atomy waiting upon him in the outward court, thanks him for his love and labour and, considering with himself what cost he hath been at and how far he hath ridden to come to him, he knows that patrons and godfathers are to pay scot and lot alike, and therefore to cherish his young and tender Muse he gives him four or six angels, inviting him either to stay breakfast or, if the sun-dial of the house points towards eleven, then to tarry dinner.

How the Bird is Dressed.

But the fish being caught for which our Heliconian angler threw out his lines, with thanks and legs and kissing his own hand he parts. No sooner is he horsed but his ostler, who all this while walked the jades and travels up and down with him like an undeserving player for half a share, asks this question: 'Straws or not?'

'Straws!' cries the whole sharer and a half.

'Away, then!' replies the first. 'Fly to our nest!' This 'nest' is never in the same town but commonly a mile or two off, and it is nothing else but the next tavern they come to. But the village into which they rode being not able to maintain an ivy-bush, an alehouse was their inn where, advancing themselves into the fairest chamber and bespeaking the best cheer in the town for dinner, down they sit and share before they speak of anything else. That done, he that ventures upon all he meets and discharges the paper bullets (for, to tell truth, the other serves but as a sign and is merely Nobody) begins to discourse how he carried himself in the action, how he was encountered, how he stood to his tackling and how well he came off. He calls the knight 'a noble fellow', yet they both shrug and laugh and swear they are glad they have gulled him.

More arrows must they shoot of the same length that this first was of, and therefore their trunk full of trinkets—that's to say, their budget of books—is opened again to see what leaf they are to turn over next; which whilst they are doing, the ghost that all this space haunted them and heard what they said, having excellent skill in the black art— that's to say, in picking of locks—makes the door suddenly fly open which they had closely shut. At his strange entrance they being some-what aghast began to shuffle away their books, but he knowing what cards they played withal offered to cut, and turned up two knaves by this trick.

'My masters,' quoth he, 'I know where you have been. I know what you have done. I know what you mean to do. I see now you are falconers indeed, but by the—' and then he swore a damnable oath— 'unless you teach me to shoot in this birding-piece I will raise the village, send for the knight whom you boast you have gulled, and so disgrace you. For your money I care not.'

The two freebooters, seeing themselves smoked, told their third brother he seemed to be a gentleman and a boon companion; they prayed him therefore to sit down with silence and, sithence dinner was not yet ready, he should hear all.

'This new kind of Hawking,' quoth one of them, 'which you see us use can afford no game unless five be at it, viz.

(i) He that casts up the 'Lure' is called the 'Falconer'.

(ii) The 'Lure' that is cast up is any idle pamphlet.

(iii) The 'Tercel-Gentle' that comes to the Lure is some knight or some gentleman of quality.

(iv) The 'Bird' that is preyed upon is money.

(v) He that walks the horses and hunts dry-foot is called a 'Mongrel'.

The Falconer and his Spaniel.

'The Falconer having scraped together certain small parings of wit, he first cuts them handsomely in pretty pieces and of those pieces does he patch up a book. This book he prints at his own charge, the Mongrel running up and down to look to the workmen and bearing likewise some part of the cost, for which he enters upon his half-share. When it is fully finished the Falconer and his Mongrel, or it may be two Falconers join in one—but, howsoever, it is by them revised what shire in England it is best to forage next. That being set down, the Falconers deal either with a herald for a note of all the knights' and gentlemen's names of worth that dwell in that circuit which they mean to ride, or else by enquiry get the chiefest of them, printing off so many Epistles as they have names, the Epistles Dedicatory being all one and vary in nothing but in the titles of their patrons.

'Having thus furnished themselves and packed up their wares, away they trudge like tinkers with a budget at one of their backs. Or it may be the circle they mean to conjure in shall not be out of London, especially if it be Term-time or when a Parliament is holden, for then they have choice of sweetmeats to feed upon. If a gentleman seeing one of these books dedicated only to his name suspect it to be a bastard that hath more fathers besides himself and, to try that, does defer the presenter for a day or two, sending in the meantime (as some have done) into Paul's Churchyard amongst the stationers to enquire if any such work be come forth and, if they cannot tell, then to step to the printer's—yet have the Falconers a trick to go beyond such Hawks, too, for all they fly so high, and that is this: the books lie all at the printer's but not one line of an Epistle to any of them (those bugbears lurk *in tenebris*). If then the spy that is sent by his master ask why they have no dedications to them Monsieur Printer tells him the author would not venture to add any to them all saving only to that which was given to his master until it was known whether he would accept of it or no.

'This satisfies the patron, this fetches money from him, and this cozens five hundred besides. Nay, there be other bird-catchers that use stranger quail-pipes. You shall have fellows, four or five in a covent that, buying up any old book, especially a sermon or any other matter of divinity, that lies for waste paper and is clean forgotten, add a new printed Epistle to it and, with an alphabet of letters which they carry about them being able to print any man's name for a dedication on the sudden, travel up and down most shires in England and live by this Hawking. Are we not excellent Falconers now?' quoth three half-shares.

'Excellent villains!' cried the Devil's deputy. By this the meat for dinner came smoking in, upon which they fell most tyrannically to it, yet for manners' sake offering first to the Bailiff of Beelzebub the upper end of the table. But he, fearing they would make a Hawk or a buzzard of him, too, and report they had ridden him like an ass as they had done others, out of doors he flung with a vengeance as he came.

O sacred Learning! Why dost thou suffer thy seven-leaved tree to be plucked by barbarous and most unhallowed hands? Why is thy beautiful maiden body polluted like strumpets' and prostituted to beastly and slavish Ignorance? O you base brood that make the Muses harlots, yet say they are your mothers! You thieves of wit, cheaters of art, traitors of schools of learning, murderers of scholars! More worthy you are to undergo the Roman *furca* like slaves, and to be branded i' th' forehead deeper than they that forge testaments to undo orphans! Such do but rob children of goods that may be lost, but you rob scholars of their fame, which is dearer than life. You are not worth an invective, not worthy to have your names drop out of a deserving pen; you shall only be executed in picture as they use to handle malefactors in France, and the picture, though it were drawn to be hung up in another place, shall leave you impudently arrogant to yourselves and ignominiously ridiculous to after-ages. In these colours are you drawn:

The True Picture of these
Falconers.

There be fellows
Of coarse and common blood, mechanic knaves,
Whose wits lie deeper buried than in graves
And indeed smell more earthy, whose creation
Was but to give a boot or shoe good fashion.
Yet these, throwing by the apron and the awl,
Being drunk with their own wit, cast up their gall
Only of ink and in patched, beggarly rhymes
As full of foul corruption as the times
From town to town they stroll in soul as poor
As th'are in clothes. Yet these at every door
Their labours dedicate. But as at fairs,
Like pedlars, they show still one sort of wares
Unto all comers with some filed oration.
And thus to give books now's an occupation.
One book hath sevenscore patrons. Thus desart
Is cheated of her due; thus noble Art
Gives Ignorance, that common strumpet, place;
Thus the true scholar's name grows cheap and base.

CHAPTER VI

Jacks of the Clockhouse: a new and cunning drawing of money from gentlemen.

There is another fraternity of wandering pilgrims who merrily call themselves 'Jacks of the Clockhouse' and are very near allied to the Falconers that went a-hawking before. The Clerk of Erebus set down their names too in his tables, with certain brief notes of their practices, and these they are.

The jack of a clockhouse goes upon screws and his office is to do nothing but strike. So does this noise (for they walk up and down like fiddlers) travel with motions, and whatsoever their motions get them is called 'striking'. Those motions are certain collections or witty inventions sometimes of one thing and then of another (there is a new one now in rhyme in praise of the Union). And these are fairly written and engrossed in vellum, parchment or royal paper, richly adorned with compartments and set out with letters both in gold and in various colours.

This labour being taken, the master of the motion hearkens where such a nobleman, such a lord or such a knight lies that is liberal. Having found one to his liking, the motion, with his patron's name fairly texted out in manner of a dedication, is presented before him. He receives it and, thinking it to be a work only undertaken for his sake, is bounteous to the giver, esteeming him a scholar and knowing that not without great travail he hath drawn so many little straggling streams into so fair and smooth a river; whereas the work is the labour of some other copied out by stealth, he an impudent, ignorant fellow that runs up and down with the transcripts, and every alehouse may have one of them hanging in the basest drinking-room if they will be but at the charges of writing it out. Thus the liberality of a nobleman or of a gentleman is abused; thus learning is brought into scorn and contempt; thus men are cheated of their bounty, giving much for that, out of their free minds, which is common abroad and put away for base prices.

Thus villainy sometimes walks alone as if it were given to melancholy. And sometimes knaves tie themselves in a knot because they may be more merry—as, by a mad sort of comrades whom I see leaping into the saddle, anon it will appear.

CHAPTER VII

Rank Riders: the manner of cozening innkeepers, postmasters and hackney-men.

There is a troop of horsemen that run up and down the whole kingdom. They are ever in a gallop; their business is weighty, their journeys many, their expenses great, their inns everywhere, their lands nowhere. They have only a certain freehold called Tyburn situate near London, and many a fair pair of gallows in other countries besides, upon which they live very poorly till they die, and die for the most part wickedly because their lives are villainous and desperate. But what race soever they run, there they end it; there they set up their rest; there is their last bait whither soever their journey lies. And these horsemen have no other names but 'Rank Riders'; to furnish whom forth for any journey, they must have riding-suits cut out of these four pieces:

   (i) The innkeeper or hackney-man of whom they have horses is called a 'Colt'.

   (ii) He that never alights off a rich farmer or country gentleman till he have drawn money from him is called the 'Snaffle'.

   (iii) The money so gotten is the 'Ring'.

   (iv) He that feeds them with money is called the 'Provender'.

These Rank Riders, like butchers to Romford Market, seldom go under six or seven in a company, and these careers they fetch: their purses being warmly lined with some purchase gotten before and they themselves well booted and spurred and in reasonable good outsides, arrive at the fairest inn they can choose either in Westminster, the Strand, the City or the suburbs. Two of them, who have clothes of purpose to fit the play, carrying the show of gentlemen, the other act their parts in blue coats as if they were their serving-men, though indeed they be all fellows. They enter all dirtied or dustied according as it shall please the highway to use them, and the first bridle they put into the Colt's mouth—that's to say, the innkeeper's—is at their coming in to ask aloud if the footmen be gone back with the horses.

'Tis answered, 'Yes'. Here the Rank Riders lie three or four days, spending moderately enough, yet abating not a penny of any reckoning to show of what house they come; in which space their counterfeit followers learn what countryman the master of the house is, where the ostlers and chamberlains were born and what other country gentlemen are guests to the inn. Which lessons being presently gotten by heart, they fall in study with the other general rules of their knavery, and those are: first, to give out that their master is a gentleman of such and such means, in such a shire (which shall be sure to stand far enough from those places where any of the house or any of the other guests were born); that he is come up to receive so many hundred pounds upon land which he hath sold; and that he means to inn there some quarter of a year at least.

This brass money passing for current through the house, he is more observed and better attended, is worshipped at every word. And, the easier to break and bridle the Colt, 'his worship' will not sit down to dinner or supper till the master of the house be placed at the upper end of the board by him.

In the middle of supper or else very early in the following morning comes in a counterfeit footman, sweatingly delivering a message that such a knight hath sent for the headmaster of these Rank Riders and that he must be with him by such an hour, the journey being not above twelve or fourteen miles. Upon delivery of this message—from 'so dear and noble a friend'—he swears and chafes because all his horses are out of town, curseth the sending of them back, offers any money to have himself, his cousin with him and his men but reasonably horsed. Mine host, being a credulous ass, suffers them all to get up upon him, for he provides them horses either of his own, thinking his guest to be a man of great account and being loath to lose him because he spends well, or else sends out to hire them of his neighbours, passing his word for their forthcoming within a day or two. Up they get and away gallop our Rank Riders as far as the poor jades can carry them.

The two days being ambled out of the world and perhaps three more after them, yet neither a supply of horsemen or footmen as was promised to be set eye upon, the lamentable innkeeper—or hackney-man, if he chance to be saddled for this journey, too—lose their Colt's teeth and find that they are made old arrant jades. Search then runs up and down like a constable half out of his wits upon a Shrove Tuesday and hue and cry follows after, some twelve or fourteen miles off round about London, which was the farthest of their journey as they gave out. But alas! the horses are at pasture fourscore or a hundred miles from their old mangers. They were sold at some blind drunken thievish fair, there being enough of them in company to save themselves by their Toll Book. The serving-men cast off their blue coats and cried 'All fellows!' The money is spent upon wine, upon whores, upon fiddlers, upon fools (by whom they will lose nothing) and the tide being at an ebb, they are as ready to practise their skill in horsemanship to bring Colts to the saddle in that town, and to make nags run a race of threescore or a hundred miles off from that place as before they did from London.

Running at the Ring.

Thus so long as horseflesh can make them fat they never leave feeding. But when they have beaten so many highways in several countries that they fear to be overtaken by tracers, then like soldiers coming from a breach they march fair and softly on foot—lying in garrison, as it were, close in some out-towns till the foul rumour of their villainies, like a stormy dirty winter, be blown over; in which time of lurking in the shell they are not idle neither but like snails they venture abroad, though the law hath threatened to rain down never so much punishment upon them. And what do they? They are not bees, to live by their own painful labours, but drones that must eat up the sweetness and be fed with the earnings of others. This, therefore, is their work: they carelessly enquire what gentlemen of worth or what rich farmers dwell within five, six or seven miles of the fort where they are ensconced, which they may do without suspicion, and having got their names they single out themselves in a morning and each man takes a several path to himself. One goes east, one west, one north and the other south, walking either in boots with wands in their hands or otherwise, for it is all to one purpose. And note this by the way, that when they travel thus on foot they are no more called Rank Riders but 'Strollers', a proper name given to country players that without socks trot from town to town upon the hard hoof.

Being arrived at the gate where the gentleman or farmer dwelleth, he boldly knocks, enquiring for him by name, and steps in to speak with him. The servant, seeing a fashionable person, tells his master there is a gentleman desires to speak with him. The master comes and salutes him but, eyeing him well, says he does not know him.

'No, sir,' replies the other, with a face bold enough, 'it may be so. But I pray, sir, will you walk a turn or two in your orchard or garden? I would there confer.' Having got him thither, to this tune he plays upon him.

How the Snaffle is Put on.

'Sir, I am a gentleman born to better means than my present fortunes do allow me. I served in the field and had command there but long peace, you know, sir, is the canker that eats up soldiers, and so it hath me. I lie here not far off in the country at mine inn where, staying upon the despatch of some business, I am indebted to the house in moneys, so that I cannot with the credit of a gentleman leave the house till I have paid them. Make me, sir, so much beholden to your love as to lend me forty or fifty shillings to bear my horse and myself to London, from whence within a day or two I shall send to you many thanks with a faithful repayment of your courtesy.'

The honest gentleman or the good-natured farmer, beholding a personable man, fashionably attired and not carrying in outward colours the face of a cogging knave, give credit to his words, are sorry that they are not at this present time so well furnished as they could wish; but if a matter of twenty shillings can stead him he shall command it, because it were pity any honest gentleman should for so small a matter miscarry.

Haply they meet with some chapmen that give them their own asking—but howsoever, all is fish that comes to net. They are the most conscionable market folks that ever rode between two panniers, for from forty they will fall to twenty, from twenty to ten, from ten to five—nay, these mountebanks are so base that they are not ashamed to take two shillings of a plain husbandman, and sometimes sixpence, which the other gives simply and honestly, of whom they demanded a whole fifteen.

In this manner do they dig silver out of men's purses all the day, and at night meet together at the appointed rendezvous, where all these Snaffles are loosed to their full length, the Rings which that day they have made are worn, the Provender is praised or dispraised as they find it in goodness—but it goes down all, whilst they laugh at all. And thus does a commonwealth bring up children that care not how they discredit her or undo her. Who would imagine that birds so fair in show and so sweet in voice should be so dangerous in condition?

But ravens think carrion the daintiest meat, and villains esteem most of that money which is purchased by baseness.

The Under-Sheriff for the County of the Cacodemons, knowing into what arrearages these Rank Riders were run for horseflesh to his master of whom he farmed the office, sent out his writs to attach them, and so narrowly pursued them that, for all they were well horsed, some he sent post to the gallows and the rest to several gaols. After which, making all the haste he possibly could to get to London again, he was waylaid by an army of a strange and new-found people.

Moon-Men: a discovery of a strange wild people very dangerous to towns and country villages.

A 'moon-man' signifies in English a 'madman' because the moon hath greatest domination above any other planet over the bodies of frantic persons. But these 'Moon-Men' whose images are now to be carved are neither absolute mad nor yet perfectly in their wits. Their name they borrow from the moon because, as the moon is never in one shape two nights together but wanders up and down heaven like an antic, so these changeable-stuff companions never tarry one day in a place but are the only, and the only base, runagates upon earth. And as in the moon there is a man that never stirs without a bush of thorns at his back, so these Moon-Men lie under bushes and are indeed no better than hedge-creepers.

They are a people more scattered than Jews and more hated—beggarly in apparel, barbarous in condition, beastly in behaviour, and bloody if they meet advantage. A man that sees them would swear they had all the yellow jaundice or that they were tawny-moors' bastards, for no red ochreman carries a face of a more filthy complexion. Yet are they not born so, neither has the sun burnt them so, but they are painted so. Yet they are not good painters neither, for they do not make faces but mar faces.

By a byname they are called 'gypsies'; they call themselves 'Egyptians'; others in mockery call them 'Moon-Men'. If they be Egyptians, sure I am they never descended from the tribes of any of those people that came out of the land of Egypt. Ptolemy King of the Egyptians, I warrant, never called them his subjects—no, nor Pharaoh before him. Look, what difference there is between a civil citizen of Dublin and a wild Irish kern, so much difference there is between one of these counterfeit Egyptians and a true English beggar. An English *rogue* is just of the same livery.

They are commonly an army about fourscore strong, yet they never march with all their bags and baggages together but like boothalers they forage up and down countries four, five or six in a company. As the Switzer has his wench and his cock with him when he goes to the wars, so these vagabonds have their harlots with a number of little children following at their heels, which young brood of

3. Gypsy Children on Horseback.

beggars are sometimes carried like so many green geese alive to a market in pairs of panniers, or in dossers like fresh fish from Rye that comes on horseback, if they be but infants. But if they can straddle once, then as well the she-rogues as the he-rogues are horsed seven or eight upon one jade, strongly pinioned and strangely tied together.

One shire alone and no more is sure still at one time to have these Egyptian lice swarming within it, for like flocks of wild geese they will ever more fly one after another. Let them be scattered worse than the quarters of a traitor are after he's hanged, drawn and quartered, yet they have a trick like water cut with a sword to come together instantly and easily again. And this is their policy: which way soever the foremost ranks lead, they stick up small boughs in several places to every village where they pass which serve as ensigns to waft on the rest.

Their apparel is odd and fantastic, though it be never so full of rents. The men wear scarfs of calico or any other base stuff, hanging their bodies like morris-dancers with bells and other toys to entice the country people to flock about them and to wonder at their fooleries, or rather rank knaveries. The women as ridiculously attire themselves and, like one that plays the rogue on a stage, wear rags and patched filthy mantles uppermost when the under-garments are handsome and in fashion.

The battles these outlaws make are many and very bloody. Whosoever falls into their hands never escapes alive, and so cruel they are in these murders that nothing can satisfy them but the very heart-blood of those whom they kill. And who are they, think you, that thus go to the pot? Alas! innocent lambs, sheep, calves, pigs, etc.! Poultry-ware are more churlishly handled by them than poor prisoners are by keepers in the Counter i' th' Poultry. A goose coming amongst them learns to be so wise that he never will be goose any more. The bloody tragedies of all these are only acted by the women who, carrying long knives or skeans under their mantles, do thus play their parts: the stage is some large heath or a fir-bush common far from any houses upon which, casting themselves into a ring, they enclose the murdered till the massacre be finished. If any passenger come by and, wondering to see such a conjuring circle kept by hell-hounds, demand what spirits they raise there, one of the murderers steps to him, poisons him with sweet words and shifts him off with this lie, that one of the women is fallen in labour. But if any mad Hamlet, hearing this, smell villainy and rush in by violence to see what the tawny devils are doing, then they excuse the fact, lay the blame on those that are the actors and perhaps, if they see no remedy, deliver them to an officer to be had to punishment. But by the way a rescue is surely laid and very valiantly, though very villainously, do they fetch them off and guard them.

The cabins where these land-pirates lodge in the night are the out-barns of farmers and husbandmen in some poor village or other, who dare not deny them for fear they should ere morning have their thatched houses burning about their ears. In these barns are both their cook-rooms, their supping-parlours and their bed-chambers, for there they dress after a beastly manner whatsoever they purchased after a thievish fashion. Sometimes they eat venison and have greyhounds that kill it for them, but if they had not they are hounds themselves and are damnable hunters after flesh—which appears by their ugly-faced queans that follow them, with whom in these barns they lie as swine do together in hogsties. These barns are the beds of incests, whoredoms, adulteries and of all other black and deadly damned impieties. Here grows the cursed Tree of Bastardy that is so fruitful; here are written the Books of all Blasphemies, Swearings and Curses that are so dreadful to be read.

Yet the simple country people will come running out of their houses to gaze upon them whilst in the meantime one steals into the next room and brings away whatsoever he can lay hold on. Upon days of pastime and liberty they spread themselves in small companies amongst the villages and, when young maids and bachelors—yea, sometimes old doting fools that should be beaten to this world of villainies and forewarn others—do flock about them, they then profess skill in palmistry and forsooth can tell fortunes. Which for the most part are infallibly true, by reason that they work upon rules which are grounded upon certainty: for one of them will tell you that you shall shortly have some evil luck fall upon you and, within half an hour after, you shall find your pocket picked or your purse cut. These are those Egyptian grasshoppers that eat up the fruits of the earth and destroy the poor cornfields; to sweep whose swarms out of this kingdom there are no other means but the sharpness of the most infamous and basest kinds of punishment. For if the ugly body of this monster be suffered to grow and fatten itself with mischiefs and disorder, it will have a neck so sinewy and so brawny that the arm of the law will have much ado

4. Gypsies on the Road.

to strike off the head, sithence every day the members of it increase and it gathers new joints and new forces by *priggers*, *anglers*, cheaters, *morts*, yeomen's daughters that have taken some by-blows and to avoid shame fall into their sins, and other servants both men and maids that have been pilferers, with all the rest of that damned regiment marching together in the first army of the Bellman who, running away from their own colours, which are bad enough, serve under these, being the worst.

Lucifer's *lanceprisado*, that stood aloof to behold the musterings of these hell-hounds, took delight to see them double their files so nimbly but held it no policy to come near them, for the Devil himself durst scarce have done that. Away therefore he gallops, knowing that at one time or other they would all come to fetch their pay in Hell.

CHAPTER IX

The infection of the suburbs.

The infernal promoter, being wearied with riding up and down the country, was glad when he had gotten the City over his head, but the City being not able to hold him within the freedom because he was a foreigner, the gates were set wide open for him to pass through and into the suburbs he went.

And what saw he there? More alehouses than there are taverns in all Spain and France! Are they so dry in the suburbs? Yes, pockily dry. What saw he besides? He saw the doors of notorious carted bawds like Hell-gates stand night and day wide open, with a pair of harlots in taffeta gowns like two painted posts garnishing out those doors, being better to the house than a double sign. When the door of a poor artificer, if his child had died but with one token of death about him, was close rammed up and guarded for fear others should have been infected, yet the plague that a whore-house lays upon a city is worse, yet is laughed at—if not laughed at, yet not looked into or, if looked into, winked at. The tradesman having his house locked up loseth his customers, is put from work and undone, whilst in the meantime the strumpet is set on work and maintained perhaps by those that undo the others. Give thanks, O wide-mouthed Hell! Laugh, Lucifer, at this! Dance for joy, all you devils!

Beelzebub keeps the register book of all the bawds, panders and courtesans and he knows that these suburb sinners have no lands to live upon but their legs. Every prentice passing by them can say 'There sits a whore!' Without putting them to their book they will swear so much themselves. If so, are not constables, churchwardens, bailiffs, beadles and other officers pillars and pillows to all the villainies that are by these committed? Are they not parcel bawds to wink at such damned abuses, considering they have whips in their own hands and may draw blood if they please? Is not the landlord of such rents the Grand Bawd, and the door-keeping mistress of such a house of sin but his under-bawd, sithence he takes twenty pounds rent every year for a vaulting-school which from no artificers living by the hardness of the hand could be worth five pound? And that twenty pound rent he knows must be pressed out of petticoats. His money smells of sin, the very silver looks pale because it was earned by lust.

How happy therefore were cities if they had no suburbs, sithence they serve but as caves where monsters are bred up to devour the cities themselves. Would the Devil hire a villain to spill blood? There he shall find him. One to blaspheme? There he hath choice. A pander that would court a matron at her prayers? He's there. A cheater that would turn his own father a beggar? He's there, too. A harlot that would murder her new-born infant? She lies in, there.

What a wretched womb hath a strumpet which, being for the most part barren of children, is notwithstanding the only bed that breeds up these serpents! Upon that one stalk grow all these mischiefs. She is the cockatrice that hatcheth all these eggs of evils. When the Devil takes the anatomy of all damnable sins he looks only upon her body. When she dies he sits as her coroner. When her soul comes to Hell all shun that there as they fly from a body struck with the plague here. She hath her door-keeper and she herself is the Devil's chambermaid.

And yet, for all this that she's so dangerous and detestable, when she hath croaked like a raven on the eves then comes she into the house like a dove: when her villainies, like the moat about a castle, are rank, thick and muddy with standing long together, then to purge herself is she drained out of the suburbs as though her corruption were there left behind her, and as a clear stream is let into the City.

What Armour a Harlot Wears
Coming out of the Suburbs
to Besiege the City within
the Walls.

Upon what perch then does she sit? What part plays she then? Only the Puritan. If before she ruffled in silks, now is she more civilly attired than a midwife. If before she swaggered in taverns, now with the snail she stirs not out of doors. And where must her lodging be taken up but in the house of some citizen whose known reputation she borrows or rather steals, putting it on as a cloak to cover her deformities? Yet even in that hath she an art, too, for he shall be of such a profession that all comers may enter without the danger of any eyes to watch them—as for example, she will lie in some scrivener's house and so under the colour of coming to have a bond made she herself may write *noverint universi*. And though the law threaten to hit her never so often, yet hath she subtle defences to ward off the blows. For if gallants haunt the house, then spreads she these colours: she is a captain's or a lieutenant's wife in the Low Countries and they come with letters from the soldier her husband. If merchants resort to her, then hoists she up these sails: she is wife to the master of a ship and they bring news that her husband's put in the Straits or at Venice, at Aleppo, Alexandria or Iskenderun, etc. If shopkeepers come to her with 'What do you lack?' in their mouths, then she takes up such and such commodities to send them to Rye, to Bristol, to York, etc., where her husband dwells. But if the stream of her fortunes run low and that none but apron-men launch forth there, then keeps she a politic sempster's shop or she starches them.

Perhaps she is so politic that none shall be noted to board her. If so, then she sails upon these points of the compass: so soon as ever she is rigged and all her furniture on, forth she launcheth into those streets that are most frequented, where the first man that she meets of her acquaintance shall without much pulling get her into a tavern. Out of him she kisses a breakfast and then leaves him. The next she meets does, upon as easy pulleys, draw her to a tavern again. Out of him she cogs a dinner and then leaves him. The third man squires her to a play, which being ended and the wine offered and taken (for she's no recusant, to refuse anything) him she leaves, too. And being set upon by a fourth, him she answers at his own weapon, sups with him and drinks *upsy Friese* till, the clock striking twelve and the drawers being drowsy, away they march arm in arm, being at every footstep fearful to be set upon by the band of halberdiers that lie scouting in rug gowns to cut off such midnight stragglers. But the word being given and 'Who goes there?' with 'Come before the Constable!' being shot at them, they vail presently and come, she taking upon her to answer all the billmen and their leader; between whom and her suppose you hear this sleepy dialogue:

'Where have you been so late?'

'At supper, forsooth, with my uncle here'—if he be well bearded, or 'with my brother'—if the hair be but budding forth, 'and he is bringing me home.'

'Are you married?'

'Yes, forsooth!'

'What's your husband?'

'Such a nobleman's man' or 'Such a Justice's Clerk'—and then names some Alderman of London to whom she persuades herself one or other of the Bench of Brown Bills are beholding.

'Where lie you?'

'At such a man's house.' *Sic tenues evanescit in auras*: and thus by stopping the Constable's mouth with sugar-plums, that's to say, whilst she poisons him with sweet words, the punk vanisheth. O Lantern and Candlelight, how art thou made a blind ass because thou hast but one eye to see withal! Be not so gulled, be not so dull in understanding! Do thou but follow aloof those two tame pigeons and thou shalt find that her new 'uncle' lies by all that night to make his kinswoman one of mine 'aunts'. Or if she be not in travail all night they spend some half an hour together. But what do they? Marry, they do that which the Constable should have done for them both in the streets—that's to say, commit, commit!

You guardians over so great a princess as this eldest daughter of King Brutus, you twice twelve fathers and governors over the noblest city: why are you so careful to plant trees to beautify your outward walks, yet suffer the goodliest garden within to be over-run with stinking weeds? You are the pruning knives that should lop off such idle, such unprofitable and such destroying branches from the vine. The beams of your authority should purge the air of such infection, your breath of justice should scatter these foggy vapours and drive them out of your gates as chaff tossed abroad by the winds.

But stay! Is our walking spirit become an orator to persuade? No, but the Bellman of London, with whom he met in this perambulation of his and to whom he betrayed himself and opened his very bosom (hereafter you shall hear) is bold to take upon him that speaker's office.

CHAPTER X

Of Jinglers, or the knavery of horse-coursers in Smithfield discovered.

At the end of fierce battles the only rendezvous for lame soldiers to retire unto is an hospital, and at the end of a long Progress the only ground for a tired jade to run in is some blind country fair where he may be sure to be sold. To those markets of unwholesome horseflesh, like so many kites to feed upon carrion do all the horse-coursers that roost about the City fly one after another. But whereas in buying all other commodities men strive to have the best, how great soever the price be, only the horse-courser is of a baser mind, for the worst horse-flesh so it be cheap does best go down with him. He cares for nothing but a fair outside and a handsome shape—like those that hire whores, though there be a hundred diseases within. He, as the other, ventures upon them all.

The first lesson therefore that a horse-courser takes out when he comes to one of these markets is to make choice of such nags, geldings or mares especially as are fat, fair and well-favoured to the eye. And because men delight to behold beautiful colours and that some colours are more delicate even in beasts than others are, he will so near as he can bargain for those horses that have the daintiest complexion, as the milk-white, the grey, the dapple-grey, the coal-black with his proper marks—as the white star in the forehead, the white heel, etc.—or the bright bay with the like proper marks also. And the goodlier propor-tion the beast carries or the fairer marks or colour that he bears are or ought to be watchwords, as it were, to him that afterwards buys him of the horse-courser that he be not cozened with an overprice for a bad pennyworth, because such horses, belonging for the most part to gentlemen, are seldom or never sold away but upon some foul quality or some incurable disease which the beast is fallen into. The best colours are therefore the best cloaks to hide those faults that most disfigure a horse. And next unto colour his pace doth oftentimes deceive and go beyond a very quick judgment.

Some of these horse-hunters are as nimble knaves in finding out the infirmities of a jade as a barber is in drawing of teeth and, albeit without casting his water, he does more readily reckon up all the aches, cramps, cricks and whatsoever disease else lies in his bones, and for those diseases seems utterly to dislike him. Yet if by looking upon the dial within his mouth he find that his years have struck but five, six or seven and that he proves but young, or that his diseases are but newly growing upon him if they be outward, or have but hair and skin to hide them if they be inward, let him swear never so damnably that it is but a jade, yet he will be sure to fasten upon him.

So then a horse-courser, to the merchant that out of his sound judgment buys the fairest, the best bred and the noblest horses, selling them again for breed or service with plainness and honesty, is as the cheater to the fair gamester. He is indeed a mere jadish none-opolitan and deals for none but tired, tainted, dull and diseased horses; by which means, if his picture be drawn to the life, you shall find every horse-courser for the most part to be in quality a cozener, by profession a knave, by his cunning a varlet, in fairs a haggling chapman, in the City a cogging dissembler and in Smithfield a common forsworn villain. He will swear anything, but the faster he swears the more danger 'tis to believe him. In one forenoon and in selling a jade not worth five nobles will he forswear himself fifteen times, and that for-swearing, too, shall be by equivocation. As for example, if an ignorant chapman coming to beat the price say to the horse-courser 'Your nag is very old' or 'Thus many years old' and reckon ten or twelve, he claps his hand presently on the buttock of the beast and prays he may be damned if the horse be not under five—meaning that the horse is not under five years of age, but that he stands under five of his fingers when his hand is clapped upon him.

These horse-coursers are called 'Jinglers'; and these Jinglers having laid out their money on a company of jades at some drunken fair, up to London they drive them and upon the market day into Smithfield bravely come they prancing. But lest their jades should show too many horse-tricks in Smithfield before so great an audience as commonly resort thither, their masters do therefore school them at home after this manner.

How a Horse-Courser Works upon a
Jade in his own Stable, to Make
him Serviceable for a Cozening
Race in Smithfield.

The glanders in a horse is so filthy a disease that he who is troubled with it can never keep his nose clean, so that when such a foul-nosed jade happens to serve a horse-courser he hath more strange pills than a pothecary makes for the purging of his head. He knows that a horse with such a quality is but a beastly companion to travel upon the highway with any gentleman. Albeit therefore that the glanders have played with his nose so long that he knows not how to mend himself, but that the disease, being suffered to run upon him many and sundry years together, is grown incurable, yet hath our Jingling mountebank Smithfield rider a trick to cure him five or six ways; and this is one of them.

In the very morning when he is to be rifled away amongst the gamesters in Smithfield, before he thrust his head out of his master's stable, the horse-courser tickles his nose, not with a pipe of strong tobacco, but with a good quantity of the best neezing powder that can be gotten, which with a quill being blown up into the nostrils, to make it work the better he stands poking there up and down with two long feathers plucked from the wing of a goose, they being dipped in the juice of garlic or in any strong oil and thrust up to the very top of his head so far as possibly they can reach, to make the poor dumb beast avoid the filth from his nostrils, which he will do in great abundance. This being done, he comes to him with a new medicine for a sick horse and, mingling the juice of bruised garlic, sharp biting mustard and strong ale together, into both the nostrils with a horn is poured a good quantity of this filthy broth which, by the hand, being held in by stopping the nostrils close together, at length with a little neezing more his nose will be cleaner than his master's the horse-courser, and the filth be so artificially stopped that for eight or ten hours a jade will hold up his head with the proudest gelding that gallops scornfully by him, and never have need of wiping.

This is one of the comedies a common horse-courser plays by himself at home, but if when he comes to act the second part abroad you would disgrace him and have him hissed at for not playing the knave well, then handle him thus: if you suspect that the nag which he would jade you with be troubled with that or any other suchlike

disease, gripe him hard about the weasand-pipe close toward the root
of the tongue and, holding him there so long and so forcibly that he
cough twice or thrice, if then after you let go your hold his chaps
begin to walk as if he were chewing down a horse-loaf, shake hands
with old Monsieur Cavaliero Horse-Courser but clap no bargain upon
it, for his jade is as full of infirmity as the master is of villainy.

*Other Gambols that Horse-Coursers
Practise upon Foundered
Horses, Old Jades,
etc.*

Smithfield is the stage upon which the mountebank English horse-
courser, advancing his banner, defies any disease that dares touch his
prancer, insomuch that if a horse be so old as that four legs can but
carry him, yet shall he bear the marks of a nag not above six or seven
years of age. And that counterfeit badge of youth he wears thus. The
horse-courser with a small round iron, made very hot, burns two
black holes in the top of the two outmost teeth of each side (the outside
of the horse's mouth upon the nether teeth, and so likewise of the
teeth of the upper chap which stand opposite to the nether) the quality
of which marks is to show that a horse is but young. But if the jade
be so old that those teeth are dropped out of his head, then is there a
trick still to be fumbling about his old chaps and, in that stroking his
chin, to prick his lips closely with a pin or a nail till they be so tender
that albeit he were a given horse none could be suffered to look into
his mouth (which is one of the best calendars to tell his age). But a
reasonable-sighted eye without help of spectacles may easily discover
this juggling because it is gross and common.

If now a horse having been a sore traveller happen by falling into a
cold sweat to be foundered so that, as if he were drunk or had the
staggers, he can scarce stand on his legs, then will his master before
he enter into the lists of the Field against all comers put him into a
villainous chafing by riding him up and down a quarter or half an hour
till his limbs be thoroughly heated. And this he does because so long
as he can discharge that false fire or that, being so cholericly hot, he
tramples only upon soft ground, a very cunning horseman shall hardly
find where his shoe wrings him or that he is foundered. And to blind
the eyes of the chapman the horse-courser will be ever tickling of him

with his wand, because he may not by standing still like an ass show of what house he comes.

If a horse come into the Field like a lame soldier halting, he has not crutches made for him as the soldier hath but, because you shall think the horse's shoemaker hath served him like a jade by not fitting his foot well, the shoe shall be taken off purposely from that foot which halts, as though it had been lost by chance. And to prove this, witnesses shall come in, if at least twenty or thirty damnable oaths can be taken, that the want of that shoe is only the cause of his halting. But if a horse cannot be lusty at legs by reason that either his hoofs be not good or that there be splints or any other eyesore about the nether joint, the horse-courser uses him then as cheating swaggerers handle novices—what they cannot win by the dice they will have it by foul play. And in that foul manner deals he with the poor horse, riding him up and down in the thickest and the dirtiest places till that dirt, like a ruffled boot drawn upon an ill-favoured gouty leg, cover the jade's infirmity from the eyes of the buyer.

How a Horse-Courser Makes a Jade that has no Stomach to Eat 'Lam-Pie'.

Albeit lamb-pie be good meat upon a table, yet it is so offensive to a horse's stomach that he had rather be fed a month together with musty oats than to taste it. Yet are not all horses bidden to this lamb-pie breakfast, but only such as are dieted with no other meat. And those are dull, blockish, sullen and heavy-footed jades. Whensoever therefore a horse-courser hath bought such a dead commodity as a lumpish slow jade that goes more heavily than a cow when she trots, and that neither by a sharp bit nor a tickling spur he can put him out of his lazy and dogged pace, what does he with him then? Only he gives him 'lam-pie'. That is to say, every morning when the horse-courser comes into the stable he takes up a tough round cudgel and never leaves fencing with his quarterstaff at the poor horse's sides and buttocks till with blows he hath made them so tender that the very shaking of a bough will be able to make the horse ready to run out of his wits. And to keep the horse still in this mad mood, because he shall not forget his lesson, his master will never come near him but he will have a fling at him. If he do but touch him, he strikes him; if he speaks to him, there is but a word and a blow; if he do but look upon him, the horse flings and takes on as though he would break through the walls or had been a horse bred up in Bedlam amongst mad folks.

Having thus gotten this hard lesson by heart, forth comes he into Smithfield to repeat it, where the rider shall no sooner leap into the saddle but, the horse-courser giving the jade, that is half scared out of his wits already, three or four good bangs, away flies Bucephalus as if young Alexander were upon his back. No ground can hold him, no bridle rein him in. He gallops away as if the Devil had hired him of some hackney-man and scuds through thick and thin as if crackers had hung at his heels. If his tail play the wag and happen to whisk up and down (which is a sign that he does his feats of activity like a tumbler's prentice, by compulsion and without taking pleasure in them) then shall you see the horse-courser lay about him like a thresher till with blows he make him carry his tail to his buttocks (which in him, contrary to the nature of a dog, is an argument that he hath mettle in him and spirit, as in the other it is the note of cowardice).

These and such other base jugglings are put in practice by the horse-coursers; in this manner comes he armed into the Field; with such bad and deceitful commodities does he furnish the markets. Neither steps he upon the Devil's stage alone, but others are likewise actors in the selfsame scene and sharers with him, for no sooner shall money be offered for a horse but presently one snake thrusts out his head and stings the buyer with false praises of the horse's goodness, another throws out his poisoned hook and whispers in the chapman's ear that upon his knowledge so much or so much hath been offered by four or five and would not be taken. And of these ravens there be sundry nests, but all of them as black in soul as the horse-courser with whom they are yoked is in conscience. This regiment of horsemen is therefore divided into four squadrons, viz.

(i) When horse-coursers travel to country fairs they are called 'Jinglers'.

(ii) When they have the leading of the horse and serve in Smithfield they are 'Drovers'.

(iii) They that stand by and coney-catch the chapman either with outbidding, false praises, etc. are called 'Goads'.

(iv) The boys, striplings, etc. that have the riding of the jades up and down are called 'Skipjacks'.

CHAPTER XI

Of Jack-in-a-Box, or a new kind of cheating, teaching how to change gold into silver; unto which is added a map by which a man may learn how to travel all over England and have his charges borne.

How many Trees of Evil are growing in this country! How tall they are! How mellow is their fruit, and how greedily gathered! So much ground do they take up and so thickly do they stand together that it seemeth a kingdom can bring forth no more of their nature. Yes, yes! there are not half so many rivers in Hell in which a soul may sail to damnation as there are black streams of mischief and villainy (besides all those which in our now two voyages we have ventured so many leagues up for discovery) in which thousands of people are continually swimming and every minute in danger utterly to be cast away.

The horse-courser of Hell, after he had dirtied himself with riding up and down Smithfield, and having his beast under him, galloped away amain to behold a race of five miles by a couple of running-horses upon whose swiftness great sums of money were laid in wagers. In which school of horsemanship, wherein for the most part none but gallants are the students, he construed out strange lectures of abuses. He could make large comments upon those that are the runners of those races, and could teach others how to lose forty or fifty pound politicly in the forenoon, and in the afternoon with the selfsame gelding to win a thousand marks in five or six miles' riding. He could tell how gentlemen are fetched in and made younger brothers, and how your new knight comes to be a cozen of this race. He could draw the true pictures of some fellows that diet these running-horses who for a bribe of forty or fifty shillings can by a false dye make their own masters lose a hundred pound in a race. He could show more crafty foxes in this wild goose chase than there are white foxes in Russia, and more strange horse-tricks played by such riders than Banks his curtal did ever practise—whose gambols, of the two, were honester. But because this sort of birds have many feathers to lose before they can feel any cold, he suffers them to make their own flight, knowing that prodigals do but jest at the stripes which other men's rods give them and never complain of smarting till they are whipped with their own.

In every corner did he find serpents engendering. Under every roof some impiety or other lay breeding. But at last perceiving that the most part of men were by the sorcery of their own devilish conditions transformed into wolves and, being so changed, were more brutish and bloody than those that were wolves by nature, his spleen leaped against his ribs with laughter, and in the height of that joy resolved to write the villainies of the world in folio and to dedicate them in private to his lord and master, because he knew him to be an open-handed patron, albeit he was no great lover of scholars. But having begun one picture of a certain strange beast called 'Jack-in-a-Box', that only (because the City had given money already to see it) he finished; and in these colours was Jack-in-a-Box drawn.

It hath the head of a man, the face well-bearded, the eyes of a hawk, the tongue of a lapwing which says 'Here it is!' when the nest is a good way off; it hath the stomach of an ostrich and can disgest silver as easily as that bird does iron. It hath the paws of a bear instead of hands, for whatsoever it fast'neth upon it holds. From the middle downwards it is made like a greyhound and is so swift of foot that if it once get the start of you a whole kennel of hounds cannot overtake it. It loves to hunt dry-foot and can scent a train in no ground so well as in the City, and yet not in all places of the City, but he is best in scenting between Ludgate and Temple Bar, and 'tis thought that his next hunting shall be between Lombard St and the Goldsmiths Row in Cheapside. Thus much for his outward parts; now shall you have him unripped and see his inward.

This Jack-in-a-Box or this devil in man's shape, wearing like a player on the stage good clothes on his back, comes to a goldsmith's stall, to a draper's, a haberdasher's, or into any other shop where he knows good store of silver faces are to be seen. And there drawing forth a fair new box hammered all out of silver plate, he opens it and pours forth twenty or forty twenty-shilling pieces in new gold. To which heap of worldly temptation thus much he adds in words: that either he himself or such a gentleman's man to whom he belongs hath occasion for four or five days to use forty pound but, because he is very shortly—nay, he knows not how suddenly—to travel to Venice, to Jerusalem or so, and would not willingly be disfurnished of gold, he doth therefore request the citizen to lend upon those forty twenty-shilling pieces so much in white money but for five or six days at most; and for his good will he shall receive any reasonable satisfaction. The citizen, knowing the pawn to be better than a bond, pours down forty pound in silver; the other draws it and, leaving so much gold in hostage, marcheth away with bag and baggage.

Five days being expired, Jack-in-a-Box according to his bargain, being a man of his word, comes again to the shop or stall at which he angles for fresh fish and, there casting out his line with the silver hook—that's to say, pouring out the forty pound which he borrowed, the citizen sends in or steps himself for the box with the golden devil in it. It is opened and the army of angels being mustered together, they are all found to be there. The box is shut again and set on the stall whilst the citizen is telling of his money. But whilst this music is sounding, Jack-in-a-Box acts his part in a dumb show thus: he shifts out of his fingers another box of the same metal and making that the former bears, which second box is filled only with shillings and, being poised in the hand, shall seem to carry the weight of the former, and is clapped down in place of the first. The citizen in the meantime, whilst this pit-fall is made for him, telling the forty pounds, misseth thirty or forty shillings in the whole sum, at which the Jack-in-a-Box starting back as if it were a matter strange unto him, at last making a gathering within himself for his wits, he remembers, he says, that he laid by so much money as is wanting of the forty pounds to despatch some business or other and forgot to put it into the bag again. Notwithstanding, he entreats the citizen to keep his gold still; he will take the white money home to fetch the rest and make up the sum; his absence shall not be above an hour or two, before which time he shall be sure to hear of him. And with this the little devil vanisheth, carrying that away with him which in the end will send him to the gallows—that's to say, his own gold and forty pound besides of the shopkeeper's which he borrowed—the other being glad to take forty shillings for the whole debt, and yet is soundly boxed for his labour.

This Jack-in-a-Box is yet but a chicken and hath laid very few eggs. If the hangman do not spoil it with treading, it will prove an excellent hen of the game. It is a knot of cheaters but newly tied; they are not yet a company. They fly not like wild geese in flocks but like kites single, as loath that any should share in their prey. They have two or three names (yet they are no Romans but arrant rogues) for sometimes they call themselves 'Jacks-in-a-Box' but, now that their infantry grows strong and that it is known abroad that they carry the philosopher's stone about them and are able of forty shillings to make forty pound, they therefore use a dead march, and the better to cloak their villainies do put on these masquing suits, viz.

(i) This art or sleight of changing gold into silver is called 'Trimming'.

(ii) They that practise it term themselves 'Sheep-Shearers'.

(iii) The gold which they bring to the citizen is called 'Jason's Fleece'.

(iv) The silver which they pick up by this wandering is 'White Wool'.

(v) They that are cheated by Jack-in-a-Box are called 'Bleaters'.

O Fleet St, Fleet St! How hast thou been trimmed, washed, shaven and polled by these dear and damnable barbers! How often hast thou met with these Sheep-Shearers! How many warm flakes of wool have they pulled from thy back! Yet if thy bleating can make the flocks that graze near unto thee and round about thee to lift up their eyes and to shun such wolves and foxes when they are approaching, or to have them worried to death before they suck the blood of others, these misfortunes are the less, because the neighbours by them shall be warned from danger. Many of thy gallants, O Fleet St, have spent hundreds of pounds in thy presence, and yet never were so much as drunk for it. But for every forty pound that thou layest out in this Indian commodity of gold thou hast a silver box bestowed upon thee to carry thy tobacco in it, because thou hast ever loved that costly and gentlemanlike smoke.

Jack-in-a-Box hath thus played his part. There is yet another actor to step upon the stage, and he seems to have good skill in cosmography, for he holds in his hand a map wherein he hath laid down a number of shires in England and with small pricks hath beaten out a path teaching how a man may easily, though not very honestly, travel from country to country and have his charges borne. And thus it is.

He that undertakes this strange journey lays his first plot how to be turned into a brave man, which he finds can be done by none better than by a trusty tailor. Working therefore hard with him till his suit be granted, out of the City, being mounted on a good gelding he rides upon his own bare credit, not caring whether he travel to meet the sun at his rising or at his going down. He knows his kitchen smokes in every county and his table covered in every shire. For when he comes within a mile of the town where he means to catch quails, setting spurs to his horse away he gallops with his cloak off (for in these besiegings of towns he goes not armed with any), his hat thrust into his hose as if it were lost, and only an empty pair of hangers by his side, to show that he has been disarmed. And you must note that this Hotspur does never set upon any places but only such where he knows by intelligence there are store of gentlemen, or wealthy farmers at the least. Amongst whom when he is come, he tells with distracted looks and a voice almost breathless how many villains set upon him, what gold and silver they took from him, what woods they are fled into, from what part of England he is come, to what place he is going, how far he is from home, how far from his journey's end or from any gentleman of his acquaintance; and so lively personates the lying Greek Sinon in telling a lamentable tale that the mad Trojans the gentlemen of the town, believing him, and the rather because he carries the shape of an honest man in show and of a gentleman in his apparel, are liberal of their purses, lending him money to bear him on his journey, to pay which he either offers his bill or bond, naming his lodging in London, or gives his word as he's a gentleman—which they rather take, knowing the like misfortune may be theirs at any time.

And thus with the feathers of other birds is this monster stuck, making wings of sundry fashions with which he thus basely flies over a whole kingdom. Thus doth he ride from town to town, from city to city, as if he were a landlord in every shire and that he were to gather rents up of none but gentlemen.

There is a twin brother to this false galloper, and he cheats innkeepers only or their tapsters by learning first what countrymen they are and of what kindred and then, bringing counterfeit letters of commendations from such an uncle or such a cousin, wherein is requested that the bearer thereof may be used kindly, he lies in the inn till he have fetched over the master or servant for some money; to draw whom to him he hath many hooks. And when they hang fast enough by the gills, under water our shark dives and is never seen to swim again in that river.

Upon this scaffold also might be mounted a number of quacksalving emperics who, arriving in some country town, clap up their terrible bills in the market-place and, filling the paper with such horrible names of diseases as if every disease were a devil and that they could conjure them out of any town at their pleasure, yet these beggarly

I

mountebanks are mere cozeners and have not so much skill as horse-leeches, the poor people not giving money to them to be cured of any infirmities but rather with their money buying worse infirmities of them.

Upon the same post do certain straggling scribbling writers deserve to have both their names and themselves hung up instead of these fair tables which they hang up in towns as gay pictures to entice scholars to them. The tables are written with sundry kinds of hands but not one finger of these hands, not one letter there, drops from the pen of such a false wandering scribe. He buys other men's cunning good cheap in London and sells it dear in the country. These swallows brag of no quality in them so much as of swiftness. In four and twenty hours they will work four and twenty wonders, and promise to teach those that know no more what belongs to an A than an Ass to be able in that narrow compass to write as fair and as fast as a country vicar, who commonly reads all the town's letters. But wherefore do these counterfeit masters of that noble science of writing keep such a flourishing with the borrowed weapons of other men's pens? Only for this, to get half the birds which they strive to catch into their hands—that's to say, to be paid half the money which is agreed upon for the scholar; and his nest being half filled with such goldfinches, he never stays till the rest be fledge but suffers him that comes next to beat the bush for the other half.

At this career the rider that set out last from Smithfield stopped and, alighting from Pacolet, the horse that carried him, his next journey was made on foot.

CHAPTER XII

The Bellman's second night-walk:
[night prizes of villainy.]

Sir Lancelot of the Infernal Lake or the Knight Errant of Hell, having thus like a young country gentleman gone round about the City to see the sights not only within the walls but those also in the suburbs, was glad when he saw Night, having put on the vizard that Hell lends her called darkness, to leap into her coach, because now he knew he should meet with other strange birds and beasts fluttering from their nests and crawling out of their dens. His prognostication held current and the foul weather which he foretold fell out accordingly.

For Candlelight had scarce opened his eye to look at the City like a gunner shooting at a mark but, fearfully, their feet trembling under them, their eyes suspiciously rolling from every nook to nook round about them and their heads, as if they stood upon oiled screws, still turning back behind them, came creeping out of hollow trees, where they lay hidden, a number of cozening bankrupts in the shapes of owls who, when the Marshal of light the sun went up and down to search the City, durst not stir abroad for fear of being shouted at and followed by whole flocks of undone creditors. But now when the stage of the world was hung in black they jetted up and down like proud tragedians. Oh, what thanks they gave to darkness! What songs they balladed out in praise of Night for bestowing upon them so excellent a cloak wherein they might so safely walk muffled! Now durst they, as if they had been constables, rap aloud at the doors of those to whom they owed most money and brave them with high words, though they paid them not a penny. Now did they boldly step into some privileged tavern and there drink healths, dance with harlots and pay both drawers and fiddlers after midnight with other men's money, and then march home again fearless of the blows that any shoulder-clapper durst give them.

Out of another nest flew certain murderers and thieves in the shapes of screech-owls who, being set on by the Night, did beat with their

249

bold and venturous fatal wings at the very windows of those houses and sat croaking at those very doors where in former times their villainies had entered.

Not far from these came crawling out of their bushes a company of grave and wealthy lechers in the shapes of glow-worms who, with gold jingling in their pockets, made such a show in the night that the doors of common brothelries flew open to receive them, though in the day-time they durst not pass that way for fear that noted courtesans should challenge them of acquaintance, or that others should laugh at them to see white heads growing upon green stalks.

Then came forth certain infamous earthy-minded creatures in the shapes of snails who, all the day-time hiding their heads in their shells lest boys should with two fingers point at them for living basely upon the prostitution of their wives' bodies, cared not now before candle-light to shoot out their largest and longest horns.

A number of other monsters like these were seen, as the sun went down, to venture from their dens only to engender with darkness but, Candlelight's eyesight growing dimmer and dimmer and he at last falling stark blind, Lucifer's watchman went stumbling up and down in the dark.

How to Wean Horses.

Every door on a sudden was shut. Not a candle stood peeping through any window. Not a vintner was to be seen brewing in his cellar. Not a drunkard to be met reeling. Not a mouse to be heard stirring. All the City showed like one bed, for all in that bed were soundly cast into a sleep. Noise made no noise, for everyone that wrought with the hammer was put to silence. Yet notwithstanding, when even the Devil himself could have been contented to take a nap, there were few innkeepers about the town but had their spirits walking.

To watch which spirits what they did, our spy that came lately out of the Lower Countries stole into one of their circles where, lurking very closely, he perceived that when all the guests were profoundly sleeping, when carriers were soundly snorting, and not so much as the chamberlain of the house but was laid up, suddenly out of his bed started an ostler who, having no apparel on but his shirt, a pair of slip-shoes on his feet and a candle burning in his hand like old Hieronimo, stepped into the stable amongst a number of poor hungry jades as if that night he had been to ride post to the Devil. But his journey not lying that way till some other time, he neither bridled nor saddled any of his four-footed guests that stood there at rack and manger but, seeing them so late at supper and knowing that to over-eat themselves would fill them full of diseases (they being subject to above a hundred and thirty already), he first without a voider after a most unmannerly fashion took away not only all the provender that was set before them but also all the hay at which before they were glad to lick their lips. The poor horses looked very ruefully upon him for this but he, rubbing their teeth only with the end of a candle instead of a coral, told them that for their jadish tricks it was now time to wean them. And so wishing them not to be angry if they lay upon the hard boards, considering all the beds in the house were full, back again he stole to his couch till break of day. Yet, fearing lest the sun should rise to discover his knavery, up he started and into the stable he stumbled, scarce half awake, giving to every jade a bottle of hay for his breakfast. But all of them, being troubled with the greasy tooth-ache, could eat none; which their masters in the morning espying, swore they were either sullen or else that provender pricked them.

This ostler for this piece of service was afterwards preferred to be one of the grooms in Beelzebub's stable.

Another Night-Piece Drawn in Sundry Colours.

Shall I show you what other bottoms of mischief Pluto's beadle saw wound upon the black spindles of the night in this his privy search? In some streets he met midwives running till they sweat and, following them close at heels, he spied them to be let in at the back-doors of houses seated either in blind lanes or in by-gardens; which houses had rooms builded for the purpose where young maids being big with child by unlawful fathers, or young wives in their husbands' absence at sea or in the wars, having wrestled with bachelors or married men till they caught falls, lay safely till they were delivered of them. And for reasonable sums of money the bastards that at these windows crept into the world were as closely now and then sent presently out of the world, or else were so unmannerly brought up that they never spake to their own parents that begot them.

In some streets he met servants in whose breast albeit the arrows of the plague stuck halfway, yet by cruel masters were they driven out of doors at midnight and conveyed to garden-houses where they either died before next morning or else were carried thither dead in their coffins, as though they had lain sick there before and there had died.

Now and then at the corner of a turning he spied servants purloining fardels of their masters' goods and delivering them to the hands of common strumpets.

This door opened and Lust with Prodigality were heard to stand closely kissing and, wringing one another by the hand, softly to whisper out four or five good-nights till they met abroad the next morning.

A thousand of these comedies were acted in dumb show and only in 'the private houses'; at which the Devil's messenger laughed so loud that Hell heard him and for joy rang forth loud and lusty plaudits. But being driven into wonder why the Night would fall in labour and bring forth so many villainies (whose births she practised to cover, as she had reason), because so many watchmen were continually called and charged to have an eye to her doings, at length he perceived that bats more ugly and more in number than these might fly up and down in darkness, for though with their leathern wings they should strike the very bills out of those watchmen's hands, such leaden plummets were commonly hung by sleep at all their eyelids that hardly they could be awakened to strike them again.

On therefore he walks with intent to hasten home, as having filled his table-books with sufficient notes of intelligence. But at the last, meeting with the Bellman and not knowing what he was because he went without his lantern and some other implements, for the man in the moon was up the most part of the night and lighted him which way soever he turned, he took him for some churlish hobgoblin, seeing a long staff on his neck, and therefore to be one of his own fellows. The bell-ringer, smelling what strong scent he had in his nose, soothed him up and, questioning with him how he had spent his time in the City and what discovery of land villainies he had made in this Island Voyage, the mariner of Hell opened his chart which he had lined with all abuses lying either east, west, north or south; he showed how he had pricked it, upon what points he had sailed, where he put in, under what height he kept himself, where he went ashore, what strange people he met, what land he had discovered and what commodities he was laden with from thence; of all which the Bellman drawing forth a perfect map, they parted.

Which map he hath set out in such colours as you see, though not with such cunning as he could wish. The pains are his own, the pleasure —if this can yield any pleasure—only yours on whom he bestows it.

To him that embraceth his labours he dedicates both them and his love; with him that either knows not how or cares not to entertain them, he will not be angry but only to him says thus much for a farewell:

> Siquid novisti rectius istis,
> candidus imperti; si non, his utere mecum.

FINIS

[*Here Endeth the Bellman.*]

[But, calling to mind the particular points of his commission, of which a principal one was that he should visit prisons in his progress, into a gaol our infernal catchpole the next morning conveyed himself. And looking to hear there nothing but sighing, lamenting, praying and cryings out of afflicted and forlorn creatures, there was no such matter but only a clamorous noise of cursing creditors, drinking healths to their confusion, swaggering, roaring, striking, stabbing one another as if that all desperviews of sixteen armies had been swearing together. Considering the desperate resolutions of some, he wished himself in his own territories, knowing more safety there than in this Hospital of Incurable Madmen, and could not till about dinner-time be persuaded but that the gaol was Hell, every room was so smoky with tobacco, and oaths flying faster about than tapsters could score up their frothy reckonings. But the time of munching being come, all the sport was to see how the prisoners, like sharking soldiers at the rifling of a town, ran up and down to arm themselves against that battle of hunger— some whetting knives that had meat, others scraping trenchers aloud that had no meat, some ambling downstairs for bread and beer meeting another coming upstairs carrying a platter more proudly aloft, full of powder beef and brewis, than an Irishman does his enemy's head on the top of his sword, every chamber showing like a cook's shop where provant was stirring, and those that had not provender in the manger nor hay in the rack walking up and down like starved jades new over-ridden in Smithfield. This set at maw being played out, all seemed quiet. The water under London Bridge at the turning was not more still.

But locking-up being come, that every cock must go to his roost, the music of that (in the judgment of the black spy) might well enough serve to rock Gran Beelzebub asleep. For nothing could be heard but keys jingling, doors rapping, bolts and locks barring in, gaolers hoarsely and harshly bawling for prisoners to their bed, and prisoners reviling and cursing gaolers for making such a hellish din. Then to hear some in their chambers singing and dancing, being half drunk, others breaking open doors to get more drink to be whole drunk, some roaring for tobacco, others raging and bidding Hell's plague on all tobacco because it has so dried up their mouths—with as many other frantic passions as there be several men: the very report of this antic dance would, he thought, be better than a comedy to his infernal audience, and therefore took especial note of all the mad passages.

In the end the Bedlamites being drowned more in beer than cares, and the Devil's fly buzzing about every prisoner's candle to spy what they did besides, he saw one sitting on his bed and reading a discovery which he had made in a long voyage; of which, whilst the other fell asleep, he stole the papers and, placing them together, sent them to the Bellman, who afterwards thus attired sent them into the world.]

CHAPTER XIII

Of a prison: certain discoveries of a prison by way of essays and characters written by a prisoner.

I am with dim water-colours to line a chart and in it to lay down the bounds of those tempestuous seas in which ten thousand are every day tossed, if not overwhelmed. Some do but cross over the waters and are sea-sick but not heart-sick: such are happy. To others it is longer than an East Indian voyage and far more dangerous, for in that if of threescore men twenty come home it is well, but in this if four-score of a hundred be not cast overboard it is a wonder.

More now than a three years' voyage have I made to these Infortu-nate Islands. A long lying have I had under hatches, during which time my compass never went true, no star of comfort have I sailed by, no anchor to cast out. Topsail, fore-sail, spritsail, mizzen, main-sheet, bowlines and drabblers are all torn by the winds, and the barque itself so weather-beaten that I fear it shall never touch at the *Capo Buona Speranza*. What have I hereby gotten but a sad experience of my own and others' miseries? I can only say what I have seen and tell what others have felt. This man hath spread a full sail and by help of skilful pilots made a safe arrival. That man, having as fair a wind, hath been cast away in the same haven. A fly-boat hath brooked that sea in which an argosy hath been drowned. For the greatest courages are here wrecked; the fairest revenues do here run aground; the noblest wits are here confounded.

So that I may call a prison an enchanted castle by reason of the rare transformations therein wrought, for it makes a wise man lose his wits, a fool to know himself. It turns a rich man into a beggar, and leaves a poor man desperate. He whom neither snows nor alps can vanquish but hath a heart as constant as Hannibal's—him can the misery of a prison deject. And how brave an outside soever his mind carries, open his bosom and you shall see nothing but wounds.

Art thou sick in prison? Then art thou sick, in health: into a con-sumption art thou fallen in thy best strength, when thy body is most able, fullest of blood, courage and vivacity. And when a fit of this ague takes thee, thou growest more tame than a bull tied to a wild fig-tree.

Art thou old and in prison? By a bad compass hast thou sailed that, having gone round about the troubles of the world without shipwreck, art now cast away in sight of shore.

Art thou young and in prison? Be not like a drunkard set in the stocks, insensitive of thine own harms. It is but a surfeit of riot, and a good diet may restore thee. Fortune hath cozened thee with false dice and therefore take heed how thou playest again. A happy chance may set up the young man, the old man never. Imprisonment is an audit-book to both: the one casts up his account and finds himself in arrear-ages irrecoverable; the other hath but mistook a sum and so made a false reckoning.

Hast thou gotten other men's goods into thy hands and so livest on them in prison? Thou deservest no pity, that tiest thine own hands and makest thyself a voluntary galley-slave only to wear golden fetters. The gallows whereon the poor thief hangs is fitter for thee. He robs but one, thou whole families. He is a felon to man only, thou to God and man. Every angel of gold that flies into thy coffers with such stolen wings will be turned into a devil and stand round about thy death-bed to torment thee and hale away thy soul to an everlasting prison. Imprisonment to thee is a sanctuary. Thou art a robber borne out by law, and art worthy by law to be borne to one execution more which may take off all the rest.

Art thou full of money in prison? Thou art a ship fraught full of wines in a tempest. It makes the Master Pilot and our owner drunk, and then all is cast away. Avoid these draughts, for riot in a prison is dancing in shipwreck, it is blasphemy in thunder and cursing in a time of pestilence. The name of a good fellow is thereby gotten, but thou payest too dear to a Lapland witch for a knot full of wind. The silver here saved is to thy wife a dowry, to thy children portions, to thyself a revenue. Prodigal expense in a gaol is to call for more wine in a tavern when thou canst not stand.

Art thou in prison and full of wants? Then art thou a field of unripe corn lodged by the wind and rain, thy glory defaced and thy golden ear emptied. Yet a sun may shine; and when it dries, ply it and thou mayest bring home a plentiful harvest.

Art thou poor and hast not health? Health in prison is wealth.

Art thou sick? Then art thou at the lowest step of poverty, having never so much. In a prison two armies bend their forces against thee—

Poverty and Death. They march in one and the same wing, Poverty in the front and Death in the rear. If thou escapest the first and breakest through his shocks, yet the other, which hath abroad a hundred, is here furnished with ten thousand arrows to pay thee home.

Art thou poor and in prison? Then art thou buried before thou art dead. Thou carriest thy winding-sheet on thy back up and down the house. Thou liest upon thy bier and treadest upon thy grave at every step. If there be any Hell on earth, here thou especially shalt be sure to find it. If there be degrees of torments in Hell, here shalt thou taste them. The body is annoyed with sickness, stench, hunger, cold, thirst, penury, thy mind with discontents, thy soul with inutterable sorrows; thine eye meets no object but of horror, wretchedness, beggary and tyranny.

Yet to thee that art in prison one comfort remaineth, being the same which makes banishment easy to a man exiled, for he shall find some, to what country soever he be confined, that live there for their pleasure; and so in a gaol are door-keepers, officers, messengers, etc., in respect of whom thy life comparatively is not miserable.

I make not an orchard but a private walk, or rather a small garden-plot set with pot-herbs for the kitchen. This which I write is not a book but a mere rhapsody of mine own disturbed cogitations. This first is no tree but a young plant new budded from whose tender branches thus much I gather: that imprisonment is a distillation, for at one and the same limbeck do we draw forth the bitter waters of men's oppressions with our own sorrows, and the sweet waters of patience if we can have the stomach to bear them.

CHAPTER XIV

Of prisoners.

Hope to escape this wreck, albeit thou swimmest sitting on a mast. The ocean hath both a shore and a bottom. Cities on fire burn out, of themselves. No misery is endless. It behoveth a prisoner to say as Caesar did to the pilot when he was afraid—'Thou carriest,' quoth he, 'Caesar'. So every generous mind ought to be armed with noble resolution to meet all storms of adversity and, having met them, to bid them welcome and, being once entertained, to be rid of them as wisely as he can. *Redime te captum quam queas minimo*—if thou canst purchase ransom, beat the market and buy as cheap as thou canst. But if thou must be forced to row in the galleys, settle to thine own oar with patience and, spitting in her face, let this triumph be thine— *maior sum quam cui possit Fortuna nocere*. Oppose a naked bosom against all her darts and, since thou art in the wolves' paws, be contented for saving of the flesh to have wool and skin torn off.

For know thou art not in a prison to dance on rushes, but to climb craggy rocks, to tread on thorns and to march over stony mountains; in which thy feet and mind must travel together and both keep a steady pace, so that thou must be armed to endure this battle with dauntless resolution, for this is a war that affordeth no rest and therefore we must not only play the manly but the wise soldiers—fight and stand sentinel, too.

But why is the name of a prison loathsome to thee? Is it because thou art cooped up under lock and key? Or is it because thou feelest wants? Hadst thou the air free as the fowls of it have, yet thy soul must be a prisoner to thy body and thy body commonly be a subject and slave to base and vicious passions. It is not imprisonment that is evil unto thee but the evil in thyself makes that so distasteful. A bird in the cage sings as sweetly as that in the field; and thou, being in prison, mayest so physic thy sick fortunes that thy mind never took hold of more noble liberty. Dost thou grieve because thou hast not sea-room enough? A poor wherry on the Thames is safer than a vast argosy dancing on the main ocean.

As for wants: hadst thou all things in the world, thou wouldst wish more and lack much more than thou wishest for. No king hath always content, and no poor man is ever sad. If thou hadst free scope to walk the streets, of some crosses thou wouldst complain. But in prison thou shouldst not fear nor fret to be hit with any bullet, because thou knowest how many can be shot against thee. What want dost thou grieve at? It is no other sun shines on thee but the same; no other air breathes in thy face but the same; no other earth bears thee but the same; and in the same shalt thou be buried. That mother will never change her love. None in this portion are disinherited for bastards.

But art thou in prison and do friends forsake thee? Yet do not thou forsake thyself. The farther they fly from thee, the closer stick thou to thine own guard.

Lie in an unwholesome bed, foul sheets and with a loathsome bed-fellow? There will be a lodging one day for thee where thou shalt have no cause to complain of these abuses.

Art thou clapped in irons and thrown currishly into a dungeon out of which the sun is shut? Care not, mourn not: there is an eye can pierce through locks and doors of iron to look upon and pity thee, and a hand which, without bribing the frozen palm of a gaoler, can turn all keys and through the narrowest grate can put in bread of comfort to feed thee whilst thou art drinking the waters of thine own affliction.

Varlets and catchpoles arrest thee? Fret not at it. If the Law hath power to whet an axe, she must pick out a hangman to smite. The mace that arresteth thee is in a Hand Omnipotent—that is thy sergeant —and His mace is the mace of office not of anger. Yes, it is of anger, but not of indignation. An action is brought against thee only to draw thee to a reckoning, and make thee know what thou owest to Heaven as well as to man. Thou art beaten with a rod not to draw blood but tears, not to drive thee into despair but amendment.

Summon a parley therefore and, although thou hast a heart never to yield unto thine enemy, yet make a rendition of that strong fort of resolution thou keepest, be it upon terms somewhat ignoble and inclining to loss. How valiantly soever thou couldst be armed even to the death to hold out for thine own proper end, yet have a care of those that are within thee. Few trees are shaken down by a storm and fall alone but others kiss the earth with them. I verily think that the bravest-spirited prisoner in the world would with a cheerful look thrust his neck into the yoke of adversity and manfully defy the threats of an insulting creditor, were not more veins to be cut than his own. But the poorest wretch dying in a prison hath someone or other lying in the coffin with him. With thine eye-strings, whosoever thou art, crack at the last gasp the heart-strings of a wife, of children, of a father or mother, of friends or allies. For these art thou bound in the bonds of nature to take pity of thyself and to hang out a flag of truce to thy bloody-minded creditor and for ransom to pay all, so thou mayest march away with life only.

But say thou hast none of these respects to tie thee yielding. Thou art a traitor to thy country if thou givest up thyself into thy enemy's hands when upon noble terms thy peace may be made. Live not in a prison but come forth that thou mayest benefit thyself. Die not there but live that thou mayest do service to thy country.

Pay thy debts so far as thou canst, because the most heavy debts that ever thy soul did owe were paid for thee. If one man would be chained to the galley all his lifetime to free all Christians from Turkish thraldom, have all the scorns scored on his head, all their blows on his back, endure all their hunger and thirst and be laden with all their irons: what a noble friend were such a man! How much should those be engaged to him whom he had freed from such slavery! Greater bonds than these have been cancelled for thy sake. One Man was surety for all the debts of all mankind; no bail else would be taken. The principal in the bond was let go; the surety only was looked for. He was arrested by Jews, sued and taken in execution. The Jews are figures of merciless creditors, He that answered the law an emblem of the poor debtor. He was imprisoned in the grave three days and watched by gaolers, but yet arose and went abroad in despite of His keepers—a type of comfort that the miseries of a prisoner are not everlasting. A day shall come when your crucifying Jews will behold Him whom they tyrannized over triumphing in glory. Be this a sovereign balm to the deepest wound of a prisoner.

I have hitherto fitted thee that art a prisoner with armour of proof against imprisonment and poverty. I will now give thee a buckler to bear off the blows of Death. And here it is: fear not to die in the hated bed of a prison sithence that last day rids thee of all men's oppressing malice and is the birthday of eternity.

CHAPTER XV

Of creditors.

A creditor hath two pair of hands, one of flesh and blood which nature gives him, another of iron which the law gives him. The first holds a dagger to defend, the second a sword to strike. Of these two the less hath power over the great, the soft warmth of the one being able to melt the hardness of the other. And that never happens but when grace and mercy kiss law and justice. Such days are seldom set down in common calendars; for a strange meridian is that almanac calculated in which they are found.

And yet I have seen a creditor in a prison weep when he beheld the debtor, and to lay out money of his own purse to free him. He shot a second arrow to find the first. But suppose he shot both away? Think you his sheaf was the less or quiver more empty? No. I believe he scattered a handful of corn and reaped a bushel. He laid out, and God paid. And so he got more by putting it to such account than the debt came to. Nay, by this means he became debtor to his debtor, with such an overplus does the Steward of the High Court love to pay honest arrearages. Had he received the money due to him it had been spent, and perhaps done him no good. But the interest being paid out of the King of Heaven His Custom House was an everlasting monopoly to his soul.

Thou that art a creditor wilt not believe this. Do not. But instead of that man's weeping, make thou thy debtor melt into tears. Drown him in the waters of his eyes; break his heart with his own sighs; laugh, at thy full table, that thou hast him fast and wilt make him famish; and, in bed to thy wife, swear to pluck money out of his throat or he shall lie by it. And when thou hast so spoken, pray that God would forgive thee thy debts as thou forgivest others! Dost thou not sleep upon the pillow of thine own damnation? That prayer to God is a curse upon thyself. Thou mock'st Him to whom thou prayest. But He will not mock thee.

Hast thou thy debtor in prison and wilt thou keep him there? Cast up thy accounts and upon the foot of it note what thou gainest. Thou seest a tree with all the fruit beaten off, and thou hewest it down because thou canst gather no more when all is gone. A building is ready to fall, and thou dost not underprop but undermine it and, when 'tis down, mak'st no use of the timber to save, but in merciless rage utterly consumest it in fire. What is this but to kill thy brother, having him at thy mercy? To wring a stranger out of his vineyard of purpose to starve him? To compel thy vassal to make more brick when straw and stuff is taken from him? Thou dost not for a few pieces of silver betray One better than thyself, but for one piece betrayest many. What a heavy score art thou to wipe off for thy cruelty! First, for the groans, sighs and bleeding heart of a wretched husband; then for the tears, wringing of hands and condolement of a languishing wife; next for the cries, starving and beggaring of innocent children; and, lastly, for the sad looks of undone servants.

This is the score, and here's the payment: as thou pluck'st thy debtor by the throat and criest out 'He shall pay the utmost penny!', so the Devil will one day take thee by thine and cast thee into utter darkness. How much better were it for thee to give all away and find an inestimable jewel than thus, by taking all away, to lose that jewel and thine own soul. If to kill a man by conspiracy be murder in the highest degree in the eye of the Lord Chief Justice of Heaven and Earth, what does he commit who by lingering tortures is killing of a man in prison a year, two, three—yea, seven—nay, half his lifetime? At what bar will he be arraigned? I protest by my hopes of eternal inheritance I would not be guilty of a man's death after this manner, to be heir to the greatest king in the world. This *homo-daemon*— man-devil—when he is once anthropophagized and longs for human flesh, no Fury is so cruel.

Man is a sacred thing, yet by thee a man is murdered in jest. For a body fashioned to his Maker's image, a pair of dice are taken by a despiteful creditor. Such a one is a cheater of life, not of living. These words 'He shall rot in prison!' or 'I will make dice of his bones!' are worthy of a Turk, unfit for a Christian. No man speaks them, but a monster; no man, but a devil; no devil, but a thing without a name worse than a devil who, having no power given him to torment, will snatch the Divine Vengeance into his own hand. How knowest thou, whilst thou threat'nest another, thyself may be stricken, and that tongue of thine cleave to thy throat for lying?

The same minute in the very Court of the King's Bench of Heaven bail can be taken to free that poor prisoner from that tyranny of rotting, no trick of clerks or keepers shall stop his passage. He will have his *quietus est* without tearing his heart in pieces for money by a sort of hungry lawyers. Thou swearest to make dice of his bones, but the grave shall claim them and make thee forsworn. He shall lie there in peace and thou stink above ground in the nostrils of God and man. He shall die happy, and thou live miserable, daily and nightly tormented with the fury of thine own conscience and his memory. Thou art but a fool to be cruel, for thou whettest a knife to cut thine own fingers, and shalt for saying 'I will make dice of his bones!' be as infamous as the Jews are hateful for casting dice for their Lord's garment. That garment which they diced for was but a senseless thing, but thou castest dice for a piece of thy Redeemer's body.

I have heard of some pirates, who carrying in their ship the rich vessels and vestments of the church broken and cut in pieces to make money of them, a storm hath risen and, within eye-sight of shore, ship and men have been swallowed up in the sea, a quick and just trial for such thieves. Destroyers of temples never die but by such vengeance. I protest before my Maker I would not in scorn strike the picture of Christ, break in pieces the image of a holy martyr—no, nor spoil or so much as deface the monumental grave of mine enemy. But more than sacrilege dost thou commit that ruinest a temple in which thy Builder dwells. And how many of these temples dost thou lay flat with the earth in one year? Nay, perhaps in one fatal Term.

Thou takest, with one clap of a varlet's hand, from the courtier his honour, from the lawyer his tongue, from the merchant the seas, from the citizen his credit, from the scholar his preferment, from the husbandman the earth itself, from all men—so much as thou canst—the very brightness and warmth of the sun in heaven.

Rufus, a King of England, to make one forest to hunt in, pulled down four abbeys and seventeen churches. He was slain with an arrow at his sport in the same forest. But thou destroyest so many cathedral churches in one man that huntest him to death in a prison. Rufus was punished in body; take heed lest thy soul pay for it.

Do not all these hammers beating on thy heart soften it? O metal of Hell! Here is the last blow I will give it. In being cruel to thy debtor thou art worse than a common hangman. He, before he strikes, begs forgiveness. Thou takest a pride to condemn when thou mayest save and, Nero-like, dancest when the most glorious city is on fire.

But it may be thy private estate is sick and weakly and thou, to physic it, art compelled to break into gardens of thine own which are locked from thee by other men's hands. In doing thus thou dost well. If any wear thy coat and thyself goest a-cold, thou art not to be blamed if thou pluck it from his shoulders. But if he that borrowed thy coat hath now worn it out and hath not a rag to cover him, wilt thou trample upon his naked bosom? If, with the Jew, instead of money thou demandest a pound of flesh next to thy debtor's heart, wouldst thou cut him in pieces? If he offer to give thee the bed he lies on, the dish he drinks in, his own chamber for thee to sleep in, and he to sit shivering in the cold; if he turn himself, wife and children as poor into the world as they are to go out of it—nay, not so rich, neither, by a sheet; and that he leave himself nothing, to pay thee all: wilt thou for all this suffer him to die in the hands of the law? Thou wilt? What art thou? A murderer!

I will teach thee to avoid that name and that sin. One step forward does it. Be merciful. Clemency in the eye of a judge sits not more sweetly than pity in the eye of a creditor. Next to a king's, this is her throne, because life and death are their sentence. To be tender-hearted to him that cannot pay thee—what is it? Is it any more than to lift a sick man upright upon his pillow and to give him a little more ease? That man may recover and do as much for thee.

Thou art born with tears in thine eyes for thine own miseries, and shouldst whilst thou stayest here be ever weeping at the miseries of others. For in thrusting forth such soft hands thou dost but save a man from drowning, lead a blind beggar into his way, lend a glimpse of a candle to one in darkness; it is but a warming at the fire, the giving of crumbs from thy board to the starved. Wouldst thou have the sun of mercy shine on thee? Be a burning-glass then, and those beams which glance on thy face to comfort thee, reflect thou back again for the comforting of others.

CHAPTER XVI

Of choice of company in prison.

Wouldst thou read the wonderful works of God? They are largeliest written in the seas. Get then thither. Wouldst thou dive into the secret villainies of man? Lie in a prison. The good may be made better there, but the bad are sure to be worse. It is a magic book which some, reading, feel no danger; others, but turning o'er a leaf, raise up devils to tear themselves in pieces.

Society is the string at which the life of man hangs. Without it, is no music; two in this make but an unison. Adam had his Eve. And every son of Adam hath a brother whom he loves. No chariot runs with one wheel; two make it steady; a third is superfluous; four too cumbersome. Thou must choose one and but one. Who walks alone, is lame. Men of all conditions are forced into a prison as all sorts of rivers fall into the sea and when two meet, the current is more swift and easy. No prisoner should be without his twin, considering they are born so fast. For if, like a tortoise, thou hidest thyself in a shell, thou art unknown both to thyself and others. No man can take his own colour; the tincture must be given by another.

My counsel then is that thou be sociable to all, acquainted with few. Trust not to any, or if any (I sing the first note) not above one; and first make trial what the vessel holds before thou pourest thyself into it. To be a bowl for every alley, and run into all companies proves thy mind to have no bias. It is like a traveller who in several countries takes up many lodgings and hath a thousand welcomes—but they are not to him, but his money.

If thou wilt consist and dwell by thyself, be not giddy but composed, for he that is everywhere is nowhere. The wound of imprisonment is not cured with many medicines. Remember that coming to a prison thou enterest heart-sick into an inn where thou hadst more need of juleps and restoratives than of a soft bed. A dangerous fever shakes thee, and therefore take heed what physician thou lightest upon.

Thou sailest not in the main ocean but in a creek full of quicksands, and comest safe to shore or art wrecked according as thou choosest thy pilot. Thy flight from the open world profits thee nothing. What thou art gone from is with thee. The iron grates of a prison let in the same vices which flew through the gates of a city. If thou carriest the cause of evils to a close prison, they lodge in the same bed thou art laid in. Mend therefore thy companion and thou healest thyself.

I have all this while but grinded colours; now will I draw the face of him with whom I wish thee that art a prisoner to hold conversation. Disparity of mind begets difference of manners; and that difference, dissension. Since therefore thy companion must of necessity grow on the same tree with thee, it is fit he should be of the same colour and taste of which thou thyself art. Let him be like a die—even, square, smooth and true, to run so near as thou canst neither higher nor lower than thou that art to run with him. If his fortunes be above thine, yet in the carriage of thy mind lift it up to a height to equal his fortunes. Is he bad whom thou takest by the hand? Do thy best to make him good. Is he good? Be thou ashamed to be otherwise.

Let him have some learning; he will be unto thee a winged hour-glass to send away the minutes of adversity merrily. Or if thou canst not get one with learning, be sure he comes furnished with wit; his tongue will be a sweet chime to rock thy cares and his own asleep. If he hath both wit and learning and yet want honesty, venture not in a sea so dangerous into him; thou shalt sail in a goodly ship full of holes. A talkative vainglorious fool will be a disease to thee. A common drunkard will lie heavier than an execution. Lean not to a willow that bows every way nor lie in the nest where a swallow builds—it is a chattering bird and tells abroad what is done at home. And no man, I think, would dwell in a house full of nothing but windows, for every eye to spy what he is doing.

But if thou hast suffered a man to sleep long in thy bosom, albeit his conditions be full of flaws, yet rather labour to piece and cement up his vices than to cast him off, lest it call thine own judgment and choice into question. All men have imperfections and being in prison we must not look to have them stars. This place is no orb for such constellations. Their shining here, if they have any, must be to themselves. Prisoners are base minerals, hidden and buried under earth and, as all metals have their ambition, we must be contented if there they aspire to lead or tin. Mines of gold and silver are to be found in the palaces of kings.

Thy companion haply may not be thy bedfellow. Call therefore him not thy bedfellow who is familiar with thee in thy chamber and scorns to look upon thee in the parlour; part sheets with such a man; the earthy smell of such dead familiarity turns thy bed into a grave wherein thou art buried alive. Choose therefore thy bedfellow as swans do their mates. If the female company with another, the male kills him. So if he that lies by thee all night loves other company better all day than thine, leave him; such sullen birds have either peacock's feathers or daw's feathers and, when pride and ignorance fly together, wit very seldom puts out a wing.

I have given thee a pair of balance to weigh thyself and thy friend in. It must be thy care to have a steady hand to hold them. As are the weights which thou throwest in, so look to have thy counterpoise set down. Art thou conversant with an atheist? Thy name will be enrolled on the same file. Is thy companion a miserable base fellow? Niggardliness will hold her fingers on thy purse-strings. The fellowship of prodigals will draw thee to riot, of adulterers to lust, of swearers to damned oaths, of pot-companions to drunkenness.

Acquaint thyself therefore not with the most but the best—not the best in clothes or money, but the best in doing best or doing well. Are there none such in prison? Keep company then with thyself, and in thy chamber talk with Plutarch or Seneca: the one will teach thee to live well, the other to die well.

CHAPTER XVII

Of visitants.

The country that holds this nation is narrow and therefore a little chorography will describe it. I take them to be Sybarites, who are inviting their guests to a banquet a twelvemonth before; and a year after, they come. I will therefore without circumferentor or any other geometrical instrument give you the true superficies or area of this Cyprian and loving island, for you must know it is no main.

The old acquaintance of a prisoner are people standing on the shore to behold a shipwrecked man labouring in the sea for life. Everyone pities his misery but, amongst all, to have one that well may do it, for strength of body, courage and art in swimming, to leap amongst the billows and save such a forlorn creature—there's the rare pattern of true compassion.

It is no hospitality for a rich man to open his gates and bid strangers that have new-dined to eat his meat. But to pluck a hungry beggar in—that's true charity. Seldom have you seen a bottle of hay brought to a horse in the pound. It is thought he cannot stay there long, and that he hath a body able enough to endure hunger. And therefore no provender is given him. So fares it with a prisoner.

Nullus ad amissas ibit amicus opes—from a ruinous house every man flies. They that ask every day abroad how thou dost when thou art in prison and protest they are sorry for thy misfortunes, yet never come to thee, are like idle passengers pressing about a barber's door when a man is carried in wounded. They peep in and climb about the windows, but dare not enter into the shop for fear they should swoon to see him dressed. A prisoner is as much beholden to such leap-frog acquaintance as a man shaken with an ague is to every gossiping woman he meets; he shall have five hundred medicines taught him for one disease, and not one worth the taking.

They practise one of our fencer's distances called 'the lunge' and cannot abide to come to 'the close'—'tis dangerous. But when the weapon of Fortune which beats thee is out of her hand and that, after struggling with her, thou takest breath and art at liberty: then, a hundred arms will be stretched wide open to meet thine. A mariner new come from sea is no more welcome home to his wife than thou art to them. Oaths thick as hail-shot fly into thy bosom that they were coming to thee above forty times and still were intercepted. But let thy answer be to them that those ships are strangely wind-bound that cannot hoist sails once in a year and get out of the haven. The witches of Norway belike sat upon the hatches.

A small end of a cord saves a man from drowning; and a finger of a friend to a prisoner is a full hand. They that cheer up a prisoner but with their sight are Robin Redbreasts that bring straws in their bills to cover a dead man in extremity. Such acquaintances grow like strawberries in a barren country; you shall hardly in a day gather a handful. Account those therefore in whose society thy purse hath been ever open and whose hands are shut to thee in prison but as dunghills on which the sun hath shined; for his golden beams they pay stinking and unsavoury smells. Do they hold thee as dead and buried in a gaol? When thou shalt rise again and walk, appear unto them but as a shadow.

As a sick man, when he hath no stomach, will make trial if he can eat, so when thou hast least want of money be most importunate to borrow of him whose mouth hath ever been full of golden promises to thee. If then, the tree being shaken, but one apple fall into thy lap, the taste of that is sweeter than of twenty before when thou hadst a full stomach. If a man do then but rake abroad his embers to give thee heat, and does it freely, it is a noble friend. He does best; and love him best, for it is a black swan. But put not the bucket too often into the well; brewers have sometimes complained that the Thames hath been without water.

In thy wants of money let thy pen neither dig the mine too often nor in too many places. Letters are but bladders to fill which a prisoner keeps a-puffing and blowing; but they to whom they are sent let all out in the very opening. Papers are beggars' rags and not regarded. As lame soldiers, so are prisoners answered with one word—'I have not for you'. Letters are a meat only to make hope fat and to starve a prisoner.

How quickly is this maze of friends trodden out! Why should I wind any more upon this bottom when a whole kingdom can scarce afford stuff to do it? Of such pearls 'tis hard to make a bracelet to go about a man's arm. And therefore till I find a shell full of them I will string no more.

CHAPTER XVIII

Of gaolers.

As laws are the foundation on which kingdoms are grounded, so when that ground fails there follows a ruin. If therefore a member be infected, *ense recidendum est*: spare not the cutting of a hand to save a heart. To keep the sick from the sound were prisons invented, for a man in debt hath the sickness of the law upon him.

If creditors had not iron nets to fish for their money, all men in the world would still borrow but never pay. And that's the cause Justice is pictured with a sword in the one hand and a pair of balance in the other. The scales weigh out the money she lends, and if you keep not your day she must give you a cut to remember it.

She is likewise painted blind. Some say it is her own emblem against bribery, but I think rather she has lent her eyes to so many of her ministers that now she wants them herself. Of which rank a keeper of a prison, being one that most is in need of eyes and in need of most eyes, her sight doth he borrow and it may be her sword, too, with which if sometimes he strikes, the blow is to be borne because he is the executing hand of the law.

He that keeps a prison walks continually in a whirlwind and would lose his very cloak from his back, clap he not it close to his body. He must struggle and wrestle and blow and all little enough to get through, and shall be sure evermore to be in a cold sweat. It is no wonder therefore if an inclination born with innated smoothness warp here and wax crabbed. He that sails to the Indies must look to be sunburnt, and he that lives amongst the Goths and Vandals will smell of their harsh conditions. An officer of this character hath not a bosom like a dove's all downy, but rather the back of a porcupine stuck full of quills ready to be shot every minute, because every minute he shall be made angry. The very place itself will undo all the wheels of the best-composed spirit and set them out of order. It cannot choose but make a wild disposition rough, and a temperate froward. Were his heart soft as wool, in this stone quarry it will soon grow to a flint to have fire stricken out of it.

VII   A Gaoler

VIII   Tipplers of All Professions

I mislike not that a king in his wrath hangs up rebels, that a Judge of the Bench be severe, that a soldier in the field play the lion, that a master for a due fault give due punishment, nor that the keeper of a prison bear a rugged brow. For he is not the keeper of a prison but the keeper of a forest full of lions, panthers and bears who, if they were not tied up, would worry him and undo themselves.

The prisoner cries out he lies upon an ill bed. But upon what bed sleeps his keeper? I think he sleeps upon none—I think he cannot sleep, for his pillow is not stuffed with feathers but with fears. Every prisoner sinks under the weight of his own debts, but his keeper feels the burden of all. And yet it may perhaps oftentimes fall out that in a wild fury thou may'st curse thy keeper for holding thee strictly in. Why dost thou rail at thy physician for giving thee pills, and yet art sick by a voluntary surfeit? Thou hast a rotten limb, and yet stabbest thy surgeon that comes to cut it off. If thou wilt compel a man to challenge thee into a fence school, thou must be content to bear blows; and if thou wilt needs run into debt, thou must at the next step be sure to run into danger. In prison thou art in Hell, and must look for none but horned devils to torment thee. There can be no music in that instrument which is ever out of tune. And therefore how sour soever the looks or conditions of thy keepers are, find not fault with them, for they are their own and not to be altered.

The favour of a prison-keeper is like smoke out of Cold Harbour chimneys, scarcely seen once in a year. He is a bell in a time of sickness that more often rings out for burials than divine service. If his eye chance to glance out pity, it is but a painted gallipot in an apothecary's shop containing that in it that is able to kill thee. And yet notwithstanding thou art continually to handle nettles, thou may'st so touch them that they shall never sting thee.

If thou walkest abroad with a keeper, use him friendly but not respectively. So manage him that he may think himself beholden to thee, not thou to him. For howsoever he fawns upon thee with complimental standing bare and officious attendance, yet know he serves in his place but as the dog the butcher. He is to thee as a cur to a drove. If thou goest on quietly, be it to the slaughter amongst griping lawyers and cruel adversaries, he waits gently and brings thee to the very door; but if thou offer to stray, he worries thee. Remember his eye shoots at two whites—thy person and thy purse. The one he is to guard, the other must find him. Thou art compelled to protect thy carcase under his shelter as a sheep under a briar in a terrible storm, and be sure for thy standing there to have some of thy wool torn off.

Thus Seneca of the Destinies: we may accuse the Destinies longer but cannot change them, they continue obstinate and obdurate, no man can move them with upbraids or tears or persuasions, they acquit no man of anything, they pardon nothing. Spare therefore tears because they are unprofitable. So I of gaolers.

CHAPTER XIX

The abuses done to prisoners by over-cruel creditors.

Albeit I have done with prison-keepers, I must not take such an abrupt leave of prisoners. In 'The Bellman's second night walk' he told you what strange transformations men were changed into in one prison where there was nothing heard but roaring, drinking, fighting, swearing. But, going a little further, there was in the chambers of another prison the sound of tunes more tragical, more serious: here was another manner of noise, new terrors, new shrieks, new condolements—no, no, they were not new, the air is filled with them every day; they are not strange, because they are common.

The Bellman went on whither this fearful noise led him, and on a sudden came into a magical circle in which were raised none but spirits of confusion—as ululations, deplorations, groans, cries, sighs and complainings. It was not the cry at an Irish funeral, which is insufferable howling, nor the crying of English widows at the burial of their husbands, which scarce wets a handkerchief; but the cry of men which pierceth the clouds. They did cry to Heaven, to earth, to God, to man. Heaven heard all and received some; earth laid up some and fed all the rest; God pitied those whom He took and preserved those that were left; but cruel man neither regards those that are here nor respects those that are gone. The cry of these men is loud, it is heard above the stars; the cry is great, it encompasseth in two cities; it is the cry of sickness, of melancholy, madness, hunger, cold, thirst, nakedness, penury, beggary, misery. It is the cry of churchmen, tradesmen, husbandmen, men undone, of scholars, soldiers—all penniless, all prisoners.

And how far reacheth the ground, think you, in which these cries echo one to another? Let your eyes walk but over this paper and here survey is drawn. Upon one side of the Thames stand the White Lion, the King's Bench, the Marshalsea, the Clink, the Counter in Southwark; on the other side the Gatehouse, Ludgate, Newgate, Wood St Counter, Poultry Counter, Finsbury, New Prison, Lob's Pound and the Hole at St Katharine's. Fourteen Golgothas environing one city!

Fourteen charnel houses where men are buried alive! Either this must proceed from much cruelty in the creditor or much deceit in the debtor.

Howsoever, these blockhouses of the law should not strike those quite through and through that vail bonnet to their mercy and authority; yet they do. But if Truth and Mercy would take candles in their hands and show the faces of these crying prisoners—alas! what wretched, lean, starved, discoloured and dejected countenances would they behold! What a forlorn hope would this be! In some of these ragged regiments are a hundred, in some two hundred, in some eighty. In all the fourteen, one thousand at least. What a loss is this to the King! What dishonour to the country! What scandal to Christianity! What derision to policy! But remember thou, whatsoever thou art, that art a creditor and hast enclosed thy heart between walls of flint and marble—remember that a prisoner is God's image, yet man's slave and a scrivener's bondman. He is Christ's pawn, redeemed from one Hell and cast into another.

A prisoner is a bird in a cage—when he sings, he mourns; a bear at a stake—baited for money; a horse in a pound—be his courage never so great, there 'tis lost; a Daniel in the lions' den—but where's his Habakkuk? Remember, O cruel man, the prisoner pines in a gaol, his wife at home, his children beg, servants starve; his goods are seized on, reputation ruined, his name forgotten, health shaken, his wits distracted, his conversation blasted, his life miserable, his death contemptible.

If a gentleman keeps a wretch in prison he deserves to be degraded, for gentry is bound to honour, to defend the oppressed. If a citizen bars a man of his liberty, he himself is not free but hazards the danger of being a foreigner in Heaven for disfranchising his brother on earth. If a countryman stifle his neighbour in a nasty gaol, let him not be angry if God blasts his corn, kills his cattle, burns his barns, and blows down his trees when he himself defaces, dishonours and destroys a piece of work worth all the world.

If such cruel creditors should be asked what they get when such poor men, their debtors, die in prison you may very well say 'Nay—what have we not lost?' Your debtors are lost; your souls are or ought to be afflicted. Bales of dice are left for you at the prison doors; you have the lives of Christians, the bones of prisoners, the anger of your Maker, the curses of wives, the woe worths of children, the hate of good men, the praise of no man.

CHAPTER XX

The villainies and abuses committed by politic bankrupts.

Now albeit this poor Irus last spoken of is to be pitied and relieved, yet there is one kind of prisoner deserves no comfort, no commiseration. And that is the politic bankrupt. It is not the honest bankrupt undone by suretyship, casualties or losses at sea, but a politic bankrupt, a noble-in-the-pound bankrupt, a five-shillings—nay, a ten-groats-in-the-pound bankrupt, a voluntary villain, a devouring locust, a destroying caterpillar, a golden thief.

In Anno 38 Hen. VIII an Act begins thus: 'Whereas divers and sundry persons, craftily obtaining into their hands great substance of other men's goods do suddenly fly to parts unknown or keep their houses, not minding to pay or restore to any their creditors their debt or duties, but at their own wills and pleasures consume the substance obtained by credit of other men for their own pleasures and delicate living, against all reason, equity and good conscience: Be it therefore enacted ... etc.' and then follow severe courses to punish those *anthropophagi*—men-eaters.

So in Anno 13 Eliz.; so in Anno 1 Jacob. Strong and cunning nets were spread by those Parliaments to catch these foxes. Yet how many of them have been since, and at this hour are, earthed in the King's Bench, the Fleet and that abused sanctuary of Ludgate! Here they play at bowls, lie in fair chambers within the Rule, fare like Dives, laugh at Lazarus, can walk up and down many times by *habeas corpus* and jeer their creditors. There they lie barricadoed within King Lud's bulwark against gun-shot; there they strut up and down the prison like magnificoes in Venice on the Rialto, brave in clothes, spruce in ruffs, with gold-wrought night-caps on their heads. They feed deliciously, plenteously, voluptuously, have excellent wines to drink, handsome wives to lie with when they please, who come in not like the wives of prisoners but of the best and wealthiest citizens. These men command the stone walls, not the walls them. They scorn the poor miserable wretches who beg at the grate and live upon the charity of the house. On them they look as at their under-vassals, and crying 'A *fico*!'

for their creditors because there they live safe to spend other men's moneys.

How are these wholesome laws and the good Princes that made them abused by these corroding cankers that eat into the hearts of ten thousand men's estates, to the undoing of families, cozening of whole parishes and dishonouring of a noble kingdom! Such a bankrupt is a devil in a vault and, so he may stand, cares not whom he blows up. His beginning is subtlety, his middle treachery, his end beggary, if not in himself, in his posterity: for *de male quaesitis non gaudet tertius heres*—

> Goods ill-gotten,
> Ere the third heir, lie rotten.

To conclude, such a bankrupt has the head of a lamb, the eyes of a dove, the tongue of a nightingale, the arms of a freebooter, the hands of a hangman, the teeth of a lion, and the belly of an elephant.

CHAPTER XXI

The prisoners' supplication.

What with the noise, first of those roaring prisoners, then the cries of the poor distressed ones, and now lastly the thunder of this cannon discharged against this Machiavellian brood of bankrupts, the Bellman persuaded the better sort of prisoners, who had the true feeling of sorrow indeed, to draw a supplication and to let it go by this title, *The Prisoners' Supplication to Conscience*. They did so, and finished it. Not to weary you with all their tedious grievances and complaints, you shall only have some of the principal heads, leaving the bodies to lie in prison still.

The styles which they pinned upon Conscience were many and great: they called her 'brightest star in the church', 'ancient Reader of the Law', 'rare pleader', 'noblest herald to judges', 'uprightest Clerk in the Chancery', 'best mistress to the Masters in the Court of Request', 'holy palmer to good men' and 'black Recorder to bad men'. They told her that where she only had a commission from the King of Heaven to call creditors before her, they prayed her to do so, for if she stood not to them they should die in prison and have scarce any to bury them.

The petition, with all their instructions, she took and, folding up the paper, put it into her bosom, hasting with all speed convenient toward the heart of the City. At length she was entertained and welcomed into a worthy citizen's house, a gentleman that by her assistance had risen to great wealth, by her arguments grew strong in religion, by her persuasions embraced scholars, loved soldiers, made much of all men. His soul was a garden beautifully planted; his mind a palace rarely adorned; his body a temple of such admirable building that people passing by would do it reverence.

In this grave citizen's company was as sweet society of other noble spirits sitting at a table, all of them taking honour from the City to be called her sons, and she as much glorying by them to be saluted by the name of mother. At the very first sight of Conscience they all rose up, receiving her with all the graceful compliments that were due to so divine and excellent a creature, every one of them hasting with a kind of grave ceremony to take her by the hand and seat her highest at the board. Then all being silent and their eyes fixed only upon her face with an expectation of some speech from her, she drew out of her bosom *The Prisoners' Supplication*, read it openly and, repeating the particular numbers of all such miserable men as lay in prison, she fetched a deep sigh and there brake into this passionate abruption:

'Oh!' quoth Conscience, 'if amongst you (but I hope you are none of them) there be any under whom men suffer the cruelty of English execution, worse than the German wheel—imprisonment, let Conscience yet persuade you to send Mercy to speak to them at their iron grates. The last work you are to do in this world and the hardest to finish is to beg Mercy and obtain it. The Omnipotent Builder of the Heavens oftentimes squares out his platforms by your lines and your measures for, if man commiserates man, the Master and Chief Almoner of Mercy extends compassion to him—if not, not. It is one of the main petitions which you tie your souls to every morning. Dally not with the great Treasurer of Heaven and Earth to ask one thing and mean another. So your own turns be served, you care for nobody else. Not to forgive when you are forgiven is to tell a lie to Him that is all truth. You make a promise and break it. You beg a blessing and take up a curse. Such equivocation runs hand in hand with condemnation.

'Be men, be Christians, be citizens. Citizens profess generosity, affability, meekness, love, piety, pity; this is the blazon of a noble coat. Make it the escutcheon of your arms. Mercy is the best motto; clemency a crest, no herald can give a braver. Release men made captives to you by the laws of this kingdom, and the laws which are set down in the Upper House of the Celestial Parliament will make you free denizens in a more glorious kingdom—a kingdom where there is no change of kings, no alteration of state, no loss of peers, no wars, no revenges, no citizens flying for fear of infection, none dying of them that stay, no prisoners to write petitions to Conscience—yet Conscience sits there in glory. There, is true majesty, true honour, true peace, true health; there, is all life, all happiness, all immortality.'

She ended, they arose and one of the company who was a well-willer to prisoners hastened home to write down what he heard Conscience utter.

CHAPTER XXII

The abuses of keepers, nurses or charwomen.

Oh, sad and dismal music! The bells begin to toll heavily, and presently to ring out. Sickness so again threatens to invade this noble kingdom, again to lock up the doors of this populous City. Defend us, Heaven!

But if the Judge Eternal holds it fit to call another Sessions so soon after the last and to arraign our lives at the bar for our sins, of which most of our souls have ever since lain dangerously sick, then thou (whosoever thou art that art struck and must betake thee to thy pillow) pray, and pray heartily, that Heaven may send thee an honest, careful, conscionable and good keeper, for in the last and late great sickness many of that nursery were as she-wolves which howled every night at the moon, and in outward shape were tender-hearted, almost weeping to see a sick man or sick woman in their beds; but the aims of a number of them, as it proved afterward, were to wrap such bodies in their winding-sheets.

Such hard-hearted keepers are foxes and, when the shepherd is gone to rest—when all the house is fast asleep—then worry they the lambs. The sicker those are whom they keep, the more easily do they seize their prey. Their bellies are cupboards ever devouring victuals, not the worst but the best they can lay their lips on. Their tongues are lickerish as flies', eyes are quick-sighted as cats' at midnight, hands as catching as bird-lime, hearts as false as dice, yet running smoothly. They are called 'keepers' because whatsoever they get but hold of they keep it with griping paws, never to let it go. They are dry-nurses and starve so far as they dare all that come under their fingers.

They are called 'charwomen' because, when Death sits all night by the sick man's bedside, they by their good wills sit till morning by a good fire in easy *chairs*, and are therefore christened by the names of '*char*women'. Of, if you will, that word 'char' comes from the Latin word *cara*, which signifies 'dear': and they that hire these night-crows into their houses shall find them dearer ware than bullocks in Smithfield. Thousands in and about London and Westminster have bought their attendance so dear that their lives have gone for it. The watchmen of the City get not so much amongst all their chalky bills in a month as one of these scrapes to herself in one night when she plucks but a shirt over a dead man's head and ears. Those shirts are their fees; so are waistcoats, night-caps, sheets, pillow-beres, bands, handkerchiefs, anything. Rats are not such gnawers of linen, nor moths of woollen, as these are of both.

If a rich bachelor sicken it is an East Indian voyage when she hoists up sail from her own house into his; and when he dies, then she and her lading comes home. Breda is then taken and she alone has the spoil. The sight of a doctor strikes her into a paleness, an apothecary's man with his urine eyes gives her a purge, for anyone that brings health in his hand puts sickness into her. The tolling of bells is music to her. She cares not how few live, over whom she is matron; nor how many die, though in her arms. The more water she fishes in, her fare is the better.

Art thou sick and trustest one of these to make thy broths? Some of them are such cooks that what good thing soever is prescribed for thy recovery shall be sure to be left out. If hot drinks would save thy life, she will persuade thee to poor thin cold beer. Hast thou any infected part of thy body? Take heed to her plasters and her surgery, for she cares not how soon a cold strikes to thy heart if thou art to leave anything behind thee to warm her. One charitable quality she has, for at midnight if she be alone with thee and perceives any signs of death in thy speech, thy pillow will she pull away to hasten thee on thy journey.

I speak not this against all keepers. Heaven forbid! A number of them are motherly, skilful, careful, vigilant and compassionate women —good nurses indeed, necessary helpers in time of such extremity. But I write against those who, fearing neither pox nor plague, nor death, nor any danger, have been the spoil, ruin, and confusion of many a poor servant's life. Many a child hath been made fatherless by them, many a mother childless. May they repent and amend.

CHAPTER XXIII

The abuses of alehouses.

We are come now to an epidemial disease, a general calamity, an impostume as wide as a kingdom: abuses of alehouses. What pen can set them down? How many parliaments have been physicians to cure this evil? Yet they roam like tetters over the body of the commonweal.

Not to meddle with the Acts and Statutes of all our former kings, what did King James Anno 1 against these exorbitants? It was then enacted that 'Whereas the ancient, true and principal use of inns, alehouses and victualling houses was for the receipt, relief and lodging of wayfaring people, to supply the wants of such as are not able by greater quantities to make their provisions of victuals, and not to harbour idle fellows to consume their money and time in drunkenness: It was therefore enacted. . . . etc.' (see the Statute) that for every offence committed by any innkeeper, alehouse-keeper or victualler (the offences are there set down) they should forfeit ten shillings to the use of the poor, etc. If these forfeits were truly paid as they are truly made the poor in some parish would live as merry as the rich. But now for all this Act and for all the other Statutes for the same purpose established since, how many parishes in England, how many in and about London (especially throughout all the suburbs) do, like islands, swim as it were in hot waters, strong beer and headstrong ale?

For to such a height is this sin of drinking grown that cobblers, tinkers, pedlars, porters, all trades, all professions, sit tippling all day, all night, singing, dancing (when they can stand), laughing, cursing, swearing, fighting. A whole street is in some place but a continued alehouse: not a shop to be seen between a red lattice and a red lattice, no workers but all drinkers, not a tradesman at his occupation, for every tradesman keeps in that place an alehouse.

It is an easier life, a lazier life, a trade more gainful. No such comings-in as those of the tap, insomuch that in most of the suburbian outroads the best men there that command the rest, the Grand Signiors of the parish—as constables, headboroughs and other officers—are common alehouse-keepers. And he that can lay in most gyles of beer and be furnished with the strongest ale and headiest liquor carries the bucklers away from all his fellows.

Now because the fashion of downright blows in the ignoble school of drinking is grown stale, wickedness hath invented new sorts of weapons to bewitch men that love such kind of play to go reeling to destruction. In some places they have little leather jacks tipped with silver and hung with small silver bells (these are called the 'jingle-boys') to ring peals of drunkenness. In other places they have shallow brown bowls which they call 'whiskins'. Then have you another brewing called 'huff's ale' of which, because no man must have but a pot at a sitting and so be gone, the restraint makes men more eager to come on, so that by this policy one man may huff it four or five times in a day.

These quaffings hurt thousands and undo many poor men who would else follow their labours but now live in beggary, their wives (unless they tipple hard, too, as for the most part they do by their evil examples) starving at home and their ragged children begging abroad. Then in some places instead of full quarts they have jugs of a pint and a half with long necks embroidered with froth, cans not a wine pint for a penny, demi-cans of draughts a piece, and a device of six earthen pipes or hollow funnels all into one, every funnel holding about two spoonfuls.

If the Acts against these enormities were severely executed and drunkards punished as the law does sentence them, then would London be a very sober City. Constables might then sit more quietly in their watch, the two Counters and other prisons not be haunted with so many 'rats' (which are a sort of drunken vermin that come staggering in at midnight) and carpenters might be more set at work in making of more new pairs of stocks—the old ones, what by bribery and connivance, standing too idle.

O per se O.

LONDON:

Printed for *Iohn Busbie*, and are to be sould at his shop in
Fleeteftreet in S. Dunftans Church-yard.
1612.

CHAPTER XXIV

O per se—O.

And so good morrow, goodman Bellman of London! Your night-piece is drawn and my day-work is now to begin. Let my morning therefore, I pray you, be your midnight and now, when all others rise to go to their labours who could scarce sleep by reason of the noise you made with your clapper, get you to your bed and dream upon your pillow upon some new discovery. In that map of villainies which you have drawn in print already I like the handling of your pencil but not the laying on of your colours. They are smooth enough but you have not given them their true sweetening, heightening and shadowing. But I cannot blame you, because *nocte latent mendae*—women, horses and colours are not to be chosen by candlelight—and you, gaffer Bellman, having no better guide, it is a wonder you stumbled no more, considering you walked i' th' dark. If, therefore, by my spectacles being clearer than yours I have discovered more nests of blackbirds— I mean more villainies of the Devil's own hatching—than ever flew to your fist and were sold afterwards to sing in shops in Paul's Church-yard, it ought not to raise up your choler an inch higher for all that, sithence in both our land discoveries our sails are hoisted up only to do good to the commonwealth.

And because the notes which I sing may appear to be of mine own setting and not either borrowed or stolen from any other, you shall know that, serving in the late Queen's time many years together in the office of an High Constable in that county wherein I now dwell, I drew from the examination of such lewd persons as came before me the truth of all those villains which here I publish. In the mustering of this damned regiment I found that whether they were rogues taken in *romboyles* (that is to say, in 'watches' or 'wards') by the Petty *Harman Beck* (who in their company signifies a Petty 'Constable') or whether they were such as in the canting tongue are called *maunderers* (of 'begging' or 'demanding'), whether they lived in *boozing kens* 'ale-houses' or what other coarse thread of life soever any of them all spun, it was ever wound in a black bottom of the most pernicious making-up that the Devil could teach them; insomuch that, albeit the very sunbeams could possibly have written down the discovery of any gross villainies by them committed, they would as easily venture upon damning in denial of it with oaths as if there had been no Hell for such offenders.

For my better painting forth these monsters I once took one of them into my service, being a sturdy big-limbed young fellow. Of him I desired some knowledge in their gibberish, but he swore he could not cant. Yet his rogueship, seeing himself used kindly by me, would now and then shoot out a word of canting and, being thereupon asked why with oaths he denied it before, he told me that they are sworn never to disclose their skill in canting to any householder for, if they do, the other *maunderers* or 'rogues' *mill* them ('kill' them). Yet he for his part, he said, was never sworn, because he was a *clapperdudgeon* (that is to say, a 'beggar born'). This *clapperdudgeon* stayed with me so long as he durst and then *binged awast in a darkmans* 'stole away from me in the night-time'. So that what intelligence I got from him or any other trained up in the same rudiments of roguery I will briefly, plainly and truly set down as I had it from my devilish schoolmaster, whom I call by the name of *O per se—O.*

Of him I learned that the cause why so many of this wicked generation wander up and down this kingdom is the free command and abundant use they have of women. For if you note them well in their marching, not a tatterdemalion walks his round, be he young, be he old, but he hath his *mort* or his *doxy* at his heels (his 'woman' or his 'whore') for, in hunting of their rascal deer, this 'law' they hold when they come to strike a doe: if she will not *wap for a win*, let her *trine for a make* (if she will not '... *O per se—O* ... for a penny', let her 'hang for a halfpenny').

And this liberty of wenching is increased by the almost infinite numbers of tippling-houses called *boozing kens*, or of *stalling kens* (that is to say, 'houses where they have ready money for any stolen goods'), unto which nests birds fly of the same feather that the owner is of. For if the ale-seller be a horse-stealer, a cutpurse, a robber by the highway, a cheater, etc., of the same coat are his guests. These houses are the nurseries of rogues and thieves, for how could they bestow cloaks, sheets, shirts and other garments being stolen if they had not *stalling kens* to receive them? Why should *grunters* 'pigs' go whining out of the world, having their throats cut by rogues, if they had not *boozing kens* to eat them in?

In the ceremony of whose ragged assemblies the Bellman a little mistook himself, for *priggers*, *filchers* and *cloyers* (being all in English 'stealers') use neither roast meat nor spits in their feastings, as he furnisheth them. But when they intend to strike a hand they levy their damnable troops in the day, but they sally forth and share the spoils in the night. For some one sturdy hell-hound above the rest undertakes to be the *miller* (that is to say, the 'killer'—I hope this can be no disgrace to any honest miller who is no thief with a false hopper). And this killer brings to the slaughter-house of the Devil (viz. a *boozing ken*) a *bleating cheat* a 'sheep'. Another *mills a crackmans* 'breaks a hedge', and that wood heats the oven whilst the sheep is dressed, cut in pieces and put into earthen pots made for the purpose to bake their victuals in. The oven's mouth being thus daubed up, out fly the little devils (more 'dammed' than the oven) either to break an house some two or three miles off or to do as bad a villainy. The piece of service being performed, a retreat is sounded and about midnight they return merrily, fall to their good cheer manfully and then divide their spoils of stolen shirts, smocks or anything else most thievishly; in which partnership the host and hostess are chief sharers. But such subtle shopkeepers are these haberdashers of the Devil's small wares that they never set out to sell but when the coast is clear and that, as thieves do among brokers, the hue and cry's throat be stopped that went bawling after them. For about a seven-night after, when all is hushed, to the *stalling ken* goes the *duds* for *lower* (to the 'thieving house' are the stolen 'clothes' sent roundly for 'money'), which being told out and divided, away fly these ravens scatteringly, the next prey that they light upon being ever at some fair or else a market.

And now that we talk of fairs, let my pen gallop over a few lines and it shall bring you without spurring swiftlier into Gloucestershire than if you rode upon Pacolet. There if you please to alight near Tewkesbury at a place called Deerhurst Fair, being kept there upon the two Holy Rood Days, you shall see more rogues than ever were whipped at a cart's arse through London and more beggars than ever came dropping out of Ireland. If you look upon them you would think you lived in Henry VI's time, and that Jack Cade and his rebellious ragamuffins were there mustering. Dunkirk cannot show such sharks. The wild Irish are but flocks of wild geese to them. And these swarms of locusts come to this lousy fair from all parts of the land within an hundred miles' compass. To describe the booths is lost labour, for let the hangman show but his wardrobe and there is not a rag difference between them. None here stands crying 'What do you lack?' for you can ask for nothing that is good but here it is lacking. The buyers and sellers are both alike, tawny sunburnt rascals, and they flock in such troops that it shows as if Hell were broke loose. The shopkeepers are thieves and the chapmen rogues, beggars and whores, so that to bring a purse full of money hither were madness, for it is sure to be cut.

But would you know what wares these merchants of eel-skins utter? Only *duds* for the *quaroms* (that is to say, 'clothes' for the 'body') which they have pilfered from hedges or houses. And this filthy fair begins before day and endeth before nine in the same morning, at which breaking up they do not presently march away with their bags and their baggages; but he who is chosen the Lord of the Fair, who is commonly the lustiest rogue in the whole bunch, leads his tattered footmen and footwomen from alehouse to alehouse where, being armed all in ale of proof and their *bene booze* the 'strong liquor' causing them to have *nase nabs* 'drunken cockscombs', up fling they the cans, down go the booths, about fly broken jugs. Here lies a rogue bleeding, there is a *mort* cursing, here a *doxy* stabbing with her knife. And thus this fair which begins merrily ends madly, for knaves set it up and queans pull it down.

Yet to meet at this assembly, how far off soever they be, they will keep their day though they hop thither upon one crutch. And it is for seven causes that thus they bestir their stumps to be at this upsitting; which are these, viz.

> (i) Everyone, as his rogueship is of bulk or can best swagger, desireth to be chosen Lord of the Fair or, if he lose his Lordship, yet to be a retainer at least and to fight under his tattered colours.
>
> (ii) To meet with the sisterhood and brotherhood of whores and wallet-mongers.
>
> (iii) To share such money as is taken for *duds and cheats won* 'clothes and things stolen'.
>
> (iv) To know how the world goes abroad, what news in the *Deuceville* the 'country' and where is *beneship* 'good' or where *queer* 'naught'.
>
> (v) To be *boozy* 'drunken' for company.
>
> (vi) To bandy their tawny and weather-beaten forces of *maunderers*, being of their own fraternity, against any other

troop of mountebanks at any other fair or market where the lowest rendezvous is to be made.

(vii) Lastly, to enact new warm orders for fresh stealing of clothes, etc., with all manner of armour for the body, but especially *stamps* 'shoes' because, being beggars, they are seldom set on horseback.

These are the seven halters that draw these hell-hounds to this fair, for the least of which seven they will venture a hanging.

The fair is broken up and, because it is their fashion at the trussing up of their packs to trudge away merrily, I will here teach you what *O per se—O* is, being nothing else but the burden of a song set by the Devil and sung by his choir; of which I will set no more down but the beginning because the middle is detestable, the end abominable and all of it damnable. Thus it sounds:

> Wilt thou a-begging go?
> *O per se—O, O per se—O!*
> Wilt thou a-begging go?
> Yes, verily, yea!
> Then thou must God forsake
> And to stealing thee betake.
> *O per se—O, O per se—O!*
> Yes, verily, yea, etc.

This is the music they use in their *libkens* their 'lodgings' where, thirty or forty of them being in a swarm, one of the master devils sings and the rest of his damned crew follow with the burden; in which midnight caterwaulings of their nothing is heard but cursing and profanation and such swearing as if they were all knights of the post. Jews did never crucify Christ with more dishonour than these rakehells who with new-invented fearful oaths tear Him in pieces. And no marvel, for most of those who are beggars born are never christened. Besides they have in their canting a word for the 'Devil' or the 'plague', etc., as, *Ruffian* for the one and *cannikin* for the other, but for 'God' they have none; only they name Him, but it is not in reverence but abuse, all their talk in their *libkens*, where they lie like swine, being of nothing but *wapping, niggling, prigging, cloying, filching,* cursing and such stuff. Who therefore would pity such impostors, whose faces are full of dissembling, hearts of villainy, mouths of curses, bodies of sores which they call their 'great *cleymes*', but laid upon their flesh by cunning; whose going *Abr'am* (that is to say, 'naked') is not for want of clothes but to stir up men to pity and in that pity to cozen their devotion? Now whereas the Bellman in his privy search found out the nests of these screech-owls, pulling off some of their feathers only to show their ugliness but, for want of good and perfect eye-sight, not flaying off their skins as I here purpose to do, and so to draw blood, I will finish that which the Bellman by being overwatched left lame, and show those abuses naked to the world which he never discovered.

First therefore shall you behold the *Abr'am* man in his true colours, his right shape, his own rags, and then shall you hear the phrase of his *maund* or 'begging'. Next him comes marching the counterfeit soldier, with his *maunding* note too. At his tail follow *bene fakers of gybes* (that is to say, 'counterfeiters of passports'). Then *dommerars*. Then *clapperdudgeons* in their true habiliments and their true beggarly rhetoric they use in begging. Then will I show you how they hang together in fraternities, and what articles of brotherhood they are sworn to, with a note as good as any rogues' mark they carry about them, how to know these knots of knaves or these brotherhoods, their names, their *libkens* or 'lodgings', their *stalling kens* to which all stolen goods are brought; and, lastly, to show you that even in their mirth they are devils, you shall hear their true canting songs now used among them.

In setting down all which hidden villainies never till this day discovered you shall find a mixture not only of all those detestable subtleties used in making those sores which eat into their flesh, but also the tricks and medicines they have without help of surgeons to cure them. I will besides in their descriptions here and there stick words and phrases of their gibberish or beggarly language, giving them the stamp presently of true English, which labour I take of purpose to procure delight to the reader.

Of the 'Abr'am' his Description.

The *Abr'am cove* is a lusty strong rogue who walketh with a *slate* about his *quaroms* a 'sheet' about his 'body' *trining* 'hanging' to his hams bandelier-wise, for all the world as cutpurses and thieves wear their sheets to the gallows in which their trulls are to bury them; oftentimes, because he scorns to follow any fashions of hose, he goes without breeches; a cut jerkin with hanging sleeves in imitation of our gallants—but no satin or camlet elbows, for both his legs and arms are bare, having no *commission* to cover his body (that is to say, no 'shirt'); a face staring like a Saracen; his hair long and filthily knotted, for he keeps no barber; a good *filch* or 'staff' of grown ash or else hazel in his *famble* (in his 'hand') and sometimes a sharp stick on which he hangeth *ruff peck* 'bacon'.

5. A Beggar.

These walking up and down the country are more terrible to women and children than the name of Raw-head and Bloody-bones, Robin Goodfellow or any other hobgoblin. Crackers tied to a dog's tail make not the poor cur run faster than these *Abr'am* ninnies do the silly villages of the country, so that when they come to any door a-begging, nothing is denied them.

Their Marks.

Some of these *Abr'ams* have the letters E and R upon their arms; some have crosses and some other mark, all of them carrying a blue colour; some wear an iron ring, etc. Which marks are printed upon their flesh by tying their arm hard with two strings three or four inches asunder and then with a sharp awl pricking or razing the skin to such a figure or print as they best fancy. They rub that place with burnt paper, piss and gunpowder which, being hard rubbed in and suffered to dry, sticks in the flesh a long time after. When these marks fail they renew them at pleasure. If you examine them, how these letters or figures are printed upon their arms, they will tell you it is the mark of Bedlam, but the truth is they are made as I have reported.

And to colour their villainy the better, every one of these *Abr'ams* hath a several gesture in playing his part. Some make an horrid noise hollowly sounding, some whoop, some holler, some show only a kind of wild distracted ugly look, uttering a simple kind of *maunding* with these addition of words—'Well and wisely'; some dance but keep no measure, others leap up and down and fetch gambols. All their actions show them to be as drunk as beggars for, not to belie them, what are they but drunken beggars—all that they beg being either *lower* or *booʒe* 'money' or 'drink'?

Their 'Maund' or Begging.

The first begins: 'Good 'orship', 'Master' or 'Good 'orships, rulers of this place, bestow your reward on a poor man that hath lain in Bedlam without Bishopsgate three years, four months and nine days, and bestow one piece of your small silver towards his fees which he is indebted there, the sum of £3-13s-7½d'—or to such effect—'and hath not wherewith to pay the same but by the good help of 'orshipful and well-disposed people, and God to reward them for it.'

The second begins: 'Now dame, well and wisely! What will you give poor Tom now? One pound of your sheep's feathers to make poor Tom a blanket? Or one cutting of your sow' side no bigger than my arm? Or one piece of your salt meat to make poor Tom a shoeing-horn? Or one cross of your small silver towards the buying a pair of shoes? Well and wisely! Ah, God bless my good dame! Well and wisely! Give poor Tom an old sheet to keep him from the cold, or an old doublet or jerkin of my master's, God save his life!'

Then will he dance and sing or use some other antic and ridiculous gesture, shutting up his counterfeit puppet-play with this epilogue or conclusion: 'Good dame, give poor Tom one cup of the best drink! Well and wisely! God save the King and his Council and the governor of this place, etc.'

Of Counterfeit Soldiers.

These may well be called counterfeit soldiers, for not one scarce among the whole army of them ever discharged so much as a caliver. Nothing makes them soldiers but old mandilions which they buy at the broker's; the weapons they carry are short crab-tree cudgels. And these, because they have the name of soldiers, never march but in troops two or three in a company. Of all sorts of rogues these are the most impudent and boldest, for they knock at men's doors as if they had serious business there whereas, the door being opened to them, they begin this parle.

Their 'Maunding'.

'Gentle rulers of this place, bestow your reward upon poor soldiers that are utterly maimed and spoiled in Her Majesty's late wars, as well for God's cause as Her Majesty's and yours. And bestow one piece of your small silver upon poor men, or somewhat towards a meal's meat to succour them in the way of truth, etc., for God's cause.'

These fellows go commonly hurt in the left arm beneath the elbow, having a *gybe jerked* (that is to say, a 'passport sealed') with licence to depart the colours, under which (if you rightly examine them) they never fought.

Yet wheresoever the wars are and how far off soever, thus can they wound themselves at home.

Their Making of their Sores.

Take unslaked lime and soap, with the rust of old iron: these mingled together and spread thick on two pieces of leather which are clapped upon the arm, one against the other, two small pieces of wood fitted to the purpose holding the leathers down; all which are bound hard to the arm with a garter. Which in a few hours fretting the skin with blisters and being taken off, the flesh will appear all raw. Then a linen cloth, being applied to the raw blistered flesh, it sticks so fast that, upon plucking it off, it bleeds; which blood or else some other is rubbed all over the arm, by which means, after it is well dried on, the arm appears black and the sore raw and reddish but white about the edges like an old wound. Which if they desire to heal, a brown paper with butter and wax being applied, they are cured. And thus without weapon do you see how our *maundering* counterfeit soldiers come maimed.

Of Placing their Sores.

The soldier hath his sore always on his left arm unless he be left-handed (for then, because of the better use of that hand, it is upon the right) betwixt the elbow and the wrist, and is called by the name of 'soldier's *maund*'. When a sore is placed on the back of the hand and that he saith he was hurt by an horse, then it is called 'footman's *maund*'. When the sore is above the elbow as if it were broken or hurt by falling from a scaffold it is called 'mason's *maund*'. And thus the altering the place of the sore altereth the *maund*.

Of these counterfeit soldiers some of them being examined will say they were lately serving-men but, their master being dead and the household dispersed, they are compelled to this baseness of life for want of means. Some of them can play the *Abr'am*, be 'mad Toms', or else beg *rum maund*, counterfeit to be a fool or else that his tongue is tied and cannot speak, and suchlike.

Of 'Bene Fakers of Gybes'.

They who are counterfeiters of passports are called *bene fakers* (that is to say, 'good makers') and these makers, like the Devil's hackney-men, lie lurking in every country to send his messengers post to Hell. The best passports that ever I saw were made in S-shire with the hand of one M.W. subscribed unto them. There was another excellent *bene faker* about P—, a town in G-shire. In S— dwelt another who took two shillings and sixpence (two *bords* and six *wins*, or two *bords* and a *flag*) for every passport that went out of his beggarly office. He counterfeited the seal of L.D.

Of these *bene fakers* I could say much more if I would be counted a blab, but now the very best of them are made in L— to carry men from thence unto W—.

How to Know Counterfeit Passports.

The seals of noblemen, gentlemen, justices or any other who have authority to use seals are graven in silver, copper or some hard stuff, and those things which are so graven seal the arms or suchlike with

sharp edges and with a round circle enclosing it as if it were cut with
an instrument of steel, and it maketh a neat and deep impression. But
these counterfeit *jarks* or 'seals' are graven with the point of a knife
upon a stick's end, whose roundness may well be perceived from the
circle of a common turned seal; these for the most part bearing the
ill-favoured shape of a *buhar's nab* or a *prancer's nab* (a 'dog's head' or
a 'horse's') and sometimes an unicorn's and suchlike, the counterfeit
jark having no circle about the edges. Besides, in the passport you shall
lightly find these words, viz. 'For Solomon saith: "Who giveth the
poor, lendeth the Lord", etc.' and that constables shall help them to
lodgings and that curates shall persuade their parishioners, etc. Another
note is, let them be in what part of the land soever they will, yet have
they an hundred miles to go at least, every one of them having his
doxy at his heels. And thus much of *bene fakers*.

Of 'Dommerars'.

The Bellman took his marks amiss in saying that a *dommerar* is
equal to the *crank*, for of these *dommerars* I never met but one and that
was at the house of one M.L. of L—. This *dommerar's* name was W.
He made a strange noise, showing by fingers across that his tongue
was cut out at Chalk Hill. In his hand he carried a stick, about a foot
in length and sharp at both ends, which he would thrust into his mouth
as if he meant to show the stump of his tongue. But in doing so he did
of purpose hit his tongue with the stick to make it bleed; which filling up
his mouth, you could not for blood perceive any tongue at all, because
he had turned it upwards and with his stick thrust it into his throat.
But I caused him to be held fast by the strength of men until such time
that, opening his teeth with the end of a small cudgel, I plucked forth
his tongue and made him speak.

Of 'Clapperdudgeons'.

A *clapperdudgeon* is in English a 'beggar born' (some call him a
palliard), of which sorts there are two: first, natural; secondly, artificial.
This fellow above all other that are in the regiment of rogues goeth
best armed against the cruelty of winter. He should be wise, for he
loves to keep himself warm, wearing a patched *caster* a 'cloak' for his
upper robe, under that a *togemans* a 'gown' with high *stampers* 'shoes',
the soles an inch thick pegged, or else patches at his girdle ready to be

clapped on, a great *skew* a 'brown dish' hanging at his girdle and a tassel of thrums to wipe it, a brace of greasy night-caps on his head and over them, lest he should catch a knavish cold, a hat or *nab cheat*; a good *filch* or 'staff' in his hand, having a little iron peg in the end of it, a *buhar* a 'little dog' following him, with a smug *doxy* attired fit for such a roguish companion. At her back she carrieth a great pack covered with a patched safeguard under which she conveyeth all such things as she filcheth. Her skill sometimes is to tell fortunes, to help the diseases of women or children. As she walks she makes balls or shirt-strings (but now commonly they knit) and wears in her hat a needle with a thread at it. An excellent angler she is, for when her *cove maunds* at any door, if any poultry-ware be picking up their crumbs near them she feedeth them with bread and hath a thread tied to a hooked pin baited for the nonce; which the chicken swallowing, is choked and conveyed under the *caster*. Chickens, linen or woollen or anything that is worth the catching comes into her net.

Under this banner of the patched *clapperdudgeon* do I levy all *palliards*, as well those of 'the great *cleyme*' or 'sores' as others whom I term 'artificial' *clapperdudgeons*, albeit they are not beggars born.

Of their 'Maund'.

This *palliard* or 'artificial' *clapperdudgeon*, who carrieth about him 'the great *cleyme*', to stir compassion up in people's hearts thus acteth his part: he slides to the earth by his staff and, lying piteously on the ground, makes a fearful horrid strange noise, through an hoarse throat uttering these lamentable tunes:

'Ah, the 'orship of God, look out with your merciful eyne! One pitiful look upon sore, lame, grieved and impudent'—for 'impotent'!—'people, sore troubled with the grievous disease, and have no rest day nor night by the canker and worm that continually eateth the flesh from the bone. For the 'orship of God, bestow one cross of your small silver to buy him salve and ointment to ease the poor wretched body that never taketh rest, and Gawd to reward you for it in Heaven!'

These *palliards* walk two or three together and as one gives over this note the second catcheth it at the rebound, using the selfsame howling and grunting; which ended, they say the Lord's Prayer and in many places the Ave, never ceasing till something be given them.

How they Make their Great Sores
Called the Great 'Cleyme'.

They take crowfoot, spearwort and salt and, bruising these together, they lay them upon the place of the body which they desire to make sore. The skin by this means being fretted, they first clap a linen cloth till it stick fast; which plucked off, the raw flesh hath ratsbane thrown upon it to make it look ugly, and then cast over that a cloth which is always bloody and filthy. Which they do so often that in the end in this hurt they feel no pain; neither desire they to have it healed, but with their *doxies* will travel, for all their 'great *cleymes*', from fair to fair and from market to market, being able by their *maunding* to get five *bords* (that is, five 'shillings') in a week in money and corn. Which money they hide under blue and green patches, so that sometimes they have about them six pound or seven pound together. The *clapperdudgeons* that have not 'the great *cleyme*' are called *farmarly* beggars.

Of their Fraternities.

There is no lusty rogue but hath many both sworn brothers and the *morts* his sworn sisters who vow themselves body and soul to the Devil to perform these ten articles following, viz.

Articles of their Fraternities.

(i) Thou shalt my true brother be, keeping thy faith to thy other brothers as to myself, if any such thou have.

(ii) Thou shalt keep my counsel and all other my brothers', being known to thee.

(iii) Thou shalt take part with me and all other my brothers in all matters.

(iv) Thou shalt not hear me ill-spoken of without revenge, to thy power.

(v) Thou shalt see me want nothing to which thou canst help me.

(vi) Thou shalt give me part of all thy *winnings* whatsoever.

(vii) Thou shalt not but keep true pointments with me for meetings, be it by day or night at what place soever.

(viii) Thou shalt teach no householder to cant, neither confess anything to them, be it never so true, but deny the same with oaths.

(ix) Thou shalt do no hurt to any *maunder* but with thine own hands; and thou shalt forbear none that disclose these secrets.

(x) Thou shalt take clothes, hens, geese, pigs, bacon and suchlike for thy *winnings* wherever thou canst have them.

How to Know their Brotherhoods.

When at the end of a town wherein a fair or market is kept you see an assembly of them together chiding and brawling but not fighting, then those *coves* are sworn brothers. If likewise two *doxies* fall together by the ears whilst the rogues themselves stand by and fight not, that also is a brotherhood, for it is one branch of their laws to take part with their *doxies* in any wrong.

Of their Names.

Every one of them hath a peculiar nickname proper to himself by the which he is more known, more enquired after by his brothers and in common familiarity more saluted than by his own true name—yea, the false is used so much that the true is forgotten. And of these nicknames some are given to them for some special cause, as 'Olli Compolli' is the byname of some one principal rogue amongst them (being an *Abr'am*), being bestowed upon him because by that he is known to be the head or chief amongst them. In like manner these surnames following belong to other Grand Signiors and Commanders, viz. 'Dimber-Damber' and 'Hurly-Burly', 'General Nurse', 'The High Sheriff', 'The High Constable' and suchlike. And some nicknames are either upon mockery or upon pleasure given unto them, as 'The Great Bull', 'The Little Bull' and many other suchlike; 'The Great Bull' is some one notable lusty rogue who gets away all their wenches, for this 'Great Bull' by report had in one year three and twenty *doxies*, his *jockey* was so lusty, such liberty have they in sinning and such damnable and most detestable manner of life do they lead.

As the men have nicknames, so likewise have the women, for some of them are called 'The White Ewe', 'The Lamb', etc. And as I have heard, there was an *Abr'am* who called his *mort* 'Madam Wap-Apace'.

Of their 'Libkens' or Lodgings.

As these fugitive vagabonds have nicknames to themselves, so have they *libkens* or 'lodgings and places of meeting'—as, one of the meeting-places, as I have heard, being a sheepcote, is by the quest of rogues who nightly assemble there called by the name of 'Stophole Abbey'; so likewise another of their lodgings is called by the same name. Then have they others, as 'The Blue Bull', 'The Prancer', 'The Bull's Belly', 'The Cow's Udder', 'The Green Arbour', 'The Blazing Star', etc. Suchlike bynames give they also to their *stalling kens*.

And note this, that after a robbery done they lie not within twelve miles at the least of the place where they do it but, having eaten up their stolen mutton baked as aforesaid, away they trudge through thick and thin, all the havens of Hell into which they put in being always for the most part of an equal distance one from another; for look how far as the one 'Stophole Abbey' stands from the other, and just so far is 'The Bull's Belly' from 'The Cow's Udder', and so of the rest. So that what way soever these night spirits do take after they have done their deeds of darkness they know what pace to keep because, what storms soever fall, they are sure of harbour, all their journeys being but of one length.

Yet dare they not but let their *morts* and their *doxies* meet them at some of these places because, how cold soever the weather be, their female Furies come hotly and smoking from thence, carrying about them *glimmer in the prat* 'fire in the touch-bore' by whose flashes oftentimes there is *glimmer in the jockey*—the flask is blown up, too; of which dangerous and deadly skirmishes the fault is laid upon serving-men dwelling thereabouts who like freebooters are so hungry of flesh that a *doxy*, if she have a smug face, cannot peep out but she is taken up for hawk's meat. And it is no wonder there is such stealing of these wild bucks, because there is such store of them. Nor is it a marvel there is such store, sithence he is not held worthy to walk or to be counted one of the four and twenty orders but to be banished as a silly animal and a stinkard from all good fellowship, society and meetings at fairs, markets and merry *boozing kens* who when the trumpet sounds (that is to say, when the cuckoo sings) thrusts not out his head like a snail out of his shell and walks not abroad about the *Deuceville* 'the country' with his spirit of lechery and thieving, his *doxy*, at his heels.

Why the Staff is Called a 'Filch'.

Thus much for their fraternities, names, lodgings and assemblies. At all which times every one of them carries a short staff in his hand which is called a *filch*, having in the *nab* or 'head' of it a *ferm* (that is to say, a 'hole') into which, upon any piece of service when he goes *a-filching*, he putteth a hook of iron, with which hook he angles at a window in the dead of night for shirts, smocks, or any other linen or woollen. And for that reason is the staff termed a *filch*. So that it is as certain that he is an *angler for duds* who hath a *ferm* in the *nab* of his *filch* as that he is a thief who upon the highway cries 'Stand!' and takes a purse. This staff serveth to more uses than either the cross-staff or the Jacob's but the uses are not so good nor so honest, for this *filching*-staff being artificially handled is able now and then *to mill a grunter, a bleating cheat, a redshank, a Tib of the buttery* and suchlike, or *to fib a cove's quaroms in the Rome pad for his lower in his bung* (that is to say, 'to kill a pig, a sheep, a duck, a goose' and suchlike, or 'to beat a man by the highway for the money in his purse').

And yet for all these base villainies and others, of what blackness soever they be, you shall at every Assizes and Sessions see swarms of them boldly venturing amongst the prisoners. One cause of their tempting their own danger so is that, being sworn brothers in league and partners in one and the same thievery, it behoves them to listen to the prisoner's confession, which they do secretly, and so to take their heels if they spy a storm coming. Another cause is to learn what lime-twigs caught the bird i' th' cage and how he was entangled by the Justice in his examination, that thereby he abroad may shun the like. But the Devil is their tutor, Hell their school, thievery, roguery and whoredom the arts they study, before Doctor Story they dispute, and at the gallows are made graduates of Newgate and other gaols, the hangman's colleges.

To shut up this feast merrily, as sweetmeats are best last, your last dish which I set before you to digest the hardness of the rest is a canting song, not feigned or composed as those of the Bellman's were out of his own brain, but by the canters themselves and sung at their meetings.

The Canting Song.

1. Bing out, bene morts, and tower, and tower!
   Bing out, bene morts, and tower!
   For all your duds are binged awast—
   The bene cove hath the lower.

2. I met a dell, I viewed her well;
   She was beneship to my watch.
So she and I did stall and cloy
   Whatever we could catch.

3. This doxy dell can cut bene whids
   And wap well for a win,
And prig and cloy so beneshiply
   All the Deuce-a-ville within.

4. The boil was up, we had good luck
   In frost, for and in snow;
When they did seek, then we did creep
   And plant in ruffmans low.

5. To stalling ken the mort bings then
   To fetch lower for her cheats—
Duds and ruff peck, romboyled by harman beck
   And won by maunder's feats.

6. You maunders all, stow what you stall,
   To rum coves' watch so queer;
And wapping dell that niggles well
   And takes lower for her hire;

7. And gybe well jerked, tickrum comfeck
   For back by glimmer to maund;
To mill each ken, let cove bing then
   Through ruffmans lag or laund

8. Till cramp-rings queer tip cove his hire
   And queer kens do them catch;
A cannikin mill queer cuffin,
   So queer to bene cove's watch!

9. Bene darkmans then, booze, mort and ken!
   The bene cove's binged awast
On chates to trine by rum cove's dine—
   For his long lib at last.

10. Bing out, bene morts, and tower, and tower!
     Bing out of the Romeville
     And tower the cove that cloyed your duds
     Upon the chates to trine.

FINIS

*Thus, for Satisfaction of
the Readers, Englished.*

1. Go forth, brave girls, look out, look out!
   Look out, I say, good coneys!
   For all your clothes are stol'n, I doubt—
   Mad shavers share the moneys.

2. I met a drab, I liked her well
   (My bowls did fit her alley).
   We both did vow to rob pell-mell
   And so abroad did sally.

3. This bouncing trull can rarely talk;
   A penny will make her . . .;
   Through any town which she doth walk
   Nought can her filching scape.

4. The house being raised, aside we stepped
   And through the mire did wade;
   To avoid hue and cry, to a hedge we crept
   And under it close were laid.

5. To th' broker's then my hedge-bird flies,
   For stol'n goods bringing coin—
   Which, though the Constable after hies,
   Our tricks away purloin.

6. You *maunding* rogues, how you steal beware,
   For privy search is made;
   Take heed thou, too, thou hackney mare
   Who ne'er art ridden but paid;

7. A licence got with counterfeit seal
   To beg as if undone
   By fire; to break each house and steal,
   O'er hedge and ditch then run

8. Till shackles soundly pay us home
   And to the gaol compel us;
   Hell's plague the Justice' heart consume,
   So cruel to good fellows.

9. Sweet punk, beer-house and beer, good night!
   The honest rogue's departed
   To hanging by the Justice' spite—
   To his long home he's carted.

10. Away, sweet ducks, with greedy eyes
    From London walk up Holborn!
    Sue him who stole your clothes—he flies
    With hempen wings to Tyburn.

FINIS

[*Another.*

1. Doxy O! Thy glaziers shine
   As glimmer! By the Solomon,
   No gentry mort hath prats like thine,
   No dell e'er wapped with such a one.

2. White thy fambles, red thy gan,
   And thy quaroms dainty is.
   Couch a hogshead with me, than,
   In the darkmans clip and kiss!

3. What though I no caster wear
   Nor commission—no, nor slate?
   Store of strommel we'll have here
   And i' th' skipper lib in state.

4. Niggling thou, I know, dost love—
    Else the Ruffian cly thee, mort!
From thy stampers then remove
    Thy drawers and let's prig in sport!

5. When the lightmans up does call
    Margery prater from the nest
And her cackling cheats withal,
    In a boozing ken we'll feast.

6. There if lower I want, I'll mill
    A gage or nip for thee a bung.
Bene booze thou shalt booze thy fill,
    And crash a grunting cheat that's young.

7. Bing awast to Romeville then,
    O my doxy, O my dell!
We'll heave a booth and dock again,
    And trining scape, and all is well.]

[*Thus Englished.*

1. O my chuck, by th' mass I swear,
    Thine eyes than fire do shine more clear!
No rustling girl hath thighs like thine,
    No doe was ever bucked like mine.

2. White thy hand is, red thy lip,
    Thy dainty body I'll not skip.
To sleep, then, down ourselves let's lay
    And coll i' th' dark and kiss and play!

3. Say, I a Plymouth cloak do wear,
    Say that nor shirt nor sheet I bear;
Yet straw we'll have both fresh and sweet
    And tumble when i' th' barn we meet.

4. Thou dost, I know, the old sport love—
    Else may the foul Fiend in thee move!

Doff thou, then, thy shoon and hose
And let's to't with downright blows.

5. When the morning up shall call
From his roost the cock and all
His cackling wives, then thou and I
At tap-house will for strong ale cry.

6. There if we want our shot to pay,
I'll filch or nip and steal away.
Suck off thy liquor, then, thy fill;
Some sucking-pig for thee I'll kill.

7. To London therefore up let's hie,
O thou, my sweet bewitching eye!
There we'll rob and to't pell-mell,
And Tyburn scape, and all is well.]

[*Another.*

1. Now my kinchin cove is gone,
By the Rome pad maundered none
In quaroms both for stamps and bone
Like my clapperdudgeon.

2. Dimber-Damber, fare thee well!
Palliards all thou didst excel,
And thy jockey bare the bell—
Glimmer on it never fell.

3. Thou the cramp-rings ne'er didst scour,
Harmans had on thee no power,
Harman becks did never tower
For thee, though drawers still had lower.

4. Duds and cheats thou oft hast won,
Yet the cuffin queer couldst shun,
And through the Deuce-a-ville didst run;
Else the chates had thee undone.

5. Crank and dommerar thou couldst play
    Or rum maunder in one day,
  And like an Abr'am cove couldst pray,
    Yet pass, with gybes well jerked, away.

6. When the darkmans have been wet,
    Thou the crackmans down didst beat
  For glimmer, whilst a quacking cheat
    Or Tib o' th' buttery was our meat.

7. Redshanks then I could not lack,
    Ruff peck still hung at my back,
  Grannam ever filled my sack,
    With lap and poplars held I tack.

8. To thy buhar and thy skew,
    Filch and gybes, I bid adieu;
  Though thy togeman were not new,
    Yet the ruffler in't was true.]

[*Another, thus Englished.*

1. Now my little rogue is gone,
    By the highway begs there none
  In body both for leg and bone
    Like my *clapperdudgeon*.

2. Pretty rascal, fare thee well!
    All beggars born thou dost excel;
  Thy threshing flail still bare the bell—
    For into th' fire it never fell.

3. Bolts my boy did never wear,
    Never thou the stocks didst fear,
  For thee no constable did swear,
    For in thy purse thou cash dost bear.

4. Clothes by stealth thou oft hast won,
   Yet the Justice' fingers shun,
   And up and down the country roam;
   The gallows else had thee undone.

5. Dumb and mad man thou couldst play
   Or a slavering fool all day,
   And like a lusty rogue couldst pray,
   Yet scape, with passes sealed, away.

6. When the evening has been wet,
   Thou the hedges down didst beat
   For fire, and some of ducks wouldst cheat,
   Or else a fat goose was our meat.

7. Mallards then I could not lack,
   Bacon hung ever at my back,
   Corn likewise always filled my sack,
   With good milk pottage held I tack.

8. To thy cur and dish adieu,
   Thy staff and pass I ne'er must view;
   Though thy *caster* was not new,
   My brave strong rogue in't yet was true.]

[*Another.*

1. A queer cove of the Deuceville
   Did dock a dell in Turvey.
   He gave her cheats and duds and lower
   But his niggling was but scurvy.
   Yet would he wap
   With a mort, with a dell,
   With an autem mort, with a doxy,
   And not bing awast fro' the boozing ken
   Till his nab cheat all were foxy.

2. This cuffin, getting glimmer
    I' th' prat, so cleymed his jockey,
The nab was queer, the bube him nipped,
    His quaroms all was pocky.
Yet would he wap
With a mort, with a dell,
With an autem mort, with a doxy,
And not bing awast fro' the boozing ken
Till his nab cheat well were foxy.

Enough of this, and he that desires more pieces of such pedlary ware may out of this little pack fit himself with any colours. *Vale!*

FINIS]

NOTES ON SOURCES AND TEXTS

EACH note falls into three parts. The first, on 'Sources', deals with the literary origins of each work. The second, on the 'Text', gives the publishing history up to the present day and identifies the copies used for this edition. The basis of each text is a single copy, usually of the first edition, though in some cases the reprint includes material which was added in subsequent editions and which is therefore transcribed from single copies of these editions too. The third part of the note, the 'Collation', is an account in list-form of such substantive emendations as have been adopted or are tentatively proposed, or of omissions, additions and revisions relevant to the text actually printed; there is no intention of giving a general conspectus of variants throughout the whole range of editions and copies. Literal and other clearly mechanical errors have been silently corrected. Where modernization obscures the issue, the old spelling has been given. Numerical references are to pages, and sufficient of the context is quoted to aid location.

The Wonderful Year

Sources

An earlier work often mentioned in connection with *The Wonderful Year* is William Bullein's *A Dialogue, both pleasant and pitiful, wherein is a goodly regimen against the fever pestilence, with a consolation and comfort against death*, first published in London in 1564 and several times reprinted. It has little in common with Dekker's pamphlet beyond the fact that it also belongs to what may loosely be called plague-literature and is very miscellaneous in its contents—with a semi-dramatic fictional situation, medical advice, scientific teaching, emblems, fables, allegory, etc. Bullein's style, in which sprightliness and wit cloak learning and pessimism, anticipates that of both Nashe and Dekker. But the reader's attention is often directed well away from the plague into various other moral and literary matters.

In the main *The Wonderful Year* does not derive from any literary source, though it might be said to owe general debts to the moralizing ballad and to the jest-book—with the all-important difference that, whereas the jest-book is commonly built round one historical or pseudo-historical figure, *The Wonderful Year* is built round one group of historical events.

As a reading of Johannes Nohl's work[1] shows, many of the ideas, reactions and even incidents found in *The Wonderful Year* are commonplaces of the European plague. The nature of the disease was not of course properly understood, but an outbreak was most frequently blamed on the sinfulness of the community affected, and especially on usury and hence on the Jews (the Wandering Jew included). The medical profession was seen to be quite helpless in the face of its greatest challenge, and the way was left open for the sharp practices of the quacks and for the hawking of all the pet nostrums of herbs and flowers that the desperate scrambled for. There was a theory, one amongst many, that newly-weds were particularly vulnerable to the plague. Observers were astonished at the suddenness with which epidemics broke out, and the ways in which society tended to collapse under the strain. The unscrupulous or stupid tried to conceal the corpses that would have brought the plague regulations down on their houses, and the very numbers of the dead rapidly led to an abandonment of any pretence at decency in the burial rites. Those who tried to flee the city ran the risk of being repulsed by the

[1] *The Black Death*, trans. C. H. Clarke (London, 1926; abridged 1961). For the Elizabethan English scene, see F. P. Wilson, *The Plague in Shakespeare's London* (Oxford, 1927).

310

frightened countryfolk and perhaps of dying in the open fields. Some met the threat of death with asceticism and prayers, others (either from medical principle or from despair) with revelry; there was a widespread story of a drunk thrown into a plague-pit for dead. The deaths of parents brought unexpectedly early legacies to young heirs who, it is said, sometimes took the opportunity to embark on a course of dissipation in the midst of all the horror. The recurrence of the plague was to give an impetus on the Continent to the sometimes democratic sentiments of the Dance of Death.

Text

There is some irregularity in the publication. An order was entered in the *Stationers' Register* on 5th December 1603 that Ling, Smethwick and Browne were each to pay a ten-shilling fine for printing *The Wonderful Year* without licence or entrance, 'contrary to the ordinances for printing', that they were henceforth disqualified from printing or selling it, and that they were to surrender such copies as they still had. The *Register* records that Smethwick and Browne each paid five shillings of these fines in April 1605; a fine of £10 paid by Ling in October 1604 is probably for some other offence.

Bibliographical discussion must centre on F. P. Wilson's valuable short study of the text in his edition. All the extant copies of *The Wonderful Year* lay claim on the title-pages to have been printed by Creede in 1603. The unchanging date helps to conceal the fact, discovered by Wilson, that there are no fewer than three successive editions (which he designates *A, B, C,* and which we designate Q1, Q2, Q3). By plotting the variant readings Wilson shows that, except for one detail, the three editions form a simple reprint series in which Q2 is the middle term. The detail is a minute piece of revision, presumably by the author: in Q2 and Q3 the sexton of Stepney, who found a drunk amongst the corpses, is said not to have gone mad and died, as in Q1, but to have *nearly* died. Q1 and Q2 are linked in that they have in common most of the outer forme of the first sheet; one edition must therefore have followed so closely on the other that some of the type had not yet been distributed and could be used again. Wilson is rather less convincing than he could have been in showing that the chronological order of the editions was Q1, Q2, Q3 rather than Q3, Q2, Q1. It is hardly self-evident that the longer reading (that in Q1) about the drunk must come first, and the fact that the shorter reading (in Q2 and Q3) is set on a page shorter by one line than is normal does not clinch the matter. The principal evidence to favour the order Q1, Q2, Q3 remains the preponderance of preferable readings in Q1.

The printer's device on all three editions is that of Ling, and this inevitably raises the difficult question as to how they are related to the copies confiscated. Wilson's conjecture is that Q1, of which only one copy survives—Wood 616(i) in the Bodleian—is the confiscated edition; the fact that the type in which the preliminaries were set was still standing when work began on Q2 indicates that the Q1 preliminaries had been printed last, the normal procedure with a first edition but not with a reprint. In printing Q2 and Q3, Wilson goes on, Ling must have overcome the disqualification laid upon him in some way not now known to us. The argument is far from watertight. Why single out Q1? No great significance can be attached to the existence of only one copy. Wilson asks us to suppose that, disqualified as Ling was from printing Q1, he scarcely (if at all) halted the presswork on it, and probably at once proceeded into further editions; that, ordered to surrender all the copies of Q1, he retained at least one for his compositors' use; and that, fined for not having made a proper entry in the *Stationers' Register*, he did not make one. This is to fly in the face of what evidence we have. Similarly with dates. Is one to credit the title-page dates of all three editions? Why not? Wilson's dating of Q1 1603, Q2 1603–04 and Q3 1604–07? is puzzling. It is true of course that 1603 can legitimately be taken to include the first quarter of 1604; but this applies just as well to Q1 as to Q2 and Q3. The 1607? of Wilson's Q3 date derives from the not strikingly relevant fact that Ling gave up business in November 1607. Wilson does not argue the case, though it is obvious that he intends to open still wider the gap between Q1 and QQ2–3. But the three quartos actually form an exceptionally close-knit reprint series, as he himself reveals, and it is tempting to say that, for all we know to the contrary, what is true of one quarto as to its date and as to its being authorized or unauthorized is likely to be true of them all.

There are several hypotheses that might be made. All three quartos might be regarded as authorized editions and consequently dated between 5th December 1603, when the Company took action, and 24th March 1604. The objection to this, that (as Wilson points out) Q1 appears to be an original edition set up from manuscript, is not insuperable, since in the circumstances it is conceivable that the confiscated edition might have been totally suppressed, and a subsequent authorized edition might not have reprinted it but have reverted instead to manuscript for copy. One would find this rather more credible if Ling had not remained the printer. On the other hand, this hypothesis does not allow us to assume anything about the precise contents of the confiscated books, and so we cannot be too dogmatic about the need or otherwise for manuscript copy later. The second hypothesis, that advanced by Wilson, cannot be ruled out; at the same time we might observe that, because of the particular kinship of Q1 and Q2, his hypothesis has less to recommend it than a somewhat similar one, that QQ1–2 were confiscated before 5th December, and Q3 was the first authorized edition afterwards. But undoubtedly the most economical interpretation of the facts we have must be that all three of the quartos preceded 5th December, that they were all confiscated, and that the trouble with the Stationers' Company was sufficient to kill the pamphlet altogether.

Five modern reprints have preceded the present one. J. Morgan in *Phœnix Britannicus*, I (London, 1732), 27–50, A. B. Grosart in *The Non-Dramatic Works of Thomas Dekker*, The Huth Library (London, 1884–86), I, 71–148, and G. B. Harrison in the Bodley Head Quartos (London, 1924) all follow Q3. F. P. Wilson in *The Plague Pamphlets of Thomas Dekker* (Oxford, 1925), pp. 1–61, is the only editor to follow Q1 exclusively. G. R. Hibbard in *Three Elizabethan Pamphlets* (London, 1951), pp. 160–207, shows on balance a preference for Q3 over Q1. The present edition has been prepared from a microfilm of the unique copy of Q1, Wood 616(i) in the Bodleian. The one sentence of revision has been adopted from Q2.

Collation

42 get you gone: I invocate] *Morgan;* get you gone, Inuocate *Q.*

43 hair are fallen] *Wilson;* haire falne *Q;* hair have fallen *conj. this ed.*

52 a *ne exeat regnum*] *This ed.;* an *exeat regnum Q.*

59 had like to have died presently after] *Q2;* died in a short time after because he was not able to live without them *Q.*

60 had like to have turned up] *Morgan;* had liked to have turned up *Q.*

62 pick a crown off it] *Q* (pick a crowne of it)*;* pick a crown out of it *conj. this ed.*

63 pockets] *Grosart;* pocket *Q.*

The Gull's Horn-Book

Sources

The Gull's Horn-Book is essentially a parody of the courtesy-book which was popular throughout Europe for the instruction of the rising middle classes in the manners of their betters. But Dekker himself acknowledges a more particular source in Friedrich Dedekind's *Grobianus*, first published in Frankfurt in 1549 and afterwards augmented and much reprinted. It was translated into English by one R.F., entered in the *Stationers' Register* on 15th December 1602 and 21st May 1604, and published in London as *The School of Slovenry* in 1605. The general similarity of title and some minor similarities in ideas and phrases in the translator's comic dedication and *The Gull's Horn-Book* make it more than likely that Dekker glanced at R.F.'s version as well as translating, as he says, 'many books' (he must mean 'chapters'—there are only three books altogether) of the German into English verse himself. Dekker apologizes for his 'ditty' and 'feet' as though he were writing verse.

The distaste which Dekker felt for the German work and which his commentators have shared with him is understandable. Dedekind, who took a pathological delight in his subject, attempted to ridicule the kind of boorishness which makes itself felt in the charging and discharging of the bowels and the bladder. It must be said that *Grobianus* is not totally lacking in entertainment, and Dedekind has a capacity here and there for a developed irony. But the connection of the work with *The Gull's Horn-Book* is slight. Even in his early chapters Dekker owes no more than a few hints to the brief first chapter of the first book of *Grobianus*, and elsewhere he owes nothing. Were it not for the fact, which is forced upon us, that the basic conception of a *Gull's Horn-Book* came from Dedekind, we might be tempted to say that Dedekind was a bad influence on Dekker and merely confused him.

In his opening pages where, as is his custom, he is running in, Dekker must uneasily have sensed the existence of complications that Dedekind had no inkling of. He found himself actually in favour of rustic simplicity: he would rather have the old world with all its wrinkles than the new one, tarted up; it is not urban sophistication he admires but innocence, and innocence may, confusingly, be another name for the folly he is supposed to be mocking. The result is that Dekker is never clear in his mind as to the sort of man to cast in the rôle of gull. Is it to be a mere lout? Is it the uncouth fool who may waste time and money pursuing high life in town and should be given a talking-to? Is it, only a step away from him, the fop, the lifeman of the smart set, who should be taken down a peg or two? Is it, only a step away from him, the society shark, who should be exposed? That Dekker's choice insensibly gravitated towards the last may of course be partly due to his general preference for clear moral issues, or simply to the fact that he had so recently been working on his Bellman pamphlets.

At all events *The Gull's Horn-Book*, nowadays regarded as one of Dekker's best pamphlets, cannot have been very popular in its own day, and his tantalizing offer of a sequel was never taken up.

Text

The Gull's Horn-Book was printed by Nicholas Okes for Richard Sergier in 1609 without entry in the *Stationers' Register*; there seems to have been no call for a second edition. In 1674 Samuel Vincent abridged it to bring it up to date and published it as *The Young Gallant's Academy*. No further reprints followed until the 19th century. J. Nott was first in the field with his still useful edition (Bristol, 1812); after him came an editor who was probably Halliwell (London, 1862); Charles Hindley in *The Old Book Collector's Miscellany*, II (London, 1872), 23–77; A. B. Grosart in *The Non-Dramatic Works of Thomas Dekker*, The Huth Library (London, 1884–86), II, 193–266; George Saintsbury in *Elizabethan and Jacobean Pamphlets*, The Pocket Library of English Literature (London, 1892), pp. 209–75; R. B. McKerrow in The King's Library (London, 1904) and The King's Classics (London, 1905); O. Smeaton in *The Guls Hornbook and The Belman of London In Two Parts by Thomas Dekker*, The Temple Classics (London, 1904), pp. 1–64; and J. Loiseau in his parallel-text edition of *Le Jour de Fête des Cordonniers (The Shoemakers Holiday) suivi de L'Abécédaire des Benêts (The Guls Hornbook)* (Paris, 1957), pp. 228–325.

The present edition has been prepared from a microfilm of a copy in The British Museum.

Collation

71 for brokers] *Vincent;* from brokers *Q.*
71 save the charges] *Vincent;* have the charges *Q.*
73 haunting taverns] *Nott;* heating taverns *Q;* frequenting taverns *Vincent.*
73 write] *Vincent;* waite *Q.*
74 ruse] *This ed.;* Rowsa *Q;* romla *conj. this ed.*
77 Birchin Lane] *Nott;* Burchin-Law *Q.*
78 Helen's] *conj. Nott;* Hattens *Q.*
78 cos] *McKerrow;* os *Q.*
79 gunpowder threatens] *Nott;* gunpowder brings threatens *Q;* gunpowder brings threaten[ing]s *Grosart;* gun powder brings treasons *coni. this ed.*

79 way, smells worse] *Nott;* way, & smels worse *Q;* way, are smells worse *conj. this ed.*

79 Timonists] *Nott; Pimonists Q;* Pyrrhonists *conj. Nott.*

80 stage] *Nott;* stay *Q.*

83 But yon baboons and yon jackanapes] *This ed.;* But you baboons and you jackanapes *Q;* But your jackanapes *Vincent;* But your baboons and your jackanapes *Nott.*

83 grey, than at noon] *Nott;* gray) at noone *Q.*

84 thy scorched skin] *Nott;* thy scorched shin *Q.*

84 right side of the rainbow] *Q;* bright side of the rainbow *conj. this ed.*

84 to fetch thee boots] *Nott;* to fetch three boots *Q.*

84 strolling] *This ed.;* strawling *Q;* straddling *Nott.*

86 Be thou a reveller] *This ed.;* But thou a reveller *Q;* But be thou a reveller *Vincent.*

86 ground eaten bare] *Q;* ground beaten bare *conj. this ed.*

92 your charge in maintaining] *Nott;* your change in maintaining *Q.*

94 unwittingly] *Halliwell;* vomittingly *Q;* as it were against your consent *Vincent;* unwillingly *conj. this ed.*

95 speak of their leaves] *This ed.* (leeues)*;* speake of their wiues *Q;* speak of their wines *Nott.*

98 Players are] *conj. Nott; Halliwell;* Players and *Q;* To players and *conj. Nott.*

100 marry, very scurvily] *Grosart* (mary very scuruily)*;* many very scuruily *Q.*

102 Euphuized] *Grosart (Euphuiẓd); Euphuird Q;* Euphuesed *Nott;* Euphuied, Euphuine *conj. this ed.*

103 CHAPTER VII] *Nott;* CHAPTER VIII *Q.*

104 stranger drunk] *Nott;* stranger drink *Q.*

104 mist] *Q;* moist *conj. this ed.*

107 in the Constable's look] *Loiseau;* in the Constable's book *Q.*

Penny-Wise, Pound-Foolish

Sources

It is not impossible that *Penny-Wise, Pound-Foolish* was, so to say, the book of the play. There is a lost play entitled *The Bristol Merchant* written by Dekker in collaboration with Ford for the Palsgrave's Men and licensed for acting on 22nd October 1624. But the ultimate source is non-dramatic. There are two medieval manuscript versions of the tale *A Pennyworth of Wit* (the later being entitled *How a Merchant Did His Wife Betray*), which is related to Continental folk-tale and probably derives from a French original—though this is not, as sometimes said, the extant fabliau *De la Bourse Pleine de Sens* by Jean de Galois.[1] In England the story had a popular currency for centuries in chapbook form; but although it was entered on the *Stationers' Register* on 14th August 1560 and was mentioned in Laneham's Letter in 1575, it is not found in print before Dekker.

Text

'A book called *Penny-Wise, Pound-Foolish* by Thomas Dekker' was entered in the *Stationers' Register* on 17th December 1630 to Edward Blackmore, who published it in 1631. No more than the one edition is known, and this is represented by only two copies, one of them in the Henry E. Huntington Library and the other, lacking sig. D, in the Bodleian. The latter was reprinted as it stood by W. Bang as an Appendix to his *John Fordes Dramatische Werke* (Louvain, Leipzig and London, 1908), I, 177–210, in *Materialien zur Kunde des älteren Englischen Dramas*, vol. XXIII.

The present edition, the first reprint of the work in its entirety, has been prepared from a microfilm of the Huntington copy and has been collated with the Bodleian copy, which proves to have no substantive variants.

Collation

121 pleasure, he tasted] *This ed.;* pleasure, tasted *Q.*
133 music kept dumb] *This ed.;* music keep dumb *Q.*

[1] J. E. Wells, *A Manual of the Writings in Middle English 1050–1400* (London, 1916), pp. 179–80.

Tales

Sources

Of the three tales 'A Medicine', 'An Excellent Stratagem' and 'The Fields of Joy', the first may derive from a play, since in *Henslowe's Diary* we read of a comedy entitled *A Medicine for a Curst Wife* for which Dekker received payments between 31st July and 27th September 1602 amounting to the impressive total of ten guineas—of which the last ten shillings was explicitly over and above his price.[1] The story, if not the play, is related to *The Taming of the Shrew* in resembling a considerable body of folk-tales recommending the violent treatment of unruly wives. 'A Medicine' and 'An Excellent Stratagem' (which no doubt comes from some collection of Italian—rather than Spanish—tales) are divertissements in *The Raven's Almanac*, a miscellany of Dekker's which is made up as a mock prognostication, i.e. a parody of a type of publication still popular today in the shape of Old Moore.

'The Fields of Joy' is an extract from Dekker's *A Knight's Conjuring*. Nashe had written a highly successful pamphlet, *Pierce Penniless his Supplication to the Devil* (London, 1592), a satiric visit to the underworld, and had promised a sequel which in fact never appeared. Several writers tried to supply the deficiency, even while Nashe was still alive. Later T.M. brought out *The Black Book* (London, 1604), and in 1606 there were two attempts, one of them Dekker's *News from Hell*. Dekker considerably revised his work and published it again the following year with a new title, *A Knight's Conjuring*.

His debt for the idea of 'The Fields of Joy' passage as such is a fairly general neoclassical one, but it has been suggested that he owes something more specific to William Bullein. In his *Dialogue* (London, 1564) Bullein has a vision of Parnassus, with the Muses sitting on one side, and poets 'sittyng under the grene trees with Laurell garlandes besette with Roses about their heades' on the other. There are both classical writers and leading English writers, including Chaucer 'accompanied with the Spirites of many kynges, knightes, and faire Ladies' and Barclay, about whom were 'many Shepherdes and Sheepe with pleasaunt Pipes; greatly abhorryng the life of Courtiers, Citizens, Usurers, and Banckruptes, &c.'[2]

[1] *Henslowe's Diary*, ed. R. A. Foakes and R. T. Rickert (Cambridge, 1961), pp. 204(2), 214, 215(2), 216.

[2] William Bullein, *A Dialogue, etc.*, ed. M. W. and A. H. Bullen, The Early English Text Society (London, 1888), Extra Series, LII, pp. 15–18. See A. H. Bullen, *Elizabethans* (London, 1924), pp. 166–7.

Text

'A Medicine' and 'An Excellent Stratagem' are from *The Raven's Almanac*, sigs. C2v–C4v and D4–E4v respectively. 'A book called *The Raven's Almanac, etc., foretelling of a plague, famine and civil wars*' was entered in the *Stationers' Register* to Laurence Lisle on 7th July 1608, and was published in London the following year as by Edward Allde for Thomas Archer. Three editions of 1609 have been identified. In modern times *The Raven's Almanac* is to be found only in A. B. Grosart, *The Non-Dramatic Works of Thomas Dekker*, The Huth Library (London, 1884–86), IV, 167–266, but there it is the second edition that serves as copy. For the preparation of the present texts a microfilm of the first edition in the British Museum has been used. On several doubtful readings it has been necessary to consult photostats of the first edition in the Bodleian.

'The Fields of Joy' is on sigs. K2–L1v, i.e. almost all Chap. IX, of *A Knight's Conjuring*, which was printed in London by Thomas Creede for William Barley in 1607. But, as we have seen, the book as a whole should be regarded as a revised and augmented version of *News from Hell, brought by the Devil's carrier*; this had been published by Ralph Blower and others for William Ferbrand in 1606, and had led to trouble in Stationers' Hall. Two works purporting to be sequels to Nashe's *Pierce Penniless* had been entered within a few days of one another in January 1606: the first of these, entered to Nathaniel Butter on the 15th and still extant, was 'a book called *The Return of the Knight of the Post from Hell, with the Devil's Answer to Pierce Penniless's Supplication*; the second, entered to Ferbrand on 25th, was 'a book called *The Devil's Let Loose*' (the head-title to the text of *News from Hell* is *The Devil Let Loose, with his Answer to Pierce Penniless*). Both entries are cancelled—by order, so a note states, of a Court held on 17th February. It appears from a transcript of Court Book 'C'[1] that on the court-day in question it was determined that, 'in recompence of the hindrance' he had done Mr East, Mr Windet (the printer of *The Return of the Knight of the Post from Hell*) was to pay him 40s. Nothing is said of printers or publishers known to be associated with Dekker's work. But it seems a reasonable conjecture that East held the copyright of Nashe's pamphlet, and regarded the publication of sequels as an infringement of it.

The passage from *A Knight's Conjuring* is represented in *News from Hell* solely by the following:

let me carry you up into those *Insulae Fortunatae* which are embraced about with waters sweet, redolent and crystalline—the tears of the vine are not so precious, the nectar of the gods nothing so sweet and delicious. If you walk into the groves you shall see all sorts of birds melodiously

[1] W. A. Jackson, *Records of the Court of The Stationers' Company 1602 to 1640* (London, 1957), p. 17.

singing, shepherds' swains deftly piping and virgins chastely dancing. You shall behold the trees ever flourishing, the fruits ever growing, the flowers ever springing. For the very benches whereon they sit are beds of violets, the beds[1] whereon they lie banks of musk-roses, their pillows are heart's-ease, their sheets the silken leaves of willow; upon which, lest my entranced soul lie too long and forget herself, let me here, like one started out of a golden dream, be so delighted with these treasures which I found in my sleep that for a while I stand amazed and speak nothing. *I am desine, tibia, versus.*

News from Hell has been reprinted only by A. B. Grosart, II, 83–153. *A Knight's Conjuring* has been reprinted only by E. F. Rimbault for the Percy Society (London, 1842), although in 1677 it formed the basis of a pamphlet of uncertain authorship, *Poor Robin's Visions, wherein is described the present humours of the times, the vices and fashionable fopperies thereof, and after what manner men are punished for them hereafter: discovered in a dream.* Poor Robin deliberately paraphrases, expands and abridges his copy to bring it up to date and perhaps to disguise his plagiary. In preparing the present text a microfilm of a copy of *A Knight's Conjuring* in the Henry E. Huntington Library has been followed.

Collation

149 balls] *This ed.;* ball *Q.*
153 Ideaques Bartolos] *Grosart;* Peagnes Bontolus *Q.*
155 Juliana] *This ed.;* Julia *Q.*
155 your sweet surgery] *Q3;* your sweete sugery *Q.*
156 her twenty nuns profited] *conj. Grosart;* her twelve nuns profited *Q.*
156 opprobratious] *This ed.;* opprobrious *Grosart;* approbatious *Q.*
161 their dortours] *Q3;* these dortours *Q.*
165 'The Fields of Joy' ... 'The Bay-Tree Grove'] *The chapter-heading Q.*
165 tears] *News from Hell* (Teares); leaues *Q.*

---

[1] buds of violets, the buddes *Q.*

English Villainies Discovered by Lantern and Candlelight

Sources

Lantern and Candlelight, which scored Dekker's greatest publishing success, was originally designed as a sequel to his *Bellman of London*. Published anonymously in London in March 1608, *The Bellman of London* was so well received that before the end of the year three further impressions had been called for, and in October Dekker was sufficiently encouraged to bring out *Lantern and Candlelight*.

The success of *The Bellman of London* occasioned a literary quarrel of which the details remain obscure but which has left its trace in *Lantern and Candlelight*. It would appear from 'To my Nation' that some unnamed writer attempted to pass off his work as by the Bellman or the Bellman's brother, the Beadle of Bridewell. Although nothing survives of what provoked Dekker's protests at this stage, the interloper was to publish again: in March 1610 *Martin Markall, Beadle of Bridewell, his Defence and Answers to the Bellman of London* appeared in London under the teasing initials of S.R., which may stand for 'Sa: Rid.'[1], author in 1612 of the underworld pamphlet *The Art of Juggling*. Martin Markall revealed that the Bellman had plundered a book then over forty years old—*A Caveat for Common Cursitors* (London, 1566) by Thomas Harman, a Justice of the Peace in Kent who had described the life and language of the vagabonds he had personally observed. The accusation is well merited. Indeed it does not go far enough: *The Bellman of London*, although it has a really fine original opening section, is a compendium of borrowings and adaptations from most of Dekker's predecessors in the art of the rogue pamphlet.

Lantern and Candlelight also has its sources. Much of the first chapter on canting is based on Harman,[2] eked out with a single untranslated (and perhaps untranslatable) set of 'canting rhythms' from Robert Copland's *The Highway to the Spital-House* (London, ?1536), one of the earliest English rogue pamphlets. Chapter II, like Dekker's *News from Hell*, doubtless owes

---

[1] Both letter-groups might be abbreviations. The authority for the expanded form 'Samuel Rid' is the Bodleian catalogue for 1620.

[2] Dekker's citing the types of vagabonds known 'four hundred years now past' shows that he did not use the lost first edition nor the last (1592) edition of Harman, in neither of which would he have found the relevant source passage.

something to the example of Nashe's *Pierce Penniless his Supplication to the Devil* (London, 1592), but it may also take its place in a long tradition of flippant mythologizing that goes back to Lucian and Aristophanes; possibly significant in Dekker's case is the fact that infernal satire was a common feature of German literature. Chapter X comes from Gervase Markham's *Cavelarice: or, The English Horseman* (London, 1607). For the rest, there may well be something in Dekker's clear statement in 'To my own Nation' and 'To the Reader' that the sequel to *The Bellman of London* was made possible by all the well-wishers who provided him with the suggestions or materials he needed. Certainly the section 'O per se—O' added in 1612 was, according to a marginal note printed in 1632, 'sent from a stranger to the author'. As it stands, it is a curious mixture of fresh, doubtless genuine information and mere padding. It is a response to, and a criticism of, *The Bellman of London* rather than *Lantern and Candlelight*. But either Dekker touched it up or else—and this is a rather more attractive guess—the writer or some redactor did what he could to imitate Dekker's style, perhaps with the possibility of publication in mind. But who was the writer? Presumably what he says, a former High Constable in the country—in fact an observer placed very much as Harman was. An analogue to parts of 'O per se—O', and evidence of the likelihood of its authenticity as social observation, is a letter written on 25th September 1596 to Burghley by Edward Hext, a Justice of the Peace in Somersetshire.[1]

It is reasonable to suppose that there is some foundation of truth to the tales told. Doubts have been raised about the Falconers of Chapter V and their planned exploitation of patrons by means of multiple dedications. One must admit that before the middle of 17th century there is no bibliographical proof of their activity; but on the other hand Dekker's feelings do seem to be genuinely aroused, and he has something further to say on the subject elsewhere, in a dedication of his own to *The Seven Deadly Sins of London*. Chapter VIII is historically important as an early account of English gypsies. One wonders if in Chapter XXIII a personal note is struck when Dekker complains that

> in most of the suburbian outroads the best men there that command the rest, the Grand Signiors of the parish—as constables, headboroughs and other officers—are common alehouse-keepers. (p. 281)

Middlesex County Records tell of a Robert Dickers who was both innholder and Constable of St Giles-in-the-Fields.

In *The Plague Pamphlets of Thomas Dekker* (Oxford, 1925), F. P. Wilson shows that the peroration of *The Black Rod and the White Rod* (London,

---

[1] Preserved among the Lansdowne MSS in the British Museum; reprinted in F. Aydelotte, *Elizabethan Rogues and Vagabonds* (Oxford, 1913), pp. 167–73, and in *Tudor Economic Documents*, ed. R. H. Tawney and Eileen Power (London, 1924), II, 339–46.

1630), one of the pamphlets which he attributes to Dekker, is very like the peroration of Conscience's speech in Chapter XXI of the augmented edition of *Lantern and Candlelight*. It is hard to decide which is the original. The absence from Conscience's speech of the phrase 'No Women-keepers to rob you of your Goods, nor to hasten you to your End', which one finds in *The Black Rod*, unfortunately proves nothing one way or the other. If *The Black Rod* came first, then the phrase may have been cut out in *Lantern and Candlelight* because of the proximity of Chapter XXII, 'The abuses of keepers, nurses or charwomen', which it may even have suggested. On the other hand, if *Lantern and Candlelight* came first, then of course the phrase in *The Black Rod* may instead have been suggested by Chapter XXII. Publishing evidence (discussed in the section following, on the 'Text') raises the possibility that Chapter XXI may have been printed, as in any case it may have been written, before *The Black Rod*.

It was chiefly the old material from Harman that caught the fancy of the public. As Martin Markall relates, *The Bellman of London* started a fashion:

> There hath been of late days great pains taken on the part of the good old Bellman of London in discovering, as he thinks, a new-found nation and people. Let it be so for this time. Hereupon much ado was made in setting forth their lives, order of living, method of speech, and usual meetings, with divers other things thereunto appertaining. These volumes and papers now spread everywhere, so that every jack-boy now can say as well as the proudest of that fraternity: 'Will you wap for a win, or trine for a make?'[1]

This question must have been a popular catchphrase on every smart Alec's lips; it is echoed by the author of 'O per se—O' (p. 286). But it is not from Dekker.

Not only pamphleteers but playwrights as well tried to make hay while the sun shone. First in the field no doubt was Dekker himself, who with Middleton wrote *The Roaring Girl* (c. 1610). This was followed by Fletcher's *Beggars' Bush* (before 1622), and at some distance by Brome's *Jovial Crew* (1641). Two lost plays may be conjectured to use the material: *The Bellman of London* (1613) by Robert Daborne and Cyril Tourneur, and *The Bellman of Paris* (1623) by Dekker and Day. The most distinguished literary outcome of the fashion may well be a single character—Autolycus.

The more original part of *Lantern and Candlelight*, the prison chapters, also had an impact upon other writers.[2] Explicit admiration for Dekker's *Bellman of London* is voiced in 1616 by William Fennor in *The Counter's Commonwealth: or, A Voyage Made to an Infernal Island, discovered by many*

[1] A. V. Judges, *The Elizabethan Underworld* (London, 1930), p. 386.
[2] See P. Shaw, 'The Position of Thomas Dekker in Jacobean Prison Literature,' *PMLA*, LXII (1947), 366–91.

captains, seafaring men, gentlemen, merchants and other tradesmen. Dekker's fellow-prisoner and plagiarist was Geffray Mynshul, who based much of his *Certain Characters and Essays of Prison and Prisoners* (London, 1618) on the prison chapters. John Taylor made his own contribution to the new genre with his *Praise and Virtue of a Gaol and Gaolers* (London, 1623).

Lantern and Candlelight is associated in its title and in the title-page woodcut of its first quarto with Samuel Rowlands's *Diogenes's Lantern* (entered in the *Stationers' Register* on 5th December 1606 and published in London in 1607), a very popular satirical miscellany mainly composed of allegory and fables. Rowlands's title alludes to the legend, derived from Diogenes Laertius, that Diogenes the Cynic took a lantern and candle in broad daylight in order to look for one honest man in Athens. The woodcut shows him beside his remarkably well-furnished barrel, setting out with the lantern in his left hand. Dekker's first title-page reproduces the same figure without the barrel and with a bell added to the right hand. A lantern had of course manifold associations (see *bell, lantern and candlelight*, in the Glossary).

Text

In the course of forty years this work passed through at least eight editions, of which only the last two were unsophisticated reprints. The first (Q1) was entered on the *Stationers' Register* to John Busby Junior on 25th October 1608 as 'a book called *Lantern and Candlelight: or, The Second Part of "The Bellman"* ', and it was published by his father the same year. The second edition (Q2), which followed in 1609, claimed to be 'newly corrected and amended', and it is clear from some of the many changes made—such as the provision of a name, Pamersiel, for the Devil's messenger where Q1 leaves a blank—and from errors of misreading that Q2 was in fact set up from a copy of Q1 that had been corrected either by the author or with reference to his manuscript. The third edition (Q3), dated 1612, reprinted Q2 without the original dedication and commendatory verses but added a substantial new section, 'O per se—O', which gave its title to the whole work: *O per se—O: or, A New Crier of Lantern and Candlelight, being an addition or lengthening of 'The Bellman's Second Night-Walk' in which are discovered those villainies which the Bellman because he went i' th' dark could not see, now laid open to the world together with the shooting through the arm used by counterfeit soldiers, the making of the great sore commonly called 'the great cleyme', the madmen's marks, their phrase of begging, the articles and oaths given to the fraternity of rogues, vagabonds and sturdy beggars at their meetings; and, last of all, a new canting song*. Though the greater part of the fourth edition (Q4) in 1616 was a reprint of Q3, a number of changes were made: six chapters on prison life (Chapters XIII–XVIII in the present text), 'The Bellman's Cry' and three canting songs appeared for the first time; one line was replaced in a canting song; the address to the reader was revised; the chapter on canting was moved to a position immediately before 'O per se—O', occasioning thereby some minor adjustments to the text; and the general title was recast to *Villainies Discovered by Lantern and Candlelight and the help of A New Crier Called 'O per se—O', being an addition to 'The Bellman's Second Night-Walk' and a laying open to the world of those abuses which the Bellman because he went i' th' dark could not see; with canting songs never before printed*. On 27th September 1619 the copyright of 'a book called *O per se—O: or, The Bellman of London*' was assigned by Busby Senior to Augustine Mathewes, a transaction which was Busby's last and Mathewes's first to be recorded in the *Stationers' Register*. Mathewes very quickly substantiated his right by printing the fifth edition (Q5) early in 1620, representing it to have 'new conceits' and to be 'newly corrected and enlarged by the author'; apart from a trifling change in the Term-times mentioned in the address to the reader, half a dozen comparatively minor insertions and the addition of one longer passage describing the Impostor and the Deluder, it was in actuality no more than an unrevised, uncorrected reprint of Q4.

Internal evidence suggests that an edition now lost followed in about 1626. The title-page of Q6 shows that there had been not five, but six previous editions: *English Villainies, six several times pressed to death by the printers but, still reviving again, are now the seventh time as at first discovered by Lantern and Candlelight and the help of A New Crier Called 'O per se—O', whose loud voice proclaims to all that will hear him another conspiracy of abuses lately plotting together to hurt the peace of this Kingdom—which the Bellman because he then went stumbling i' th' dark could never see till now; and because a company of rogues, cunning canting gypsies and all the scum of our nation fight here under their own tattered colours, at the end is a canting dictionary to teach their language, with canting songs. A book to make gentlemen merry, citizens wary, countrymen careful; fit for all Justices to read over, because it is a pilot by whom they may make strange discoveries*. The address to the reader of Q4, on the other hand, speaks as we should expect of 'a fourth set battle' and, rather misleadingly, this phrase is reprinted in Q5. It would therefore seem probable that a sixth edition was brought out between Q5 and Q6—that is, between 1620 and 1632. This would fit quite well into the general publishing history of the work, which one would suppose too popular to lie unreprinted for twelve years just at this time. Now the Q6 address to the reader recalls that 'a bed of strange snakes'—English villainies—were *first* discovered eighteen years before. If this is to be taken at its face value, then it wrongly asserts that the year 1614, which actually fell midway between Q3 and Q4, was the date of publication of Q1. But if instead we assume that the year 1608 was the date meant, then it may well be argued that the Q6 address to the reader is merely a reprint of a text which was first written and presumably also first published in 1626. One result of accepting the conjecture of an edition in 1626 would be a loss to Dekker biography. The possibility would have to be entertained that the 1632 dedication to the Justices of the Peace for Middlesex, with its passing reference to Dekker's 'threescore years' that is our principal if already vague evidence for his date of birth, might have originated as much as six years earlier.

Be that as it may, the next edition after 1620 which has come down to us and which for the present we are to designate as Q6 is dated 1632, and for all one can say to the contrary it appears to have reprinted a copy of Q5 to which a number of alterations great and small had been made. Now entitled *English Villainies*, as we have seen, it contained the dedication to Middlesex J.P.s, a revised address to the reader partly based on that of QQ4–5, and five new chapters taking the place of the six that had first appeared in Q4; two canting songs were newly translated, but a third was omitted; some adjustments were made to the text to allow the chapter on canting to be again moved, this time to a position between the bulk of 'O per se—O' and its accumulated songs (which were thus made to follow the song in the chapter on canting); and there were some isolated and trivial instances of cutting and rewording here and there, some of which seem to have been the result of moral and religious censorship.

The two final seventeenth-century editions were that for Marmaduke Parsons in 1638 (Q7) and that for Nicholas Gamage in 1648 (Q8). They are parallel reprints of Q6. Of the two, Q7 alone differs significantly from copy, and then only in one very minor particular. The first sentence of the address to the reader is altered so as to suggest that the original edition of the work had been printed not *eighteen* (as in Q6) but *twenty* years earlier. In this Parsons may be betraying his anxiety over the strength of his copyright, which he had only recently acquired along with a printing-press from the much impoverished Mathewes.

The present edition is the first attempt to reprint the whole work. Q2 has been reprinted by A. B. Grosart in *The Non-Dramatic Works of Thomas Dekker*, The Huth Library (London, 1884–86), III, 171–303, and by O. Smeaton in *The Guls Hornbook and The Belman of London In Two Parts by Thomas Dekker*, The Temple Classics (London, 1904), pp. 159–273. In *The Elizabethan Underworld* (London, 1930), pp. 312–82, A. V. Judges gives a text which is based substantially on Q2 but which has been collated on some points with Q1; to save space he omits the chapter on canting. Judges also provides the first modern reprint of the 'O per se—O' section from Q3. Additions, such as the prison chapters, subsequent to Q3 have not been reprinted since their own day.

In preparing a complete text it is well-nigh impossible to assess Dekker's own final intentions as to the order and contents of his work although, as the successive changes in it go to show, he was to some degree personally responsible for it over the twenty-five years from 1608 to 1632. Two particular problems may illustrate the difficulties. Thus, the chapter on canting alone has a curious textual history. What is virtually advance notice of its first publication is given at the end of the third edition of *The Bellman of London* in 1608, but in the event it must have been submitted much later than planned to the printer, who was obliged to make an allowance of space for it—that was, as it proved, far from generous enough—and to start work on the rest of *Lantern and Candlelight*. The course of events is revealed by the run of signatures and the position of the watermarks, and by the setting up before Chapter II of what was probably half-intended to be a regular general head-title—'The Bellman's Second Night's Walk' (which was to remain the alternative to 'Lantern and Candlelight' on the title-page and in the true head-title, and was also to be the heading of Chapter XII, the only part of the book to which it was really appropriate). Twice, in the editions of Q4 and Q6, the chapter on canting was shifted, though it is difficult to say why this should have been so. Was it to give a specious appearance of freshness to the opening pages of the new editions? Was it because the material had become notorious as plagiary and was better tucked out of sight? Or were the reasons more stylistic than commercial—was the editor dissatisfied with the design of the book? After all, it had two seemingly unrelated opening chapters, and indeed the first of these had few obvious affinities with anything that it was supposed to introduce unless it was the final 'O per se—O' section, which was an oddity itself even more difficult to assimilate. So perhaps, by combining the incongruous chapter and the incongruous section, he was trying to kill his two gawky birds with one stone. The question as to whether Dekker was the editor who made these decisions must remain unanswered.

Doubt also surrounds the first appearance in Q6 of the five chapters which in the present edition have been numbered XIX–XXIII. Of these, XIX–XXI need to be considered as a separate trio. Each of them begins with a reference to what has gone before, and these references link them not only to one another in the order they now have but also, as a continuation, to the group of six chapters (XIII–XVIII in the present edition) that had been printed sixteen years earlier in Q4: it had plainly been the intention that all nine chapters should form a single series about imprisonment. But as it turned out the later three did not follow the six; they replaced them. Some confusion in Q6 Table of Contents is no doubt an incidental sign of some trouble with the new material. There is no reason to assume that the three chapters of Q6 were written at the same time as the six of Q4. Indeed, if the chapter on nurses (Chapter XXII in the present edition) is strictly contemporary in composition with the three prison chapters of its Q6 group, then it is noteworthy that it contains a specific allusion to the fall of Breda in 1625 and, less conclusively, what is probably a general allusion to the outbreak of plague in 1625 (easily the most severe since 1603 and in fact second in severity only to the Great Plague of 1665). Were Chapters XIX–XXIII originally written then for the supposed lost edition of 1626?

Even in a reprint the modern editor has to take into account all the additions, omissions and rewordings to be found in QQ3–8, and to come to some working hypothesis about them. Fortunately, the instances of omission and rewording that can with any confidence be attributed to Dekker are confined to the address to the reader, and one line in the canting songs. The most convenient procedure is therefore to adopt Q1 corrected against Q2 as initial copy, and to incorporate all subsequent additions wherever possible, in the earliest form in which they occur.

Except for omissions, all departures found in succeeding editions from what may be termed accumulative copy are recorded in the textual notes, whether or not they are regarded as authorial, provided they are regarded as intentional and not simply the result of compositorial error. Within the present text itself additions are not marked if they constitute self-contained units, but if they are insertions in older passages they are enclosed in square brackets. Side-notes have not been reprinted.

In deciding when differences between Q1 and Q2 are due to corrections by the author or to carelessness in the printing-house, unexpected aid is to be found in the fact that some of the new substantive readings in Q2 are set up in roman type in a context of black letter where Q1 has black letter alone. This is presumably because the annotations were in an italic hand. One such annotation which gave the correct reading 'sergeants' in place of 'servants' (see textual note below for p. 203), besides being adopted (in roman) within the text itself, was also erroneously set up in roman in the margin as for a side-note, and this was slavishly reprinted in all the following six editions. The textual notes below specify the character of the fount where it supports the case for emendation.

Also recorded below are a few certain or probable errors which Dekker has committed in using his sources and which a modern editor is of course obliged to leave uncorrected in the text.

It has been beyond the scope of the present project to collate all copies of each edition, and it is likely enough that further investigation would show that some copies which bear the same date and appear at first glance to belong to the same edition are bibliographically distinct from one another. The present reprint has been prepared from microfilms of Q1 and Q2 in the Folger Library; Q3, Q5 and Q7 in the British Museum; Q4 and Q8 in the Henry E. Huntington Library; and Q6 in the Harvard University Library.

Collation

173   *The Bellman's Cry* . . . mine eyes] *Q4; not in QQ1–3.*

174–5   *A Table*] *The chapter numbering of Chaps. XIII–XXIV, this ed.; the titles of Chaps. XIII–XVIII from Q4 Table, those of Chaps. XIX–XXIII from the text of Q6, that of Chap. XXIV from the text of Q3; 'O per se—O' is first presented as a numbered chapter in Q6 Table and text. For the present Chaps. XIX–XXIII, Q6 Table offers the following three titles:* The abuses of women-keepers; Abuses of alehouses; Abuses in the suburbs by common strumpets, etc.

177   in this our school] *Q2;* in ⟨ . . . . ⟩ school *clipped in Q.*

178–9   *To the Glory of Middlesex* . . . THOS. DEKKER] *Q6; not in QQ1–5.*

180   doth in a fourth set battle once again bravely] *Q4;* doth now bravely *Q.*

180   Easter Term and Trinity Term] *Q5;* Michaelmas Term *Q.*

180   To furnish this army . . . mettle they are] *Q4; not in QQ1–3.*

182–3   *To the Reader* . . . Farewell] *Q6; not in QQ1–3; QQ4–5 has under the title of 'To the Reader' a rewriting of Q 'To my own Nation' with an ending similar to that of Q6 'To the Reader', namely,* All that before was written or now newly added is to yield thee both profit and pleasure. Here is physic and counsel; to lay hold upon which I leave them, if by knowing the secret mischiefs, abuses, villainies and disorders of the world, thou at least desirest to arm thyself against them, or to guard thy friend by advice from them. Read and laugh: read seriously, and get knowledge. Farewell.

182   eighteen years past] *Q6 (18);* twenty years past *Q7.*

187   When all the world] *Q;* Because in this discourse ensuing much speech is had of canting, you shall therefore know how it grew to be a language. When all the world *Q4; in QQ4–5 the chapter on canting immediately precedes 'O per se—O'.*

190   soldiers of these tattered] *Q2;* soldier of these tattered *Q.*

192   prounce's] *Q from Copland* prounces; *prance's or prancer's conj. this ed. (praunces or prauncers).*

193   to cut bene] *Q (to cutt bene);* to cutte benle *or* benie *Harman.*

194   butter, milk or whey] *Q from Harman, for* butter-milk or whey.

194   *poplars,* pottage] *Q;* poppelars porrage *Harman. But Dekker consistently substitutes* pottage *for* porrage *both here and in 'The Bellman of London'.*

195   *Rome booze*] *Q2 (Rome-bowse);* Rome-bowsie *Q.*

195   *stuling ken*] *Q;* staulig ken *Harman.*

196   stamps in the harmans] *Q2;* stamps in the harman *Q.*

196   heave a booth] *Q2;* have a booth *Q.*

196   gentry cofe's ken] *Q2;* country cofe's ken *Q.*

197   sound as of men] *Q2;* sound of men *Q.*

198   clients that complain] *Q2;* clients that complained *Q.*

198 their wives for pride and servants for stealth] *Q5; not in QQ1–4.*

200 lay their heads together] *Q2;* lay their heards togither *Q;* beards *conj. this ed.*

200 with his night rimes] *Q5; not in QQ1–4.*

201 of the Grand Sophy] *Q2;* of Grand Sophy *Q.*

202 Hereupon Pamersiel the messenger] *Q2;* Hereupon —— the messenger *Q.*

202 Fly, Pamersiel, with speed] *Q2;* Fly —— with speed *Q.*

202 if an Irishman, flatter] *Q5; not in QQ1–4.*

203 nimble of his heels] *Q2;* nimble of heels *Q.*

203 sergeants] *Q2 (rom.* Serieants)*; servants Q (b.l.* seruants)*; Q2 also sets up* sergeants *(rom.* serieants) *in the margin.*

204 Here he heard fools . . . wise men dumb] *Q5; not in QQ1–4.*

204 perceived knaves solicit] *This ed.;* perceiu'd knaues solleit *Q5;* perceiu'd knaues collect *Q6.*

205 or 'Impost-Taker'] *Q5; not in QQ1–4.*

208–9 To these there is another . . . curses of undone people] *Q5; not in QQ1–4.*

208 Impostor's friend and half] *This ed.;* Impostor's friend half *Q5;* Impostor's friend's half *Q6.*

209 take money for jewels] *This ed.;* take money, jewels *Q5.*

210 CHAPTER IV] *Q2; this heading not in Q.*

210 the pursuers never give over] *Q2 (rom.* Pursuers)*;* the Pursnets neuer giue ouer *Q (b.l.* Pursnets).

210 these are barbarous] *Q2;* thse are barbarous *Q.*

211 wounds the deer of the land] *Q2;* wound the deer of the land *Q.*

211 makes such havoc] *Q3;* make such havoc *Q.*

211 goodliest herds] *Q2 (rom.* goodliest)*; b.l.* headlese Heards *Q.*

211 these Rabbit-Suckers run] *Q2;* this Rabbit-Suckers run *Q.*

211 out of their holes] *Q2;* out of the their holes *Q.*

212 those to come] *Q2* (thos to come)*;* thus to come *Q.*

212 dabbing on the necks] *Q2;* dubbing on the necks *Q.*

213 do now more trouble their wits] *Q2;* do now trouble their wits *Q.*

213 is lost £30] *Q6;* is lost 30 *Q.*

214 add £10 more] *Q2;* and £10 more *Q.*

214 remaineth only £330] *This ed.;* remaineth only 330 *Q.*

214 Nay, it hath been verily reported . . . but not wonderful] *Q5; not in QQ1–4.*

214 lie scouting] *Q2;* lies scouting *Q.*

214 into any statute] *Q2;* into statute *Q.*

215 CHAPTER V] *This heading from Judges; not in QQ1–5;* CHAPTER IV *Q6.*

215 Doctor] *Q2;* Doctors *Q.*

217 which our Heliconian angler] *Q2;* which Heliconian angler *Q.*

218 England] *Q2 rom.; b.l.* Holland *Q.*

219 saving only to that] *Q2;* having only to that *Q.*
219 cozens five hundred] *Q2 (rom.* Cozens*);* cozened five hundred *Q (b.l.* cozned*).*
219 smoking in,] *Q2;* smoking, *Q.*
220 smell more earthy] *Q2;* smell more earth *Q;* smell more of earth *conj. this ed.*
220 throwing by the apron] *Q2;* thriving by the apron *Q.*
220 cast up their gall] *Q2;* cast up the gall *Q.*
221 CHAPTER VI] *Q2; this heading not in Q.*
221 in praise of the Union] *Q2 (rom.* Vnion*);* in praise of the rhymer *Q (b.l.* rimer*).*
223 CHAPTER VII] *Q2; this heading not in Q.*
223 ever in a gallop] *Q2;* even in a gallop *Q.*
225 where the gentleman or farmer dwelleth] *Q2;* where the gentleman— farmer dwelleth *Q.*
226 these Snaffles are loosed] *Q2;* this Snaffles are loosed *Q.*
228 CHAPTER VIII] *Q2; this heading not in Q.*
229 pairs of panniers] *Q2;* paiers of panieles *Q.*
229 hanging their bodies] *Q2 (rom.* hanging*);* having their bodies *Q (b.l.* hauing*).*
230 enclose the murdered] *Q2;* enclose the murderers *Q.*
232 their pay in Hell] *Q;* their pay where it was due *Q6.*
233 CHAPTER IX] *Q2; this heading not in Q.*
233 Grand Bawd] *Q2;* ground bawd *Q.*
237 CHAPTER X] *Q2; this heading not in Q.*
239 Jingling mountebank Smithfield rider] *Q2;* jangling mountebank Smithfield rider *Q.*
240 root of the tongue] *This ed.;* roof of the tongue *Q; Markham has* root of the tongue.
241 by foul play. And] *Q2;* by foul. And *Q.*
241. lamb-pie breakfast] *Q2;* lamb-pie breakfasts *Q.*
242 tumbler's prentice, by compulsion] *Q2;* tumbler's prentice, by com- position *Q.*
243 for the most part none but gallants] *Q2;* for the most none but gallants *Q.*
243 cozen of this race] *Q2;* cozen of this races *Q.*
243 by a false dye] *Q2 (rom.* Dye*);* by a false diet *Q (b.l.* diet*).*
245 glad to take forty shillings] *Q2;* glad to take forty pounds *Q.*
249 CHAPTER XII] *Q2; this heading not in Q.*
249 *night prizes of villainy*] *Q6; not in QQ1–5.*
249–50 beat with their bold] *Q2;* bear with their bold *Q.*
250 Candlelight's eyesight] *Q2;* Candlelight eyesight *Q.*
251 stole to his couch] *Q3;* stole to his coach *Q.*
252 four or five good-nights] *Q3;* four of five good-nights *Q.*

253 *Here Endeth the Bellman*] *Q3; not in QQ1–2.*

253–72 But, calling to mind . . . So I of gaolers] *Q4; not in QQ1–3.*

255 CHAPTER XIII] *This ed.;* CHAPTER XI *Q4; and so consecutively for Chaps. XIV–XVIII.*

255 bowlines] *This ed.* (bollings); bottings *Q4, but probably Dekker means* bonnets.

269 Of such pearls 'tis hard] *This ed.;* Of such pearl 'tis hard *Q4.*

270 As laws are the foundation] *This ed.;* As laws are the sound action *Q4;* As laws are the found action *Q5.*

273 CHAPTER XIX] *This ed.;* CHAPTER XII *Q6; and so consecutively for Chaps. XX–XXIII.*

273–82 *The abuses done to prisoners* . . . standing too idle] *Q6; not in QQ1–5.*

277 was as sweet society] *This ed.;* was asweete societie *Q6.*

285 CHAPTER XXIV] *This ed.;* CHAPTER XVIII *Q6.*

285 *O per se—O*] *Q3;* And now to our discourse of 'O per se—O', under which name the author disguising and shadowing himself thus begins *Q4.*

285–303 And so good morrow . . . With hempen wings to Tyburn. FINIS] *Q3; not in QQ1–2.*

286 denial of it with oaths] *Q4;* denyall of it with oates *Q3.*

291 more terrible to women and children] *Q5;* more terribly to women and children *Q3.*

292 shoeing-horn] *This ed.;* sharing horn *Q3.*

293 Her Majesty's late wars, as well for God's cause as Her Majesty's] *Q3;* His Majesty's late wars, as well for God's cause as His Majesty's *Q6.*

293 which are clapped upon the arm] *Q4;* which are clap upon the arm *Q3.*

300 To shut up this feast . . . sung at their meetings] *Q3;* All these fore-named monsters of a kingdom, with many others like them, as they are differing from others in their manner of life, so have they begotten among themselves as strange a gibberish language which they call canting *Q6; in QQ6–8 the canting songs from 'O per se—O' are transferred to the end of the chapter on canting, which is otherwise made to follow 'O per se—O'; the song beginning* Bing out, bene morts *is then re-entitled 'Another Sung by the Canters at their Meeting'.*

302 10. Bing out] *Judges;* 10 Bingd out *Q3.*

303 Hell's plague the Justice' heart consume] *Q4;* Ill may the Justice ever thrive *Q3.*

303–4 *Another.* 1. Doxy O! . . . And trining scape, and all is well] *Q4; not in QQ1–3.*

304 And her cackling cheats withal] *This ed.;* And her cackling cheat withal *Q4.*

304 7. Bing awast] *Q5;* Bing awast *Q4.*

304–5 *Thus Englished.* 1. O my chuck . . . And Tyburn scape, and all is well] *Q6; not in QQ1–5.*

305 6. There if] *Q7;* 5. There if *Q6.*

305 7. To London] *Q7;* 6. To London *Q6.*

305–6 *Another.* 1. Now my kinchin cove . . . Yet the ruffler in't was true] *Q4; not in QQ1–3.*

305 And through the Deuce-a-ville] *This ed.;* And thy Deuce-a-ville *Q4.*

306–7 *Another, thus Englished.* 1. Now my little rogue . . . My brave strong rogue in't yet was true] *Q6; not in QQ1–5.*

307–8 *Another.* 1. A queer cove . . . *Vale!* FINIS] *Q4; not in QQ1–3.*

308 2. This cuffin] *This ed.;* 2. Thus cuffin *Q4.*

308 FINIS] *Q4; unique to Q7 is the concluding permit of the censor* Febru. 27. 1637 Recudatur Matth. Clay.

GLOSSARY

Page numbers refer usually to the first or only instance of any expression or sense, but sometimes to the most problematical instance when this is not the first. To save space, some entries are grouped together under the most convenient word, and cross-references are kept to the minimum.

There are two kinds of gloss: first, such definition or translation as is basic to understanding, secondly (introduced by 'i.e.' or enclosed in square brackets) a note giving the background or further implications of the word or expression in the specific reference. Semi-colons mark off distinct senses of a word except where a longer expression repeating the word is separately quoted and glossed. The designation 'pun' has been freely used to cover many different kinds of multiple sense.

An asterisk(*) indicates that the occurrence of an expression or sense is earlier than any other given by the New English Dictionary; *an obelus (†) that this or some other occurrence in Dekker is given by the* New English Dictionary *as the first anywhere.*

*about with, have: ? deal with 63.

Abraham man: beggar pretending to be mad [from the name of a ward in Bedlam, q.v.] 189. Also *Abr'am,* 290.

abroad: in all directions 81; at large 257.

absit: 'may it be averted'; far from it 83.

absolute: perfect 121.

account, make: take into account, calculate 28.

Acheley, Thomas: poet and translator of high repute in Nashe's day 168.

*aconited: poisoned 28.

acquit: requite 159. acquittance: settlement of debts 57.

Actæon: mythological hunter turned into a stag by Diana [see horns] 56.

action: histrionic gesture and movement [pun] 41. action at the case: proceedings (commonly vexatious) taken for debt, on the grounds that it is an offence against rightful expectation of repayment rather than simply a breach of contract 134.

Adage and Apophthegm: proverb and maxim [? with reference to Erasmus's *Adagia* (Paris, 1500) and *Apothegmata* (Basle, 1531)] 72.

admiral: chief ship of a merchant fleet 60.

admiration: wonder 50.

advantage: opportunity 228. advantage of compliment: pretext of courtesy, e.g. by bowing 89.

adventure: speculative investment 125.

Æolus: mythical controller of the winds 51.

again: repeatedly; with abandon 55.

Age, Golden: idyllic earliest Age of the four progressively degenerating Ages in myth (Gold, Silver, Brazen, Iron) under the reign of the god Saturn

[pun] 41, cf. 176–7. Thus Saturnian, 78. Saturnist: one of saturnine temperament—morose, cold, dull 87.

aim, give: observe and direct the shooting 39.

Aisle, Mediterranean, Middle: main concourse of St Paul's Cathedral [pun] 51, 176, Plate IV.

al savio mezza parola basta: 'to the wise, a brief word is enough' [Italian] 67.

ale, huff's: see huff. Pinder's ale: ? ale sold at the *Pinder of Wakefield* tavern, near Gray's Inn 49. aleconner: inspector of ale 61.

aloes, syrup of: bitter medicine 73.

aloof: at some distance 62.

amazed: terrified, bewildered 44.

Amphitruo: play by Plautus, the Roman comedy-writer 28.

angel: gold coin worth about ten shillings [pun] 62. light angels: i.e. light-weight, counterfeit [pun] 200.

answerable: suitable 117.

*anthropophagized: turned into a man-eater 42.

antic: clown, grotesque 73.

Antiquity: ? i.e. such satires as those by Ovid and attributed to Virgil. But Erasmus's *Moriae Encomium* (Strasburg, 1511) might be meant 79.

apes of the kingdom: ? political gossips; ? performing apes [such as jump over a chain if the king is named] 96.

Apollo (Phœbus): classical god of poetry 29, 167, like King James in being associated both with the north and the sun 39, cf. 28, being the patron of poets 40, being himself a poet 41. sit at the table of the Sun: be in the select company of great writers 168. by Apollo's sign: ? by what Apollo stands for (i.e. ideal poetry); ? by intimation of the god-king [proclamations in May and July restrained access to London and the Court to prevent the spread of the plague] 40.

apothecary: chemist and grocer, seller of wine and tobacco [where the gallant might resort for his morning drink] 207, cf. 95.

apple-squire: procurer 77.

aqua cælestis: restorative, distilled from wine 41. *aqua-vitæ:* spirits 53.

aquila non capit muscas: 'the eagle does not catch flies' (Erasmus) [they are beneath his dignity] 216.

Arcadian and Euphuized gentlewomen: ladies of fashion who affect the wit and style of Sidney's *Arcadia* (London, 1590) and Lyly's *Euphues* (London, 1578) [very démodé and bourgeois by this time] 102.

argosy: merchant vessel of the greatest size 255.

arms, give: show armorial bearings, i.e. be a gentleman [pun] 34.

ars homicidiorum: 'the art of murders' 81.

artificial: deliberate, imitation 76. artificially: craftily 300.

*ass*afœtida: asafœtida, a stinking resinous gum used in medicine [pun on 'ass'] 79.

atomy: atom, pigmy 216.

attach: arrest 198.

Attic: Athenian 167.

audita querela: writ to stay execution of judgment on a debtor to hear further argument 198.

Augeas: mythical king whose enormous filthy stables were cleansed by Hercules 78.

aunt: prostitute [pun] 236.

aurum potabile: 'drinkable gold'; a medical preparation containing gold [pun] 49.

autem mort: married woman vagrant 189.

Avaro, Signior: 'Mr Miser' [Italian] 206.

ave: shout of welcome 33.

Averroës (1126–98): Spanish physician famous for his handbook of medicine, and commentary on Avicenna [q.v.] 151.

Avicenna (980–1037): Persian physician famous for codifying medical knowledge; an authority on the plague 49.

avoid: expel 239.

away: go away, not persist 29.

back, have by the: lay hold of, seize [? pun] 52. backside: back yard 52.

bait: ? contentiousness; food [pun] 34; halt for refreshment 223.

bald: graceless [pun] 78.

bale (of dice): set of nine pair 96.

Bales, Peter: famous writing-master b. 1547. In 1575 he wrote the Lord's Prayer and much else on a penny and presented it to the Queen 39.

Balthazar: in Kyd's *Spanish Tragedy* (= *Hieronimo*) II. i. 111–15 he speaks alternately of being 'glad' and 'sad' at learning he has a successful rival, Horatio, for the hand of Bel-imperia—glad to be able to revenge himself on him, sad at not being able to enjoy his success [the cobbler has more rivals but will do less about them] 57. In a famous night-scene, II. v., Hieronimo is roused from his 'naked bed' to find his son Horatio murdered 250.

ban: curse 49.

band: collar, ruff 280.

bandog: mastiff 62.

Banks: trainer of the famous performing horse Morocco that ascended Paul's steeple in 1600 and did other much-discussed tricks such as counting numbers, identifying the owners of objects, etc. 29, cf. 91.

banquet: dessert, delicacy 134.

Barathrum: pit of hell 199.

barber: dentist as well as hairdresser 238.

barely: with apparent candour 216.

*Bartholomew-babies: dolls sold at Bartholomew Fair at West Smithfield on 24th August 212.

basilisk: mythical reptile whose look was fatal 45. Thus basilisk-eyed, 34.

bastinado, baston: beating [pun] 57, 28.

battledore: ? *horn-book [q.v.]; ? the shape of the lower-case letter 'b'. Hence, distinguish a B from a battledore: be able to read; have intelligence 74.

bavin: brushwood 115.

bawd, parcel: see parcel.

bawdy-basket: thieving whore who pretends to be a pedlar 189.

beadle: law officer whose duties included the whipping of vagabonds and other offenders 178.

bear away the bell: outstrip the others 76.

beast, the great, the many-headed, of many heads: the mob, the masses 98, 178, 96.

beaten to this world: broken-in, experienced 231. beaten together: slammed shut

[? so forcibly as to shatter the timbers] 52. beating the price: haggling 204.

Bedlam: Hospital of St Mary of Bethlehem outside Bishopsgate, a lunatic asylum 51.

bees: i.e. according to traditional belief, swarms could be reclaimed by beating on kettles and pans 62.

beg for a concealment: see concealment. swear by no beggars: i.e. swear fiercely 34.

bell, bear away the: see bear. bellman: one of two nightwatchmen appointed under Queen Elizabeth to patrol the City streets to guard against fire and robbery, and give the time 108. The official cry was 'Remember the clocks,/Look well to your locks,/Fire and your light,/And God give you good night,/For now the bell ringeth.' Cf. 173. He made a din by ringing his bell and knocking on doors 199. The Bellman in his first voyage, in his first round: Dekker's persona, as one versed in the ways of various criminals, was first assumed in *The Bellman of London* (1608) 189, the third edition of which gives a sample of thieves' cant and promises more 195. the Bellman's brother, 180, see 321.

Bentley, John: popular actor of the Queen's Men 168.

bewray: divulge 155.

Bi*ass:* see Seven Wise Masters.

bill: placard; indictment [pun] 48; promissory note 77; halberd [pun] 77. brown bills: ? i.e. rusty, ? painted brown 107. chalky bills: ? i.e. treated with chalk against rust [pun] 280. billmen: men armed with bills 64, nightwatchmen 235.

bing awast: go away 307.

Birchin Lane: quarter by Cornhill for drapers and clothes dealers 49.

birding-piece: gun for shooting birds 78.

Black Dog of Newgate: legendary spectral dog who haunted the prison at execution-time [the legend had recently been dramatized] 201. black guard: menials [? pun] 201.

blain: sore 46.

blaze: expose 184.

blazon: heraldic shield 278.

blind: imperceptive; inconsiderate; deceitful 198; out of the way, secret 225; without a light 96.

block: mould for a hat; a style, fit or shape of hat [pun] 88.

blow: shot, go [pun] 85. downright blows: plain deeds, 'brass tacks' [pun] 282.

bodily fear: fear for their physical well-being 38.

*boil: search 301.

bolt: arrow 28.

bombasted: ? coated, plated 41.

bones: dice 205. ten bones: fingers 62. make dice of other men's bones: let them rot in prison [proverbial] 198.

book: account-book. crossed the book: marked the account as settled 141, cf. 89. be great in, exalted in, somebody's books: have run up a big account 77, 90. fight by the book: see Saviolo, Vincentio. Toll Book: see Toll.

boot: use [pun] 46. ruffled boot: see ruffled. boot-haler: highwayman [pun] 150.

bottle: bundle 251.

bottom: reel, ball of thread 56; ship 124.

Boulogne: i.e. captured by Henry VIII in 1544—an event that was once a great historical landmark 60.

boxed: given a good hiding [pun] 47.

brave: splendid 116. bravery: finery [pun] 41.

Breda: see Maurice, Graf.

brewis: bread and gravy 253.

Bridewell: first House of Correction in England, associated with whipping and hard labour. Staff (beadles) and inmates wore blue 180.

briskly: smartly 216.

Bristol diamond: counterfeit diamond, rock crystal [not Ferdinand, but his mistresses] 111.

brook: endure [pun] 255.

bruit: rumour 140.

Brutus, King: see Troynovant.

bube: abscess in the groin 308.

Bucephalus: Alexander the Great's horse 242.

buck: a wash, wash-tub 193.

buckler: shield 260. take up the bucklers: take arms 80. carry the bucklers away from: get the better of 282.

Bucklersbury: street of grocers and chemists near Cheapside 47.

budget: (doctor's) bag 49; bundle 217.

bugbear: spook 218.

bull tied to a wild fig-tree: emblem of a man subdued by calamity [the fig-tree was supposed so repugnant to a bull in rut that it would instantly tame him] 256.

buonaroba: 'wench' [Italian] 131.

burden: offspring; mournful song, refrain [pun] 42.

*burned: affected by V.D. [pun] 60; heated [of wine] 58. burnt: diseased [of seed] 35.

bush natural: i.e. from the proverbial jibe at the long-haired, 'Bush natural, more hair than wit' 86.

buskined: in the thick-soled boot worn by actors in ancient Athenian tragedy [figurative] 41.

butter-box: [literally] container for imported Dutch butter; Dutchman 87. butter-firkin: cask of butter 51. spirit of the buttery: see spirit.

buxom: cheerful 167.

by-blow: incidental mishap; bastard 232.

cacodemon: evil spirit 227.

Cade: Jack (d. 1450): leader of Kentish insurrection [dramatized by Shakespeare] 287.

cælum pettmus stultitia: 'we aspire to Heaven in our folly' (Horace). [The 'Heaven' to which the would-be gallant aspires is really supreme folly, but even this is beyond his powers unaided. Likewise the dolt commonly thought fit to be Constable does not always measure up even to that unexacting office] 72.

cage: lock-up in each ward 50.

caliver: light musket 49.

Cambyses, King: subject of a popular old play by Thomas Preston 98.

camlet: fine material of silk and goat's hair 290.

can: pint tankard 60. Hence *demi-can, 282, *half-can, 74.

canary: lively Spanish dance; light sweet wine from the Canaries [pun] 58.

*cane: variety of tobacco 109.

canvas: attack 49; toss in a blanket [pun] 81; discuss 58.

cap, doctor's: physician's headgear [of velvet, which was also used for patches to cover sores] 150. Also velvet cap, night-cap, 49, 152. flat cap: woollen cap which was the uniform of a London citizen 49. throw Plato's cap at: see Plato's. thrummed cap: see thrums.

capias (ad respondendum): writ to arrest the defendant to secure his attendance at court 198.

capital: principal [? *pun] 47.

Capo Buona Speranza: 'Cape of Good Hope' [in bad Italian] 255.

career, fetch a: manœuvre a galloping horse with precision; carry through a tricky stratagem [pun] 223.

caroach: small, luxurious carriage 46.

carriage: conduct, bearing [pun] 199.

carry it away: get away with it [pun] 59. carry the bucklers away from: see buckler.

carted: exposed to public censure on a cart [a common punishment for prostitution] 233.

case: *house, ?*brothel 192; suit 103. action at the case: see action. pull their blue cases over their ears: dismiss them [servants' livery was commonly blue] 107, cf. 216.

cast: reckon 59; defeat at law [pun] 199; analyse 238; cast-off 34. cast up: vomit 57. cast beyond the moon: indulge in wild conjecture 41. *caster:* cloak 296. casting: dice-throws [pun] 59.

Castalian: belonging to the Spring Castalia on Parnassus sacred to the Muses 29.

casualty: accident 275.

catamountain: wildcat, prostitute 133.

catch a fall: see fall. catchpole: sheriff's officer (also known as sergeant, 93) who arrests for debt [as one who preys on another] 34; making his arrest by laying hand or mace [q.v.] on the debtor's shoulder. Hence shoulder-clapper, shoulder-clapping, 249, 100.

caudle: hot sweet drink 79.

censure: judge 154.

cent: card-game like piquet 125.

ceruse: white lead used as a cosmetic 78.

chamberlain: attendant at an inn in charge of bedchambers 224.

Chancellor, Lord: see lord.

changeable silk: shot silk 32. changeable-stuff: inconstant [figurative] 228. cost so much the changing: i.e. silver had been falling in valuation and consequently gold coins, which were most trusted and sought after for major transactions, were often to be had only at a premium 206.

chapless: without the lower jaw 43.

chapman: buyer and/or seller, merchant 98.

charity of the house: endowments, legacies and gifts for the relief of destitute prisoners 275.

charm: chirm, sing like a bird [? pun] 75. charms of poesy . . . at the first made the barbarous tame: i.e. according to Horace, *Ars Poetica* 192.

Charon: in classical myth the ferryman who carried the dead into Hell 209. Hence Stygian ferry, 46.

charwoman: home-help, daily woman 279.

chase: hunting-ground 211.

cheat: thing 307. *nab cheat:* see *nab*.

cheer: expression 167.

Chettle, Henry (c. 1560–>1607): printer and playwright, often collaborated with Dekker 168.

child, be with: be very much looking forward 132.

chirurgery: surgery 184.

chorography: topography 268.

circumferentor: early type of theodolite 268.

cities, two: London and Westminster 273.

civet: anal secretion of the musk-cat used in perfumery 72.

clap, at a: at one stroke 158.

clapperdudgeon: beggar born 296.

clarissimo: grandee, gentleman [Italian] 134.

Clarke, Will: witless bell-ringer of St Paul's 88.

cleanly: neatly; cleverly; completely 57.

cleft to the shoulders: 'half cut' 106.

cleyme: sore 296. **cleymed:* made sore 308.

climacterical year: critical year [supposed of any date divisible by seven] 38.

Clink: prison in Southwark [much used for religious prisoners] 273.

clip: embrace 36; pare (the edges of coins) 59.

close: secret 177. close strosser: see strosser. close up: finish 37; fill 109. close prison: strict confinement to one room or ward in prison 266. close-stool: commode 95.

closet of a woman's thoughts: private cabinet of her secrets 155.

cloth, painted: inferior tapestry worked with figures, mottoes or texts 80. clothes cut out of the same piece: bed-clothes of the same material, i.e. earth 53.

clout up: patch up 57.

clown: yokel 75.

cloy: steal 289.

coat, blue: see case. coat with four elbows: fool's costume 72.

cockatrice: whore 100; basilisk [q.v.], said to be hatched from a cock's egg 234.

cockney: 'softy' 106.

cocksure: giving no cause for anxiety 58.

cog: wheedle 28.

cognizance: heraldic device 27.

coil, keep a: make a to-do 48.

Cold Harbour: poor tenements remarkable for the numerous chimneys 271.

coll: hug 125.

College (of Critics): group apparently associated with Jonson 72, cf. 98.

colour: appearance 226; pretence 234; make plausible 292. take his own colour: see take.

*come down upon: ? hold him responsible 61.

comfortable: comforting 39.

commission . . . to call creditors, 277, see 7.

commodity: advantage 86; goods; goods sold by a money-lender on credit at an excessive price and then partly or wholly bought back for cash, in order to evade the legal restrictions on usury 211.

common gaol: ordinary part of a prison, distinct from more comfortable quarters money could buy 64. gallery commoner: see Gallery.

companion: fellow [contemptuous] 228.

Company: trade organization presided over by a Master and a number of Wardens. Head Warden: senior Warden 41. Twelve Companies: the great Livery Companies, including the Merchant Taylors 77; the ceremonial dress of each had a distinctive hood 109.

compass: limits, range 39; get hold of 209.

compliment: courtesy 88. advantage of compliment: see advantage. *complimental: ceremonious 72.

composition: peace-terms 46.

*Comus: god of revelry 75.

*concealment, beg for a: claim for oneself the grant of a property that has been improperly withheld by others from the Crown, e.g. the (profitable) guardianship of an idiot; claim as fair game 79.

conceit: fancifulness 60; device 155; form an opinion 153. poison my conceit: ? spoil [by untimely criticism] the effectiveness of my invention; ? ruin my reputation 35. conceited: fanciful 124.

condition: way of life, character 177.

coney: rabbit [of girls] 302. coney-catch: cheat, trick 242.

congé: bow ceremoniously 207.

conjuration: entreaty 94; calling up spirits by sorcery [pun] 52. Hence conjuring, [pun] 52; conjurors, [? allusion to *Doctor Faustus*] 198. conjuror in hogsheads at midnight: one who secretly adulterates the wines 103, cf. 250.

consist: stay 265.

consort: partnership; harmony; orchestra; concert 129.

conster: construe, find a significance in 36. *construe out, 243.

convent: monastery 158.

conversation: social intercourse [it could also mean 'sexual intercourse'] 153.

cope: sew up the mouth of a ferret (to prevent it biting rabbits) 212.

copy out: scrutinize 36.

*coral: teething-ring and the like 251.

cordwainer: shoemaker (worker in cordovan leather) 149.

cormorant: glutton 75.

corregidor: 'corrector', magistrate [Spanish] 208.

corrival: rival 137.

cos amoris: see Helen.

Counter: Sheriff's prison for debtors and night-walkers 64; there was one in Wood St, one in the Poultry [pun] 100, and one in Southwark 273. hunting counter: following the scent in the opposite direction—hunting the hunters 213.

counterfeit crank: beggar pretending to be an epileptic 190. nailed up for counterfeits: i.e. as tradesmen treated false coins. Money from plague-stricken London might not be acceptable tender, either 63.

country: region 88.

course, by: as a matter of course 154.

court of guard: body of soldiers on guard duty [figurative] 107. court gate of heaven, the first and principal: January 32.

cove: man 296. *rum cove:* see *rum.*

covent: company, gang 219.

cozen: fool 28.

crabbed: gnarled, knotted 151.

crack: bright boy 200. cracked: flawed 74.

craft, gentle: shoemaking 149.

cramp-ring: [literally] a finger-ring worn against cramp; fetters 195.

crazy: ailing 179.

credit: favour [in its turn conferring influence] 94; trust by creditors 122; good name 156. commission . . . to call creditors, 277, see 7.

Critic: see College.

Crookes his ordinary: famous tavern and dining-house in Cheapside [according to Smeaton] 78.

cross: coin (stamped with a cross) [pun] 116. crossed, amongst citizens, the book: see book. crossbiter: double-crosser 182. cross-staff: instrument for shooting the sun or stars 300.

cuckoo in Christmas: i.e. by tradition hibernates and moults 83. the cuckoo in June has a discordant cry, by tradition jocularly associated with cuckoldry 72.

cuffin: man 308.

curious: fastidious 117; expert 182.

curmudgeon: miser 116.

cursitor: vagrant 190.

curtail: vagrant who wears a short cloak 189.

curtal: horse with its tail docked; small horse 29.

custard: open pie, often with fancy crusts 78.

cut: slashed [ordinarily, by the tailor, to show the rich lining] 290. clothes cut out of the same piece: see cloth. cutter: swaggering swordsman 51; tailor 108.

Cyarum: i.e. an oath [meaning unknown] 192.

cypress: funereal tree 43; light transparent material like crape worn in sign of mourning 90; satin 103.

Cyprian: of Cyprus, where Venus was worshipped 268.

Dædalian: labyrinthine, with intricate folds [and, here, of several tiers] 77.

dagger: ? Dagger tavern famous for its pies 78.

Dagonet, Sir: King Arthur's fool 216.

dam: counter [pun] 36. dam the oven: see oven.

Danish sleeve: ? i.e. elaborately puffed and slashed 77.

Daphnean: of Daphne, a river-god's daughter who escaped the amorous Apollo by changing into a laurel-tree 40.

darkman: dark, night 192.

dawcock: [literally] male jackdaw; fool 99.

day, keep your: observe the day of payment in the bond 270. St Thomas his Day: see St Thomas.

de male quaesitis non gaudet tertius heres: 'the third heir does not have the ill-gotten gains to enjoy' [proverb] 276.

*dead: lying unsold, unmarketable [pun] 58. dead pay: see pay. pressing to death: see pressing. death's doors: ? i.e. those of his own house, to which he is confined by plague regulations 44. handwriting of Death: see lord.

decet novisse malum; fecisse nefandum: 'it is right to have known evil, abominable to have done it' 171.

decidis in Scyllam: 'you run on to Scylla'—one rock, in trying to avoid Charybdis, the other [proverbial] 48.

dell: virgin vagrant 190.

demi-can: see can.

demur: plea to stop a legal action in that the allegations are true but do not constitute grounds 198.

Derrick: the public hangman [responsible for disembowelling] 80.

despatch: deal with 118.

desperview: poor beggar, ? desperado 49.

Destinies; Destiny, three housewifely spinsters of: the Fates, three goddesses of classical myth, believed to spin the thread of life and to determine its course and end 53, 86, cf. 119. Hence Fatal Sisters Three, 149.

Deuce-a-ville, Deuceville: the country 192, 307.

devil in a vault: Guy Fawkes 276.

di meliora: 'God forbid!' 64.

diacatholicon (aureum): laxative cure-all 49, 79.

diacodion: sleeping-draught made of poppies 49.

diet: meals 78.

diminish: ? be selective in 88.

dimissaries: testicles 159.

dine: spite 301.

discover: reveal 57.

†disimpark: turn out of a park, i.e. sell off [? get rid of fleas and keep lice] 86.

disparagement: see goose.

dispraisest, what thou now: i.e. the evils he defames will, paradoxically, bring him fame 185.

dispute: debate in a formal academic exercise 300.

Dives: unfeeling rich man with a poor man Lazarus in the parable, Luke xvi. 19 ff 47.

divide our breath: ? cut short our lives; ? kill us in their various ways 35. the world were divided: see world. run division: play variations 120.

dock: copulate with, deflower 192.

document: teaching, admonition [pun on 'blow' and 'dock'; he does not intend to reprove but (ostensibly) to encourage blockheads] 85.

doddypoll: fool 131. Doctor Doddypoll: learned fool, ? pseudo-scholar 215.

dog left, nor a: i.e. dogs were slaughtered as carriers of the plague 47. Black Dog of Newgate: see Black. dogs of Nile: see Nile.

dommerar: beggar pretending to be deaf and dumb 190.

dorp: (Dutch) village 77.

dortour: dormitory of a monastery or convent 156.

dosser: basket 229.

double jug, double pot: large tankard [? one quart] 62.

doucets: sweet morsels (such as deer's testicles) 159.

doxy: vagrants' whore 190.

drab: whore 62.

drabbler: additional piece of canvas laced on the bonnet of a sail to give it greater depth 255.

Dragon, Mount: see Mount. *dragon-water: preparation of the dragonwort efficacious against the plague if taken warm with mithridatum [personified] 47.

draught: swallow 282.

draw: take out your money 101. draw a hand: see hand. drew on a pair of yellow hose: see yellow. draw-latch: sneak-thief (who enters through the door) 190. drawing window: ? window for ventilation 52.

drink: smoke [pun] 75.

dry tobacco: i.e. tobacco, being sold in moist cake, must be spread on waste paper and dried out on a fire-shovel before smoking 35. dry spring-time: see spring. dry-brained: sarcastic 73. hunt dry-foot: track game by scent of the foot [? with some idea of avoiding any real inconvenience] 218.

dryades: wood-nymphs 32.

Duke, Duke's Gallery, Duke's Tomb, Duke Humphrey's Walk: i.e. a tomb by the south aisle of St Paul's was the traditional rendezvous of those without the price of dinner, and debtors who enjoyed the right of sanctuary in the cathedral; popularly attributed to Duke Humphrey of Gloucester (1391–1447), a cult-hero of the needy, it was actually the tomb of Sir John Beauchamp (d. 1358) 89, 90, 92. Duke of Guise: see Guise.

Dunkirk: home-port for pirates, the dregs of many nations 46; pirate-vessel out of Dunkirk 51.

dunstical: dunce-like 74.

dust: money 36.

Dutch, High Dutch, Dutchman: German 187, 107, 70.

E: see mark, rogues'.

ears, get by the: antagonize [pun] 108. pull their blue cases over their ears: see case.

eaten up: wasted 100.

*eel, salt: rope's end used for flogging 152. merchant of eel-skins: ? rag and bone man 288.

Egyptian grasshoppers, lice: Egyptian plagues in Exodus viii. 16 ff and x. 4 ff [Geneva Bible] 231, 229.

elaborate: produced with much hard work and care 73.

Elagabalus, M. Aurelius Antoninus (A.D. 204–222): insanely voluptuous Roman Emperor who ate the tongues of birds as delicacies 77.

electuary: medicinal paste or syrup 49.

element: sky [? climate or weather conditions causing plague] 33. eye of the element: sun 81.

emperic: quack 247.

empty gaols, it is better to, etc.: ? i.e. it is better to execute justice speedily than to treat the sick; hanging a thief does more good than curing a patient 178.

Endymion: shepherd beloved of the moon-goddess and granted eternal youth and [correctly] *unbroken* sleep 81.

English great ones: Lord Grey of Wilton, Lord Cobham, Sir Walter Raleigh, etc., were committed to the Tower in July 1603 charged with conspiring to carry off the king and his son to the Tower. the same park: the Tower, traditionally founded by Julius Caesar, and used as a royal residence [James stayed there briefly on first coming to London]. that deer [pun], second Caesar: the king [a proclamation in May forbade the indiscriminate killing of deer] 39.

engross: corner 158. engrossed: formally drawn up 198.

ense recidendum est: 'it should be cut off with the sword' (Ovid) 270.

entertain: take in, accommodate 161. those that would entertain them: those willing to receive (buy and read) them 176.

†epidemial: epidemic 168.

Erebus: region between Earth and Hades 221.

Erra Pater: see Pater.

eryngo root: candied root of the Sea Holly used as a sweetmeat and regarded as an aphrodisiac 77.

et iam tempus equum fumantia solvere colla: 'it is now time to release the smoking necks of our horses' (Virgil) 64.

et me rigidi legant Catones: 'and let the most censorious read me' (Martial) 25.

Evander: legendary first settler at Rome and son of the Arcadian nymph Carmentis, who prophesied in verse 167.

even, make: reconcile, 'iron out' 38.

ever sad: always depressed 259.

exalted: see book.

excrement: outgrowth, such as hair, nails, feathers [pun] 87.

executed in picture: see France. execution: writ of execution, a sheriff's authority to carry out the judgment of the court by arresting the debtor 198; destruction in war [pun] 210.

exhibition: allowance 96.

eye, turns up the white of her: see white. urine eyes: see urinal. eye of the element: see element.

eyne: eyes 296.

Fabyan, Robert (d. 1513): English chronicler, an industrious compiler 50.

fact: crime 230. factor: agent 29.

fair and softly: quietly, steadily [? withdrawing in good order] 225.

faitor: vagrant swindler 190.

fall, catch a: be thrown on the back in wrestling 140, [pun] 251. falls into an insinuation: see insinuation. fall into . . . the Lord's (hands): see hand. fall to: make a start with 63. fall upon: come across 137. falling sickness: epilepsy [pun] 206.

familiar: close friend 89.

fardel: bundle 252.

farm an office: hire a lucrative position 227.

*farmarly: ? pitted 297.

fashionate: in the height of fashion 88. fashions: farcin, disease of horses characterized by small tumours all over the body [pun] 78.

fat: rich 131. makes his brains fat: makes a fat-head of himself 28, cf. [pun] 75.

Fatal Sisters Three, Fates: see Destinies. Wheel of Fate: common emblem for the arbitrary ups and downs of life 39.

father, ghostly: see ghostly. twice twelve fathers: the aldermen 236.

fauni: satyrs, rural deities 74.

favour: privilege 46; feature 200; charm 153. those whom Fortune favours: see Fortune.

fee, keep in: hold as one's absolute and rightful possession [pun] 105. fee-simple: estate in absolute possession of the owner and his heirs for ever [pun] 85.

fellows!, All: equals 225, cf. 223.

fencer: fencing master 79. fencer's supper: hospitality given him after his display of skill 106.

feng: ? seize 192.

feoffment: kind of conveyance of a freehold 97.

fern: i.e. supposed efficacious against plagues and sores 62.

Fernelius: Jean Fernel (1497–1558), a famous French pathologist, an authority on fevers 49.

fetch in: take in 205. fetch over: get the better of 247. fetch a career: see career.

fico: 'fig' [Italian] 275.

field-bed: camp bed [pun] 53.

file: string on which legal documents were strung for preservation or reference 198. filed: polished 220.

*fillet: plain line impressed on the cover of a book 216.

find: make his living 271.

fine: defendant's collusion in a recovery [q.v.] 97; penalty [pun] 198.

finger, with a wet: with the utmost ease 105. two fingers: see horns.

fir bushes: i.e. valued for the supposedly disinfectant resin 62.

fire, discharge false: shoot blanks, fireworks [figurative] 240.

fish-days: statutory days when fish must be eaten to benefit the fishing fleet, as opposed to flesh-days when meat might be eaten 140.

fit: escapade, scrape; strain of music [pun] 124.

five and fifty: see primero. five thousand years: i.e. since the Fall [probably in mistake for 'six thousand', since by the usual English computation the Creation took place in 4004 B.C.] 78.

flag: groat, i.e. fourpence 194; sixpence [? in error] 294.

*flake: light fleecy tuft 246.

flap-dragon: raisin floating in liquor and swallowed burning 74.

flask: powder-flask [figurative for 'penis'] 299.

Fleet: royal prison for debtors and prisoners of state, the most comfortable of prisons for those able to pay 275. Fleet St: street notable for its lawyers, especially in the Temple; for its publishers, including John Busby, publisher of *Lantern and Candlelight* 180; for its goldsmiths 244; and for its tobacco-shops 246.

flirt: jibe, 'crack' 101.

flocks: wool refuse used for stuffing mattresses 86.

Flora: Latin goddess of flowers 32.

*flounder-catcher: ? loud-mouth [? like a hawker of flounders, or with a big mouth like a flounder's]; ? someone destined to be hanged [pun] 101.

fly-boat: ship's boat 255.

foil: contrast 93.

foist: pick-pocket 200.

fondly ceremonious: foolishly formal [in always providing himself with a dedication] 176.

Fools, Feast of: burlesque festival of the Middle Ages celebrated in churches at

New Year [figurative] 76. Ship of Fools: popular literary motif originating in the German satirical poem, Sebastian Brant's *Narrenschiff* (Basle, 1494) 73.

foot, had the length of her: see length. lantern unto your feet: see lantern. foot-cloth: rich horse-cloth [a status symbol] 47.

for and: and moreover 301.

foreigner: stranger without full rights of citizenship 233.

forge testaments, they that: i.e. for this the statutory penalty was life imprisonment and disfigurement 219.

Fortune favours, those whom: i.e. are lucky enough to develop into fools instead of being born to it [euphemism] 76.

fox-furred: wearing a gown trimmed with fox-fur, the mark of the well-to-do such as usurers 213.

*foxy: drunk 307.

frame: timber structure 189. framed: constructed 85.

France, Civil Wars of: the recurrent wars of religion throughout the period of Elizabeth's reign [and title of a series of lost plays in which Dekker collaborated] 35. executed in picture (as they use to handle malefactors in France): ? executed in effigy, e.g. like an escaped heretic 219. sweating together in France: ? i.e. in part of a tennis-court [pun on the French sweating treatment for V.D.] 94. like a French lackey: ? arrogant, ceremonious 73. like your French lord to have as many tables furnished as lackeys: ? i.e. to have one attendant at each table; thus, only one at home and sometimes none when not entertaining 103, cf. 60. French standing collar: high straight collar 77. the scurvy part of the Frenchman that plucks up all by the roots: ? i.e. sells off all the timber on the estate [pun on the loss of hair due to syphilis, 'the French disease'] 85.

frater: beggar with a forged patent to collect alms for a hospital 189.

free: enjoying the full rights of membership in a company, city, etc. 77; generous [pun] 69. freedom: district over which a city exercises its rights, a liberty 200, cf. 166. freebooter: roving pirate 79.

French: see France.

freshwater (soldier): raw 29.

fret: peevishness; bar on the fingerboard of the lute [pun] 101.

friend: relative 117. maze of friends trodden out: see maze.

†frokin: little (Dutch) girl 51.

frolic: sportive 32; *spree, ? some drinking-game 74.

*furca: kind of portable pillory like a yoke, for the public discrediting of untrustworthy slaves 219.

furnished as lackeys, as many tables: see France. furniture: uniform 180.

Galen (c. 130–c. 200): very influential Greek physician, an authority on fevers 49. Galenist: student of Galen, physician 150.

gall: bile, the secretion of the liver; bitterness; oak-apple from which an ingredient of ink was made [pun] 27; harass by firing 108. liver dressed in gall: heart full of bitterness [? pun on cookery] 34.

Gallery, Duke's: see Duke. penny gallery: covered stand of the open-air public theatre, costing a second penny for admittance 75, hence probably twopenny gallery, 168. gallery commoner: spectator in the public sections of the gallery 98. galleries: ? ball-rooms [a distinction seems intended between private and public practices in fencing and dancing] 109.

galligaskin: wide hose or breeches 77.

gallipot: small earthen glazed pot to hold medicines 271.

Gallonius: public crier in ancient Rome proverbial for his gluttony 77.

Galloway nag: small strong Scottish horse 93.

gambols: sports 74.

game, hen of the: game-bird, ? breeder of game-birds 245.

gamut A re: [literally] two lowest notes of the medieval musical scale; the ABC of music 72.

gaols, it is better to empty, etc.: see empty.

gate of heaven, court: see court. gates of a Lord Mayor's house: see lord. Gatehouse: prison, largely for religious offenders, under the Dean and Chapter of Westminster 273.

gather: heart, liver and lights 140.

gatherer: money-collector at the doors of a theatre 98.

gear: matter [i.e. the scorn nowadays directed at the sound, unsophisticated citizens who have deserved well of the City] 79.

generation: category of people 47.

generous: noble, liberal 73.

Genii: attendant spirits 43.

genitories: testicles 160.

gentle craft: see craft. gentleman-usher: household official 93.

German wheel: i.e. breaking on the wheel [pun: the English execution in this sense was hanging] 278. *Germany: German 74.

*Gete: Goth 30.

ghostly father: father confessor [figurative] 57.

ging: crew 123.

gird: jibe 73.

glasses: ? chamber-pots; ? vials 108. glass-house: glass works 132.

gleek: three-handed card-game with twelve cards each and a 'stock' 125.

glimmer: fire 303; *syphilis 299. *glimmerer:* beggar with a forged begging licence representing him to have suffered losses from fire 189.

glister: shine 28.

globes: ? coins [models not of this world, like terrestrial globes, but of a finer one—that of the Silver and Golden Ages—such as the rich alone can enjoy] 177.

Glorius: a courtier satirized by Donne 208.

†glove: ? drinking vessel 74.

glow-worms, worship: seek cheap popularity 28.

Golden Age: see Age. Golden Ass: Latin novel by Apuleius, dramatized by Dekker [pun] 78. †goldfinch: rich man [pun] 47; gold coin 248. Goldsmiths Row: block on the south of Cheapside once occupied by goldsmiths but gradually abandoned for Fleet St, Holborn, the Strand 244.

goll: hand 60.

Goodfellow, Robin: Puck 291.

goodman: Mister [addressed to one below the rank of gentleman] 285.

goose, green: spring gosling 104. in the bosom of your, knuckle-deep in, goose: i.e. finishing it off. The correct order of courses was butcher's meat, poultry and game, and Dekker believed it ill-bred to eat faster than one's social better. A knight outranks a captain, a J.P. a knight's younger son [? pun on disparagement: matching an heir under his degree or against decency. And on woodcock: fool; he is well matched with fools] 95. serve in for a goose: make a fool of [pun] 28. goosecap: numskull 84. Sir Giles Goosecap: foolish hero of a recent play 49.

gorbelly: big-bellied 60.

gossip: his child's godfather; close friend 216.

Gotham, wise men of: utter fools, the inhabitants of a proverbially foolish village 85.

grate: bars from which destitute prisoners beg from passers-by 198.

Gravesend: main port of embarkation for the Continent [pun] 46.

great together: 'thick', on close terms 64. great in somebody's books: see book. English great ones: see English. Great Turk: see Turk.

Greek, merry: livewire [pun] 86.

Griselda, Patient: proverbial type of an all-enduring wife, heroine of tales by Petrarch and Chaucer, and a play by Dekker 57.

†Grobianism: literary nature of Friedrich Dedekind's *Grobianus* (Frankfurt, 1549) [see 314] 70.

grope: handle poultry in order to find whether they have eggs [figurative] 205.

groundling: poorer member of the audience who stood in the theatre-yard 98.

groutnoll: blockhead 75.

Guard: 'Beaf-eaters' 205. black guard: see Black. court of guard: see court. guard of Switzers: see Switzer.

Guise, Duke of: Henri de Lorraine (1550–88), leader of the Roman Catholic party in the French Civil Wars, who was notorious for the Massacre of St Bartholomew's Day [he was the subject of a play by Marlowe] 64.

gulch: glutton 61.

gull: fop 28; dupe 205; (vb.) cheat 214. Isle of Gulls: title of a play by John Day accused of being topical court satire in 1606 [figurative] 73.

gummy tears into mine ink, rain down your: i.e. find expression for your grief, especially since gum was one ingredient of ink 43.

guts . . . taken out by the hangman: i.e. as in hanging, drawing and quartering 61.

gybe: counterfeit begging licence or passport 194.

gyle: quantity of beer brewed at one time 281.

Habakkuk: Old Testament prophet who prophesied and lamented the taking of Jerusalem 156; according to legend, he was carried by an angel to feed Daniel in the lions' den 274.

habiliments: uniform, dress 180.

habit: dress 32.

hackney: horse kept for hire 46; hack 215.

haec mala sunt, sed tu non meliora facis: 'these are bad, but you do not make any better' (Martial) 30.

haggler: unskilful archer 28; small-time tradesman [the poorer spectators bring little money or intelligence and are likewise glad simply to take home some fragmentary impressions to talk about] 98.

hail-shot: small shot (that scatters like hail) 29.

half: partner (in betting) 208. half hams: see shadow. half-can: see can. half-sharer: see sharer.

halt: limp 241.

Ham: i.e. cursed for seeing the nakedness of his father, Noah 156. half hams: see shadow.

hamadryades: classical wood-nymphs 32.

Hamburgers: merchants of the most important continental commercial centre 60.

hand: signature 72. *draw a hand: ? play a round at dice 59. fall into . . . the Lord's (hands): ? 'go to meet your Maker' 81. on the mending hand: getting better [pun] 149–50. shall be required at his hands: he shall be held answerable for 61. strike a hand: 'do a job' 287. take the upper hand: take precedence 203. at the worst hand: if the worst comes to the worst [? pun] 100. handwriting of Death: see lord.

hang: fasten to the sword-belt [pun] 97. hanger: loop or strap on a sword-belt by which the sword is hung 247. *hanging forth the party for a sign: making a public example of any individual 182. guts . . . taken out by the hangman: see guts.

Hannibal: i.e. he broke down rock impeding his passage over the Alps by first heating it and then pouring vinegar over it [Livy] 73.

hatch: inlay [pun] 36.

hawk's meat: easy prey 299.

hazard: dice-game 96.

head: concentration of insurgents 181; tip of an arrow, drawn back to the bow [pun] 201; topic [pun] 277. Head Warden: see Company.

headborough: petty constable 56.

heart's-ease: pansy or wall-flower [pun] 166.

heated: physically excited, stirred up 78.

Hebricians: Hebrews [Dedekind on the contrary stresses the Jew's excessive courtesy] 82.

hedge!, To the: ? take to the woods! Clear off! 196. hedge-creeper: skulking rogue [pun] 228.

heels, kick up the, turn up the: die 81, 60.

height: latitude 252. *heighten: render a colour more luminous 285.

Helen, Helena: beautiful wife of the Greek Menelaus, but seduced by the Trojan Paris [thus causing the Trojan War] 58; Paris called the one flaw in her beauty *cos amoris*, the whetstone of love [but Lyly gives Helen a scar on her chin, Venus a mole on her cheek] 78.

Helicon: mountain or a fountain rising on it, sacred to the Muses; poetic inspiration 29, 41. Heliconian, 29.

hell: hole into which a tailor threw remnants and pilferings 203.

hem: clear the throat 74; ? i.e. their drawing discreet attention to their outstanding accounts [pun] 77.

henchman: one of the Lord Mayor's pages, admired for their pretty saying of grace 216.

Hermes: Mercury, god of eloquence and music 29.

heteroclite: oddity 72.

hic finis Priami: 'this Priam's end' (Virgil) [i.e. the brutal killing of the Trojan king, proverbial as a great reversal of fortune; but mainly whimsical, for 'that's the lot'] 64.

Hieronimo: see Balthazar.

hinc dolor: 'hence the grief' 28. *hinc illæ lacrimæ:* 'hence the tears' (Terence) 42. *hinc pudor:* 'hence the shamefacedness' 28. *hinc risus:* 'hence the laughter' 201.

Hippocrates: founder of Greek medicine 49.

Hobbinoll: yokel 46.

hobby, hobby-horse: pony 88, 97.

hold of, take: ? strictly obey [with reference to 'to have and to hold'] 55. hold tack: see tack.

hole: lowest grade of prison accommodation, largely financed from charity 64. Hole at St Katharine's: prison for the Precinct of the Royal Hospital of St Katharine by the Tower 273.

Holinshed, Raphael (d. 1580?): historian, published *Chronicles* (1577) in folio 39.

Holy Rood Days: 3rd May and 14th September [Deerhurst Fairs were instituted in 1319] 287.

hooker, alias *angler:* thief who steals from open windows with a hooked stick 189.

hoop: one of the bands at equal intervals on a quart pot; thus, a measure of drink 60. †hoop-girdle: support for a farthingale [figurative] 167.

horns: emblem of the cuckold, fancifully said to grow horns on his forehead [pun] 56, [in the public ridicule of a cuckold, he might be forced to wear gilt horns on his head] cf. 32. Hence Actæon, 56; swelling temples, 57; unicorn cobbler, 58; and the improper gesture of two fingers, 250. horn-mad: enraged [pun] 57. slips his horns: uncouples from the yoke 106. unicorn's horn: see unicorn. horn-book: bat-shaped board with an alphabet, syllables, etc. and the Lord's Prayer mounted under horn, used to learn reading 28; primer 65. In reading aloud, the pupil indicated a syllabic letter or character by 'per se'; hence, *O per se—O:* O on its own [possibly, reference to the interjection 'Oh!' as a cry of indignation or crier's call, or to nought (with a pun on 'naught' meaning 'evil-doing'), or more probably to a clown's clumsy reading of a charm to summon up devils in the 1616 *Doctor Faustus*] 283.

horse that went up, etc.: see Banks. horse-courser: dealer in horses 237. horse-loaf: bread made of beans, bran, etc. 240. horse-tricks: ? horse-play 74.

hose, Scotch: see Scotch. yellow hose: see yellow. hosen; hose; stockings or pants 193.

Hospital of Incurable Madmen: ? i.e with reference to Tommaso Garzoni, *L'hospidale de' Pazzi incurabili,* translated as *The Hospital of Incurable Fools* (London, 1600), a satirical survey of fools ancient and modern 253.

house, charity of the: see charity. show of what house one comes: ? reveal one's true nature 224. household-stuff: household goods 139. housewifely spinsters of Destiny: see Destinies.

hoy: small coasting vessel 72.

hue and cry: raising a whole village or neighbourhood under the Constable in pursuit of malefactors 60.

huff it: bluster [? pun]. *huff's ale: ? ale with a kick 282.

humour: bodily fluid supposed to determine mental qualities and physical condition; vagary, caprice [pun] 79. humorous: wilfully affected 88.

Humphrey, Duke: see Duke.

hundred, in the: percent [any rate of interest of over 10% on loans was illegal] 69.
The Hundred Merry Tales: popular jest-book (1525?) 64.
hyacinth: flower emblematic of those who die young 43.
Hydra: mythical many-headed snake whose heads grew as fast as they were cut off; killed by Hercules 96.
Hymen: classical god of marriage 54.

iam desine, tibia, versus: 'now cease, my flute, the song' (Virgil) 320.
ignis fatuus: Will-o'-the-wisp [personified] 107.
ille ego, qui quondam: 'I am he who once' [spurious opening of the Aeneid, announcing a change of subject-matter from the pastoral to the martial] 78.
imagine: conjecture 157.
imbroccata: 'fencing thrust over the dagger' [Italian] 51.
impost: tax, customs duty [literally. Here, the Gull pawns his belongings with the Impostor, and tries in vain to redeem them by instalments, game by game] 209.
impostume: abscess 35.
impression: pressing, moulding 102.
impudently audacious: ? i.e. in dedicating their work to those it is not worthy of 176.
in arte bibendi magister: 'master in the art of drinking' [cf. Vincentius Opsopœus, *De Arte Bibendi* (Nuremberg, 1536)] 73.
in diebus illis: 'in those days', in the fabulous past [cf. Genesis vi. 4] 143.
in dispetto del fato: 'in contempt of Fate' [Italian] 72.
in esse: 'in actual existence' 205.
in forma pauperis: 'in the form of a poor person', exempted from the costs of a legal action [figurative] 143.
in plano: in a flat projection [cf. Emery Molyneux, *The Globes Celestial and Terrestrial Set Forth in Plano* (1592). Also a pun on 'plain'] 78.
in posse: 'in potentiality' 205.
in tenebris: 'in obscurity' 219.
inamorato: 'lover' [Italian] 134.
in-and-in: gambling game played by three persons with four dice, the object being to throw two or four of the same numbers 125.
indeed-la: i.e. Puritan exclamation, ludicrously mild as an oath 28.
indentures, pair of: deed made of one parchment divided into two copies by a zigzag cut, in order to make later authentication possible [figurative for a zigzag course] 58.
Indian: American 35. Indian chimney: i.e. for tobacco-smoke 85. West Indies: i.e. gold 51.
Infortunate Islands: see *Insulae Fortunatae.*
ingle: boy-friend 108.
inhabitable: uninhabited 210.
inn, instead of an: i.e. a jocular comparison of the wedding trip to a conventional journey with its stops at inns 55.
innocent: guileless person 78; (adj.) [pun] 84.
insinuation, falls into an: begins to worm his way into his favour 208.
Insulae Fortunatae: Islands of the Blessed, Elysium 165. Hence ironically In-fortunate Islands, 255.

intelligence: (source of) information 31. intelligencer: informer, spy 201.
inventory of the kitchen: see kitchen.
Iovis summi causa clare plaudite: 'for the sake of Jove almighty, give us some loud
applause' (Plautus) 28.
Ireland, wild: regions outside English settlement [The arch-foe Hugh O'Neill,
Earl of Tyrone, who had been routed much earlier in Lord Mountjoy's
Irish campaign, did not make formal submission till April 1603] 39. wild
Irishman: uncivilized Irish peasant outside English rule 203. wild Irish kern:
such a peasant, recruited as a foot-soldier 228. Irish: old game resembling
backgammon 125. Irish funeral: i.e. women, sometimes hired for the
purpose, wailed loudly 273. *Irish toyle:* thieving pedlar with a satchel
189.
iron: sword [pun] 41. Iron Age: see Age.
Irus: beggar [Homer] 275.
Iskenderun: principal Levantine port for overland route to India 123.
ivy-bush: sign of a tavern where wine was sold [pun on hunting for sport]
105.

jack: piece of wood which jumps up to pluck a string when a key of the virginal
is struck 84; leathern tankard 282. jack (of the clockhouse): figure of a man
which strikes the bell on the outside of a clock 89, 221.
jackanapes: pet ape 83.
Jacob's (staff): instrument for measuring the height of the sun; supported on a
rod 300.
jade: horse; scoundrel [pun] 202.
Janus: two-faced classical god, doorkeeper of heaven; god of January and of the
beginnings of things [one of the allegorical figures to welcome King James
into London in *The Magnificent Entertainment*] 32.
jarkman: forger of sealed licences to beg, and passports 189.
*jeer: excreta; backside 192.
jet: strut 72.
Jew's letter: phylactery; the mark of a Jew. give his lips a Jew's letter: ? brand
him as a humbug and extortioner, in paying lip-service to his religious
office while exploiting it [a phylactery is properly worn on the arm and
forehead] 48. jew's-trump: jew's-harp 136.
*jingler: dishonest dealer in horses 238.
jobbernowl: blockish head 85.
*jockey: penis 299.
Johanan: John of Giscala, Jewish leader in the civil war against Simon bar Giora
and Eleazar in Jerusalem, when the Romans were at the gates [they put
self-interest before civic unity and the welfare of their stricken people] 48.
John in Paul's Churchyard: a dishonest hatter 88.
jolly: bold, 'cocky' 49.
journeyman: qualified craftsman 202.
Jubilee: year of celebration to be kept by the Jews every fifty years [see Leviticus
xxv] 38.
judgment, confess a: admit the case against him 206.
julep: medicated sweet drink 179.
Justice: righteousness [personified] 56.

keep a coil: see coil. keep touch: see touch. keeper: nurse [every parish appointed two] 64; gaoler, liable for the debts of those who escaped; for a fee, underkeepers escorted debtors about their business outside the prison 271. Master Keeper: head gaoler 209.

Kelley, Edward (1555–1595): disreputable alchemist who professed to turn base metal into gold 73.

Kempe, William: famous comedian, at one time with the Chamberlain's Men and creator of some of Shakespeare's earlier comic rôles 74.

ken: house 299. *stalling, stuling ken:* see *stall.*

kinchin co: boy brought up to vagabondage and stealing 189. *kinchin mort:* vagrant's infant daughter 190.

kind: soft-hearted 166.

King's Bench: Southwark prison, especially for debtors 273. apes of the kingdom: see apes.

kitchen, inventory of the: menu [it being more usual to view the fare itself before ordering] 104. kitchen-stuff wife: ? woman who deals in dripping and the like 61.

knight of the post: professional perjurer 289.

knocking: 'thumping great' 125.

lace: ornamental braid made of gold wire (or imitation gold wire) 99.

ladle: instrument for charging cannon with loose powder; snuff-spoon 95.

Lady Eve: i.e. Elizabeth was born on 7th September 1533 (the Nativity of the Virgin Mary being on 8th) and died on 24th March 1603 (the Annunciation being on 25th) 37.

Lancelot (du Lac), Sir: a knight of the Round Table [figurative] 249.

lanceprisado: 'lancecorporal' [quasi-Spanish] 232.

lantern and candlelight: lantern complete with lighted candle; carried by a bellman [q.v.]; and associated with Diogenes as a satirist [see 324]; required by law to be hung out by householders in winter [to throw light on dark places]. A crier of lantern and candlelight goes through the streets announcing lighting-up time [perhaps confused with a town crier in the title of *Lantern and Candlelight* Q6] 325. lantern unto your feet: see Psalm cxix. 105 [Geneva Bible] 107.

lapped: clothed 83.

lares: 'household gods' [figurative, for 'presences in the house'] 52.

lasciva est nobis pagina, vita proba est: 'wanton is my page; my life is good' (Martial) 183.

last: latest [an elaboration of the proverb] 215. knew the length of his last: see length.

lattice: window screen of crossed laths instead of glass 41. penny-lattice: i.e. shoddy 37. red lattice: i.e. indicating an alehouse 281.

laund: glade 301.

lawn: diaphanous dress of fine linen 83.

lawyers' walls: e.g. those of the Temple in Fleet St 34.

leaguer: besieging force [as in the Low Countries] 46.

leap-frog acquaintance: ? i.e. such as make an entertainment of others' misfortunes [? also with reference to onlookers jumping up on one another] 268.

lease: i.e. pun on 'leash' (and perhaps on 'led/let') 41.

lecture: lesson, instructive example 243.

leg: bow 32.

leman: mistress 155.

length of her foot, had the; length of his last, knew the: summed him/her up, knew how to handle him/her [pun] 150, 204.

Levant taffeta: fine silk from the East 41.

lewd: delinquent 285.

lib: sleep 301.

liberty: see freedom.

lickerish: greedy, sensual [pun] 279; tempting 77.

lieger: ambassador 199.

life, for: for dear life 46.

lightly: commonly 142.

likelihood, of: promising 208.

likeness, in his: ? in person 46.

limbeck: retort, still 257.

limbo: prison 64.

lime-bush, lime-twigs: trap for birds spread with sticky stuff 212, 300.

lin: leave off 100.

*line: sketch; fill in 255. lining: contents 200.

link: torch made of tow and pitch [? whereas a torch as such is of wax] 107.

liver: seat of violent passion 34. liver dressed in gall: see gall.

livery: legal delivery of property into a person's possession 97.

loadstone: magnet 208.

lob: bumpkin 49. Lob's Pound: ? a local lock-up 273.

lodged: flattened 256.

Log, Servingman's: see serve. loggerhead: blockish head 73.

Lombard St: street of merchants and bankers 244.

Long Lane: centre for pawnbrokers and old-clothes dealers by West Smithfield 34.

looby: lout 75.

loon: one of low rank 73.

lord, French: see France. Lord Chancellor's Tomb: the tomb of Sir Christopher Hatton (1540–91) was the most magnificent in St Paul's and boasted an epitaph of 40 lines or more—a notorious contrast with Sidney's simple wooden tablet and 8-line epitaph, a few steps away 91. new-painted gates of a Lord Mayor's house: i.e. it was customary to paint red the posts at the entrance to the house of the newly-elected Lord Mayor 85. Lord have mercy upon us: i.e. infected houses were sealed off for 28 days, the doors being marked with a red cross and a paper with these words 48. Hence handwriting of Death, 44. fall into . . . the Lord's (hands): see hand. Lord of Misrule: master of ceremonies for festivities in a great house 32. Lords' Room: gallery of boxes above and behind the stage [? once fashionable but now démodé because of its unsavoury associations, thronged with servants intriguing together, and shamelessly overcrowded]. thrust into the rear: ? deprived of their former prestige [? or perhaps with reference to architectural changes in the theatre, such as roofing over the stage] 98.

lower: money 307.

Lud, King: legendary ancient Briton and builder of Ludgate 275. Ludgate: gatehouse and debtors' prison for freemen of the City only, who enjoyed

some self-government there 273. between Ludgate and Temple Bar: i.e.
Fleet St [q.v.] 244.

lurch: get more than his fair share of the food 96.

luxurious: lecherous, debauched 80.

mace: staff of office of the catchpole [q.v.] 259.

Madcap, Pasquil's: see Pasquil's. mad-Greek: livewire [pun] 30. Hospital o
Incurable Madmen: see Hospital.

Mæcenas: generous patron [of Horace and Virgil] 216. Hence Mæcenass, [pun] 69.

magnifico: 'magnate' [Italian] 134.

main: match at dice 209; mainland, broad open space [pun] 268; full (gallop) 215;
open (sea) 258.

maior sum quam cui possit Fortuna nocere: 'I am too great for Fortune to harm'
(Ovid) 258.

make up: fill 95. make even: see even. maker: poet 167.

mandilion: loose military top-coat or cape 83.

mandrake: poisonous plant with magical properties and roots of human form,
said to shriek when plucked 43.

mandritto: 'right-handed or downright blow' [Italian] 51.

Mare Mortuum: Dead Sea [pun] 46.

mark: target 48; coin worth 13s. 4d. 203. rogues' mark: tattoo [marks of legal
branding included R for rogue, V for vagabond, T for Tyburn, etc.] 290,
cf. 291.

Marshal: law-officer answerable to the King's Bench with powers to arrest for
debt 214. Marshalsea: Southwark prison [especially for offences at sea and in
the Royal Court] 273.

match: slow-burning piece of impregnated cord (? with which to light a pipe) 99;
arrangement 208.

maund: beg, ask 192. *rum maund:* see *rum. maunder, maunderer:* beggar 298,
127.

Maurice, Graf, of Nassau (1567–1625): brilliant Dutch general and patriot
victorious against the Spanish in the Netherlands 93; captured Breda in
1590, but in 1625 it fell to Spinola after a grim, protracted siege 280.

maw, (set at): game of maw, a card-game played with a piquet pack [pun] 253.

maze of friends trodden out, is this: i.e. have I got to the end of them, or of my
account of them [? pun on early senses of maze: disappointment, deception]
269.

mazer: head, 'nut' 59.

measure: dance 120.

mechanical: labouring 41.

mends his pace: improves its speed 57. on the mending hand: see hand.

Menelaus: see Helen.

mercer: dealer in costly textiles 77.

mere: unadulterated 70.

mess: course, dish 28.

metals have their ambition: according to alchemy metals have a hierarchy through
which, under the influence of the sun, they tend to rise; lead naturally tends
to become tin, tin silver, silver gold 266.

meter: judge, especially of measure [pun] 40.

mew: i.e. derisive exclamation 98.

miching: skulking 47.

Mid*ass:* Midas [with pun on 'ass'], legendary king who turned all he touched to gold [as the gull tries to turn all he touches to scathing wit] but whom Apollo [q.v.] gave ass's ears for insensitivity to his lyre 73.

mingle-mangle: hotch-potch 79.

minion: darling 42.

mirabilis annus: see Plato's.

mist: fuzzy [? pun on 'mystical'] 104.

Mithridates (died c. 63 B.C.): King of Pontus said to have developed an antidote, composed of numerous ingredients, to poisons 79. Hence †mithridatum: a cure-all [personified] 47.

mittimus: warrant to commit to gaol 107.

modicum: ? titbit to keep one sober 75.

Molyneux, Emery: London mathematician, instrument-maker and voyager, made the first English globe (1592, revised 1603), varnished with egg-white [Dekker prefers the honest rudeness of olden times to modern sophistication and pretence] 78.

mome: fool 75.

Momus: Greek god of ridicule; captious critic 73.

money, single: see single. white money: see white. money from the bar: i.e. a loan 104.

month's mind: inclination 73.

moon, cast beyond the: see cast. man in the moon: i.e. he traditionally had a bundle of sticks visible on his back 228; figure on a clock 91.

Moorditch: notoriously unsavoury stretch of the old City moat by Moorfields 78.

Morpheus: god of dreams 80.

mort: woman vagrant 232. *autem mort, kinchin mort:* see *autem, kinchin.*

motion: puppet-play 64; mechanism with moving figures 91; mental disturbance 154; urging 155.

motley: variegated cloth traditional for a fool's dress 29.

Mount Dragon: ? some hero of romance 216.

mountebank: itinerant quack 81.

mouse: tear at, as a cat does a mouse 42.

Mouth . . . at Bishopsgate, *The:* inn with a huge gaping mouth as its sign 200.

mow: grimace [pun] 86.

mumchance: dice-game like hazard 125.

muscadine: muscatel, traditional drink after a wedding 54.

Muschamp of Peckham, Francis: probably the eventual head of this old family (1579–1617), but his father and son, both named Francis, were also alive in 1608 176.

musket shot should not reach him: ? he would be out of range 51.

musty: stale; ? sullen 59.

myrtle: plant sacred to Venus 166.

nab: head 307. *nab cheat:* hat 191; ? horse's head seal forged on a licence or passport; ? halter 192.

nam tales nusquam sunt hic amplius: 'for nowhere do such people exist any more' 29.

Naomi: 'pleasant'. Mara: 'bitter' [see Ruth i. 20] 179.

nappy: strong 116.

nase: drunk 192.

natural: fool 81. bush natural: see bush.

naught: bad 288.

ne exeat regnum: 'that he should not leave the kingdom' [a writ to restrain someone from going abroad to escape proceedings against him] 52.

neat: ? unadulterated, undiluted 104.

*nerveless: feeble 40.

never so much, having: however much you have 256.

New Bourse: fashionable shopping-centre, an unsuccessful rival of the Royal
Exchange founded in 1608 132. New Prison: House of Correction in
Clerkenwell 273. Newgate: County Prison of Middlesex [mainly for felons]
273. Black Dog of Newgate: see Black. new-painted gates of a Lord Mayor's
house: see lord.

niggling: copulating 307.

night-crow: ominous nocturnal bird, probably an owl or nightjar [figurative] 279.
night-piece: picture of a nocturnal scene 251.

Nile, dogs of: i.e. they were said to run along as they drank for fear of crocodiles
29.

Nimrod: see Gen. x. 8–9, xi. 1–9 188.

nine and thirty: see primero.

ninny-hammer: simpleton 74.

nip: cutpurse 200.

noble: gold coin worth 6*s*. 8*d*. 77.

Nobody: i.e. a reference to the sign (probably of a man with legs but no trunk) of
John Trundle, one of Dekker's publishers [a favourite word for jokes]
217.

nocte latent mendae: 'by night are blemishes hid' (Ovid) 285.

noddy: card-game resembling cribbage 125.

noise: band, 'group' 131.

noll: head 87.

nomine et re: 'in name and in reality' 179.

non minus venefica quam benefica: 'no less poisonous than beneficial' 81.

nonce, for the: for the purpose 58.

none-opolitan: ? i.e. jocular perversion of 'monopolitan' (monopolist) meaning
'one who monopolizes the worthless' 238.

noverint universi: 'let all men know'—the formula with which a bond customarily
opened [pun] 235.

novum: dice-game played by 5 or 6 persons 125.

nullus ad amissas ibit amicus opes: 'no friend will approach when wealth is lost'
(Ovid) 268.

O per se—O: see horns.

objection: contradiction 38.

ochreman, red: worker or dealer in ochre, used as a pigment 228.

octogesimus octavus annus: 'eighty-eighth year' [long predicted as a year of dis-
aster] 38.

omne bonum: 'all manner of good' 40.

only: most considerable 86.

opposed: facing; hostile 98.

*opprobratious: opprobrious 156.

order, take: take measures 156. four and twenty orders: i.e. the traditional burlesque classification of knaves (or fools) 299.

ordinary: eating-house with a standard charge for meals [pun] 72. Crookes his ordinary: see Crookes. in ordinary pay: on the regular establishment [pun] 95.

oriently: brilliantly 60.

Orleans: i.e. considered the best place to learn French 187.

outface: impudently stare out [? with reference to bluffing at cards] 101.

oven, daub up the, dam the: ? seal with clay to increase the heat 287.

overseer: supervisor of or assistant to the executor of a will 198.

overwatched: tired out from staying up too long 290.

owner: ? i.e. the person who stands to lose [her, one and the same as the Master Pilot, he whose duty it is to take the right course of action] 256.

Pacolet: dwarf in the fairy-story of *Valentine and Orson* with a magic flying horse [erroneously, for the horse] 248.

pad: toad. smell a pad in the straw: 'smell a rat' 154.

pair: set [not limited to two]. Hence, of cards, 96; of stairs, 85; of virginals, 84; of writing-tables, 39. post and pair: see post. pair of indentures: see indentures. there went but a pair of shears between: see shears. pair of yellow hose: see yellow.

palliard: vagrant who wears a patched cloak, steals in league with his wife, and makes artificial sores 189.

Pan: Greek rural god who delighted in music and sometimes caused panics [pun] 62.

pantofle: high-heeled slipper. stand on one's pantofles: stand on one's dignity [pun] 149.

Paracelsus (1490–1541): famous Swiss physician opposed to the theories of Galen [q.v.] 49.

parcel: bit 94; partly, e.g. parcel bawd, 233; parcel-gilt, 32; parcel-Greek, parcel-Latin, 81.

Paris, Sir: see Helen. old Paris Garden: former site of bear-baiting in Southwark [? laid out as gardens] 78.

parlous: dreadfully 57.

parts: qualities [pun] 41. the scurvy part of the Frenchman: see France.

Pasquil's Madcap: title of a satire by Nicholas Breton (1600) [Pasquil, a common pseudonym of satirists, was a name jocularly given to an old statue in Rome dressed up on St Mark's Day and hung with lampoons] 78.

passage: occurrence 124; dice-game with three dice for two players 125.

passion: agony of mind, overpowering emotions 45. passionate: deeply-felt 42.

passport: travel-permit issued to vagrants legally bound to return to their place of origin 29; used as a licence to beg 294, cf. 301.

patch: fool [? pun] 57.

Pater, Erra: supposed Jewish Doctor of Astronomy and Medicine, and author of a popular perpetual prognostication (c. 1536 and much reprinted) 38. *paterfamilias:* 'head of a family' 106.

patrico, patring cove: hedge-priest (who performs mock marriages) 189, 192.

Paul's (Churchyard): centre of the retail book-trade 176, [? reference to the pasting up of title-pages as adverts] 34. John in Paul's Churchyard: see John.

pay, dead: pay fraudulently drawn for soldiers no longer on the strength [pun, for extortionate burial fees] 59. Thus dear pays, [? likening cheap salads, ordered to make a show instead of more substantial dishes, to empty spaces on the pay-roll, or perhaps to men that can be produced at a muster to make good the fictitious numbers on the pay-roll] 104. in ordinary pay: see ordinary. pay home: do for 257.

pearl: pupil; tear [pun] 38; cataract [pun] 41; ? pus 60.

peck: eat 192.

Pegasus: mythological winged horse, bearing authors on flights of true inspiration 29.

pegged: with wooden pegs [instead of metal nails] 295.

pelf: filthy lucre 35.

Pelion upon Ossa, heap: pile one mountain on another [in a Titanic effort to outdo the gods, as in classical myth] 100.

pell-mell: in confused hand-to-hand fighting 152; indiscriminately 302.

pencil: brush 120.

penny, (with their): i.e. money, pretty penny 116. penny gallery: see Gallery. penny-father: skinflint 36. penny-lattice: see lattice. penny-white: beautified by her riches 116.

penthouse: sloping roof or ledge to protect a window from the weather 85.

pepper: do for, ruin [? pun on the sense *'pelt with shot'] 48.

perfect: fully versed 97.

perinado: ? 'bum-boy' [? a formation on the Spanish *perineo*, perineum; cf. also *perinola*, neat little woman] 108.

Persian lock: love-lock 99.

persuaded, was: came to the conclusion 60.

pest-cart: waggon to carry sick and dead to the Pesthouse 46.

pettifogger: minor lawyer 166.

philosopher's stone: substance sought by alchemists to change other metals into gold 73.

Phœbus: see Apollo.

Phœnix: mythical bird that periodically resurrected itself after burning to ashes on a sacred pyre of aromatic twigs [associated with James's succession] 38.

physic: medicine 78. physicked: given medicine 35. physical: medicinal 27.

pick a crown off it: i.e. gather like fruit 62.

piece: patch of leather; coin, especially the unit of 22s. [pun] 56; fire-arm [pun 57. clothes cut out of the same piece: see cloth.

pied: parti-coloured [see motley] 203.

pillow-bere: pillow-case 280.

pin: peg in the centre of a target 201.

pint, wine: somewhat less than the proper ale pint [and about five sixths of the modern imperial pint] 282.

pioneer: soldier who prepares roads and entrenchments for the main body 46.

pipe-office: [literally] office in Exchequer handling enrolled sheriffs' accounts; ? mouth; ? smoking-room or tobacconist's [pun] 73.

pitchfork: i.e. table fork, still unfamiliar in England [? regarded as a precaution against poison] 78.

plant: hide 301.

Plato's cap at, throw: admit to being outstripped ['throw one's cap at' proverbial. Here, with additional jocular reference to an academic cap; cf. the satirical prognostication *Plato's Cap, Cast at this Year 1604, being Leap Year* (1604)] 38. Plato's cock: Plato having defined Man as an animal biped and featherless, Diogenes plucked a fowl and called it 'Plato's Man' 83. Plato's *mirabilis annus:* Plato's 'wonderful year' or Great Year, completed when all the heavenly bodies have come full circle [this is continually happening, but it was wrongly thought to be at one particular future time of disaster] 38.

play with: make sport with [? pun on the sense 'bombard', used of artillery] 59. (player's) supper: hospitality given him after the performance 69; bets were then sometimes laid on competitions in acting selected rôles 106. private playhouse: indoor theatre with a fashionable clientèle. public playhouse: less expensive theatre partly out of doors, with a broadly representative audience 98, cf. [pun] 252.

pledge: respond to a toast 42.

Pliny (A.D. 23–79): Latin author of the vast encyclopedia *Historia Naturalis,* which does not mention woodcocks 83.

Plowden, Edmund (1518–85): distinguished lawyer [the association of the popular catchphrase with his name has been variously explained] 116.

Plowman, Piers: hero of William Langland's 14th-century poem; the ideal plain working man 78.

Plutarch: 1st-century Greek biographer and author of *Moralia,* ethical works concerning ordinary life 267.

Pluto: god of the underworld 215.

Plymouth cloak: no cloak at all, but a cudgel 140.

pocas palabras: 'few words' [Spanish] 57.

pocky: syphilitic 308. *pockily: 'damnably' [pun] 233.

point, full: full stop 42.

policy: cunning, strategy 157. politician: schemer 200. politicly: artfully 50.

polling: cropping; extortionate [pun] 87.

polt-foot: club-foot 204.

†polypragmonist: busybody 73.

poniard: dagger 80.

popinjay: parrot 73.

popularity: ? popular favour [probably subject of 'rejects'] 37.

port: style of living, grand style 133.

post: courier, despatch-rider 45; ride fast 122; speedily 227. knight of the post: see knight. in post: in haste 97. post and pair: card-game played with three cards each 125. postmaster: one in charge of a posting station who hired out horses 223.

posy: lettering inscribed in a ring 57.

pothecary: see apothecary.

pottage: *porridge 194.

pottle-pot: two-quart tankard [? pun on 'pot-gun': mortar; pop-gun] 107.

powder beef: powdered or salted beef 253.

power, to their: as far as they were able 52.

practice: trick 221.

prancer: horse 189.

prat: buttocks, thighs; genitals 299.

prefer: show off 90; promote 251.

presently: immediately 198.

pressing to death: torture (used to make a silent prisoner plead) [pun] 28.

Priam: King of Troy slain when the city fell 42.

Priapus: classical god of procreation 32.

prick: mark 39. provender pricked them: see provender. prick-song: written music [? i.e. elaborate vocal counterpoint with much opening and closing of the mouth] 84.

prig: drunken and thieving tinker 189; steal 289, but cf. 194.

prima vista, primero: card-game 125, 96. five and fifty: the second highest score, with a hand of ace, six, seven and knave of hearts. nine and thirty: the total points for the two highest cards (the seven and the six) and hence the makings of a strong hand to bet on. prime: four cards all of different suits, the third best hand 208.

prining-iron: wire to clear touch-holes and vents (in gunnery); stopper 95.

*print, in: complete [pun] 28; properly pleated [of ruffs], well-groomed [pun] 78, [pun] 90.

private house, playhouse: see playhouse.

prize: fencing prize-fight, public test undergone by fencing students to qualify as masters of defence 101; prey, plunder 249.

pro Troia stabat Apollo: 'in Troy's defence stood Apollo' (Ovid) [as an example of one god bringing aid against the anger of another] 39.

probatum est: 'it has been tested' [a phrase used in prescriptions] 79.

process: proceedings 198.

proface: welcome to food or drink [salutation] 75.

prognostication: weather forecast; almanac containing astrological forecasts 206.

promoter: informer 233.

proof, of: (armour) of proven strength [figurative] 62.

proper: individual 62; handsome 126; such as should be 237.

properties: accessories 215.

prosecute: execute 120; continue the enquiry 154.

Protean: like the classical Proteus in its variety of transformations 38.

prounce: ? horse 192.

provant: rations 253.

provender pricked them: good feeding made them mettlesome [proverbial] 251.

publish: make public 89.

pudding: compressed roll of tobacco 75.

pug, western: bargee plying the Thames inland from London 63.

pull: bout (at wrestling) [pun] 208. pull their blue cases over their ears: see case.

punk: prostitute, mistress 69.

puny: raw youngster (like a soldier who has never seen action) 207.

purchase: loot 223; gain 227.

purse-net: bag-shaped net with a draw-string at the mouth, for rabbit-catching [pun] 79.

pursy: short-winded; fat 61.

put to his shifts: see shift. put down: outdo 149. put off: remove the hat 90, cf. put on, 216. put up: pocket 104.

quacksalver: quack 109.
quail-pipe: lure 64.
quaint: elegant, fashionable 131.
quaroms: body 308.
quat: pimple [figurative] 103.
quean: whore 230.
queer: bad 307.
quest of enquiry: legal investigation [figurative] 99.
quick: alive 200; pregnant; teeming with ideas [pun] 155.
quietus est: 'he is quit', i.e. his account is settled [? because his creditors cannot stand the smell] 108.
quill: tube [pun] 39.
quit: repay 91.
quod: said 151.
quod supra nos, nihil ad nos: 'what is above us is nothing for us' (attributed to Socrates) 30.
quondam: former 141.
quoth a: said he 150.

rabbit-sucker: [literally] sucking rabbit; †one who lives off a rabbit or dupe [pun. Also cf. coney-catch] 211.
rase: ? become wrinkled [pun on 'erase'] 41.
Ram: zodiacal sign or house of Aries. Spring begins when the sun enters it on 23rd March. Dekker treats the Ram's horns as a kind of inn-sign [see also horns] 32.
ranger: gamekeeper 211.
rank rider: one who rides hell for leather 29.
rapier: i.e. weapon worn by a gentleman 48.
rare: outstanding, excellent 47. rarely: beautifully 82; exceptionally well 189.
rascal: inferior deer [pun] 211.
rashers o' th' coals: broiled bacon eaten to get up a thirst 75.
Raw-head and Bloody-bones: bogeymen 291.
raze: scratch 292.
reach: trick [pun] 184.
ready, make: dress 129.
rebato: stiff collar or wire frame to support a ruff 77.
recovery: breaking an entail by a suit based on a legal fiction [pun] 198.
recudatur: 'it may be reprinted' 333.
*recusant: one who refuses [pun on the sense 'Roman Catholic dissenter', with reference to wine in mass] 235.
redime te captum quam queas minimo: 'ransom yourself from captivity as cheaply as you can' (Terence) 258.
reparation: repair 28.
respectively: respectfully 271.
rest, set up one's: be fully prepared to take all the risks [pun on the propping up of a fire-arm] 28; be determined 52; come to stay 223.

return: i.e. a kind of death assurance, benefit being payable on survival and return [pun] 206; return-day, one of the (few) days each Term when the sheriff reports on writs directed to him, and so when proceedings can begin 198.

revise: reconsider 218.

Rhadamanth, Aeacus, Minos: in Greek myth the three judges of the dead 199.

Rhazes (c. 865–923 or 932): great Persian physician, authority on plague 49.

Rhenish: Rhine wine 74.

rhythm: rhyme 192.

Rialto: the Exchange in Venice 275.

Rich-mount: i.e. Richmond, where Queen Elizabeth died on 24th March 1603 33.

rifle: search 99; gamble, raffle [figurative] 239.

ring: ? smoke-ring 95. running at the ring: sport in which a rider tries to carry off on his lance a ring hanging from a post [figurative] 225, cf. [pun] 226.

ringtail: bird of prey; *lecherous person [pun] 137.

roaring boys: hooligans 125.

Robert's men: 14th-century marauders 190.

*roll (Trinidado): i.e. of tobacco 75.

Romans: i.e. honourable men [it was uncommon for Elizabethans to have, as Romans had, more than one Christian name or one surname] 245.

Romeville: London 302.

Romford: one of the principal meat markets for London butchers [in Essex] 223.

rook: scoundrel 34.

rosemary: fragrant evergreen plant used at weddings and funerals [and against plague] 55.

rough-footed: with feathered legs 84.

round: brisk 174. the Bellman in his first round: see bell.

royal paper: a paper of high quality 221.

ruffled (boot): folded down 241. *ruffler:* ex-soldier or ex-servingman newly turned beggar and robber 189.

rug: coarse woollen material 235.

*Rule: the precinct, an area legally constituting a prison (such as the Fleet or King's Bench) but extending beyond the prison buildings proper to include expensive lodgings 275.

rum: fine. *rum cove:* gentleman 301. *rum maund:* ? special begging technique 294.

ruse: 'have a booze' [Danish] 74.

rushes: ordinary floor-covering of a dwelling-house [green when fresh] 43.

rusty: ill-conditioned 29.

sack: Spanish white wine [commonly taken with sugar] 42, cf. 105.

safeguard: riding-skirt; ? a kind of cape 296.

St Clement: patron saint of the Company of Brown Bakers said to have written an epistle to the Corinthians on humility and charity [? The sexton was a baker by trade; or else was at the Church of St Clement Danes, where there were thriving charities to which Richard Beddoe left a large legacy on 3rd July 1603 and where the plague was severe. ? Having profiteered on the burial of the rich, he may face lean times now most of them are gone] 48.

St Cynog: 5th-century Brecknockshire saint whose severed head dried up a well 93.

St Giles', Cripplegate [pun], St Sepulchre's and St Olave's: three of the very worst plague-stricken parishes 48.

St Martin's (le Grand): centre by St Martin's Lane of the trade in footwear and cheap finery 84.

St Thomas his Day: 21st December, when constables were nominated for the London wards 203. St Thomas onions: ? i.e. late crop 212.

salad: hors d'œuvre 88, [? pun on 'sallet': head-piece of armour] 104.

Salerno, University of: famous for its medical school and *Regimen Sanitatis Salerni*, a medieval Latin poem in doggerel verse containing medical precepts 80.

Salmon: Solomon; the mass 192.

salt: pungency 191. salt eel: see eel. equinoctial of the salt-cellar: equator, i.e. dividing-line, between the socially important and less important, traditionally marked on the table by the salt-cellar 96.

Saturnian, Saturnist: see Age.

save one, wise enough to: see wise. saving: breaking even 207.

Saviolo, Vincentio: Italian teacher of weapon-play and the duelling code in London, author of *Vincentio Saviolo His Practice* (1595) [from which the technical terms are taken] 51, cf. 88.

scantling: distance from the mark in archery. keep much about one scantling: are much of a muchness 213.

scape: transgression 154.

scavenger: unpaid parish officer responsible for clean streets, good pavements and fire-proof chimneys 78.

scent a *train: pick up a scent 244.

sciences, liberal: the university curriculum of grammar, logic, rhetoric, music, arithmetic, geometry, astrology 29. Hence seven-leaved tree, 219.

sconce: head; fort [pun] 59.

Scotch (hose): plaid 88.

screw: threaded cylinder 221.

scrivener: professional scribe and solicitor, sometimes a moneylender 198.

†scrubbing: beggarly 46.

sea-card: chart 39.

search: examination 60; probe 178.

security: freedom from care 42.

Seneca (c. 3 B.C.–A.D. 65): Stoic philosopher, author of, e.g., *The Remedies Against All Casual Chances* 267.

sergeant: see catchpole.

serve in for a goose: see goose. Servingman's Log: ? bench for servants to sit on 89.

*set off: show to advantage 89. set off wet: give an immediate and accurate picture [? take an impression from an inked block or type on moistened paper] 182. set out a wide throat: shout 124. set: pleat, pleating; the merchant's set was said to be especially neat 49. set up one's rest: see rest. setter up of: one who makes the fortune of 59, establishes 75.

'seven!, Come on': see six. Seven Electors: German princes who chose the German King 51. Seven Wise Masters: the Seven Sages of classical Greece representative of ancient learning [also, the title of a lost collaborative play by Dekker] 72. They included Bias [Bi*ass* is a pun on 'ass'] who was called a fool for keeping quiet at a feast [but retorted that no fool could keep quiet] 73; and Solon, the Athenian legislator, who was said to have disliked acting because it was a deception [the loobies would strike even him as genuine] 75. Seventeen Provinces: Netherlands 93.

several: different 49.

shadow: keep dark, pass off, excuse 155; *shade 177; depict 182. shadowing: shading 42. with their half hams/Shadowing their calves: ? with their skinny thighs shading their calves, i.e. running hard with bended knees [pun on the senses 'conceal' and, in an image of herding cattle, 'protect'] 36.

share: share in the proceeds of each performance given by an acting company. Only principal actors had full shares. Hence sharer, half a sharer, 98, 41. half-sharer: play-actor [? pun on 'half': partner] 58.

shaver: swindler, 'bright spark' 213. shaving: swindling [pun] 87.

shears between, there went but a pair of: they were of a piece [pun] 77.

shift: expedient 53; get by somehow 47; change clothes 89; get rid of 230. put to his shifts: 'put on the spot' 156.

shock: military engagement, charge 257.

shoe awry, treading her: lapsing from virtue 56. where one's shoe wrings one: what one's trouble is [pun] 240. shoeing-horn: appetizer, thirst provoker 75. shoemaker's wax: see wax. shoon: shoes 305.

shop-board: platform on which tailors sit 203.

shot: bill [pun] 105. musket shot should not reach him: see musket.

shoulders, cleft to the: see cleft. shoulder-clapper, shoulder-clapping: see catchpole.

Shrove Tuesday: i.e. a holiday when apprentices commonly ran wild 224.

*shrug: cringe 97.

shut up: bring to an end 39.

sibyl: prophetess, witch 38.

sic tenues evanescit in auras: 'thus she vanishes into thin air' (after Virgil) 236.

Sidney, Sir Philip: see lord.

silly: unsophisticated 32.

Silvanus: god of woods, fields, cattle 74.

simple: medicine (made of one ingredient) 49; simpleton [pun] 79; simple word 191; feeble 49. simple souls: see single.

Singer, John: comedian with the Admiral's Men 74.

single money: small change 133. single-sole: [literally] with only one thickness of material in the sole; poverty-stricken [? pun on the sense 'whole-hearted, straightforward'] 32, cf. single and simple souls, [pun] 78. singlest (and the simplest): with no compounds; composed of independent elements; honest-to-goodness 187.

singular: exclusive 29.

Sinon: Greek who induced the Trojans to admit the wooden horse 247.

siquid novisti rectius istis,/candidus imperti; si non, his utere mecum: 'if you know of anything better than this, be good enough to let me in on it; otherwise make do with this, like me' (Horace) 253.

si-quis: 'if anyone . . .', the start of a public announcement, e.g. by a servant seeking employment, who would post it on the West Door of St Paul's 91.

Sisters Three, the Fatal: see Destinies.

sith, sithence: since 184, 27.

'six!, Come on', 'Come on, seven!': ? i.e. calls at dicing, derived from the highest numbers *cinque* and *sice*, and suggesting daredevil play 125. six-footed creature: louse 85.

skean: dagger 230.

skelder: cheat 97.

skills not, it: it does not matter 89.

skinker: tapster 74.

skipjack: whipper-snapper 242.

skipper: (Dutch) ship's captain 77.

slips his horns: see horns. slip-shoes: slippers 250.

smell it out: form an impression 51. smell a pad in the straw: see pad.

Smithfield: London's permanent horse and cattle market 46.

smoked: cured by smoke 35; suspected 217.

smug: trim, smooth 32.

snakeproof: impervious to malice 73.

†snaphance: spring catch like a flint-lock 60.

snort: snore 58. snorts again: snores resoundingly 59.

socks: light shoes worn on the classical stage by comic actors [pun] 225.

Solomon saith . . .: see Proverbs xix. 17 (ascribed to Solomon) 295.

Solon: see seven.

song, an old: a trifle. here's an end of an old song: i.e. that's all there is to it 64.

sophistical: specious 81.

Sophy, Grand: Shah (of Persia) 201.

sops: bread dipped in wine 54.

sound, third: see trumpets.

souter: (ignorant) shoemaker 57.

sovereign: excellent [pun] 40; supreme 74; most efficacious 260.

Spanish jennet: highly valued small horse of Arab strain 93. Spanish needle: i.e. made of the best steel in the world 203. Spanish slop: shorts 77. Spanish weapons: i.e. needles 41.

spawl: spit 75.

spawn, multitudinous: what emerged from the crisis and took many forms (was the underlying rottenness in the state that had caused the crisis by perverse hopes of destruction) [an obscure passage confounding images of birth and suppuration] 35.

speed: prosper; do for 49.

spheres: the transparent globes of the earth-centred cosmos; one within another, and each carrying a planet on its surface, supposed by their revolutions to make exquisite music inaudible to fallen man [cf. Job xxxviii. 7] 32.

spirit of the buttery: hobgoblin 203. lively spirits: vital spirits, semi-material agencies acting through the blood-stream for the 'vegetable soul', sustaining the most elementary life-processes—digestion, respiration, etc. 82.

spleen: seat of anger, laughter, etc. 244. spleenful, 137.

splint: callous tumour on a horse's leg 241.

spoiled: despoiled 214.

spring: cause to appear, well up [pun] 35; cause (a bird) to rise from cover 215. spring-time, that was dry: i.e. there was a great drought early in 1603 35.

springe: snare 83.

spurn: kick 74.

spurs, silver: i.e. it was the right of choir-boys to fine those who wore spurs in the Cathedral 90. spur-gall: make sore from spurring too hard 29. spur-royal: gold coin worth 15s. 108.

squares out his platforms: regulates his plans [pun] 278.

stage monkey, fantastic: affected fool who sits on the stage 28.

staggers: disease of domestic animals [pun] 59.

stairs: landing-stage 100. pair of stairs: see pair.

stake: butt [such as were scattered all over Finsbury Fields] 28.

stall: screen a pickpocket from observation 301, but cf. 195. *stalling ken:* house for receiving stolen goods 299, also *stuling ken,* 195.

stamp: (imprint on a) coin [pun] 63.

stand: open barrel 53. stand on one's pantofles: see pantofle. stand to: be bound by [pun] 58; back up [pun] 74. stood to his tackling: 'stuck to his guns' 217. stand upon: pride oneself on 41; give careful consideration to 46; insist on 197. French standing collar: see France.

Standard: monumental water-conduit in Cheapside [pun] 47.

standish: inkstand 27.

starch, patent for: i.e. a profitable monopoly granted by the Crown 78.

state: throne 98.

States: the Dutch government 51.

stationer: bookseller 28.

statute (merchant or staple): statute governing the making of a bond and imposing imprisonment and forfeiture of goods if the debt was unpaid 214. Statute (of Rogues): statute against masterless men of no fixed address, designed to whip them home 29.

stave's end, at the: at a distance [pun] 62.

stay: stop 157.

stead: serve his turn 226.

Stephen's . . . breeches, King: i.e. they cost him five shillings, according to an old ballad [cf. *Othello* II. iii. 91–99] 77.

stewardship: good management 143.

still: always 40.

stitch: heart-ache [pun] 57.

stoccata: 'thrust' [Italian] 51.

stock: capital 142.

stomach, stuck more in her: made a more lasting impression on her, meant more to her 57.

stool: defecation [pun] 99.

stop: block [i.e. hold] 45; repair 62; keep 209.

store: plenty 83. stored: furnished 117.

Story, Doctor (c. 1504–71): Regius Professor of Civil Law at Oxford, persecutor of protestants in England and the Netherlands; kidnapped, brought to England and executed for treason at Tyburn [the three-sided gallows on which he was the first to be hanged came to be jocularly called his cap—the mortar-board being sometimes three-cornered. To dispute is to hold a form of debate common as a university exercise] 201.

stoup: flagon 74.

Stow, John (c. 1525–1605): historian and antiquarian, published his *Summary of English Chronicles* (1565) in 8° and (1566) in 16° 39, and *The Chronicles of England* (1580) 91.

Straits: i.e. of Gibraltar 123.

stramazzone: 'downward cut' [Italian] 51.

strange woman: harlot 119. stranger: foreigner 104.

strike: make one's way, go [pun] 204. strike a hand: see hand.

strong: impossible to escape from 159.

strosser, Italian's close: tight trousers 77.

stultorum plena sunt omnia: 'the world is full of fools' (Cicero) 67.

sturdy: able-bodied; tough 190.

Stygian: of the infernal river Styx; infernal 204. Stygian ferry: see Charon.

subsidy: tax 97.

suburbs: quarters of the town outside the walls (notorious for poverty, crime, disease; the plague began there) [figurative] 98.

sugar, papers of: see sack.

Summers, Will: Henry VIII's fool 72.

sumpter-horse: pack-horse 203.

supplement: requisite 95.

sure, make: betroth 40.

surfeit: (indisposition from) eating too much [figurative] 109.

swadder: thieving pedlar 189.

sweat, make their silver: ? melt down their silverware; ? sweat in panic themselves [the same metaphor as in Casting] 35. sweating together in France: see France.

sweet water: scent 55. *sweetening: softening 285.

swelling: deeply moving; splendid [? the ludicrous language of the food-snob] 104. swelling temples: see horns.

swigman: thieving pedlar with a pack 189.

Switzer: Swiss 74. guard of Switzers: i.e. mercenaries commonly employed as bodyguards by kings 108. Switzer's blistered codpiece: prominent bag or pad over the genitals ornamented with short padded rolls 77. Switzer's breeches: knee-length baggy breeches with panes of lining hanging in puffs 29.

swound: faint 37.

Sybarites: natives of the ancient Greek city of Sybaris in southern Italy, famous as voluptuaries and said to spend the whole of one year giving invitations for the next year 268.

synodical: of the professional body or council [of doctors] 49.

table: board or panel 70. tables, table-books, writing-tables: copy-book, note-book 57, 90, 39. tables: backgammon 125. as many tables furnished as lackeys: see France. table diamond: i.e. cut thin with a large flat upper surface surrounded by small facets 209. table of the Sun: see Apollo. tableman: backgammon or other gaming piece [figurative for the sense 'diner' or 'gamester', ? implying 'blockhead', 'dummy'] 73.

tack, hold: hold one's own 306.

tailor: i.e. proverbially poor and proud, vulgar 73.

taint: infect 238; do harm to [pun on the sense 'apply ointment to'] 37.

take (his own colour): be impregnated, dyed [on his own a man is colourless, without a real identity] 265. take hold of: see hold. take the upper hand: see hand. take away: clear away 109. take up (the matter): settle amicably 58. guts . . . taken out by the hangman: see guts. taking: agitation 61.

talents: wealth; talons [pun] 202.

Tamburlaine: the ruthless conqueror in Marlowe's play, proverbial for his grandeur 46.

Tarlton, Richard: most famous of all Elizabethan comedians, died 1588 74.

tatterdemalion: ragamuffin 286.

tawny-moor: Arab 228.

tears of the vine: i.e. the sap, a medical remedy for many ailments 165. rain down gummy tears: see gummy.

tell: count 213.

Temple Bar: timber gateway at the west end of Fleet St 244. between Ludgate and Temple Bar: see Lud. Templar: barrister with chambers in the Temple 98.

tenter, on the uttermost: stretched to the utmost 209.

tercel-gentle: male falcon(s) 126.

Term, Term-time: law-term, when London was thronged and all business (including publishing) brisk 70, 197. Termer: lawyer's clerk 197.

terse: well-groomed, well turned-out 204.

tester, teston: sixpence 96, [the price of admittance to the stage] 100.

tetter: skin disease such as impetigo 281.

texted: in the formal hand used by way of capitals for headings, etc. [? with reference to bonds] 211.

than: then 303.

théâtre du monde: 'theatre of the world', the title of a book by Pierre Boaistuau [? a fleeting pun on the Globe Theatre] 78.

Theobalds: palace built in Hertfordshire by Lord Burghley [King James was received there in 1603] 42.

*Thespian: dramatic 29.

thriftily: soundly 151.

throat, set out a wide: see set. tearing money out of their throats: ? i.e. by brutal insistence 48, cf. 261.

throughly: thoroughly 184.

thrums: waste thread or yarn 296. thrummed cap: i.e. mop-like 87.

ticket: tick 101.

tickle: stir up 64. tickle under the gills: entice into danger, as a trout may be caught 57. tickling: titillating 85.

tickrum: passport [q.v.] 301.

tick-tack: old variety of backgammon 125.

tie thee yielding: keep you tractable 260. bull tied to a wild fig-tree: see bull.

tilt: stagger [? pun on the sense 'joust'] 36.

time-catcher: opportunist 41.

Timonist: misanthrope like Timon of Athens 79.

tincture: colouring 265.

tip: pay 301.

tire: dress, head-dress 135.

tobacco, dry: see dry. tobacco office: ? smoking-room or tobacconist's 89. tobacconist: smoker 41.

tocsin: alarm-bell [? pun on such words as 'toxical': poisonous] 46.

token: plague spot [pun] 44; small coin issued by tradesmen 136.

Toll Book: market register in which the true ownership of horses for sale must be first established by witnesses [pun; by so-called 'benefit of clergy' the death penalty could be evaded by convicts who proved they could read, thus saving themselves by the book] 225.

tongs: instrument with which to take a light from a live coal 95.

tongue-'travelling': see travail.

toot: peer inquisitively 81.

touch, keep: keep faith 195. *touch-bore: touch-hole [figurative for 'vagina'] 299.

toys: trash 134.

tracers: those trailing them 225.

travail: work hard, exert oneself [pun on 'travel'] 29; labour [pun] 132. tongue-'travelling': tongue-wagging; working the tongue hard [pun] 37. 'travelled' in this . . . vacation: i.e. pun on 'travailed in this . . . vocation' 50.

travel: see travail.

traverse: check 106.

tread: stamp out, crush [? pun on the sense 'copulate', with reference to the ill effect of crossing on breeding quality] 245. treading her shoe awry: see shoe. maze of friends trodden out: see maze.

tree, seven-leaved: see sciences.

Tribe of Critic: cf. College.

tributary: payable as homage 81.

trillil: 'glug-glug' [a drinking term, imitating the sound of liquid] 62.

tripos: 'stool' [? with allusion to the seat of the Delphic oracle; ? or to the fool at Cambridge Commencement] 100.

Trojan: fine chap [pun] 58.

Troynovant: London, the capital of the legendary founder of Britain, the Trojan Brutus, great-grandson of Aeneas 47, cf. 236.

truckle-bed: movable bed kept under the master's bed and suitable for servants 74.

trull: whore 290.

trumpets: i.e. they were sounded three times to give warning that the play was to begin 100, cf. 101.

trunk, hollow: speaking-tube [a quill was hollow] 43.

tumble: toss and turn 33. tumbler: dog like a small greyhound for rabbiting 211.

Turk, the Great: the Ottoman Sultan 32. (turn) Turk: traitor 57. Turkish: cruel 63.

turn: change 36. turn off the ladder, over the perch: hang [figurative] 64, 81. turned them over the thumbs: made them do just as she pleased; ? done for them 64. turn up the heels: see heels.

Turnbull: i.e. Turnmill St in Clerkenwell, one of the most disreputable quarters of London 133.

Tuscan: language of Tuscany, the classical form of Italian 187.

twelvepenny room: the best box, probably in the lowest gallery to one side of the stage [admission prices were doubled for a première] 73. twelvescore: i.e. paces—the standard archery range 166.

Tyburn: permanent site for public hangings, near the modern Marble Arch 81.

tympany: morbid swelling 155.

Tyre and Sidon: Syrian cities famous in the ancient world 42.

ululation: wail 273.

underfoot: below the real value 27.

underlay: sole or heel, repair; put up with [pun] 56.

unicorn: see horns. unicorn's horn: costly medical preparation supposed efficacious against poison, etc. 41.

Union: i.e. with Scotland 221.

unison: note of the same pitch as another, as in one instrument tuned to another 265.

unnatural: anti-social [with reference to the moral meanings of the emblems as much as to hunting in the wild] 210.

unvaluable: invaluable 129.

*upsitting: getting up after an illness 288.

upsy Friese: 'after the Frisian fashion' [Dutch: *op zijn Vriesch*], i.e. a way of drinking deep 74.

urinal: chamber-pot 81. urine eyes: uranalysis 280.

utter: sell 98; outer 262.

vail: lower (a flag, etc.) in submission; meekly take off (a hat) [pun] 59.

vale: 'farewell' 308.

varlet: scoundrel 238; catchpole [q.v.] 259.

vault, devil in a: see devil. vaulting-school: brothel [literally 'gymnasium'] 233.

vaunt-couriers: advance-guard 82.

Vecchio, Soldado: 'old soldier' [Spanish and Italian mixed] 207.

velvet cap, night-cap: physician's headgear 49, 152.

vent: sell 123.

Vertumnus: god of the changing year [one of the allegorical figures to welcome King James in *The Magnificent Entertainment*] 32.

vetus comoedia: 'the old comedy' [of a satirical character] 80.

vintner . . . brewing in his cellar: see conjuror in hogsheads at midnight.

visited: infected [pun] 48.

vizard: mask 249.

void: empty 60. voider: receptacle with which to clear away 78; *servant clearing away 205.

voluntary: volunteer 180.

voyage, The Bellman in his first: see bell. Cadiz Voyage: expedition of 1596 in which Howard and Essex sacked Cadiz. Island Voyage: unsuccessful expedition of 1597 under Essex to the Azores [figurative] 252. Portugal Voyage: unsuccessful expedition of 1589 under Norris and Drake 93.

Vulcan: Roman god of fire and metal-working, grossly deceived by Venus 57. Vulcanist: blacksmith 41.

waft: wave 229.

wagtail: whore [figurative] 125.

walk: move briskly 240. Duke Humphrey's Walk: see Duke. walking sprite: ghost haunting the place [figurative] 52.

wallet: knapsack, bag with a mouth in the middle and a pouch at each side 77.

want: lack 41, 81.

wap: copulate 286.

ward: guard, watch [q.v.] 285. Head Warden: see Company.

warrant: permit 211; grounds for thinking 152.

watch: armed picket of householders under the Constable who challenged night-walkers and rounded up vagrants [pun] 28, 285; their turn of duty 100. (his, etc.) watch: (him)self, etc. 192, [apparently misunderstood in the translation] 301, cf. 302.

water, sweet: see sweet. Water-Bailiff: conservancy and fishing officer 27. water-caster: urinologist 49. *watering-place: where a ship puts in for fresh water 62. waterman: boatman plying for passenger-hire on the Thames 46.

Watson, Thomas (1557?–92): learned poet in Latin and English (notably, sonnets), highly respected in London literary circles and under the patronage of Walsingham 168.

*wax, (shoemaker's): cobbler's heelball, a black resinous composition used to rub thread and, spread on leather, as a medical dressing 56. in wax: in sealing-wax, in the sealing of bonds 212.

We Three: i.e. three blockheads [with reference to a comic song in which two singers, in admitting their own stupidity, implicate an unsuspecting on-looker; or to an inn-sign playing a similar joke] 99.

weasand-pipe: windpipe 240.

welted: trimmed [see fox-furred] 202.

West Indies: i.e. gold 51. western pug: see pug. westward: i.e. towards Tyburn [q.v.] 201.

wherry: light rowing-boat 258.

whew: i.e. exclaim with a whistling sound 101.

whiff: ? inhaling; ? blowing the smoke down the nose 95. †whiff down: swallow down 88.

whip and a white sheet: i.e. to be whipped and dressed in the robe of penitence, a punishment for sexual transgression 156. *whipjack:* vagrant with a forged begging licence representing him to be a distressed sailor 189.

whisht: hush(ed) 157.

white: white archery target 271. turns up the white of her eye: puts on a pious expression 57. White Lion: Surrey County prison 273. white money: silver 35. white sheet: see whip.

wild fig-tree, bull tied to a: see bull. wild Ireland, Irishman, Irish kern: see Ireland. wild man: savage [a common figure in pageants and court entertainments] 34. *wild rogue:* vagrant born and bred 189.

willow: tree symbolic of grief for disappointment in love [especially when green] 166.

wind: insinuate 202.

wise, he should be: i.e. 'he is wise enough that can keep himself warm' [proverb] 295. wise enough to save one: smart enough to take care of himself [proverbial] 64. Seven Wise Masters: see seven. wise men of Gotham: see Gotham.

witch, Lapland: i.e. such women sold to becalmed sailors a string with three knots in it which, when untied, were supposed to release winds of increasing velocity 256. Thus also witches of Norway, 269.

woe worth: curse 274.

woman, strange: see strange. woman's evil: menstruation [figurative] 151. closet of a woman's thoughts: see closet.

Wood St Counter: see Counter. woodcock: fool [pun] 83. *wooden: sylvan; blockish [pun] 32. Woodpecker: i.e. in effect he insures a gamester against losing, the benefit being an overvalued article, the premiums being calculated on the alleged value and payable only on winnings 206–7.

world, beaten to this: see beaten. the world runs upon wheels: i.e. fast and headlong [proverb] 139, [alluding to the shortage of transport for refugees] 46. the world were divided: i.e. classical tradition divided the world variously into three—between sky, land and sea, between the triumvirs, between Europe, Asia and Africa. Christian tradition divided between Shem, Ham, Japheth, but there is also a fourfold division in Isaiah xi. 12 and Rev. vii. 1, and the reference may be to the discovery of the American continent 200.

worth, woe: curse 274. worthy: noteworthy 50.

writ of error: writ of Chancery issued on appeal against wrongful proceedings or judgment. writ of outlawry: writ for deprivation of all a subject's rights, including bail. writ of rebellion: writ for arrest on not answering a summons 198.

writing-tables, pair of: see pair, table.

yard: cheapest part of the public theatre, for people to stand in 99.

yellow: i.e. the colour of jealousy. drew on a pair of yellow hose: i.e. became jealous 150.

zany: ludicrous imitator 100.

Zoilus: [literally] Greek grammarian famous for severe criticism of Homer; type of small-minded and malicious critic 73. Hence Zoilist, 30.

ᶎona frigida, Frozen Zone: arctic or antarctic [figurative] 53, 38.